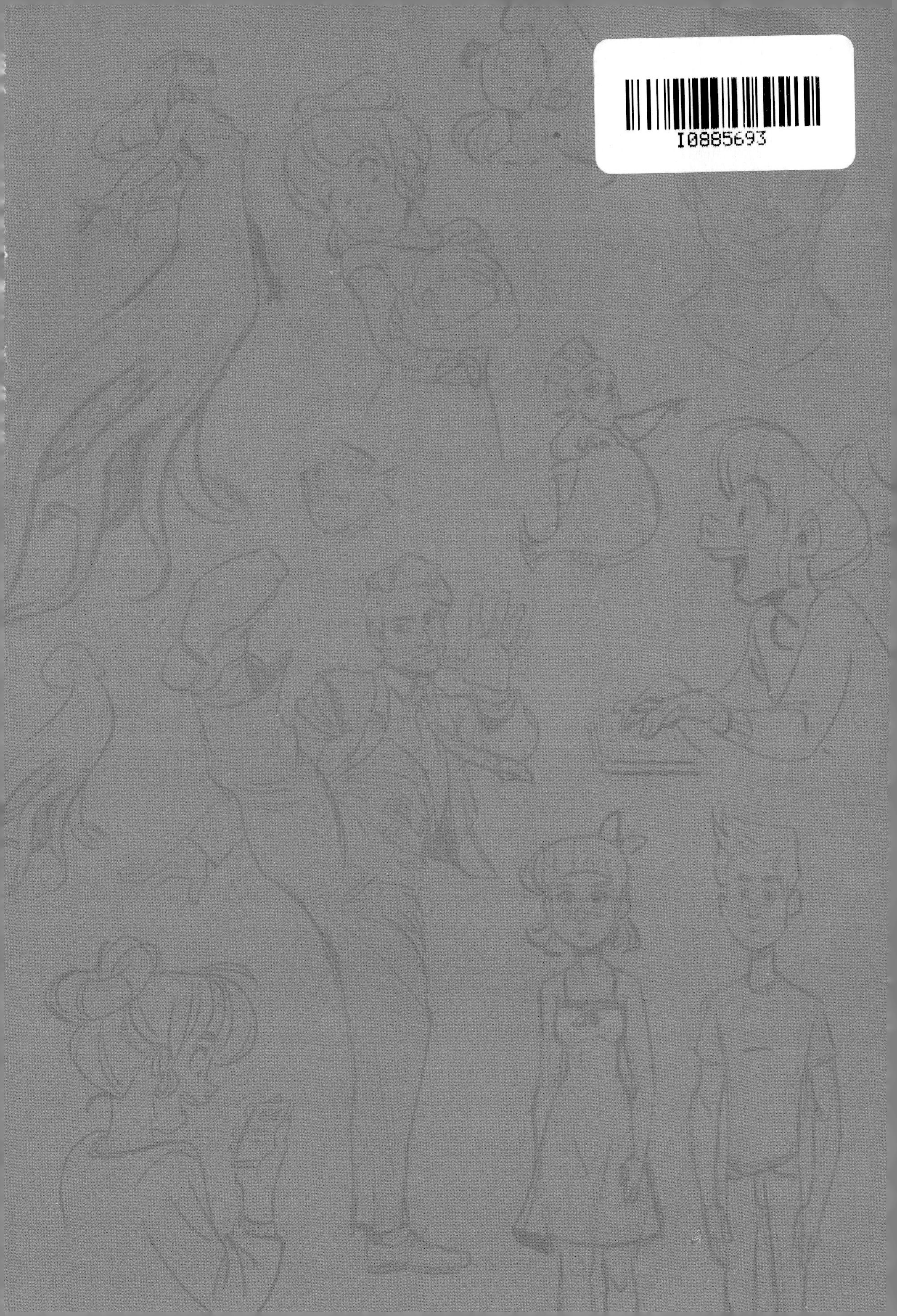

DRAW WHAT YOU LOVE

THE ART OF SIMONE GRÜNEWALD

![3dtotalPublishing]

3dtotalPublishing

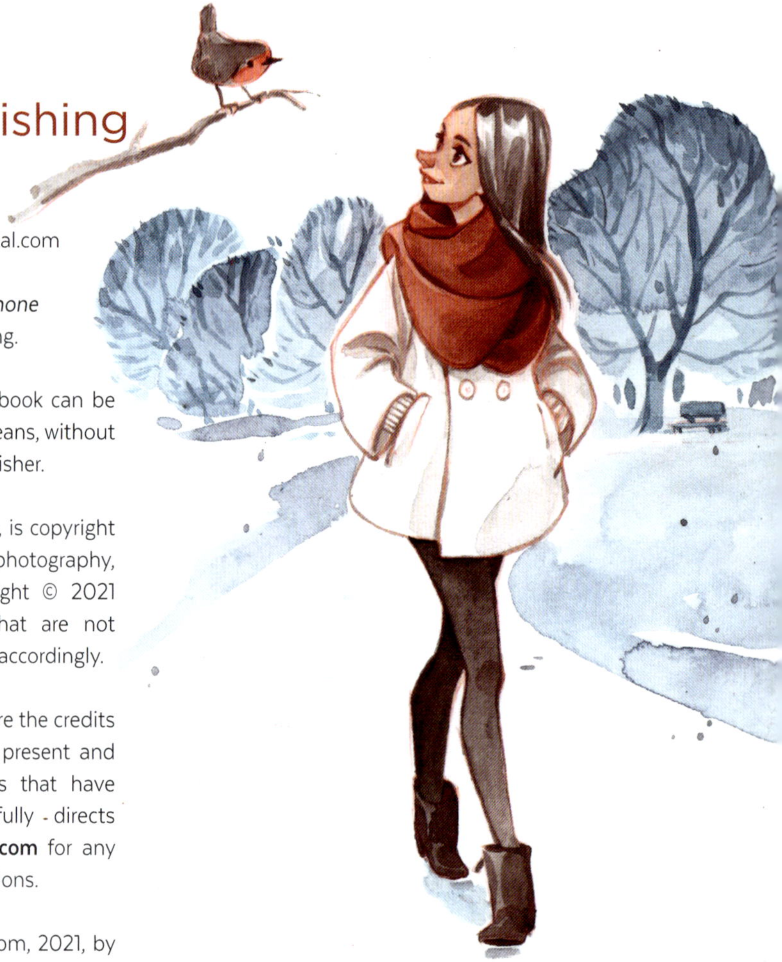

Website: www.3dtotal.com
Correspondence: publishing@3dtotal.com

First published in the United Kingdom, 2021, by 3dtotal Publishing.

Address: 3dtotal.com Ltd, 29 Foregate Street, Worcester, WR1 1DS, United Kingdom.

Hard cover ISBN: 978-1-912843-30-5
Printing and binding: Dongguan Everbright Printing Co. Ltd (China)
www.everbrightprint.com

Visit **www.3dtotalpublishing.com** for a complete list of available book titles.

Managing Director: Tom Greenway
Studio Manager: Simon Morse
Lead Editor: Samantha Rigby
Lead Designer: Fiona Tarbet
Editorial Project Manager: Sophie Symes

ONE TREE PLANTED FOR EVERY BOOK SOLD

OUR PLEDGE

From 2020, 3dtotal Publishing has pledged to plant one tree for every book sold by partnering with and donating the appropriate amounts to re-foresting charities. This is one of the first steps in our ambition to become a carbon-neutral company with carbon-neutral publications, giving our customers the knowledge that by buying from 3dtotal Publishing, they are working with us to balance the environmental damage caused by the publishing, shipping, and retail industries.

CONTENTS

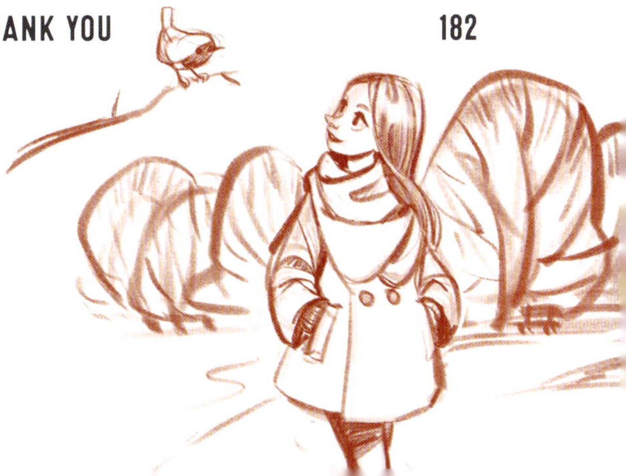

INTRODUCTION

I'd like to introduce *Draw What You Love* with a lovely little comic created by an artist friend of mine upon receiving my first art book, *Sketch Every Day*. Thank you so, so much, Marie Jo!

I'm very proud of my first ever art book, *Sketch Every Day*. Through the book I simply wanted to encourage people to create art! I wanted readers to understand that there is no right time; all it takes is the desire to create and the motivation just to dive straight into it. And, of course, sticking with it and continuing to develop and grow. To build drawing skills, you mostly just need to draw a lot. Where my first book focused heavily on the benefits of continuous sketching, within this book I delve deeper into my processes and reveal all of my personal insights, unique techniques, and trade secrets.

Since the release of my last book, I have continued to develop and share tutorials on a variety of different topics via my Patreon account. One of the great things about making this content is having the chance to explore areas I need to improve on – having an excuse to throw myself into learning and figuring a new topic out is actually what I love to do most!

My ultimate goal has never been to reach a certain point or to work on a particular project for a specific company. My drive is simply to grow as an artist, to learn and experiment with new techniques, and to continuously improve my art. My most recent fascination has been in developing backgrounds and mastering the play of color and light – both of which I will cover in more detail across the pages of this book.

With this book I share what I have learned through fun breakdowns, as well as detailed step-by-step tutorials, and I am so very grateful to 3dtotal for this opportunity to grow alongside the people I teach.

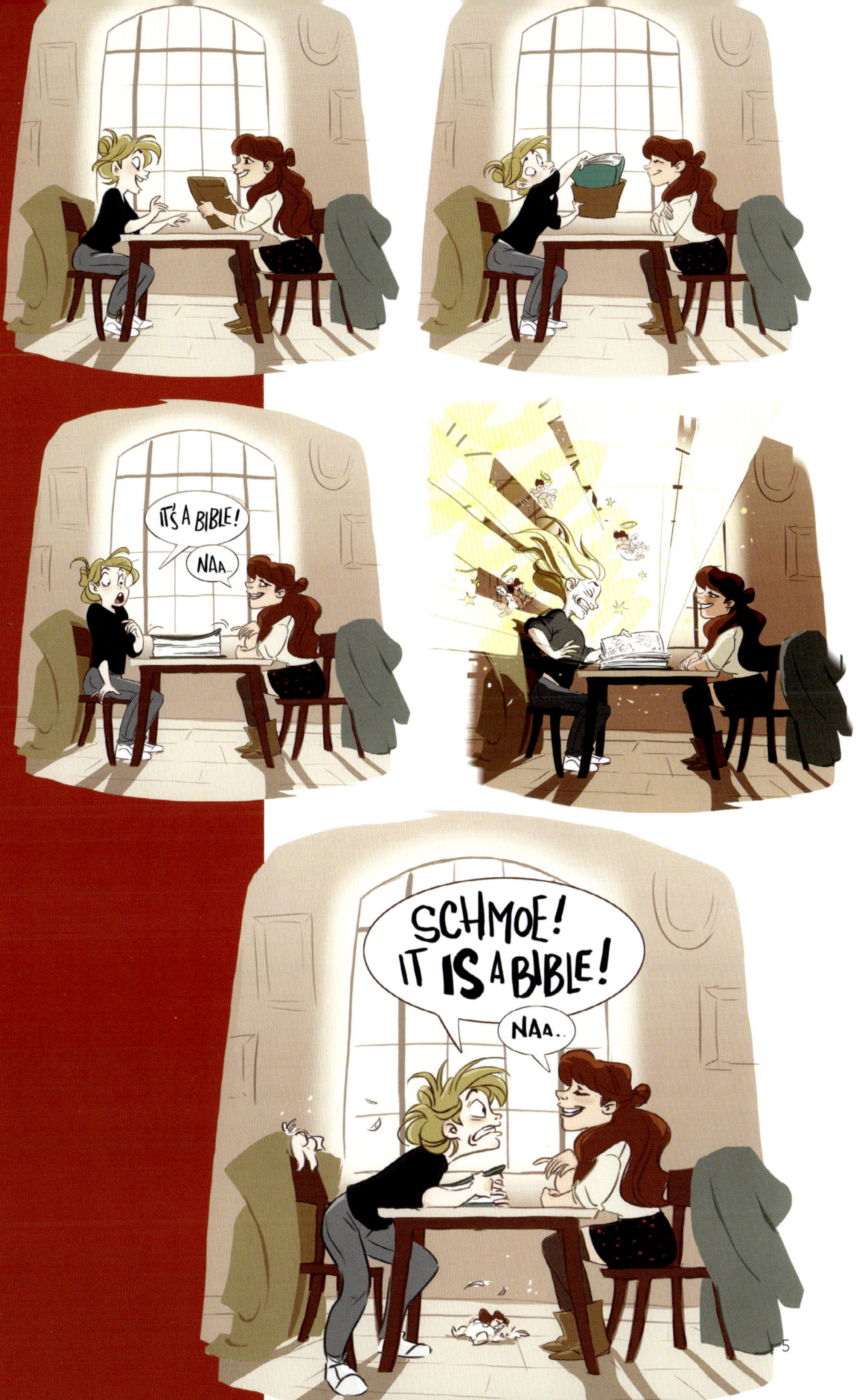

IT'S A BIBLE!
NAA...
SCHMOE! IT **IS** A BIBLE!
NAA..

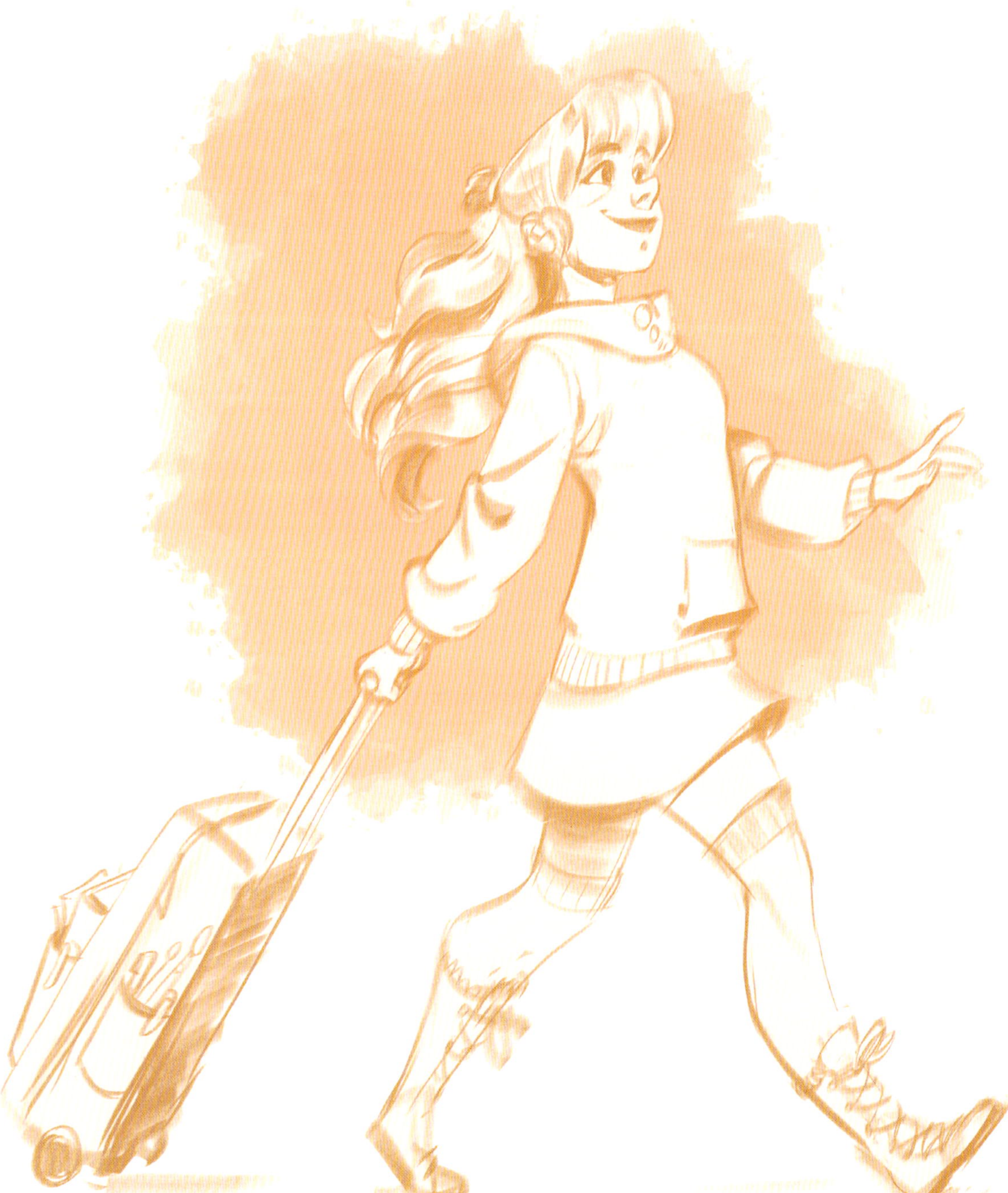

MY CREATIVE JOURNEY

After quitting my full-time job in November 2018, my exciting journey as a freelancer began. It took a lot of work and preparation for me to feel safe to go freelance. The problem is knowing when to stop working and make that leap of faith, but I'm truly happy I took this scary step — now I feel like I'm really doing my thing!

TIMELINE

The life events and career moments shown here are those that were most significant to my creative journey, and had the most long-lasting effect. I did also undertake some small commissions here and there when I had time to spare. And, of course, maintaining my social media presence was, and is, immensely important for my freelance career.

These days, I work four to five hours a day before picking up my son, Remus, from playgroup. On Fridays I work all day because my husband only works for half a day and can take over caring for Remus.

As well as being something that brings me joy, I see art as my calling card and a medium I can use to tell the world about my projects and ideas.

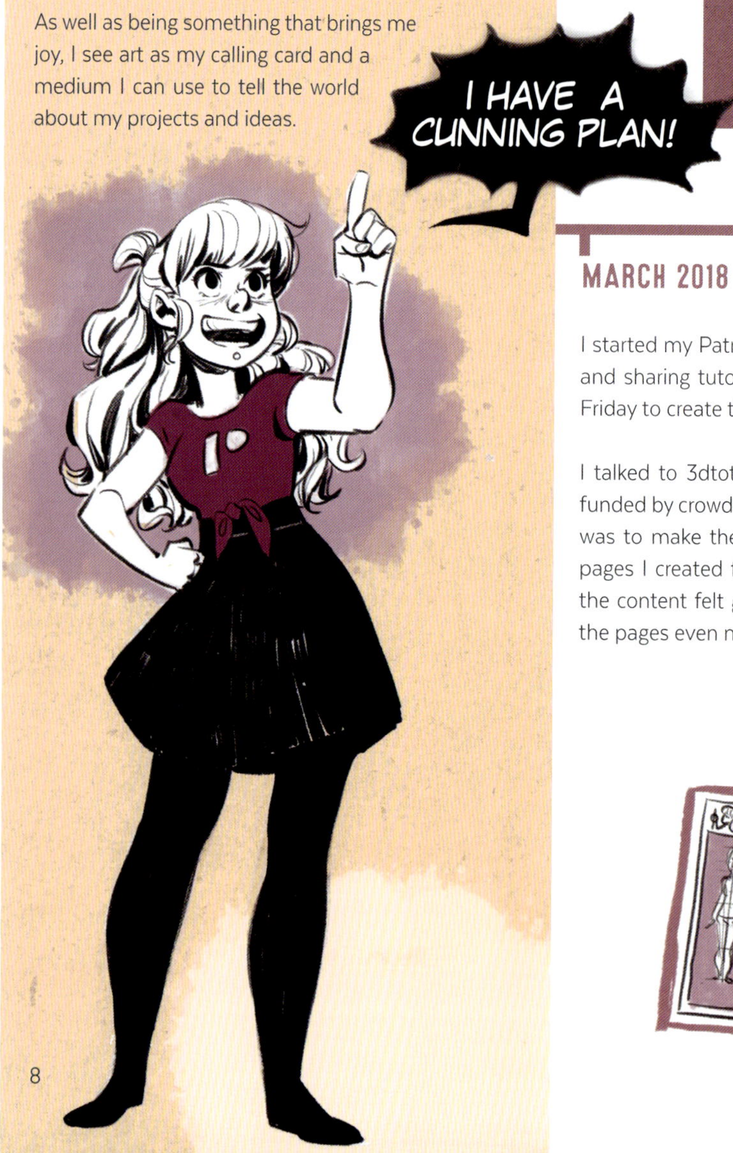

While working full-time at Daedalic, I was approached by another company to create some character designs for a 3D movie!

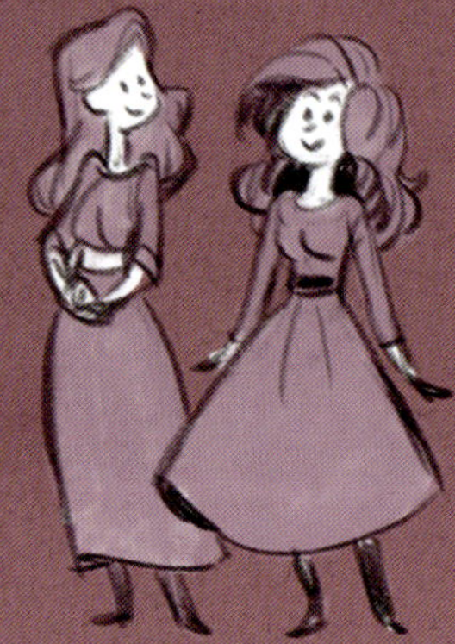

JUNE 2018

MARCH 2018

I started my Patreon account with the idea of creating and sharing tutorial pages weekly. I made time every Friday to create this content for my patrons.

I talked to 3dtotal Publishing about creating a book funded by crowdfunding platform, Kickstarter. My plan was to make the book from the collection of weekly pages I created for Patreon. Having a second use for the content felt good and made the time invested in the pages even more worthwhile.

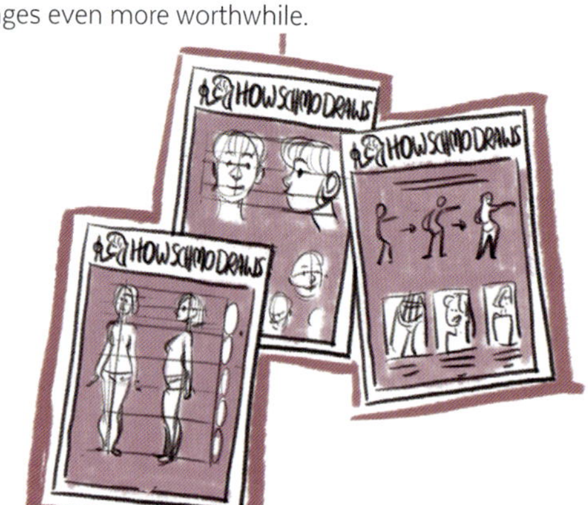

NOVEMBER 2018

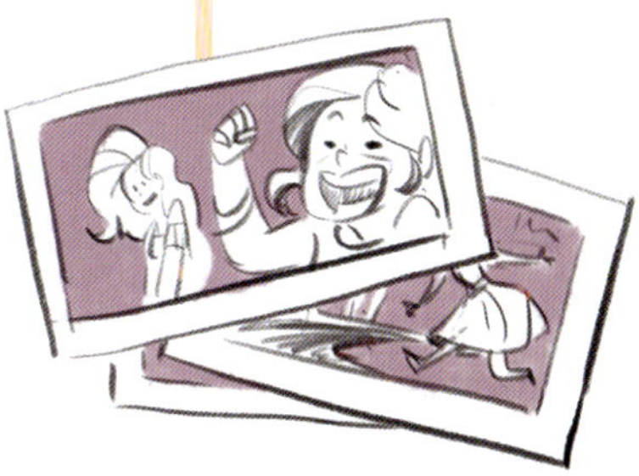

The same company asked me I if would like to design explorative story illustrations for the movie. This was a job that would be continuous for an undefined period of time.

I knew I wanted to leave my job at some point and this offer, on top of my Patreon, helped with my decision to quit. At this point, everything was aligned just right.

APRIL-MAY 2019

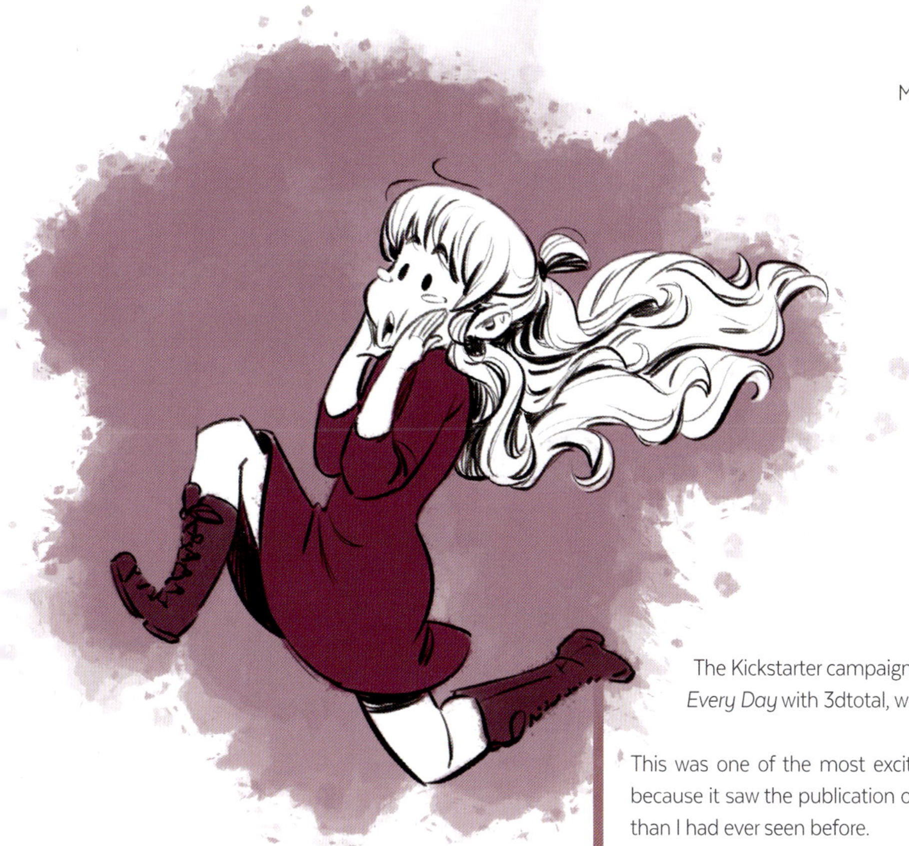

The Kickstarter campaign for my first book, *Sketch Every Day* with 3dtotal, went live.

This was one of the most exciting events of my career because it saw the publication of my art on a larger scale than I had ever seen before.

JUNE 2019

From June onward I started to sporadically but continuously contribute concept art to the indie game, *Under the Island.*

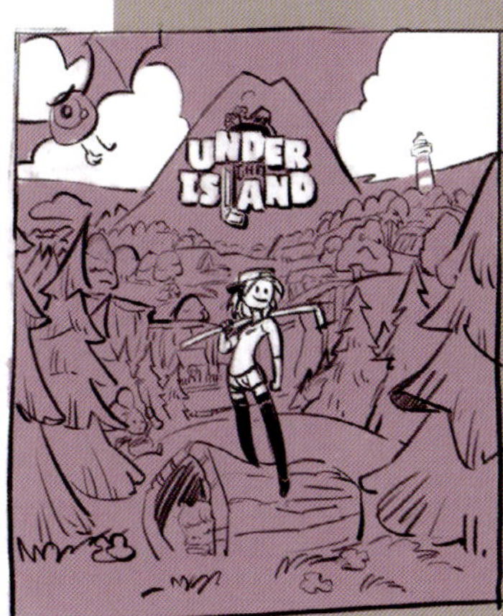

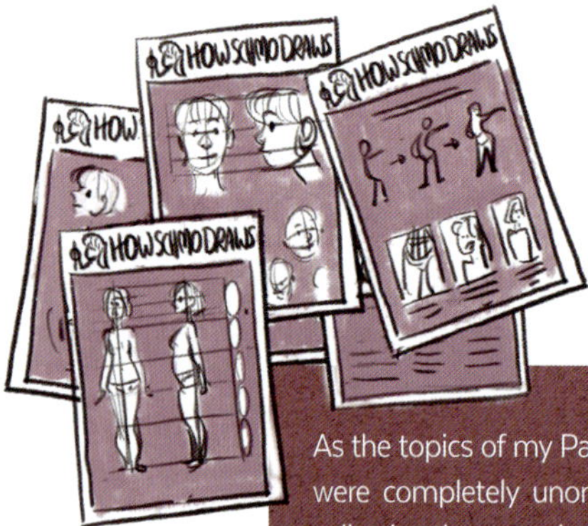

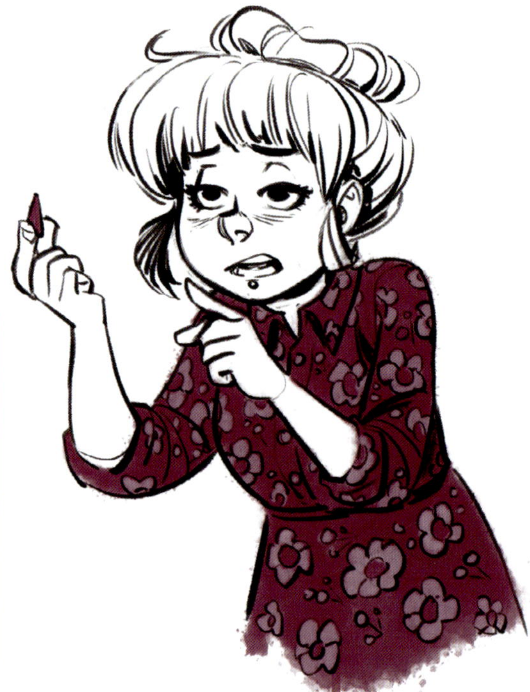

As the topics of my Patreon tutorials were completely unorderly, I began collecting the pages in PDFs that had the same topic and offering them as a monthly extra gift.

This was a bit of a turning point for my Patreon and it grew a lot for a quite a while.

NOVEMBER 2019

AUGUST 2019

I held *Sketch Every Day*, my first physical book, in my hands.

Copies started shipping out to Kickstarter backers in September and I watched gleefully as people received their books and showcased them enthusiastically in their Instagram stories.

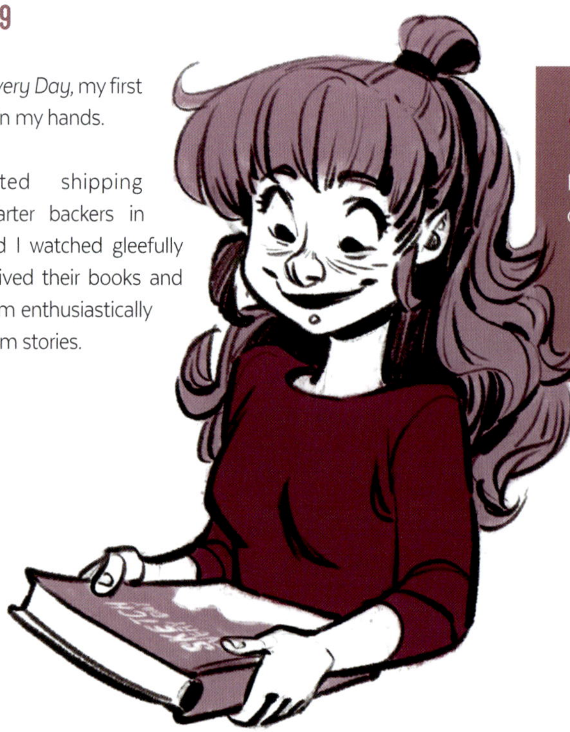

JANUARY 2020

Irrelevant to my creative development but a life landmark — Remus put a pip up his nose and we nearly had to go to hospital, but we got it out pretty ingeniously.

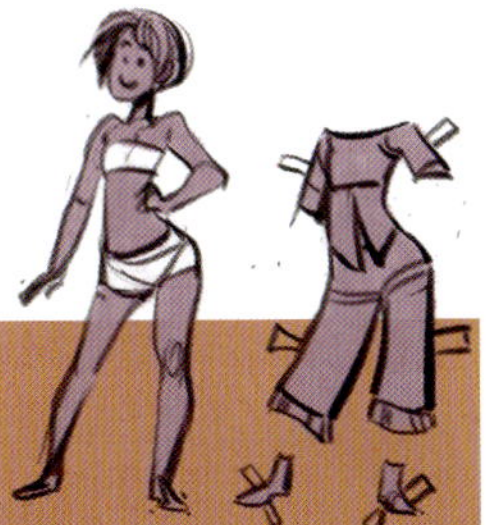

MAY 2020

The Covid-19 pandemic began and my storyboard job came to a holt, but I had been approached by another company in January and so began another indefinite long-term job.

I felt very privileged that the two long-term jobs had come my way. They didn't have difficult deadlines and I could fit the work around looking after Remus.

SEPTEMBER 2020

A German translation of my book was published at Carlsen Comics. This was a dream come true! As Carlsen Comics are a publisher whose comics and books I have always loved, having my book published by them felt amazing.

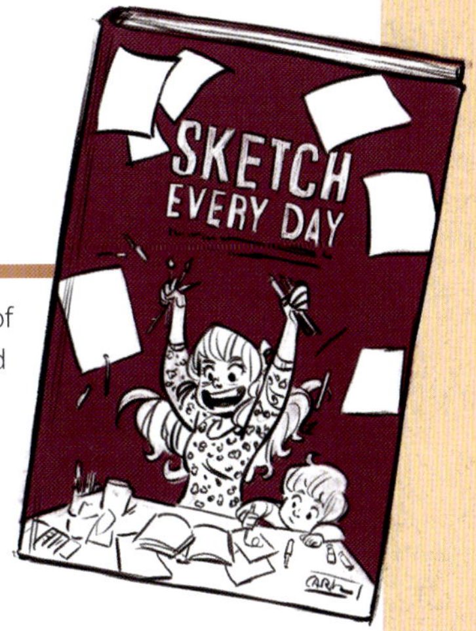

SEPTEMBER 2020

Another small but long-term job doing corrections began, covering three to four hours a week.

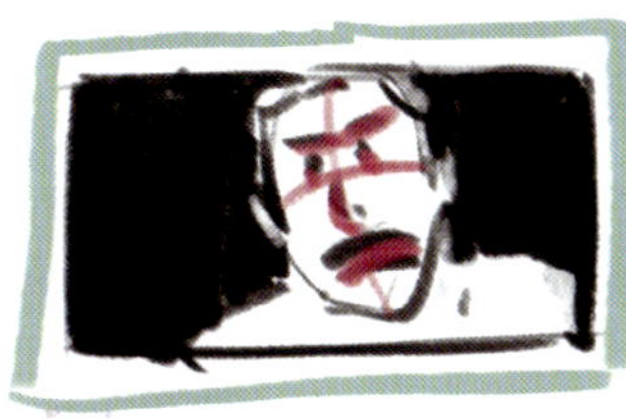

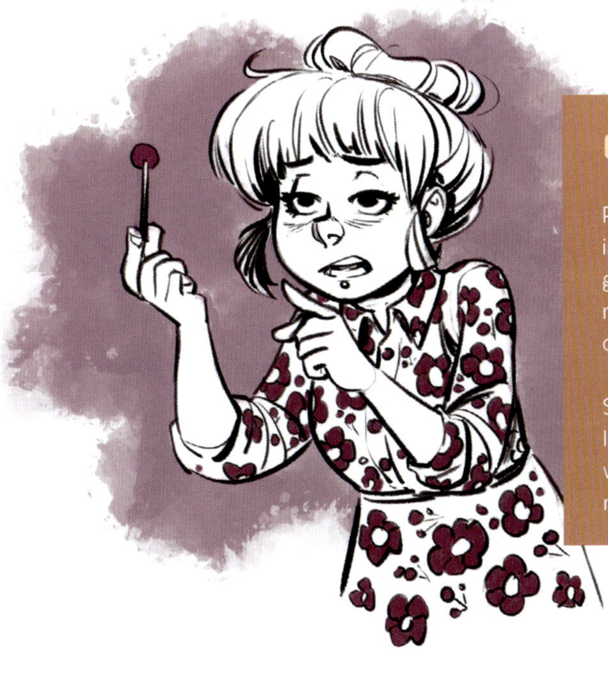

OCTOBER 2020

Remus swallowed a lollipop, including the stick! This time we did go to the hospital, but there wasn't much to be done but wait. It came out and all was fine.

Sickness or emergency moments like this can throw me off for a week, which is why I am all the more happy to find flexible jobs.

WORKSPACE

My workspace is centered around my desk. Here I work with my digital tools as well as my traditional materials, such as pens, pencils, and watercolor paints.

I need some clutter around me, so my workspace doesn't get any tidier than this! But I always make sure I'm surrounded by the stuff I love. The inspiration wall behind the desk is filled with prints – I enjoy collecting the art of other artists and collating them here.

These shelves contain a wild mix of art supplies that I can reach from where I sit, including old sketchbooks, books I've had printed, inspirational books, and graphic novels

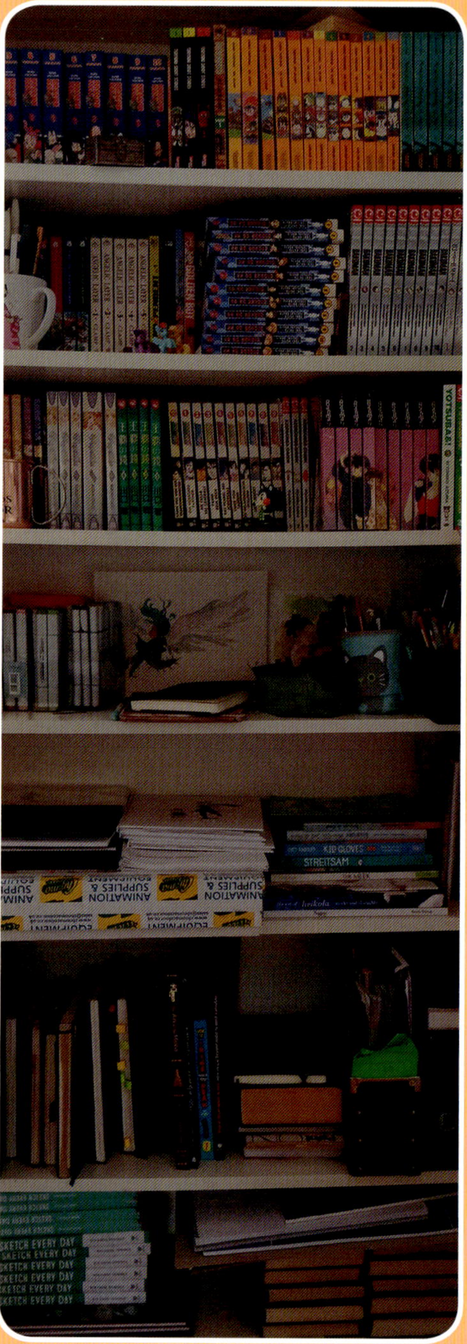

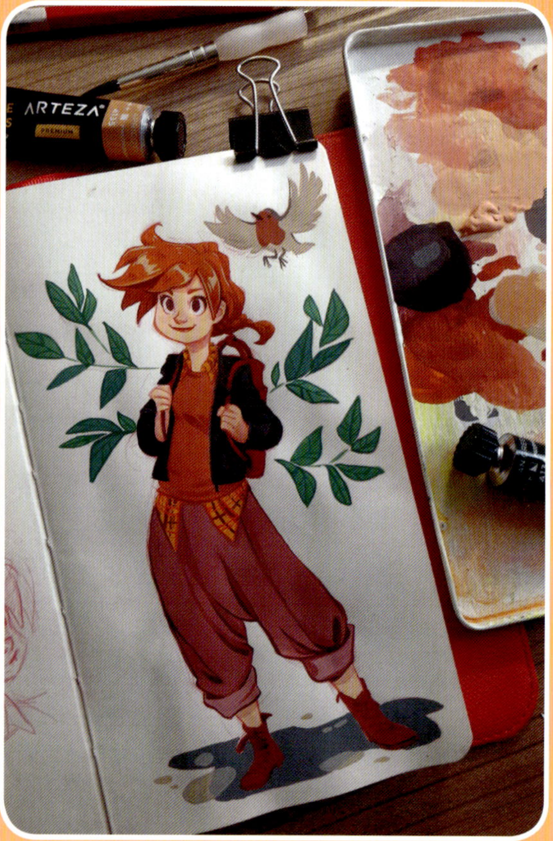

"I ALWAYS MAKE SURE I'M SURROUNDED BY THE STUFF I LOVE"

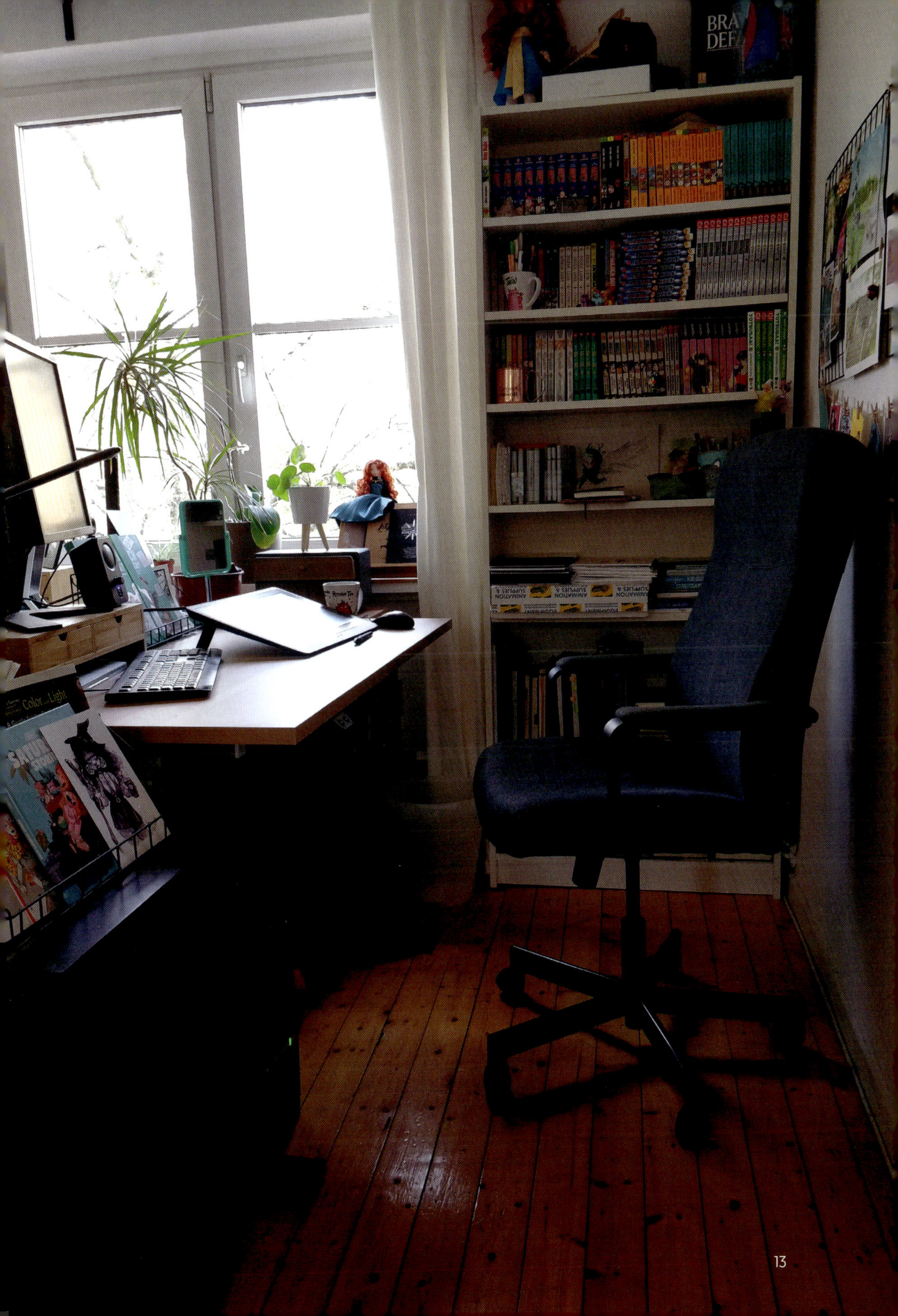

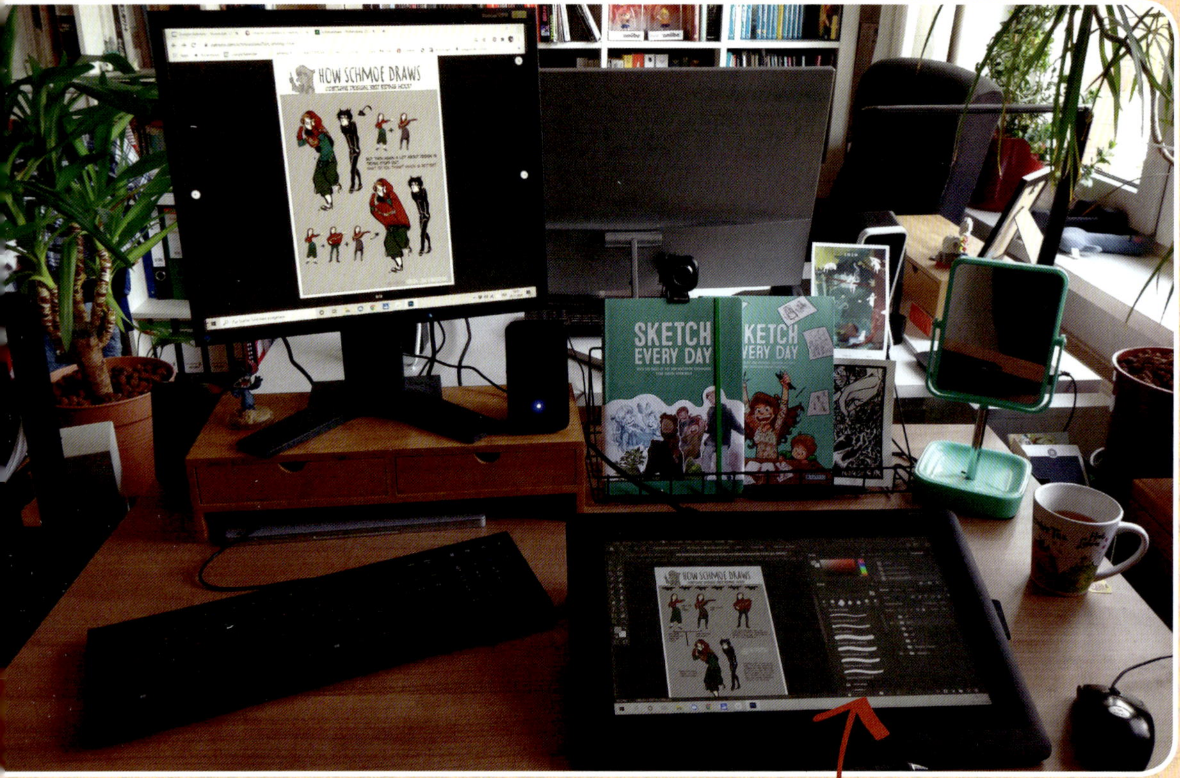

My daily digital setup – as well as my digital tools, my desk features a handy mirror for quick facial reference work and of course, a copy of Sketch Every Day!

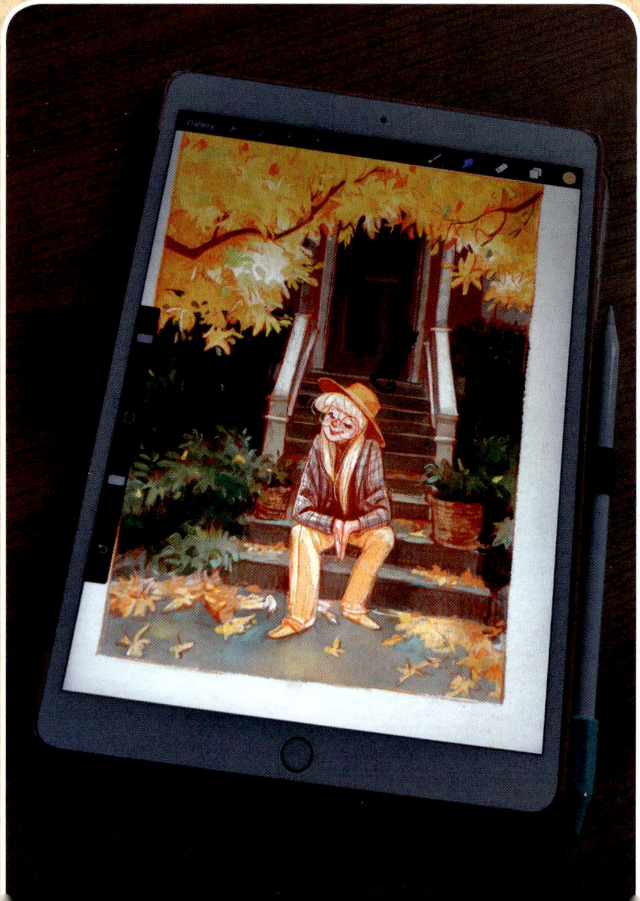

DIGITAL TOOLS

To create my digital designs, or digitally develop some of my traditional illustrations, I work with a Wacom Cintiq 16 tablet as well as an iPad Pro 10.5" from 2017. I use both Adobe Photoshop and Procreate software.

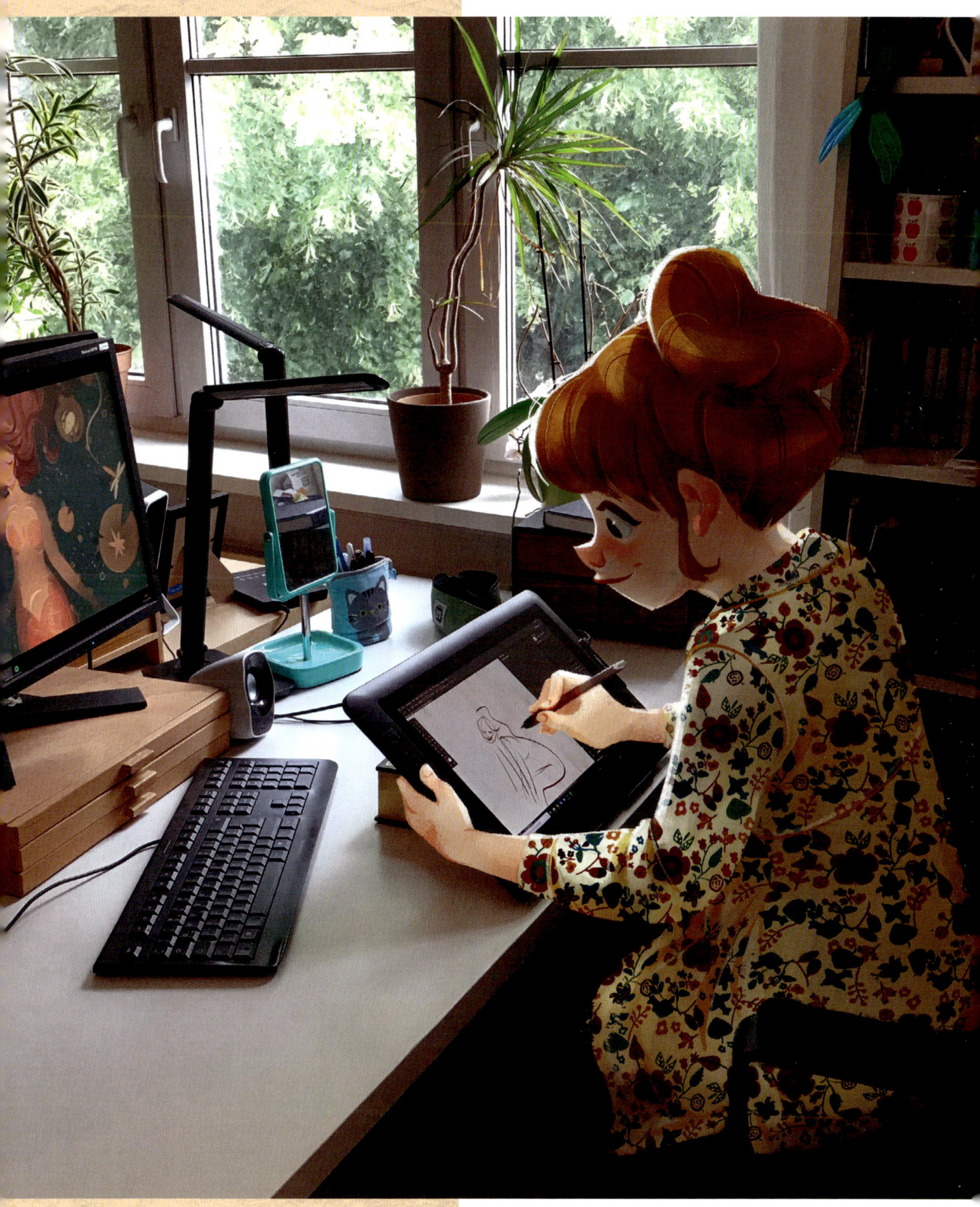

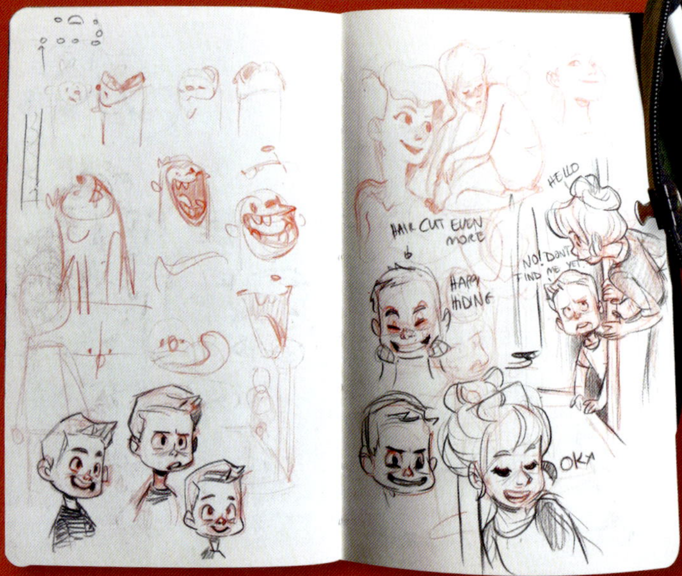

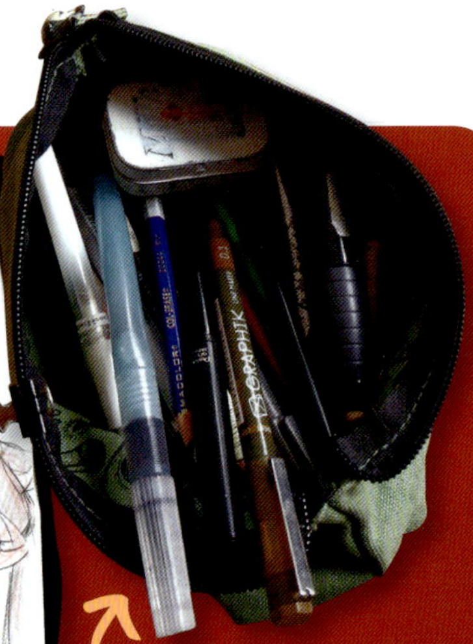

This is my favorite pencil case because it's spacious and always big enough for me to just throw in the materials I want to use

PENS AND PENCILS

I use a variety of different pens in my traditional work, such as white gel pens, fineliners, markers, and brush pens. These images feature a selection of my favorites, including Uni-Ball Signo, Japan Sakura Gelly Roll 05, Tachikawa School G for Manga Sepia, Derwent Graphik Line Maker 0.1mm Sepia, Pentel brush pen, and Zebra Sign WF1 brush pen.

I also use a range of graphite and colored pencils to build my sketches, such as Prismacolor Col-Erase erasable colored pencils (Scarlet Red, Tuscan Red, and Blue shown here), Faber-Castell Polychromos (Black and Venetian Red featured here), Faber-Castell 0.7 Poly Matic mechanical pencils, as well as 2B pencils.

To erase and perfect, I utilize Tombow Mono Zero eraser, Faber-Castell kneadable eraser, and Tombow Mono Light Touch Plastic eraser.

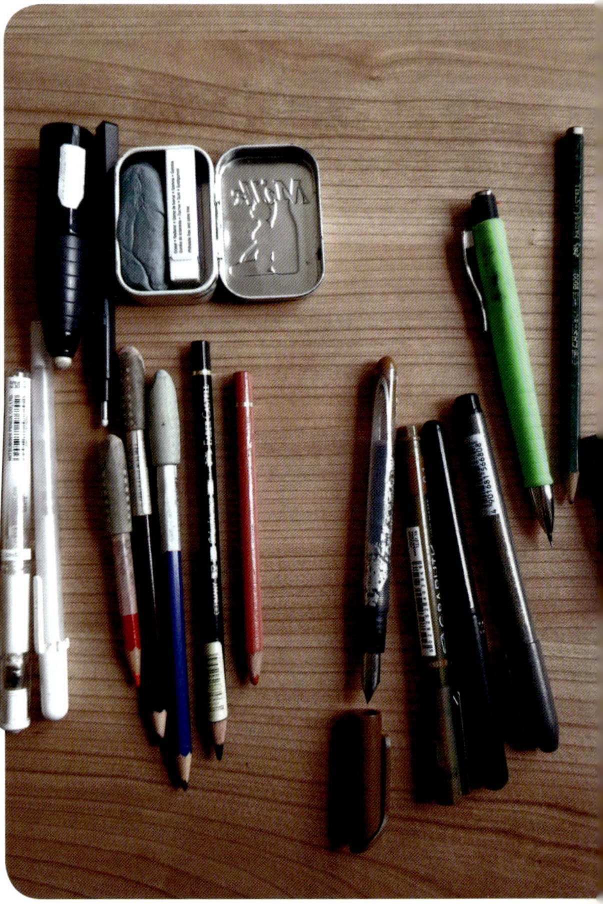

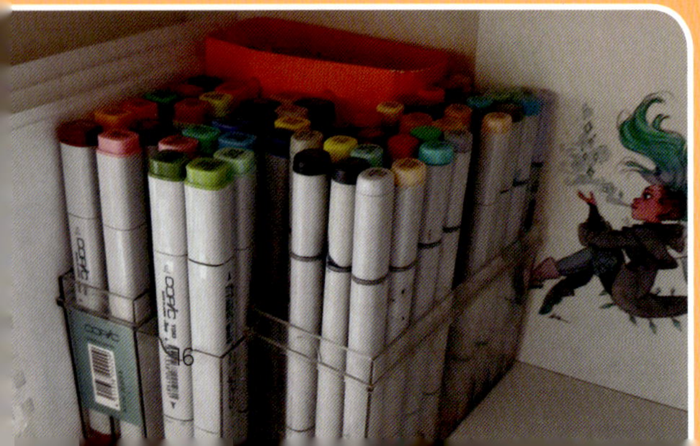

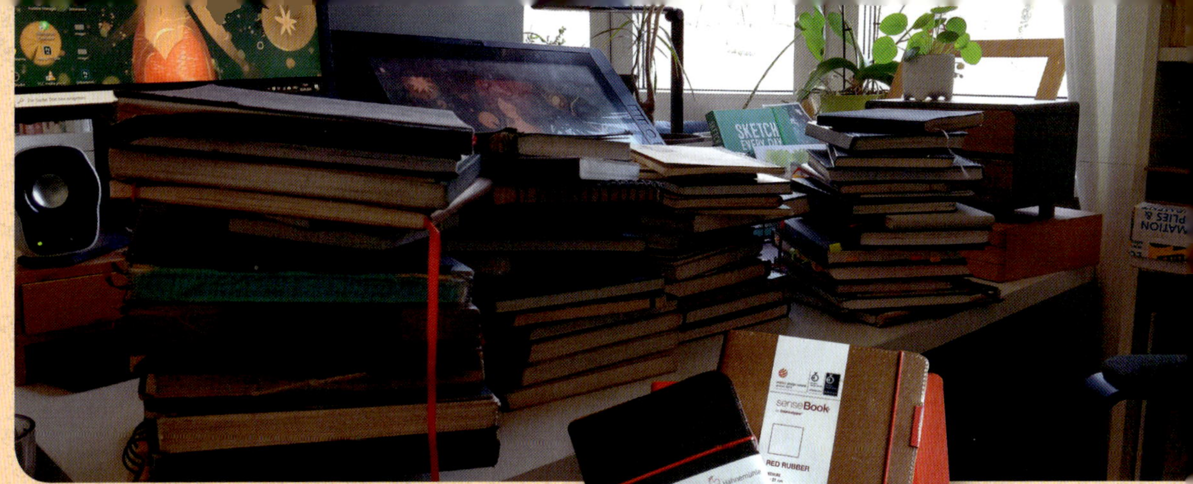

These piles of books are made up from over fifteen years of sketchbooks

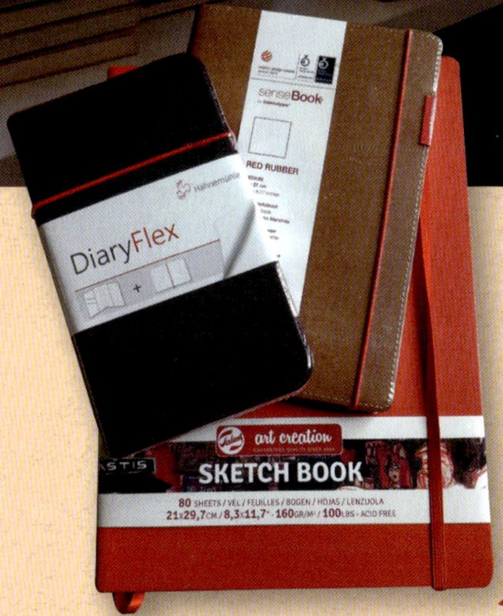

I always keep a few new sketchbooks I want to try out in a drawer

TRADITIONAL TOOLS

The drawers next to my desk contain pencils, fineliner pens, erasers, nibs, and more — I'm an art supply hamster! I use the top drawer of the set of drawers directly next to my desk as an extension of my workspace, and store my watercolor set up here.

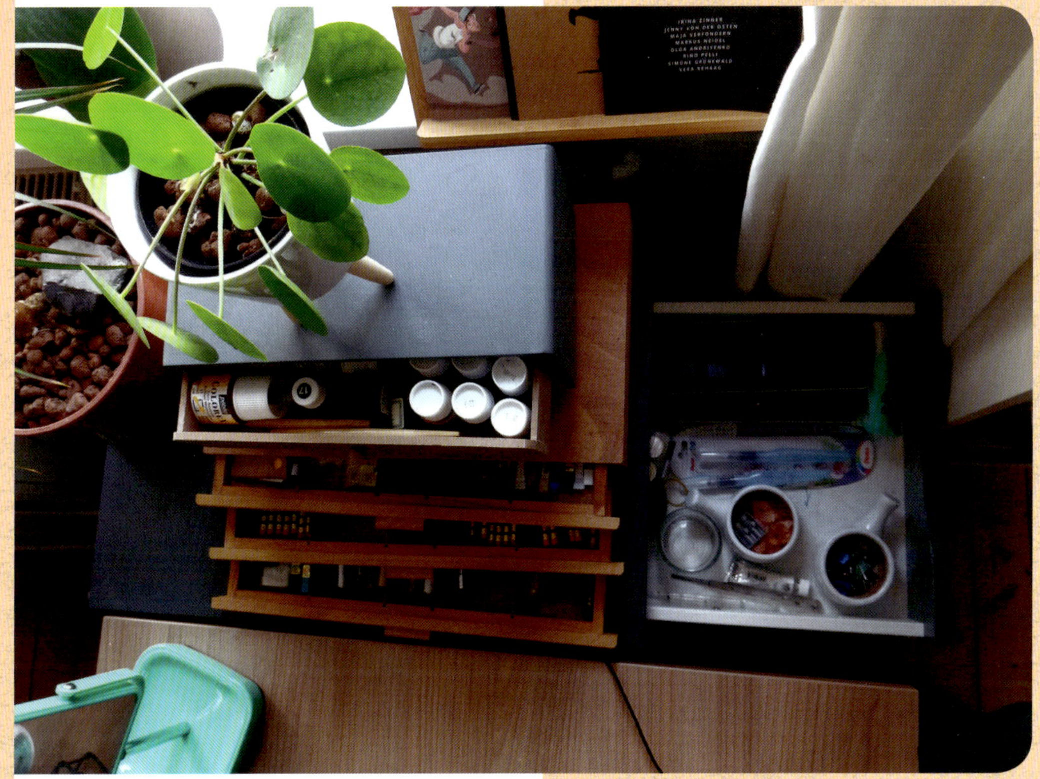

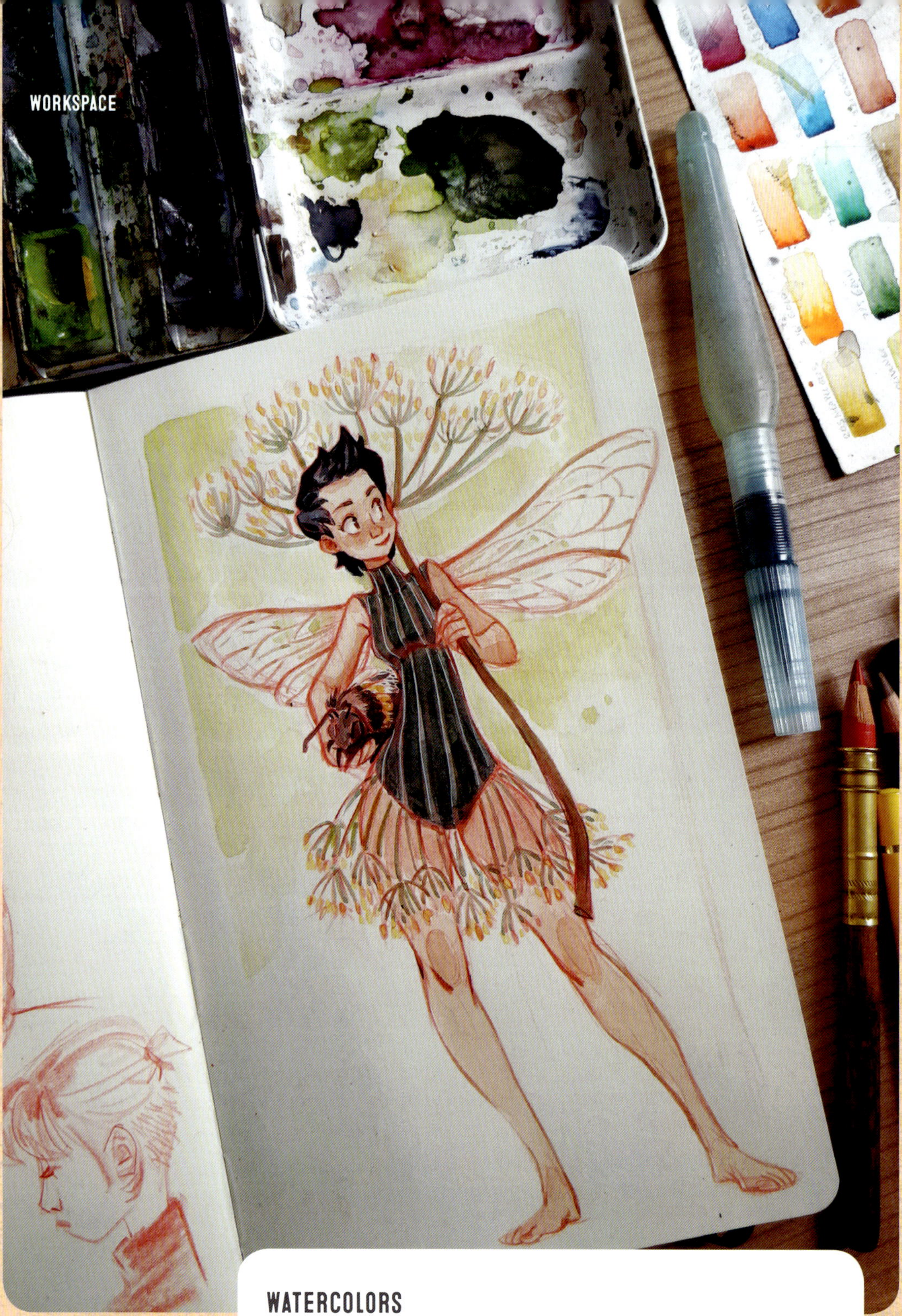

WATERCOLORS

Perfect for painting while traveling, I often use my White Nights watercolor set to develop my watercolor designs. In combination with the watercolor paints, I use a Pentel watercolor brush pen.

Pictured above is my current sketchbook, a Moleskine Art Collection sketchbook, which is solid and has served me well.

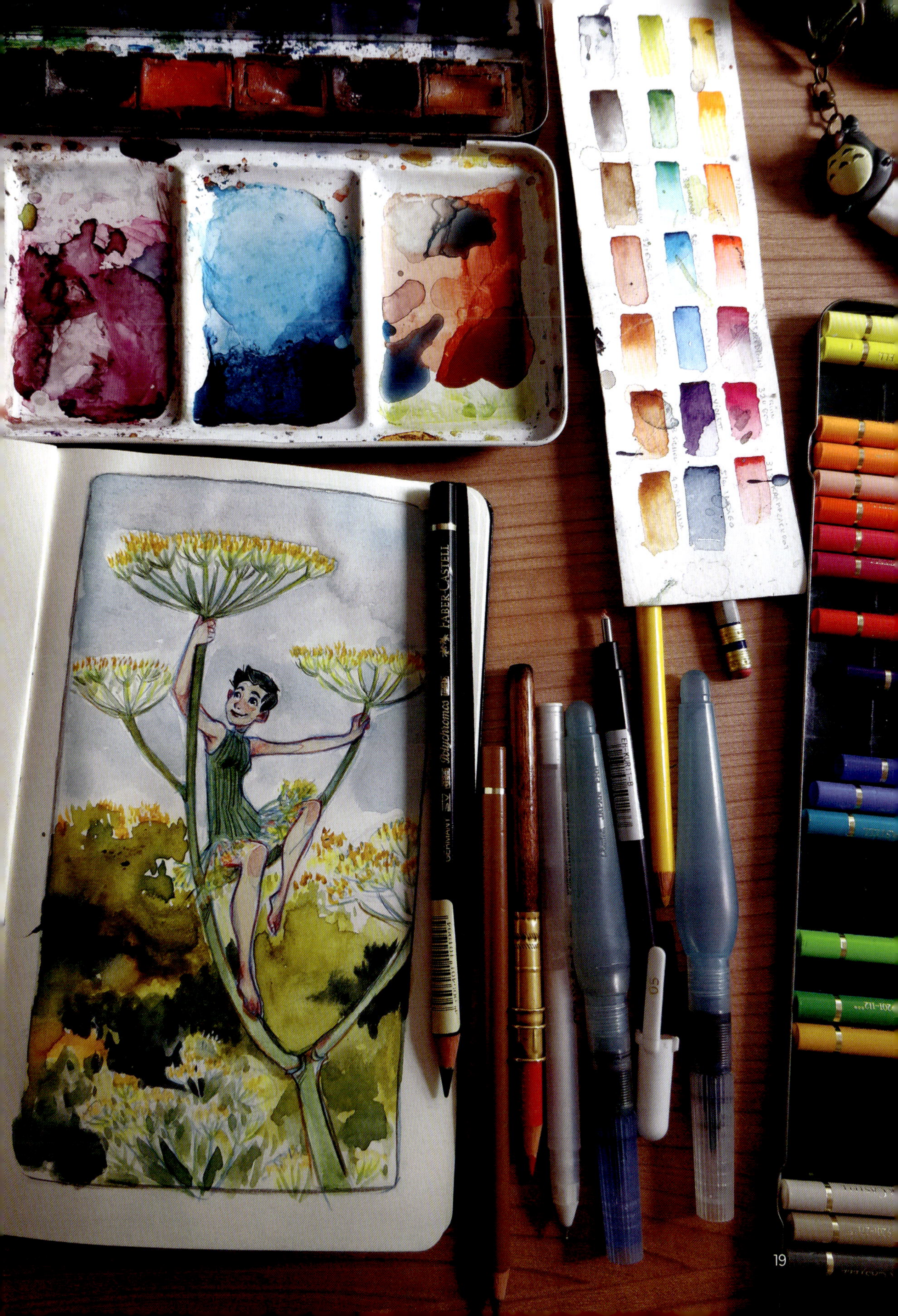

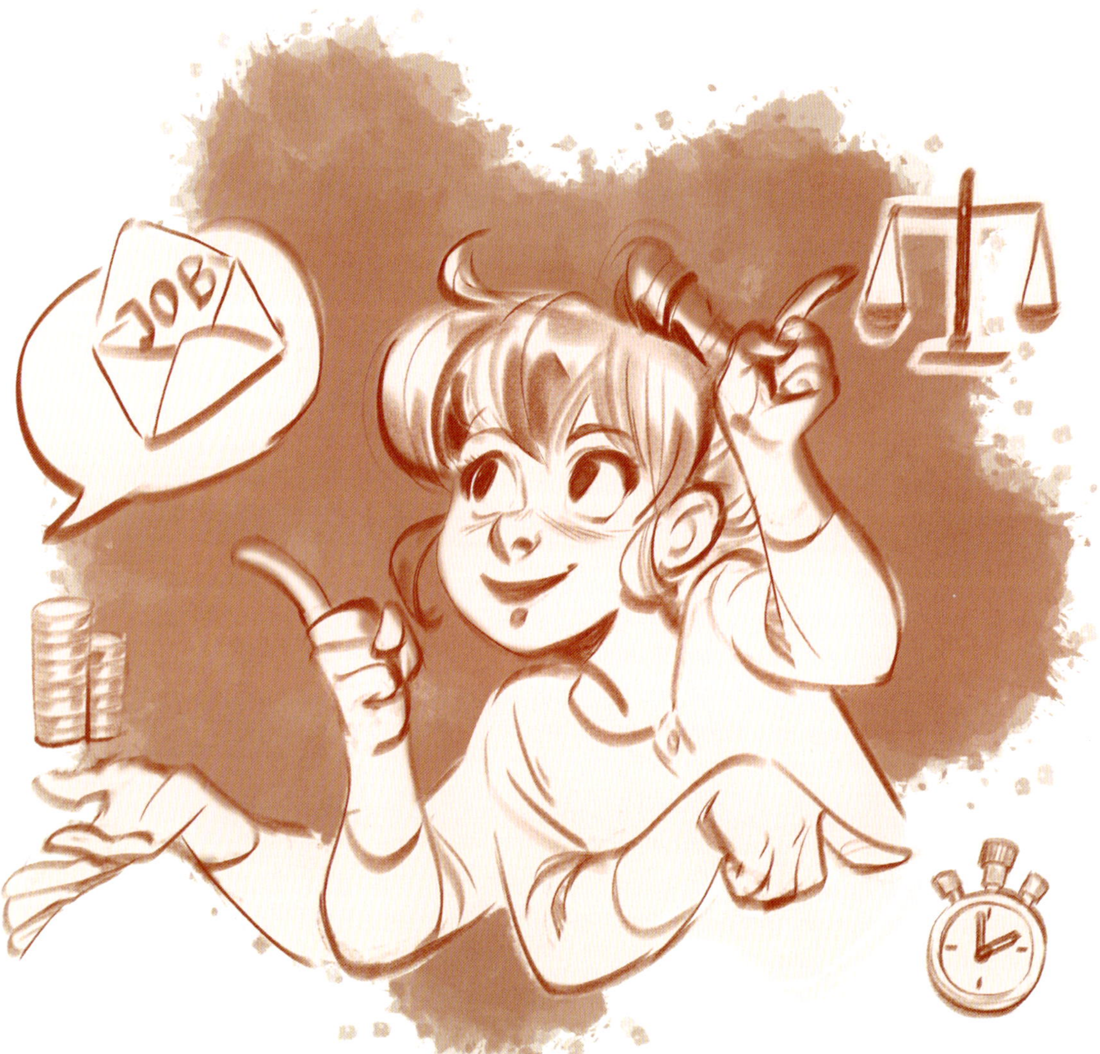
JOB

ARTIST'S ADVICE

When it comes to freelance work, there are so many unknowns and questions that need answering — for example, how to secure commissions and jobs, how to price work, and understanding license fees. In this chapter I share my first-hand experience and tried-and-tested knowledge.

MAKING A LIVING

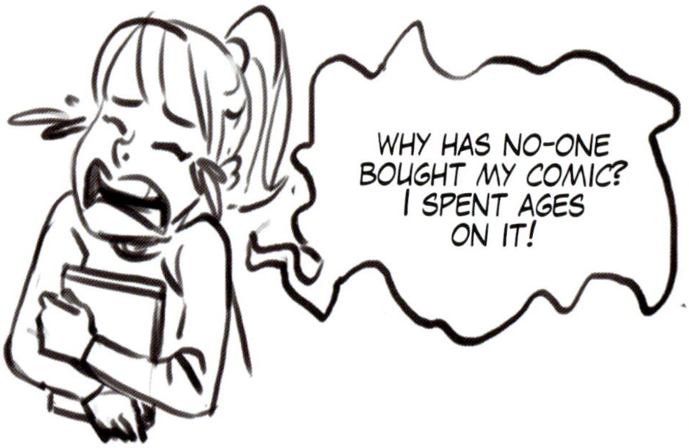

WHERE TO BEGIN?

Find what you love!

Your passion will shine through and make your work appealing.

Build your skills, but remember, there's no need to be good at everything – that takes a lifetime! Focus on achieving a professional level in a small area of interest and expand from there.

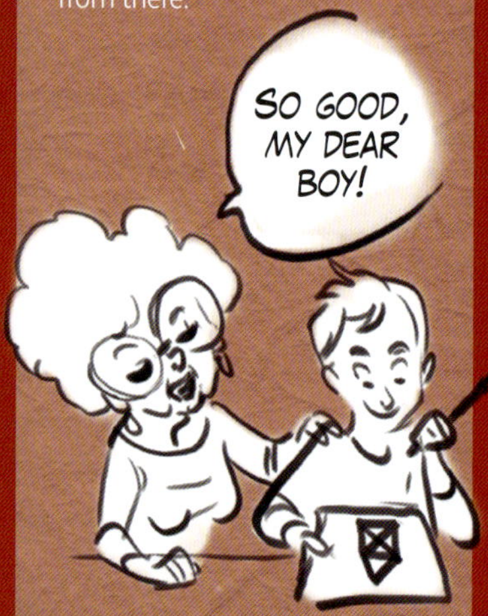

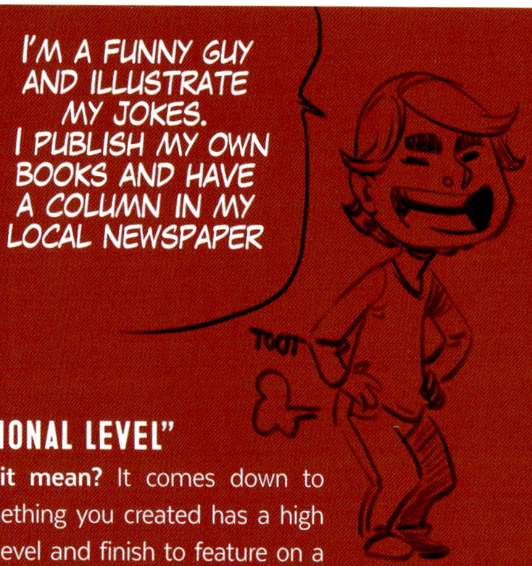

"PROFESSIONAL LEVEL"

What does it mean? It comes down to whether something you created has a high enough skill level and finish to feature on a poster, in a shop, or even as part of a book or TV show.

Your anatomy knowledge is lacking? Not a problem! Either practice until you develop the knowledge and skills or just draw something with simpler anatomy that suits your comfort zone and style. It's beneficial for your confidence if you focus on a topic or technique you can improve and hone. I often see artists that don't take the time to build their foundational skills enough and then they make a big project that just demonstrates all the flaws they still have. It's important to ask for feedback from people outside of your friends and family support network!

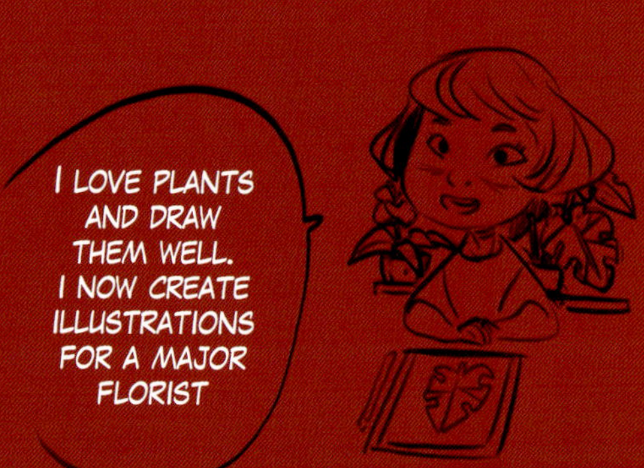

DIFFERENT AREAS OF ART

SKILL LEVEL	STYLE	STORYTELLING	VISUAL DEVELOPMENT	NATURALISTIC ART	
May vary	Illustration: Book covers Magazines Posters Advertising Merchandizing	Books Comics Animation Storyboards	Concept art Character design Set design Prop design	Paintings (in any medium)	Super-high

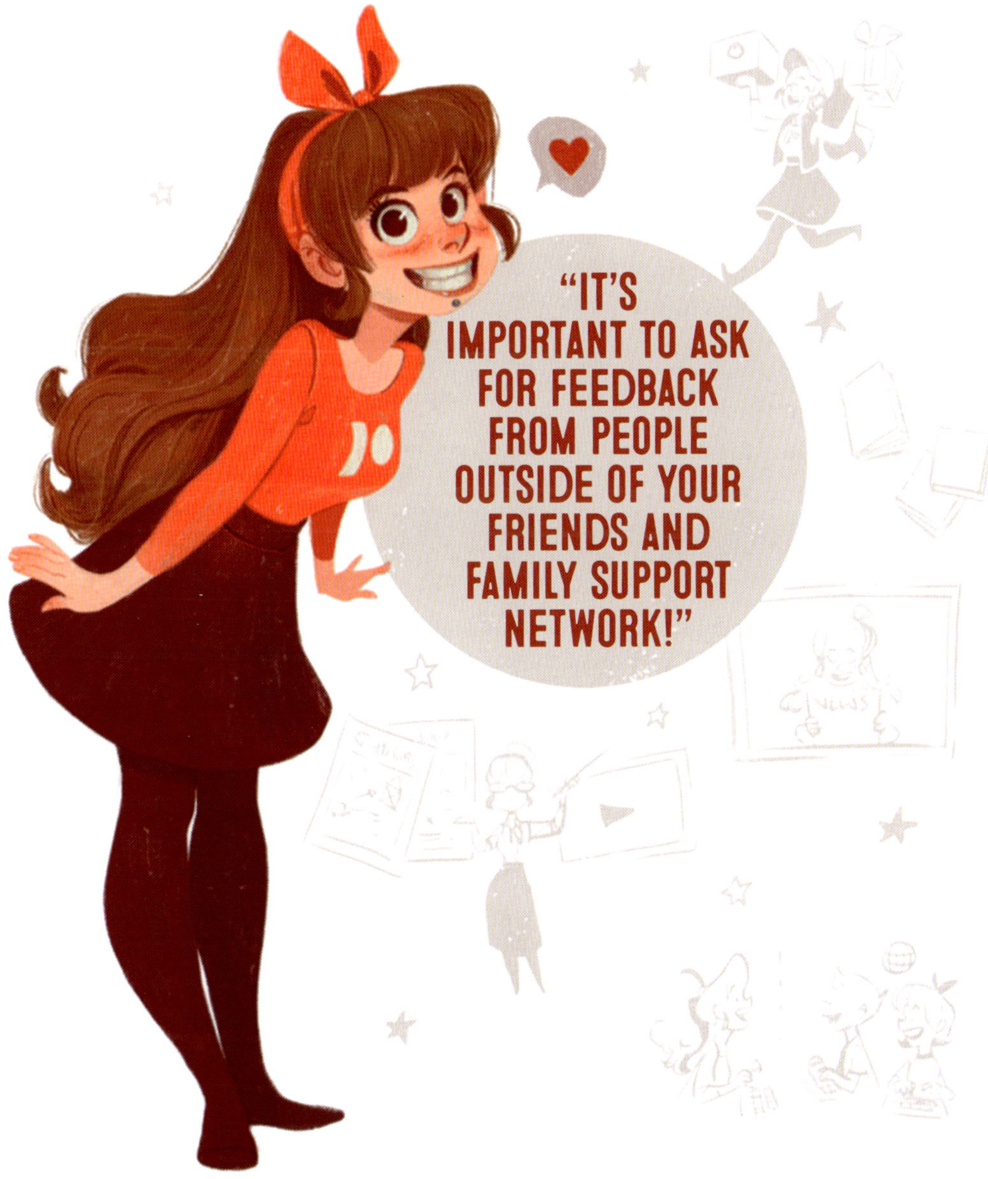

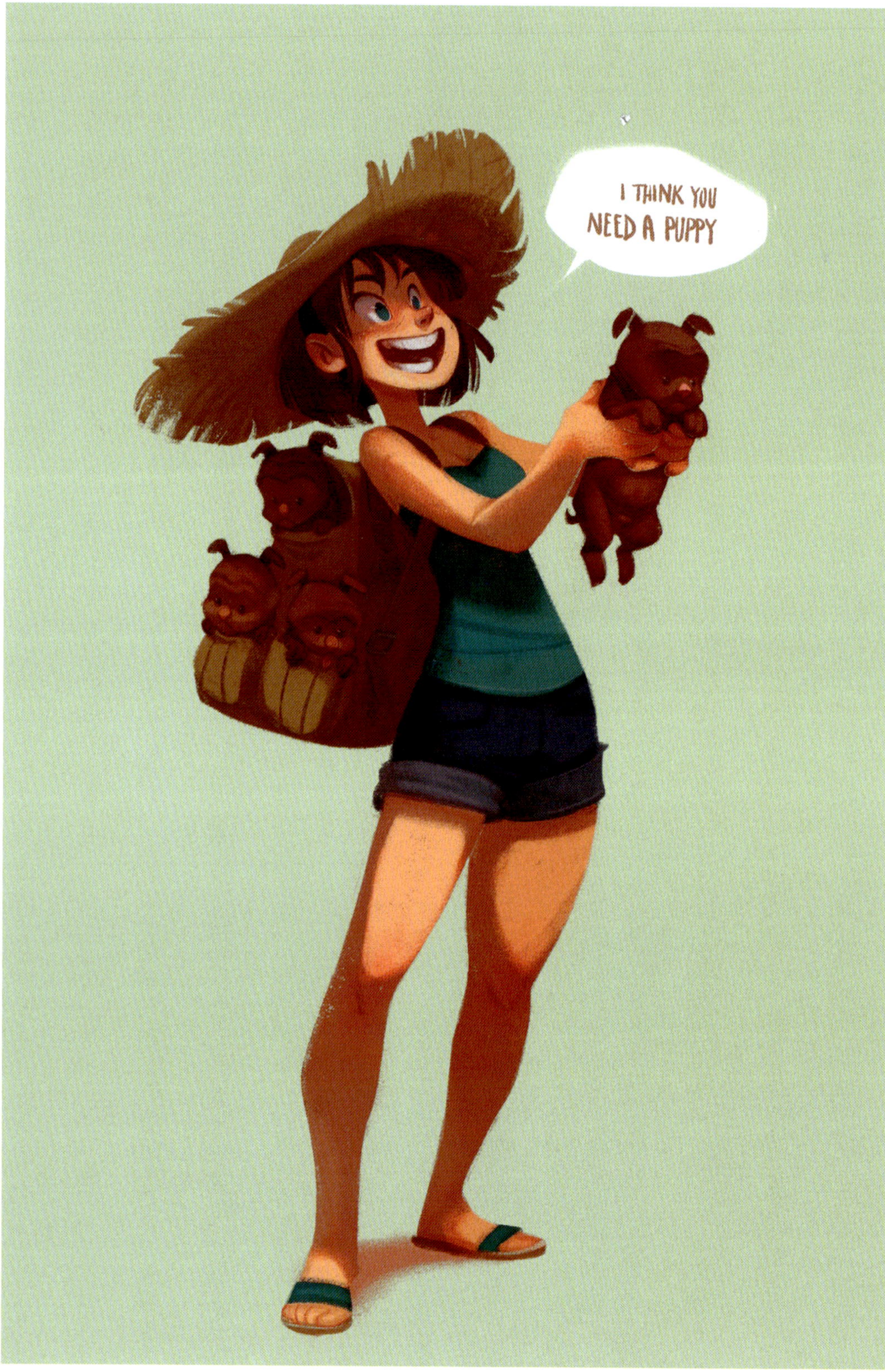
I THINK YOU
NEED A PUPPY

HOW TO MAKE A START

A certain skill level is required (however acquired: art school or self-taught). Find a project you want to pursue and finish it! Pick absolutely anything, such as:

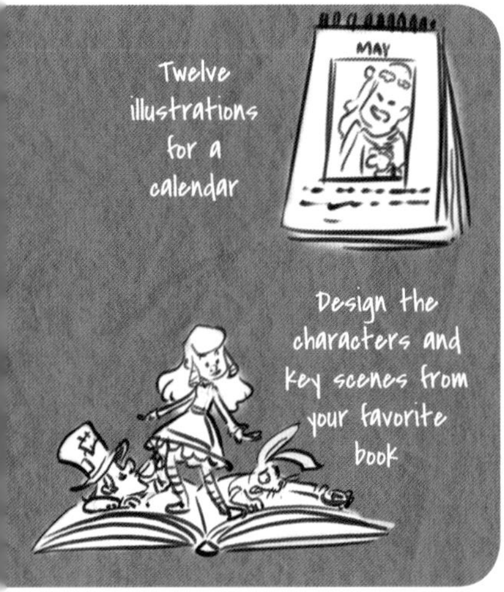

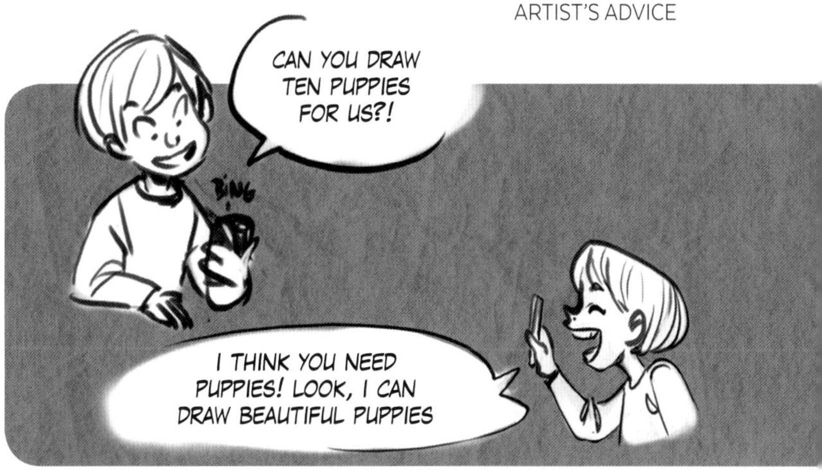

Want to tell a story? Find an art style that you are comfortable with that won't be a strain on your skills and creativity — it's fine to look to other artists for inspiration.

Next, show the world! Maybe even share your process. Take your followers on your journey. If you produce good art, people will notice, your following will grow, and opportunities will arise. With a newly developed portfolio, it is a great time to approach companies.

If you don't find work immediately, be patient and enjoy the freedom of being able to draw whatever you like while you can, before the steady flow of work begins!

BELOW ARE JUST A FEW EXAMPLES OF ARTISTS WHO WORKED HARD AND FORGED THEIR OWN PATHS:

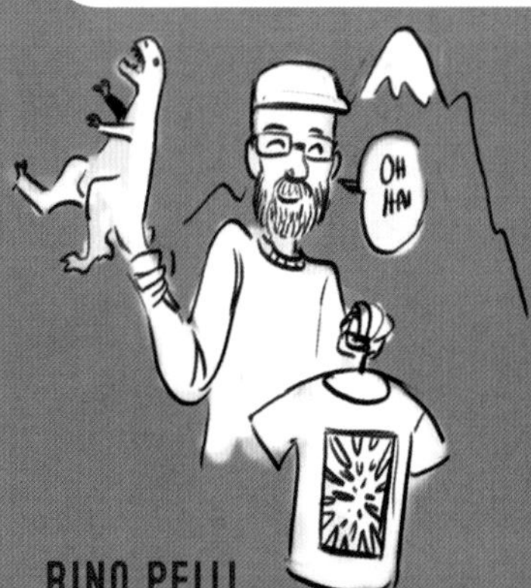

OLGA ANDRIYENKO

Loves storytelling and drawing seductive characters. She started out as a manga artist and now creates concept art storyboards. From the start of her creative journey she was very active on social media and networked with a lot of other artists.

RINO PELLI

Likes dinosaurs and mountains. Started off as a graphic designer, then became an animator, and now undertakes compositing and creates beautiful illustrations for cover and t-shirt designs for a band he loves, who approached him after an old concert-going friend recommended him.

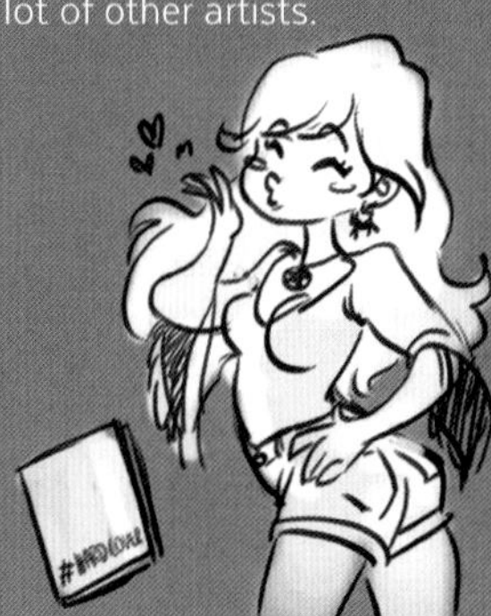

IRINA ZINNER

Makes comics and illustrations for many different companies. She found her clean, sweet comic style very early on in her career. She started as an intern at Daedalic and from there her connections grew, from which many opportunities arose. She always takes care to be reliable and deliver on time.

NETWORKING AND DEVELOPING A SUCCESSFUL PRACTICE

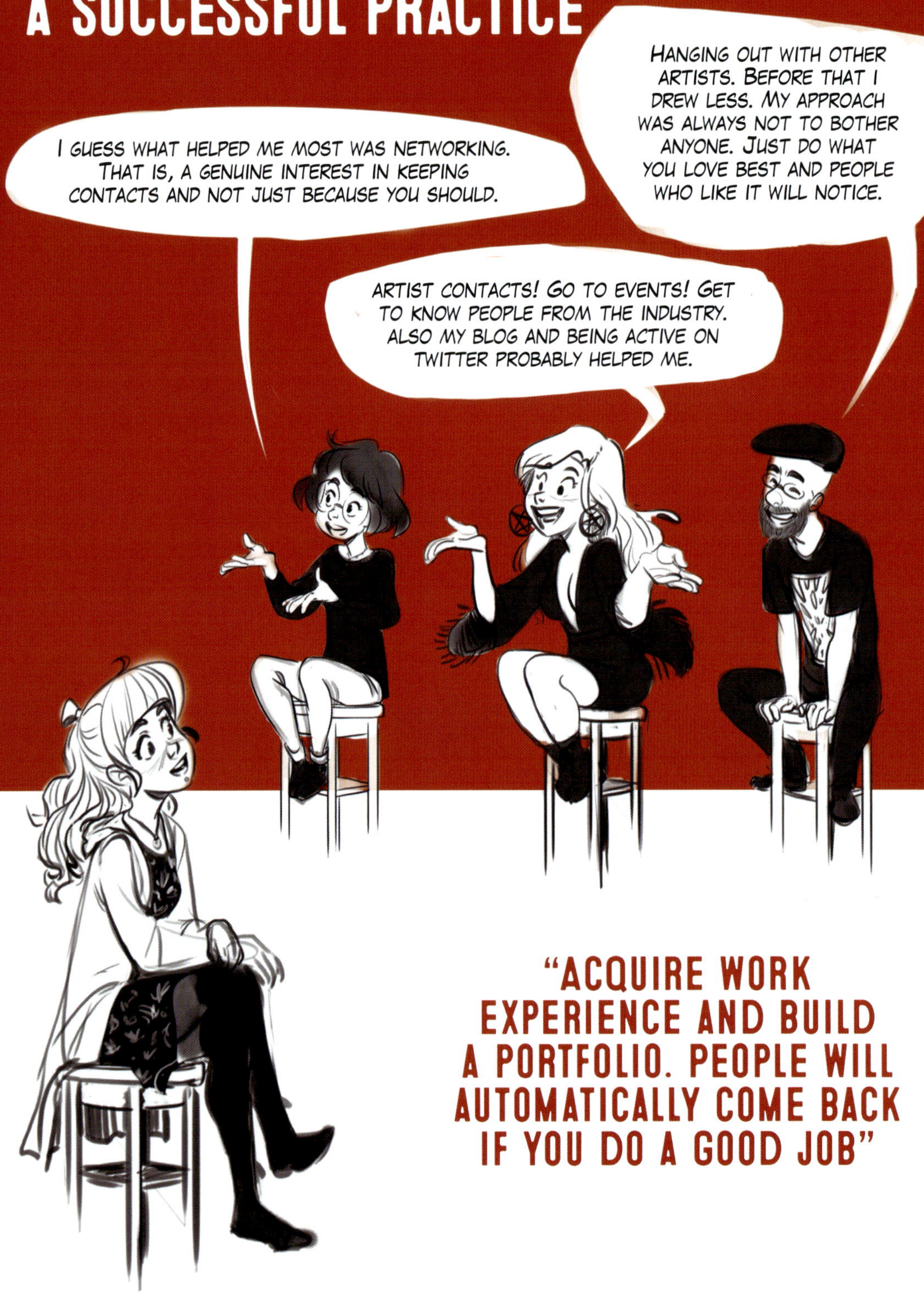

"ACQUIRE WORK EXPERIENCE AND BUILD A PORTFOLIO. PEOPLE WILL AUTOMATICALLY COME BACK IF YOU DO A GOOD JOB"

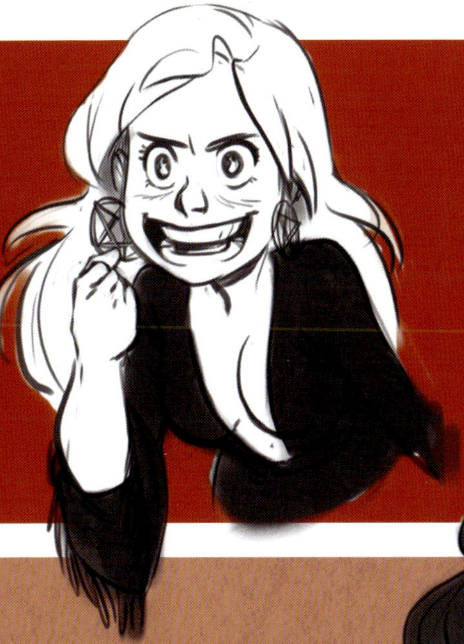

Try out as much as possible. That was how I found out what I like doing best. I drew manga, worked at different games companies, gave drawing lessons, and even tried web design. Many artists may suggest focusing on creating the perfect portfolio for your dream company, but at the beginning I believe it is more beneficial to experiment as much as possible before honing your chosen skills and style.

OLGA ANDRIYENKO

Acquire work experience and build a portfolio. People will automatically come back if you do a good job. Be reliable! At the beginning of my career, I secured plenty of jobs where other artists had left last minute.

IRINA ZINNER

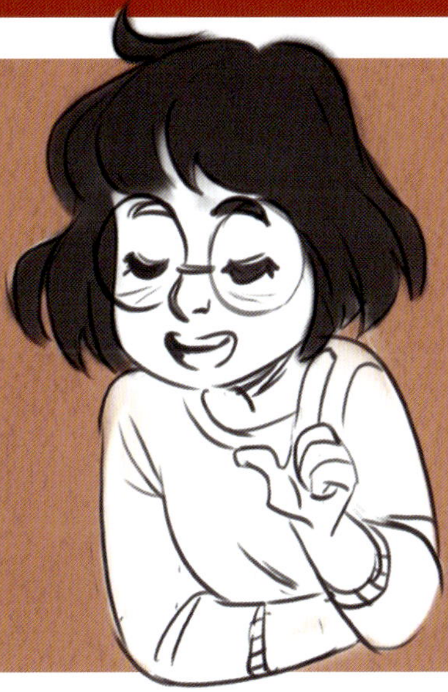

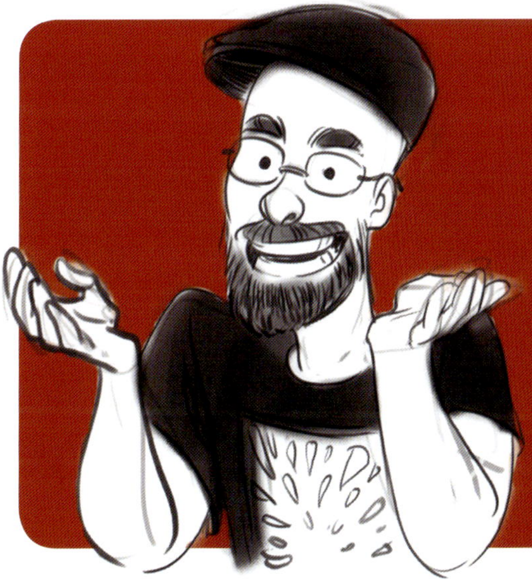

If you are unsure or stuck with where to go next with your art, show the work to other artist friends. Informed input so often solves problems for me! And don't undervalue your work. Accurately calculate what kind of hourly rates you need to receive. If the customer's budget doesn't allow for more, make suggestions that can work for both parties, for example, a simplified design. It's okay to compromise, just not so much that it won't work for you.

RINO PELLI

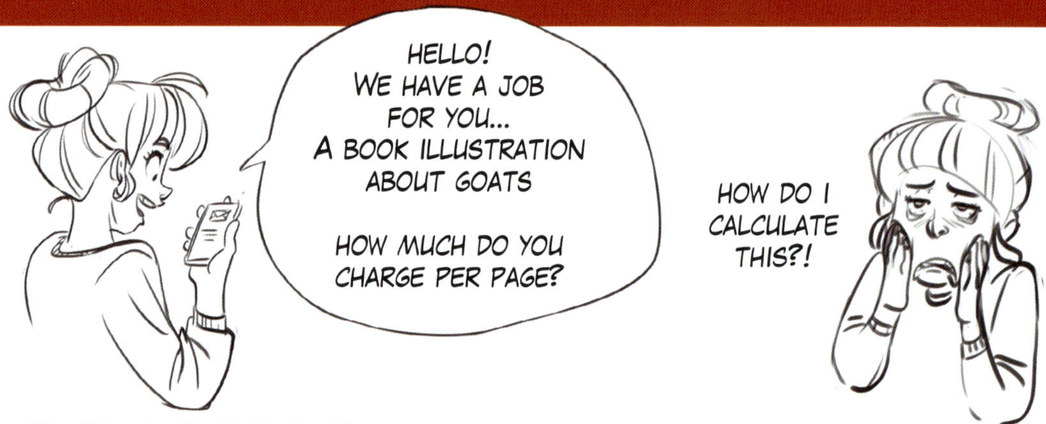

PRICING

To start, make sure to have all the information necessary to make an educated guess at how long the work will take to complete. Request detailed information from the customer to find out what they envision for the project. For example, do they have a story in mind, or a specific style? How many characters need to be designed? Are backgrounds required? What is the overall size of the project, and how detailed does it need to be? And how much freedom do you have as the designer?

THE CUSTOMER SELECTS A STYLE AND EXPLAINS THEY ARE LOOKING FOR:

Full-color illustrations

- Two double-page illustrations, of which one is the cover, front and back
- Two single-page illustrations
- Two single character illustrations

ALTERNATIVELY, THE CUSTOMER MIGHT SELECT A STYLE AND ANSWER:

Here is the story, now you offer a layout.
All creative decisions are up to you!

FOR THIS EXAMPLE, I WILL FOLLOW THE FIRST BRIEF:

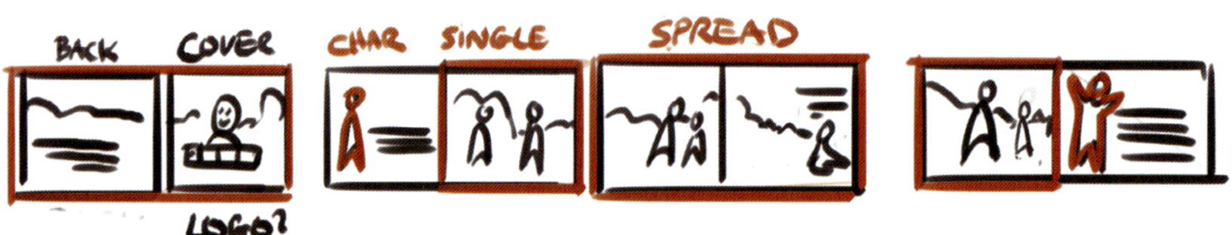

In both cases it is useful to create a rough layout to aid pricing calculations. The layouts shouldn't take more than a few minutes but will help to visualize the project as a whole and break down the workload. They are for your eyes only and don't need to detail the story. The characters I sketched above help me guestimate how many could actually be depicted. You don't want to waste time creating final work before the customer accepts the proposal.

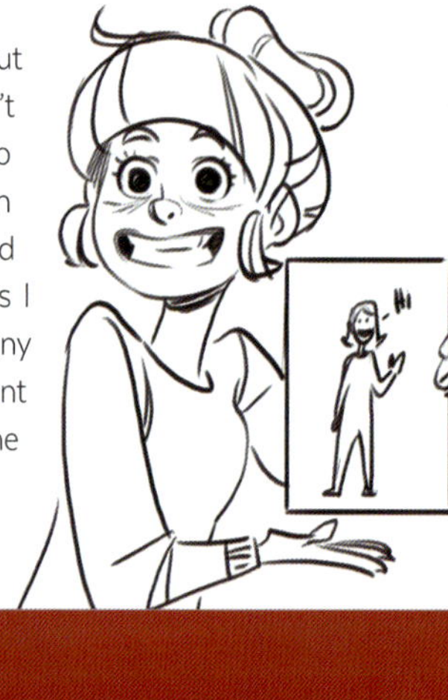

Per character design (including sketch work) I estimate a colored render to take approximately 3-4 hours and a monochrome render to take 1-2 hours.

In my imaginary layouts I count 10 characters, so I calculate 3.5 hours x 10 characters = 35 hours to produce 10 characters.

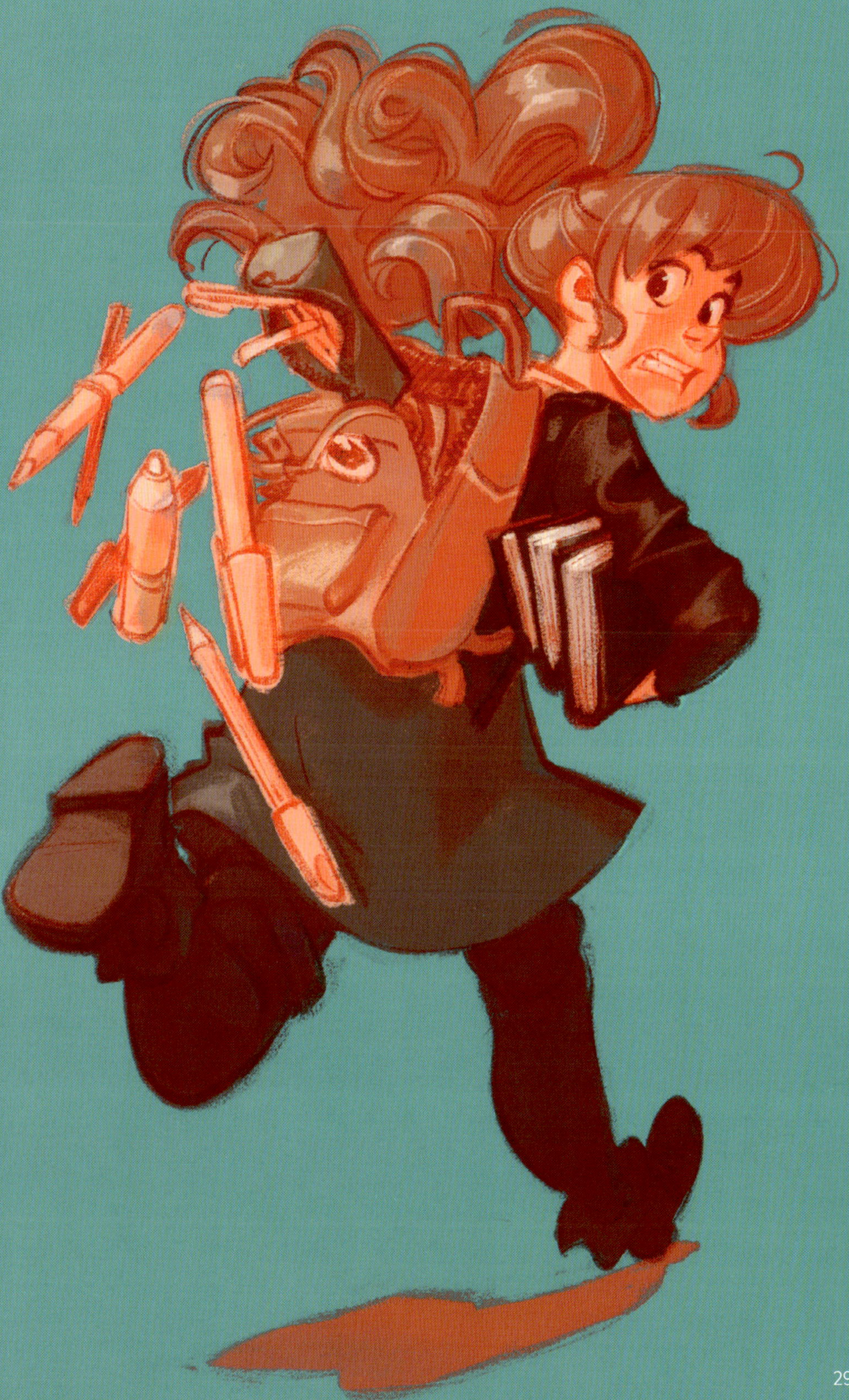

PRICING BACKGROUND DESIGNS

TIME PER BACKGROUND (INCLUDING THE SKETCH BUT NOT THE CHARACTERS)

SUPER SIMPLE: 0.5 - 1 HOUR

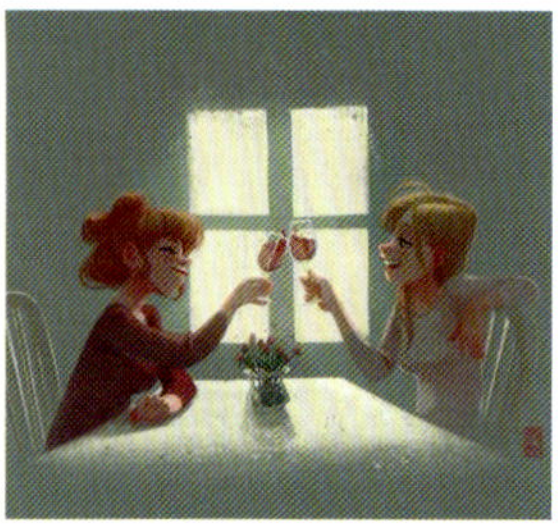

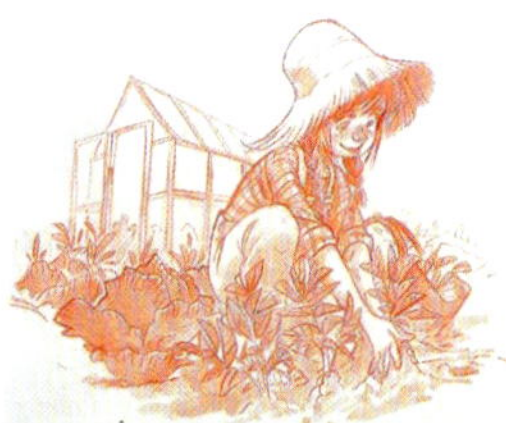

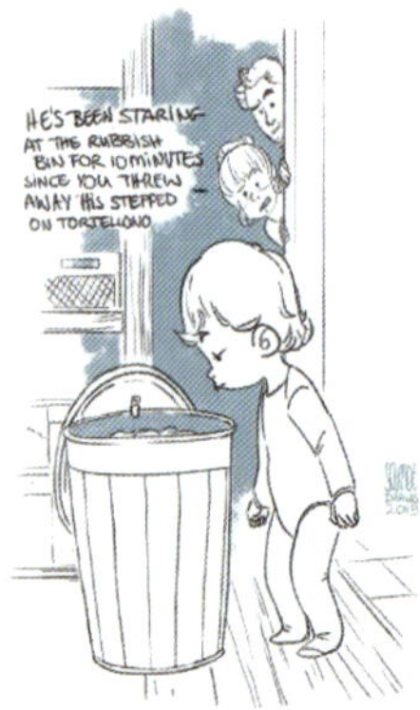

SIMPLE: 1.5 - 3 HOURS

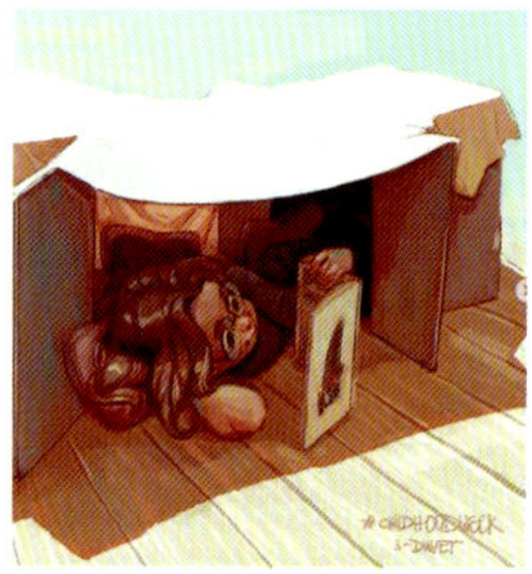

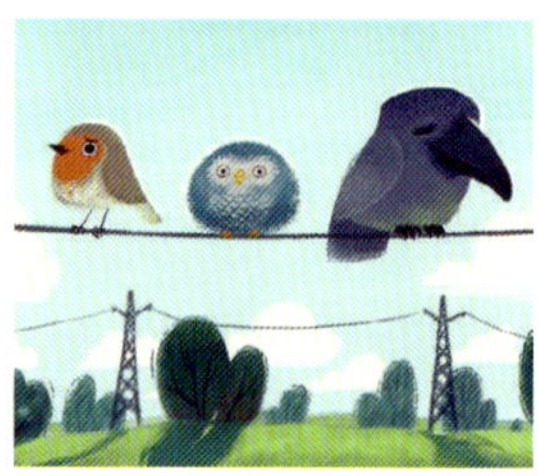

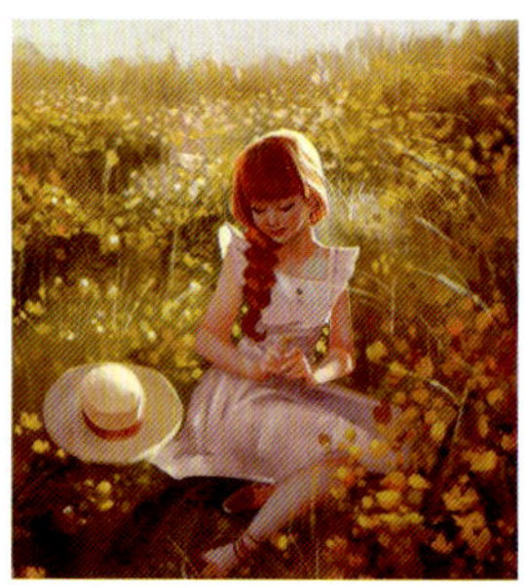

MEDIUM: 3 - 4 HOURS

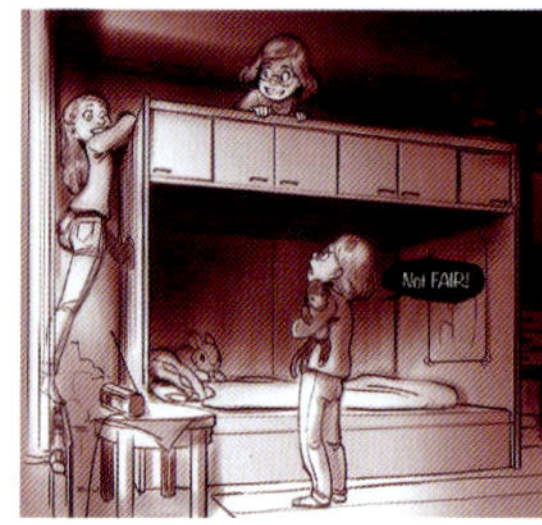

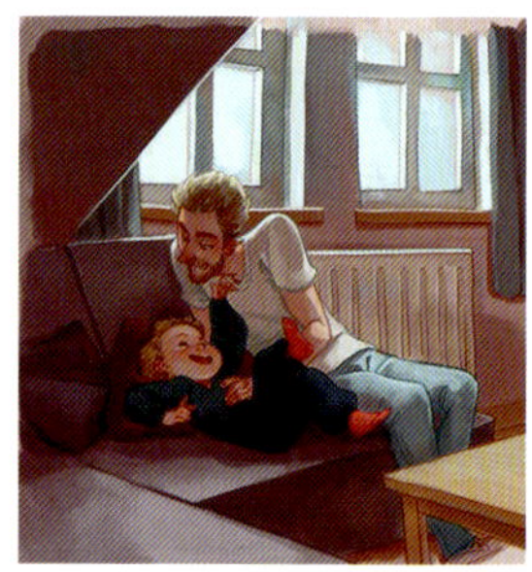

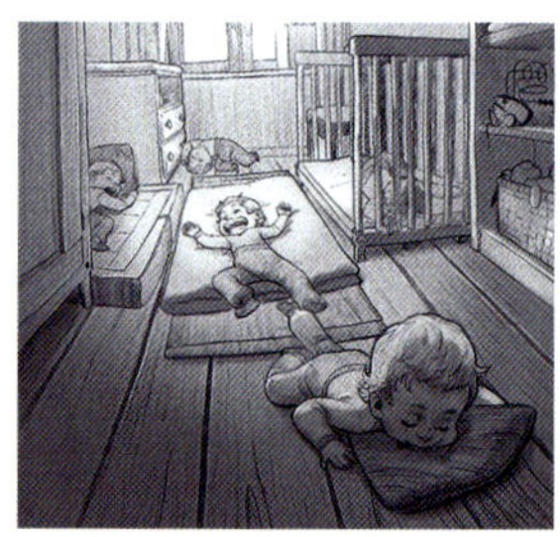

ELABORATE: 8 - 16 HOURS

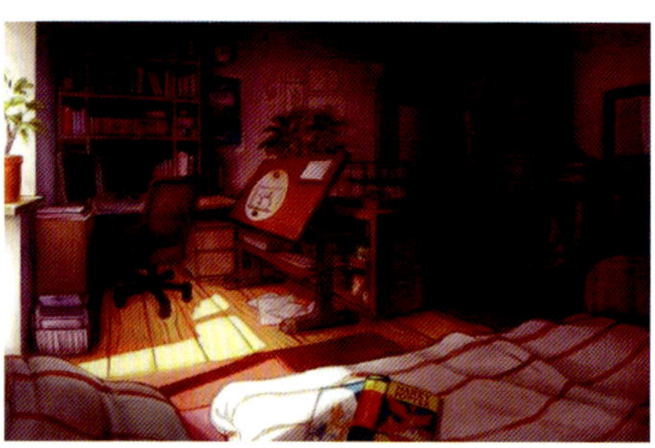

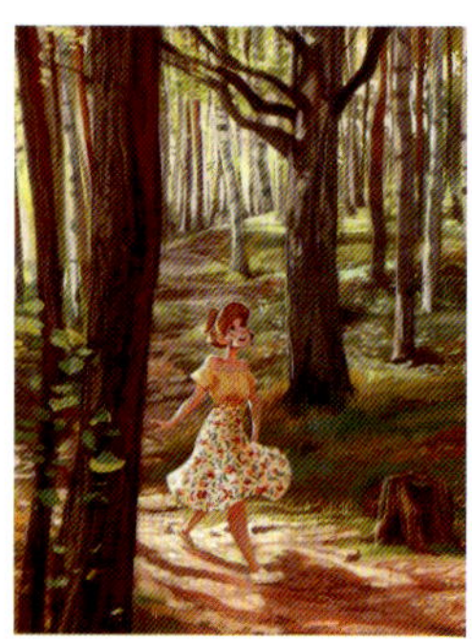

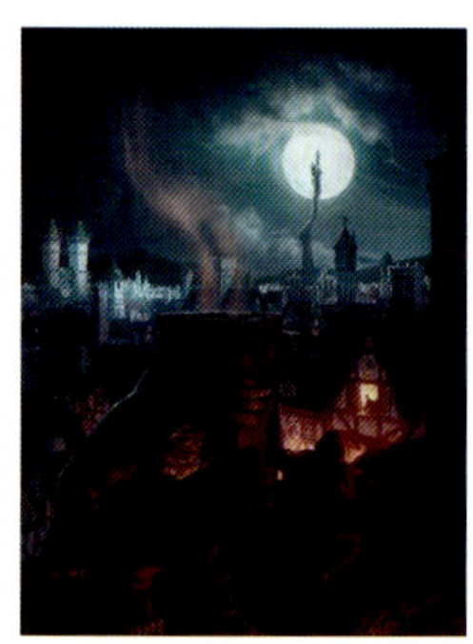

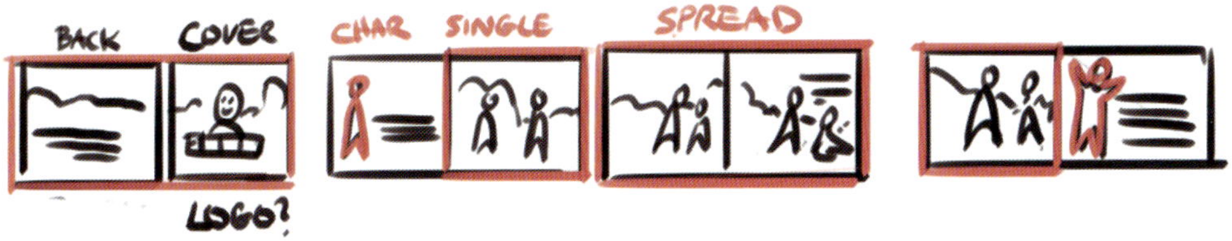

Revisit your rough layouts to make an estimate. In this example, I make calculations with two elaborate and two medium backgrounds in mind. So, the calculation would be:

2 x 12 hours (average for elaborate backgrounds) +
2 x 3.5 (average for medium backgrounds)

31 HOURS IN TOTAL

This calculation gives you an idea of the number of hours the backgrounds could take to create. Consider that the customer might require some corrections, so add another 8 hours to the total.

Next, to achieve a total fee for the work, add up the hours it will take to create the characters and backgrounds, plus extra time for making corrections.

The calculation would therefore be as follows:

35 hours to create characters +
31 hours to create backgrounds +
8 hours to make corrections

74 HOURS IN TOTAL

"CREATE A ROUGH LAYOUT TO AID YOUR PRICING CALCULATIONS... THEY WILL HELP YOU TO VISUALIZE THE PROJECT AS A WHOLE"

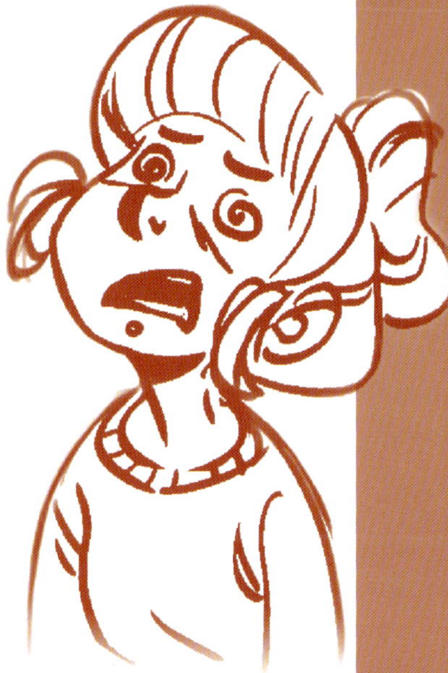

When divided by the number of pages that are required, the total hours per page can be found. As there are 8 pages required within the project, the calculation would be:

74 hours ÷ 8 pages = 9.25 hours per finished page

To find a final price per page, I multiply the number of hours required to make the design by my hourly rate, which is 60 euro. The calculation is then:

9.25 HOURS X 60 EURO = 555 EURO PER PAGE

TRACK YOUR TIME

Monitoring and making note of how long different processes take you to complete is very valuable when it comes to working out the final pricing, as you can be more accurate and realistic with timings and calculating hourly rates.

CHARACTER DESIGN PRICING BREAKDOWN

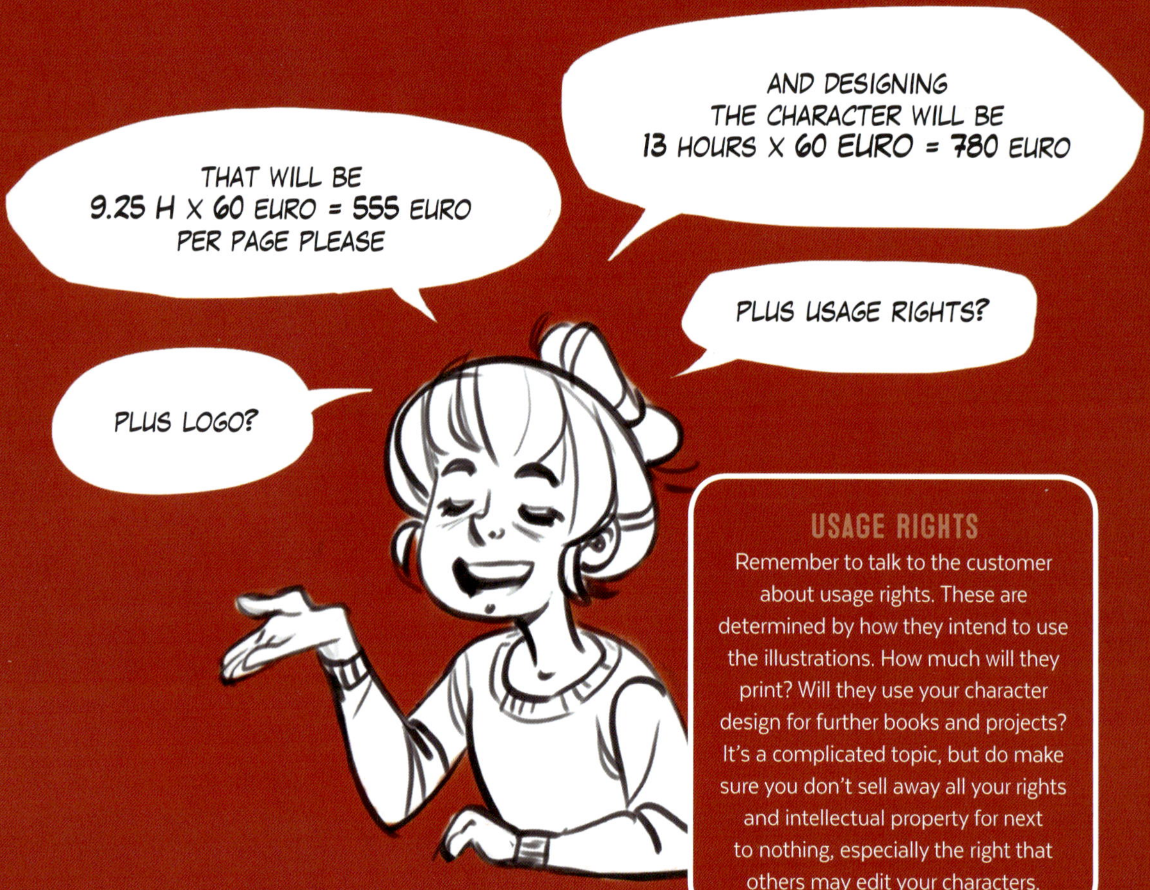

USAGE RIGHTS

Remember to talk to the customer about usage rights. These are determined by how they intend to use the illustrations. How much will they print? Will they use your character design for further books and projects? It's a complicated topic, but do make sure you don't sell away all your rights and intellectual property for next to nothing, especially the right that others may edit your characters.

As a reference for the pricing calculations for the rest of the characters, it is helpful to have one of the main characters completely designed.

My estimates for creating a character are:

3-4 SKETCHES OF THE MAIN CHARACTER, WITH CORRECTIONS = 5 HOURS

3 COLOR SUGGESTIONS, WITH CORRECTIONS = 8 HOURS

However, when asked to create special character designs such as mascots for adverts or branding, the design work and pricing will be more complex and the price should take usage rights costs into account, which can be very high.

When adding the cost of the character development together with the price per page, the whole project would cost 5,220 euro. That price may seem quite high, but it may not be a problem, and it often depends on who the customer is. You could lower the price by taking a lower hourly rate and working less elaborately on the backgrounds and characters, but it's better to plan for a contingency, as not everything works out as expected.

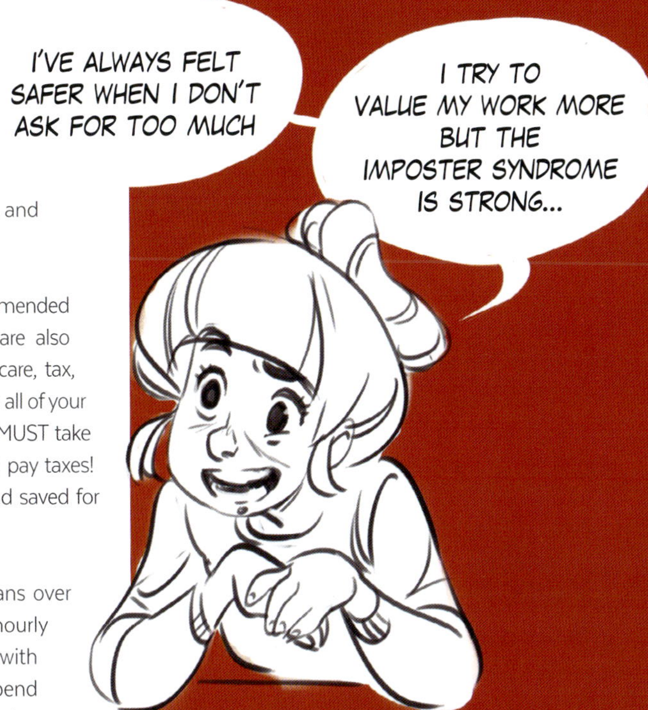

HOURLY RATES

60 euro is my highest rate at the moment, but depending on the customer, I could and should go higher. The lowest rate I apply is 30 euro an hour, and that is a bit too low.

In Germany, a rate of at least 50 euro is recommended so that you can pay for overheads. There are also additional costs to consider, such as health care, tax, and covering quieter working periods. Examine all of your expenses and calculate the hourly rates you MUST take to survive. And don't forget that you need to pay taxes! At least a third of my income is put aside and saved for paying taxes.

When working on a steady project that spans over a long period of time, I can charge a lower hourly rate because I know it will be stable work, with no quieter periods where I will need to spend time looking for more work. Whereas, for short jobs (such as one-off commissions or branding), I apply my highest rate, to make all of the communication time a new job requires worthwhile.

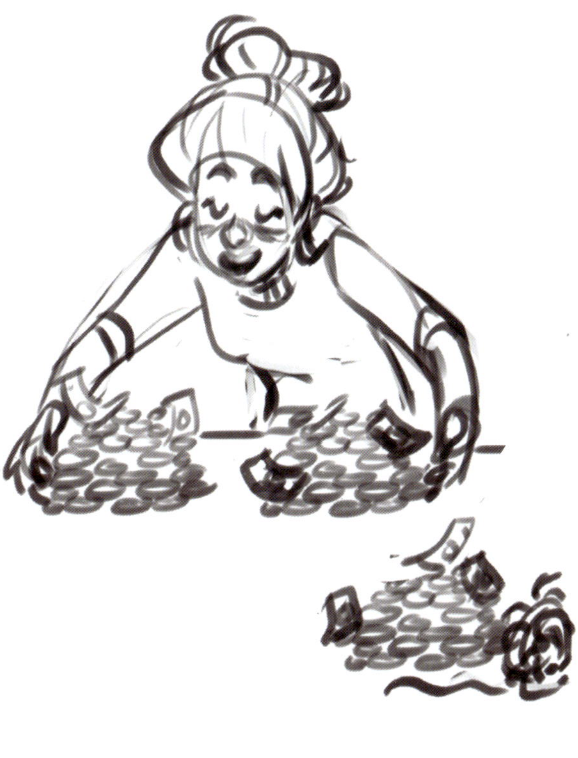

"EXAMINE ALL OF YOUR EXPENSES AND CALCULATE THE HOURLY RATES YOU *MUST* TAKE TO SURVIVE"

LICENSING

Licensing is a topic that freelancers (myself included!) are often unsure of because there are many different factors to consider. As projects and commissions differ, so do the licensing requirements.

The best place to start is by understanding that the original artist of a piece of art automatically has copyright over it. This means that you have copyright over the art you create! Art is the intellectual property of the artist and the commissioner requires a license to reproduce the art for a specific length of time.

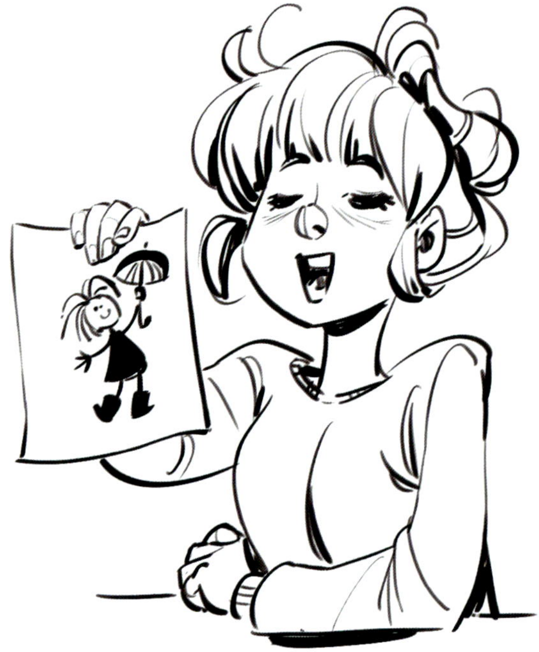

LEVEL OF LICENSING REQUIRED → **EXTRA LICENSING FEE**

PRIVATE COMMISSIONS

For example, a personal commission for an individual. These are usually for private use only and will only need to pay a licensing fee if the commissioner wants to sell or use the design commercially.

CONCEPT ART

Work could include character designs for films or storyboards. As these are often created for a company, you will usually be required to sign a contract to give the company full ownership of any work produced for the project.

ONE-OFF ILLUSTRATION FOR AN INDIVIDUAL FOR COMMERCIAL USE

For example, creating an avatar and header for a YouTuber. As the art is being used for commercial reasons, it makes sense to include a licensing fee in the price.

A COLLECTION OF ILLUSTRATIONS FOR A CALENDAR

As a commercial item, the pricing should include a licensing fee, or a royalty agreement should be in place to ensure you receive payment for the work as sales continue.

BOOK ILLUSTRATIONS

Projects created for the publishing industry will often be subject to royalties, and if a large amount of work is created for the project, an advance payment will also be offered to cover costs of early work.

LOGO DESIGN

Depending on the company the work is created for, this logo may be reproduced lots of times and for a long period of time (potentially the lifespan of the company itself!). In this case, it is sensible to carefully assess the requirements and work out the rates of licensing fees that are appropriate – often work for the advertising industry will be much higher paid than work for the entertainment industry.

CALCULATING LICENSING FEES

Once design costs have been calculated (see previous section on Pricing on pages 28-33), a licensing fee can be determined and added to the design fee to give an overall charge for the work. Make sure to ask lots of questions about the commissioned work, as the answers will help to guide the price of the licensing fee for the project. The table below, which I use for my licensing calculations here in Germany, may assist with calculations. Recognized organizations such as the Illustratoren Organisation in Germany or the Association of Illustrators in the UK share similar tables to give a guide to industry pricing standards.

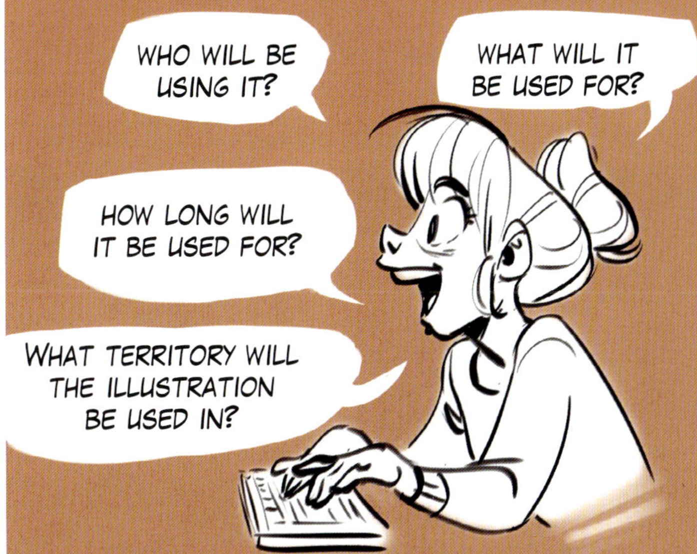

TYPE OF USE	INTENDED USE	SCOPE OF USE	DURATION	TERRITORY	EXTRA
Non-exclusive **0.1**	1 print media **0.1**	Small edition and target group **0.1**	3 months to 1 year **0.1**	Local **0.1**	Total buy-out **3.0-10** (No licensing restrictions, but the copyright remains with the artist.)
Exclusive **1.0**	5+ print media **0.5**		Up to 3 years **0.3**	Germany **0.2**	
	Online **0.5**	Large edition and target group **0.5**	Up to 10 years **0.5**	Europe **0.5**	
	Presentation **0.1**		Unlimited **1.0**	Worldwide **1.0**	
	Television **0.15**				
	Unlimited **1.0**				

Using the pricing guides above, multiply the original design fee by the sum of the rates across the specification columns.

For example, the license fee calculation for a non-exclusive project printed in 1 media in a large edition for up to 10 years worldwide would be as follows:

DESIGN FEE (FOR EXAMPLE 1000 EURO) X (0.1 + 0.1 + 0.5 + 0.5 + 1.0) = 1000 X 2.2 = 2200

With a licensing fee of 2200 euro and a design fee of 1000 euro, the total cost of the project will be 3200 euro. Once a final price has been established, set up a written agreement to include a breakdown of the design fee, licensing fee, as well as any deadlines previously agreed upon.

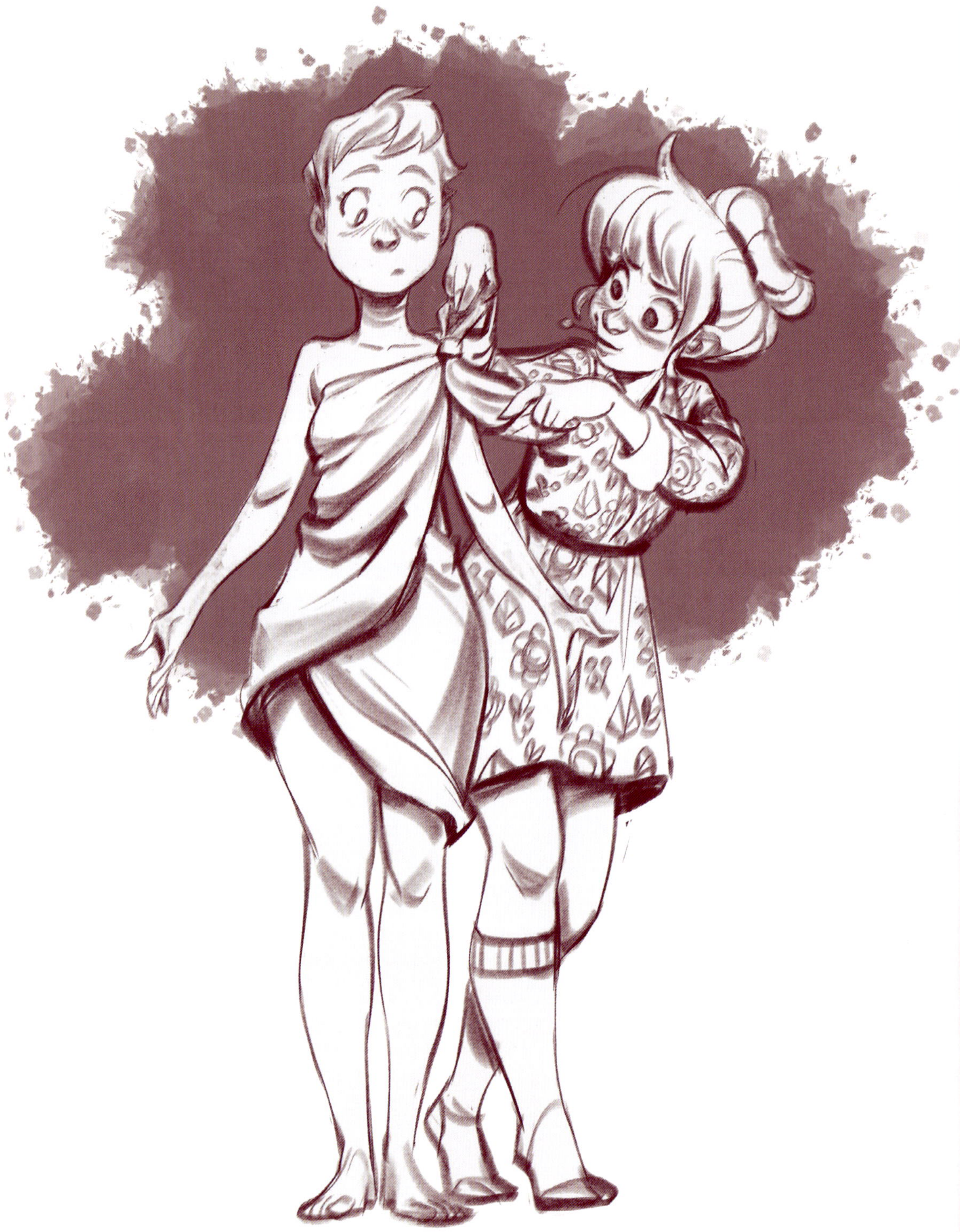

CHARACTER DESIGN

Driven by my love of character work, my first book, *Sketch Every Day*, heavily focuses on the design of characters. To extend that bank of knowledge, here I want to share more of the finer details of the inner workings of humans – our basic anatomy, as well as the way we move, act, and dress.

ANATOMY

PROFILE

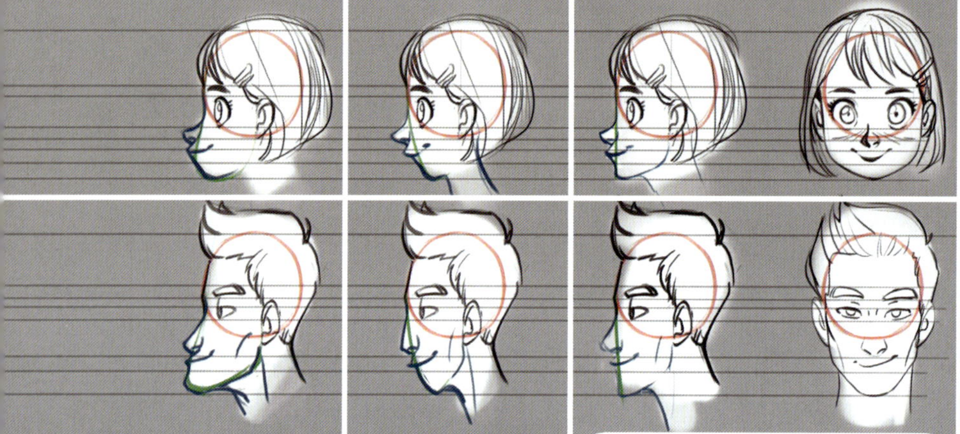

One frontal view can have myriad profiles

A profile can differ depending on the size and shape of the nose and jaw

A protruding jawline is associated with confidence, power, and brutishness

A recessed jaw and chin is often associated with the opposite traits to that of a prominent jawline

Consider the character's personality – should the profile fit a stereotype, or surprise the viewer and give the character depth?

An interesting profile can be enough to inspire an exciting original character!

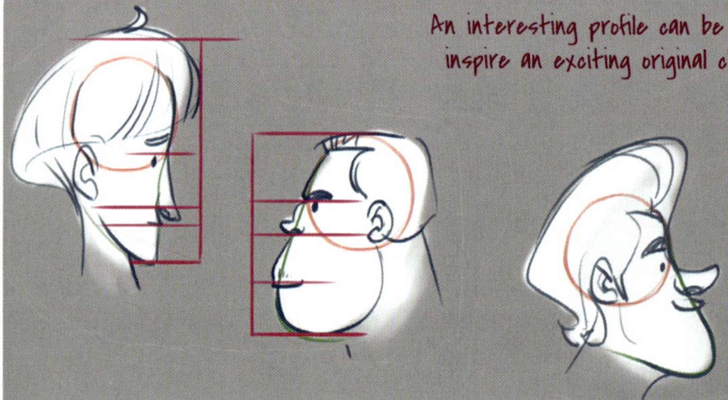

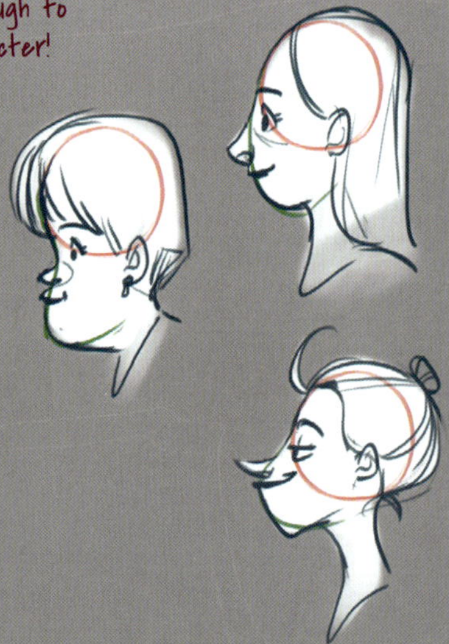

To find a starting point when drawing a head, it might help to first draw a circle. Play around with adding extra lines to the initial circle and see where the shape takes you. Just remember to vary the proportions!

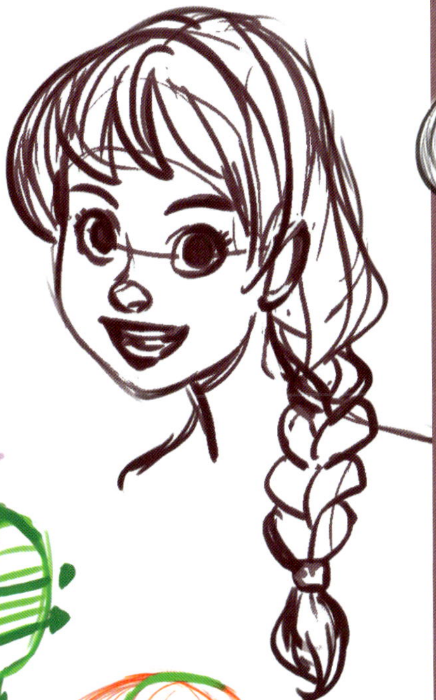

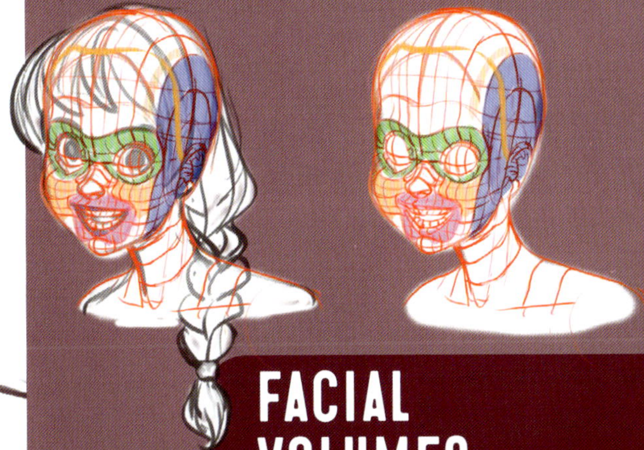

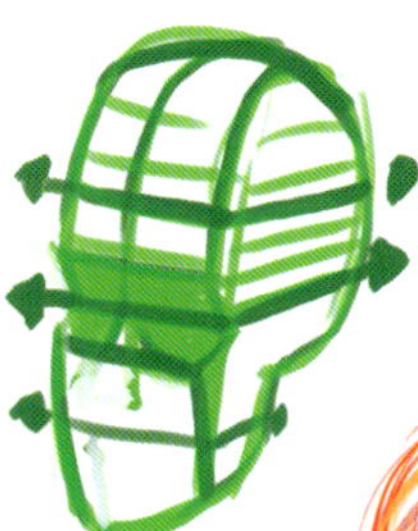

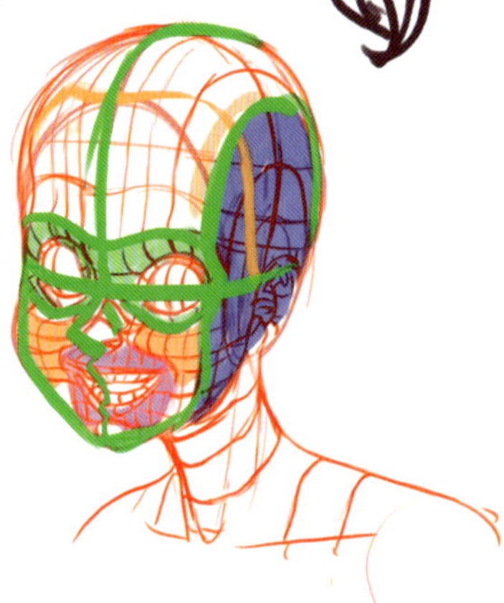

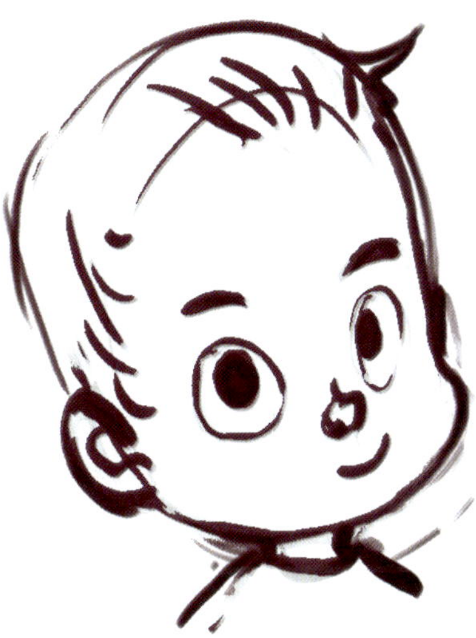

FACIAL VOLUMES

Using the underlying muscle structure as a guide to segment the face and head makes it easier to understand the volumes.

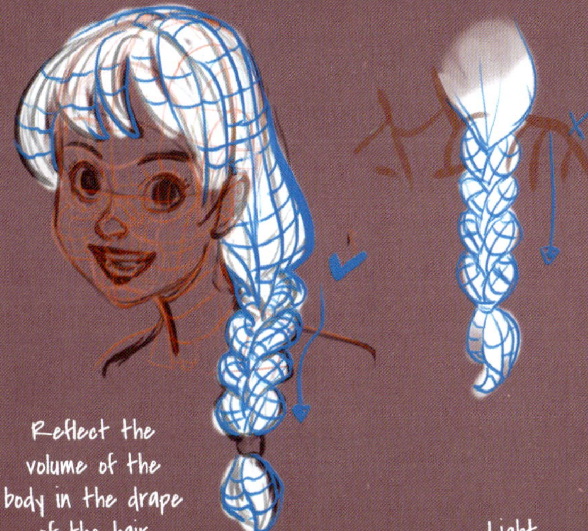

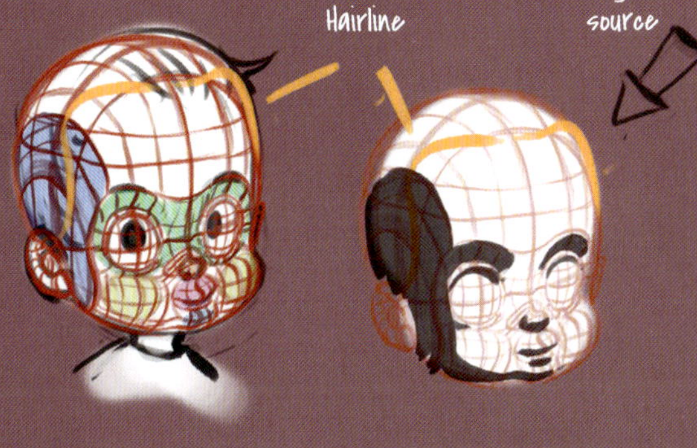

AGING

It's important to understand how to age a character, to know which traits make them appear young or old. This will help you to create believable characters. The character needs to look like they belong in the environment or company they keep.

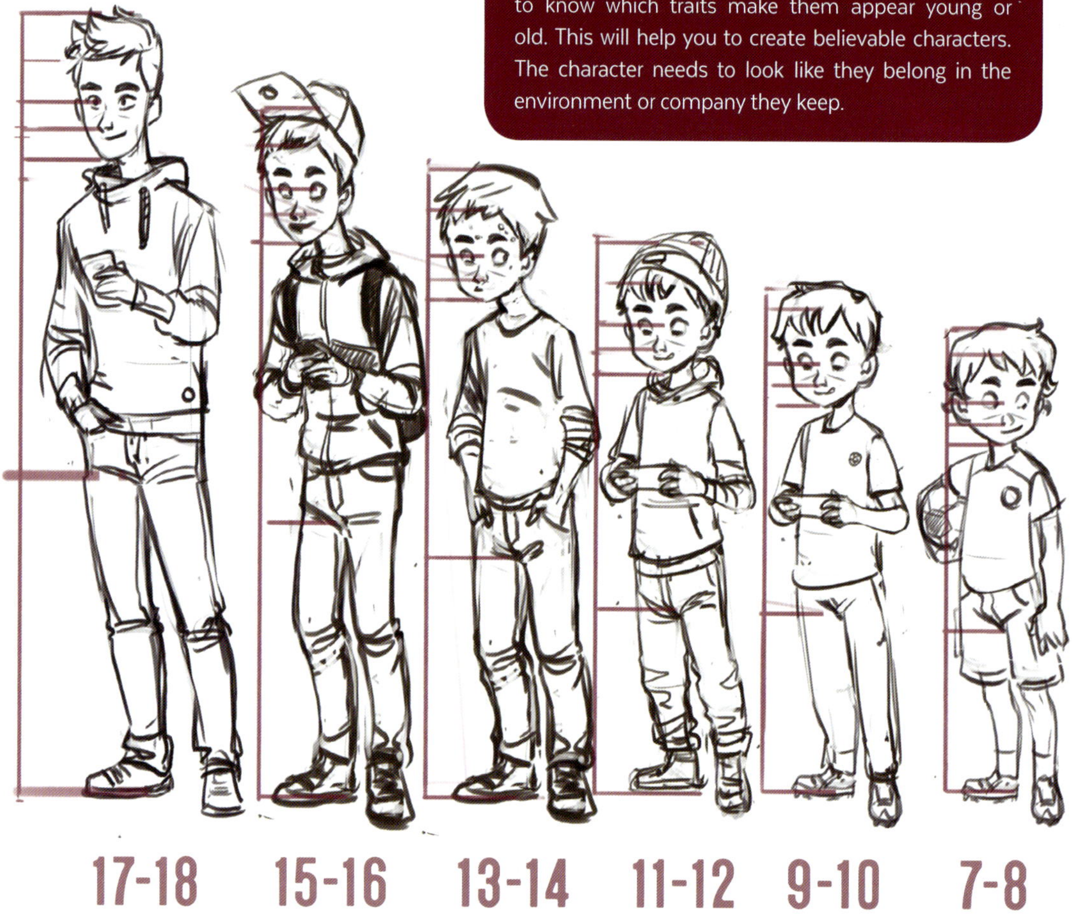

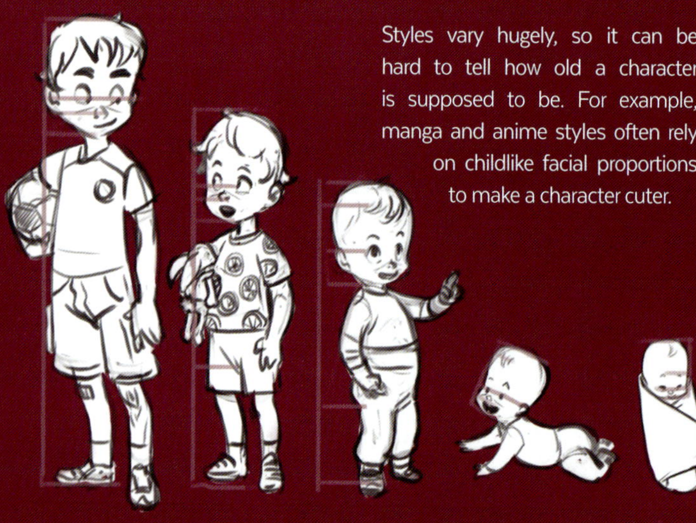

Styles vary hugely, so it can be hard to tell how old a character is supposed to be. For example, manga and anime styles often rely on childlike facial proportions to make a character cuter.

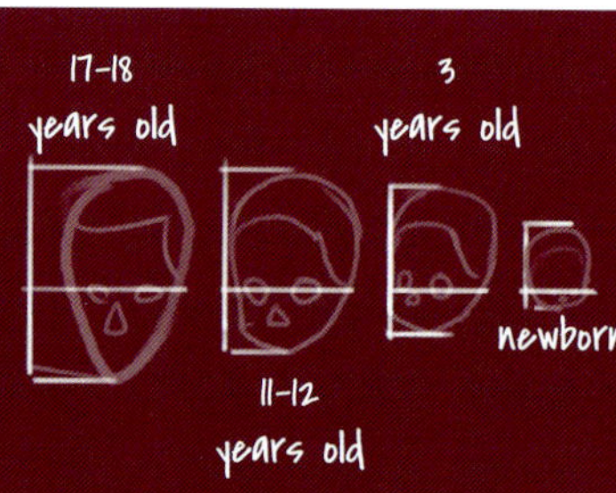

To effectively age the face of a character as they get older, I make the nose larger and the jaw more defined.

The eyes remain similar in size during most of the aging process, while the other features around them grow.

TORSO: FRONT

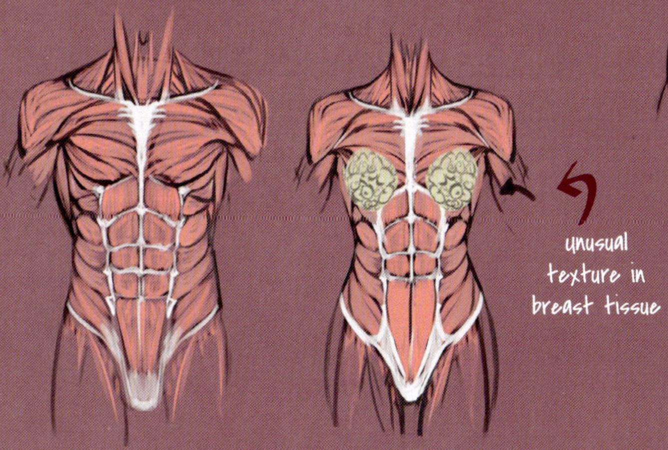

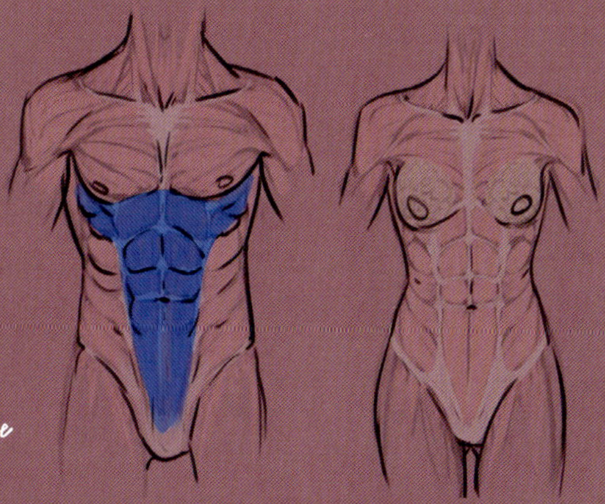

In the male chest, I imagine the stomach and under-breast muscles making a "T" shape. The female musculature is not as prominent as in a male. When drawing the female torso, I don't think much about the muscles.

Abdominal muscles can have very different shapes — don't make the mistake of drawing them straight and flat!

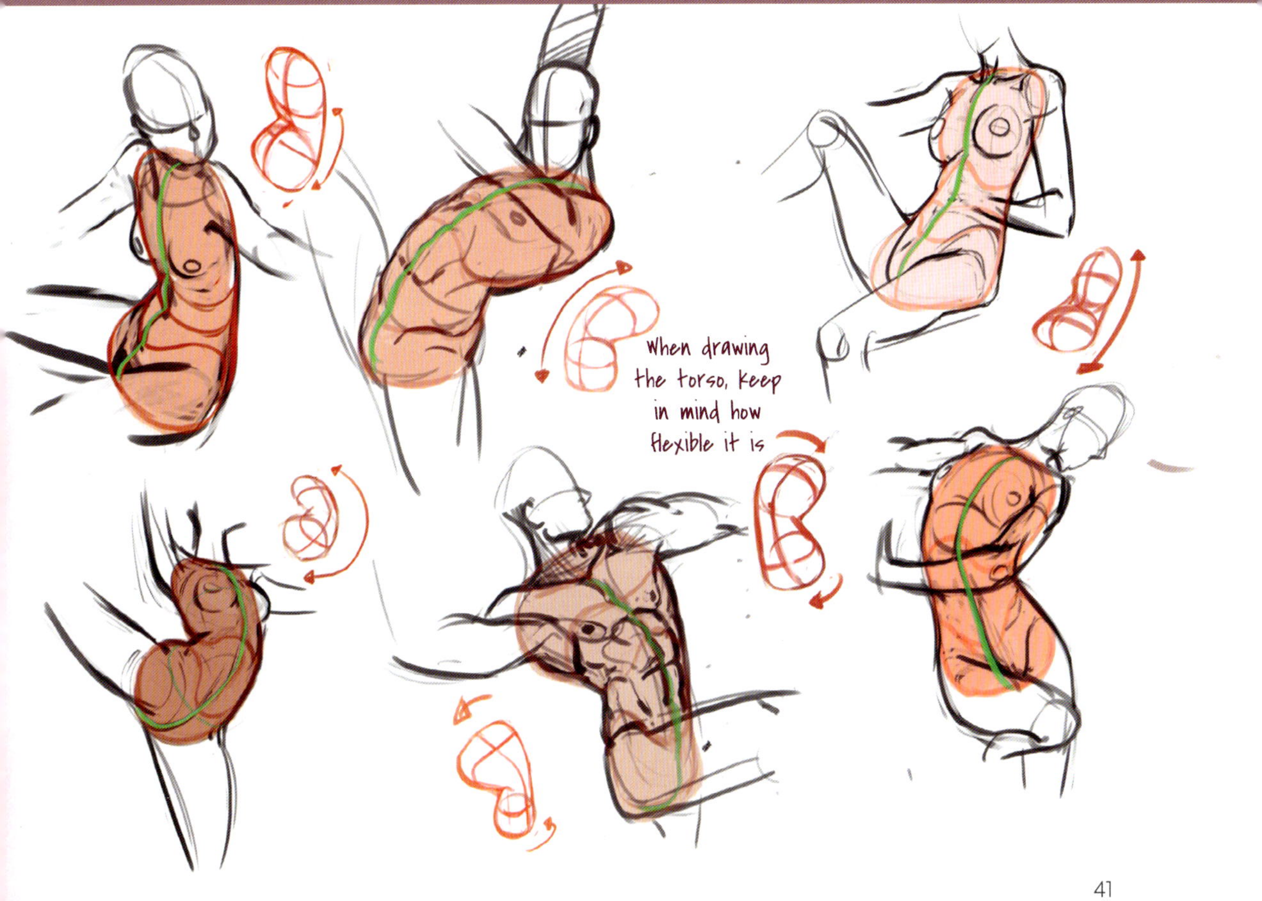

TORSO: BACK

When aiming to simply capture the aesthetic of the back, it is useful to understand how the muscles spread along the back, but knowing every individual muscle is not necessary.

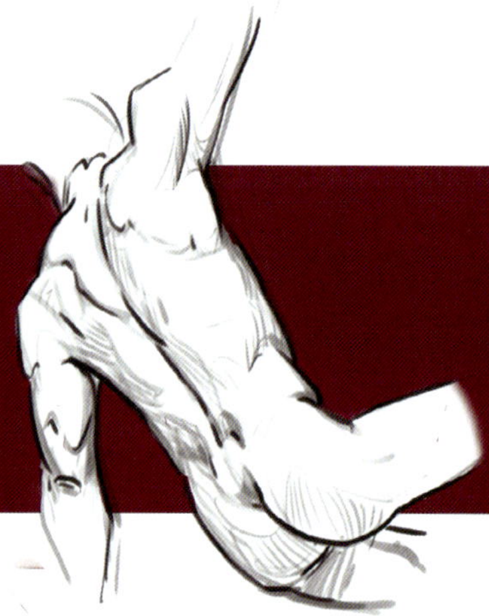

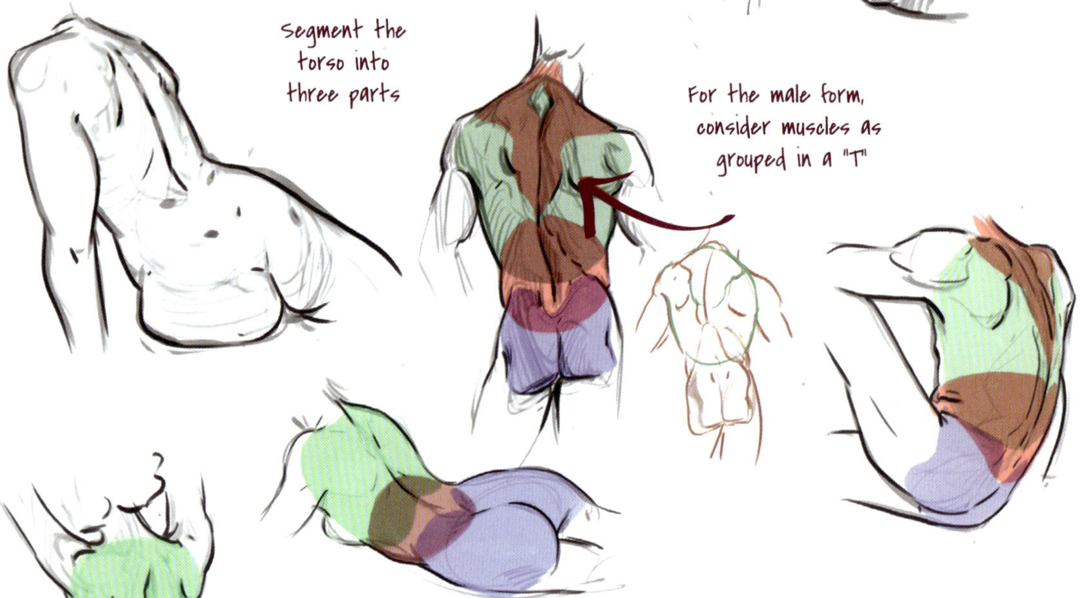

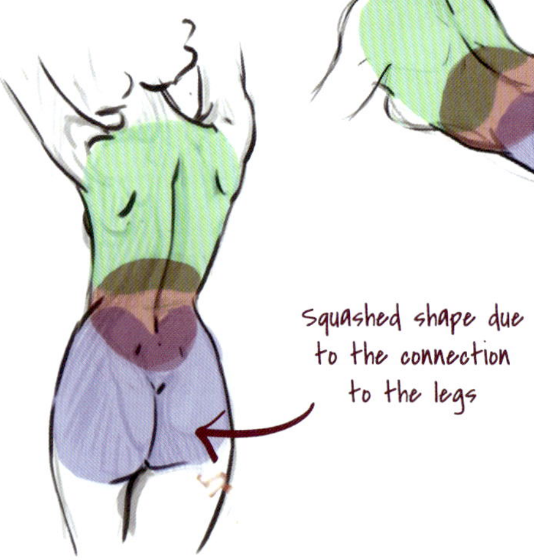

Female shapes are more rounded, while male forms are more angular and square.

When building a female figure, think less about the muscle structure than about how to layer the shapes. Consider how the fat layer on top of the muscle gets squashed and distorted with movement. Keep the shoulder blades, spine, and any dimples in mind to define the overall form.

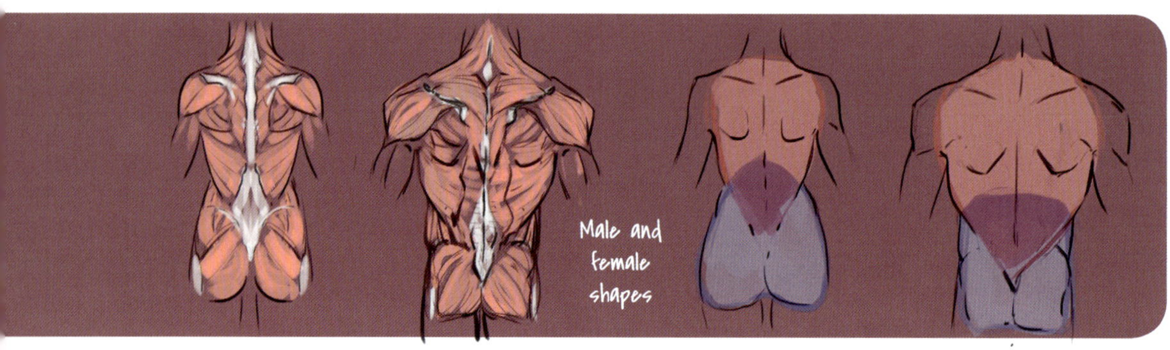

The scapula (shoulder bone) is a very mobile part of the back that moves according to the position of the arms.

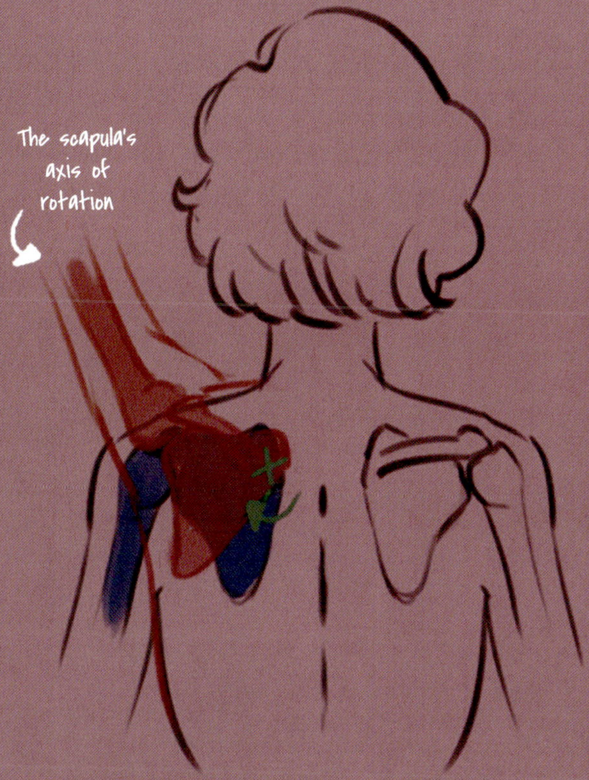

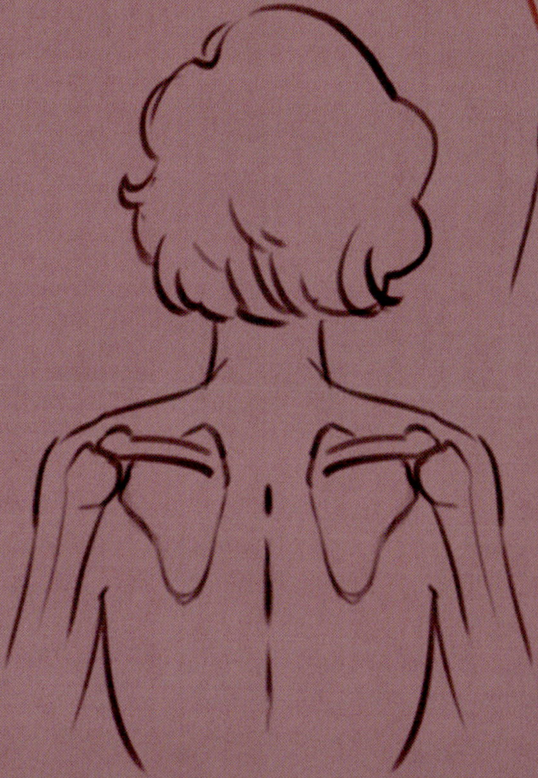

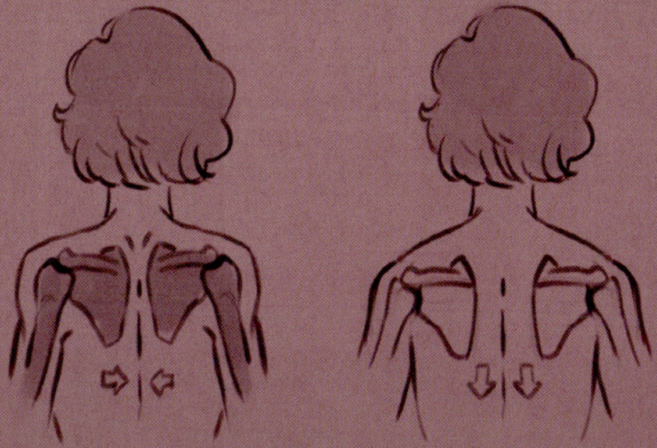

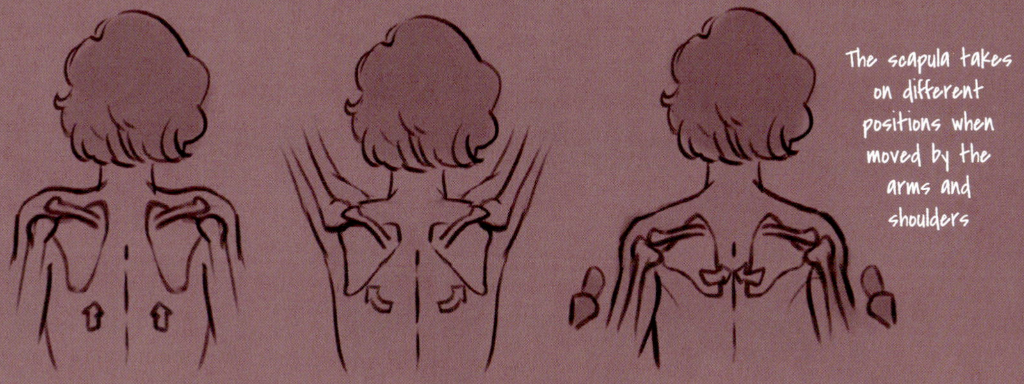

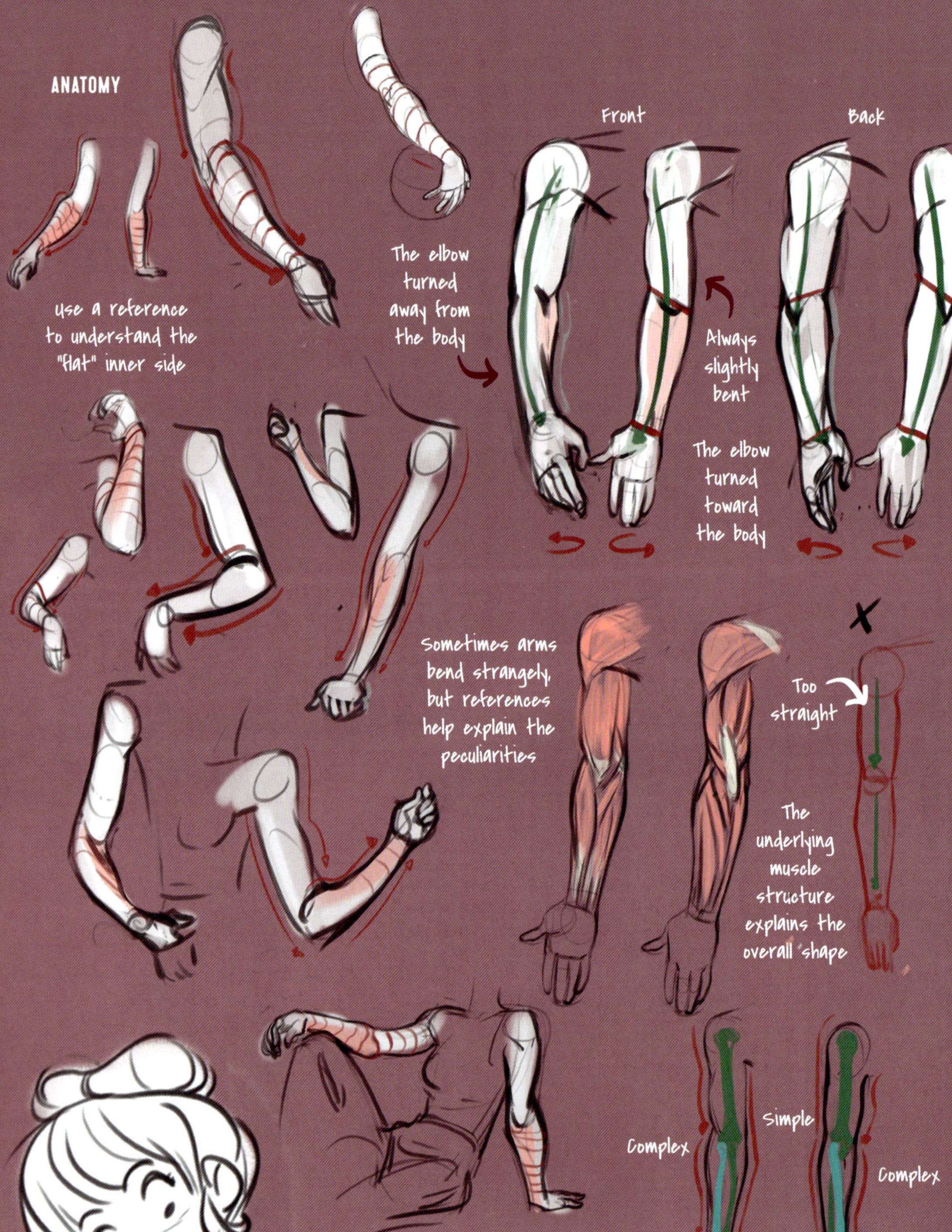

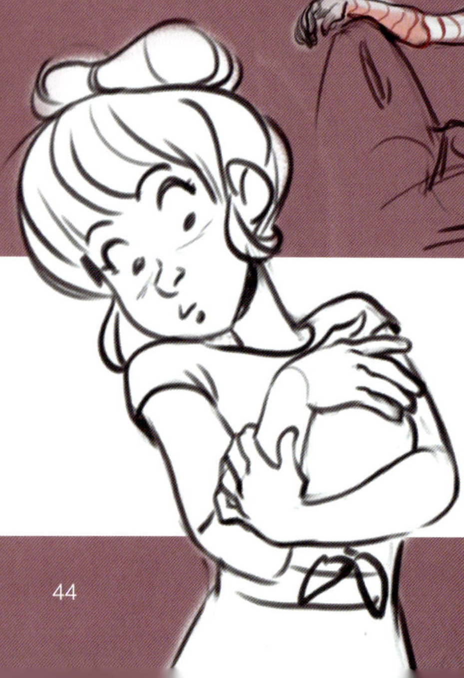

ARMS

Arms are tricky to fathom because they change their shape slightly depending on the twist of the wrist. The inside of the arm is most affected by the twist, while the back of the arm is a simpler shape.

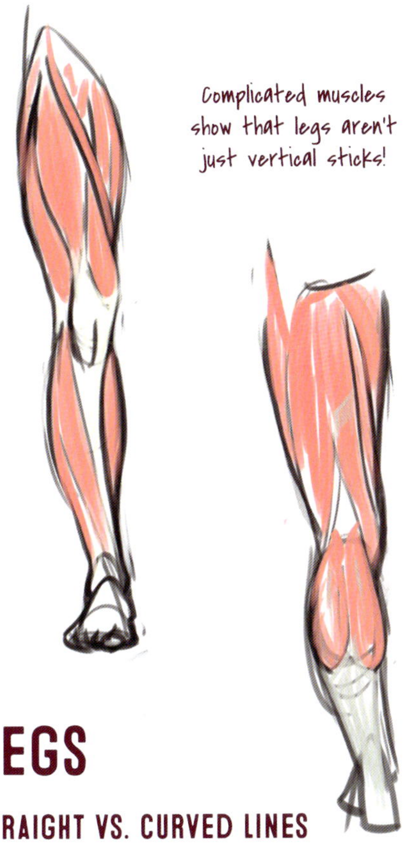

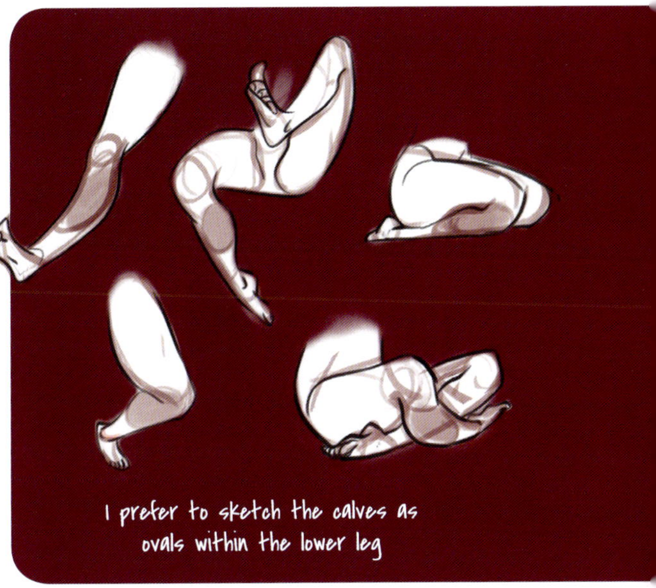

LEGS

STRAIGHT VS. CURVED LINES

Remember that legs are slightly flexible, including the bones within, so they shouldn't appear rigid and stiff. Mix curved and straight lines to achieve a more realistic form.

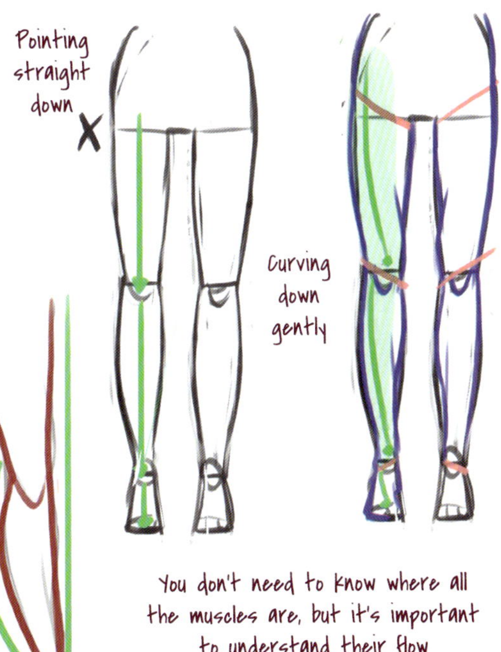

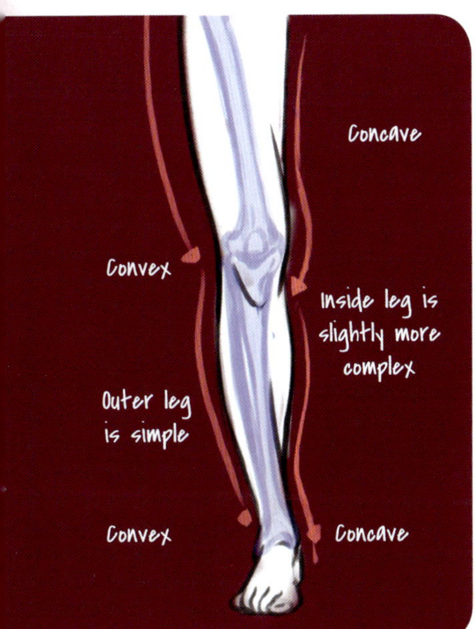

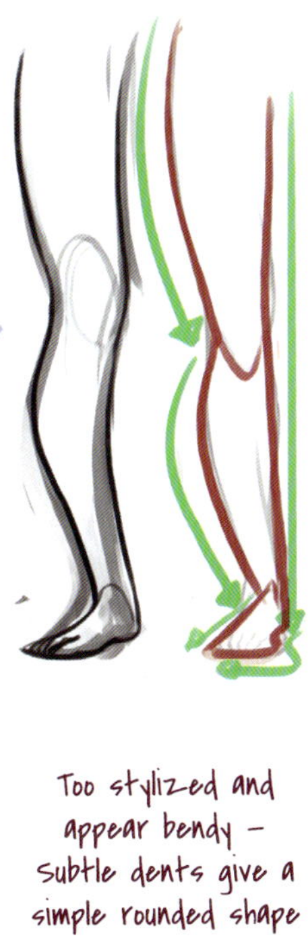

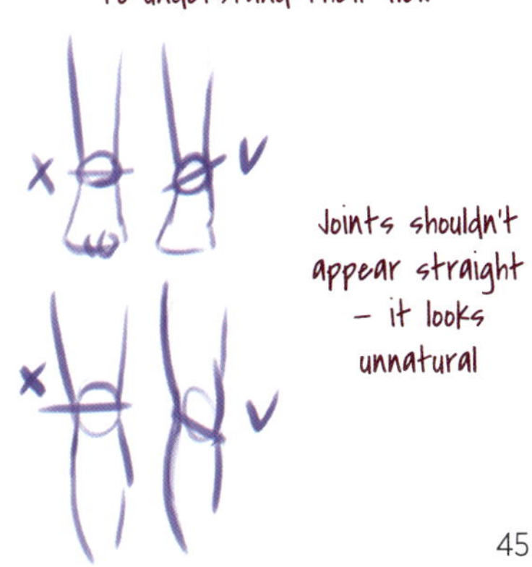

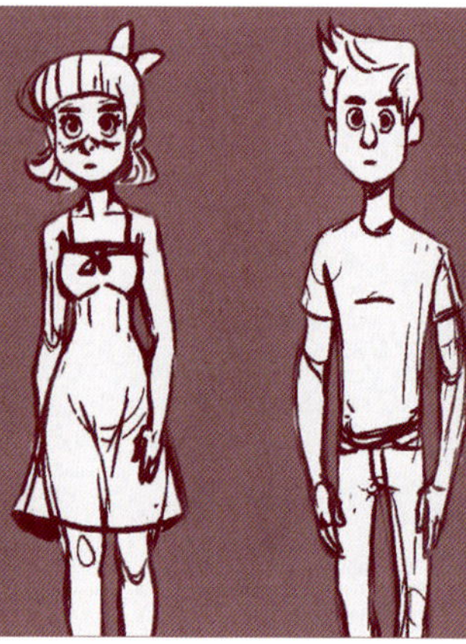

POSES

BODY LANGUAGE

Characters are brought to life through emotional expression and body language. It is important to know and understand the stereotypical poses and be able to identify which elements make them appear the way they do. These elements can be combined to create interesting body language with more depth.

THE STEREOTYPICAL ANGSTY, UNSURE TEEN

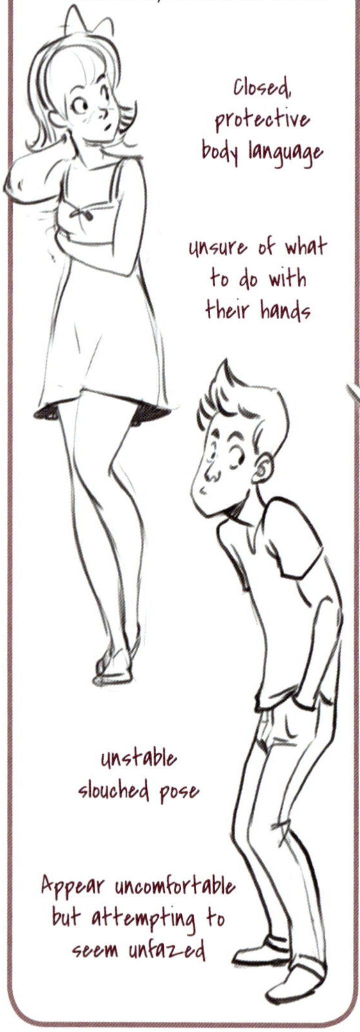

STEREOTYPICAL MALE POSTURE

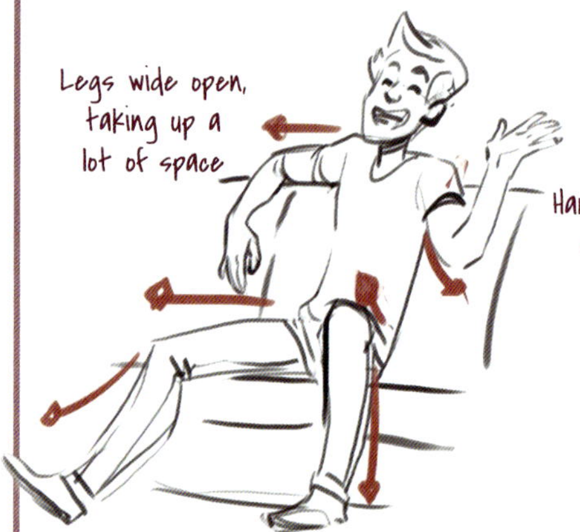

STEREOTYPICAL FEMALE POSTURE

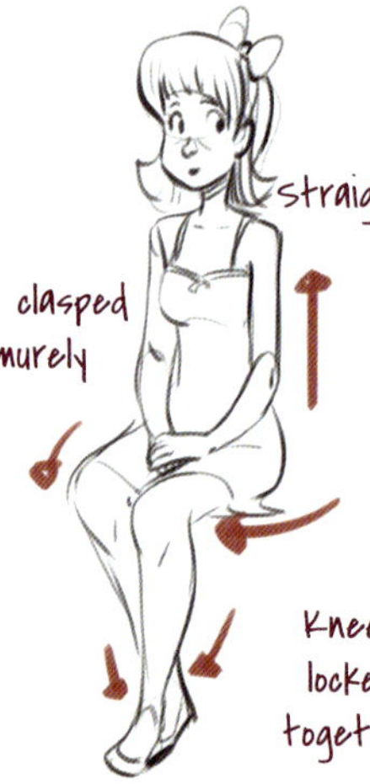

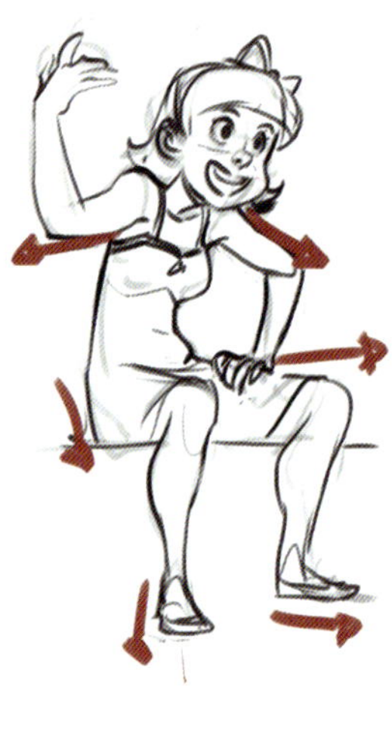

When you switch the genders around, you will achieve less clichéd characters.

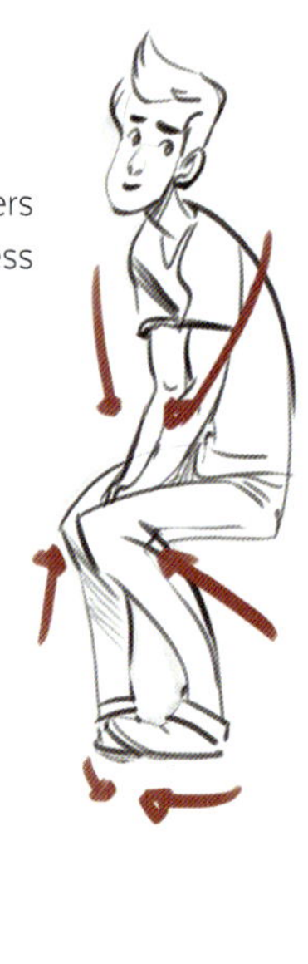

MIXED MESSAGES

Similar poses with different expressions and visible emotions can mean totally different things.

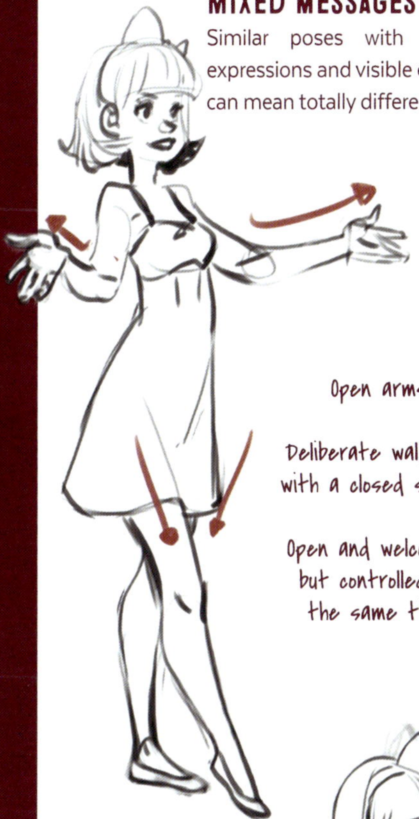

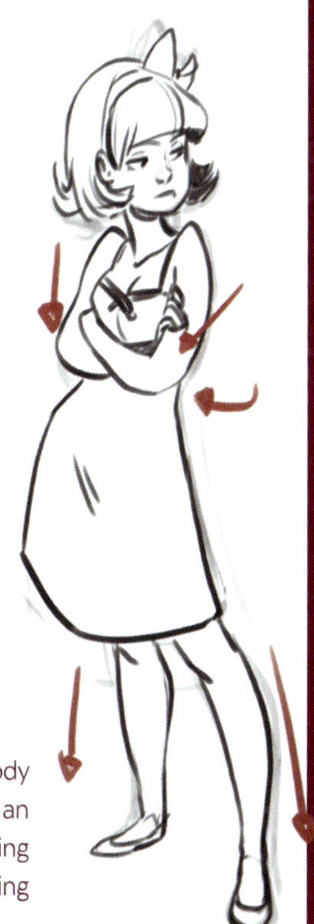

This combination of body language produces an irritated person, not willing to fight but clearly signaling dissatisfaction.

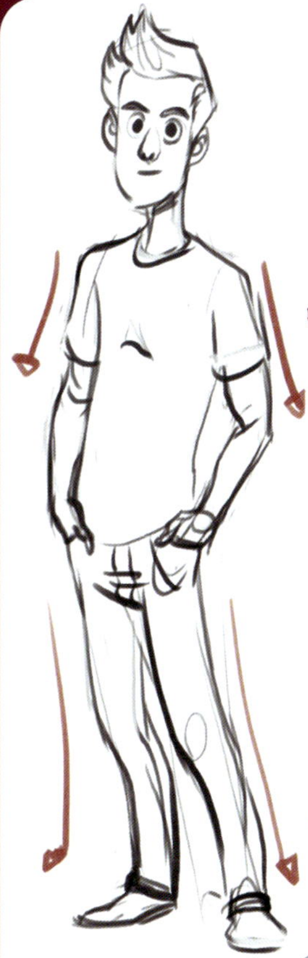

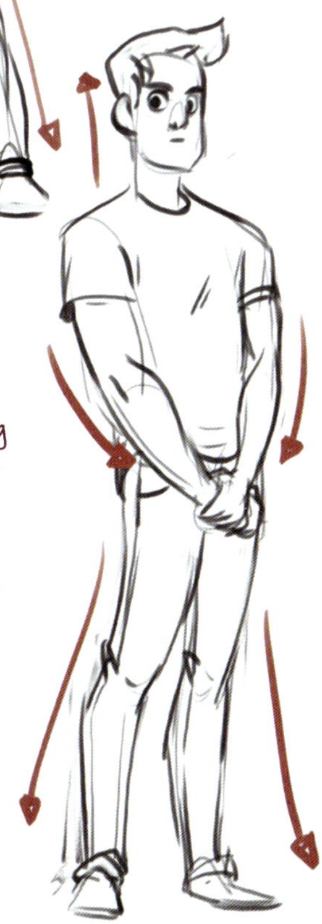

The character now appears strong and uninviting — subtle changes can make a huge difference!

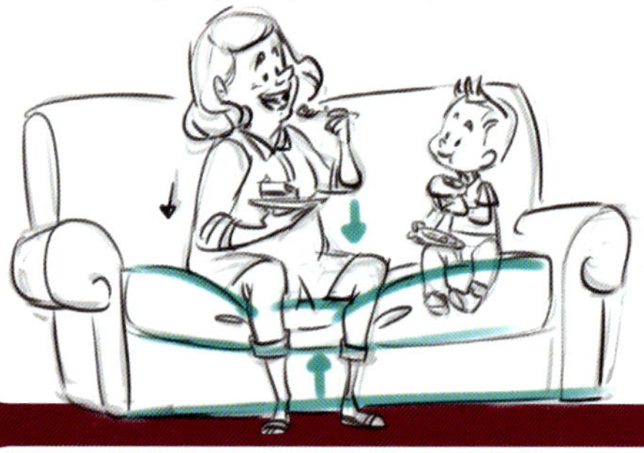

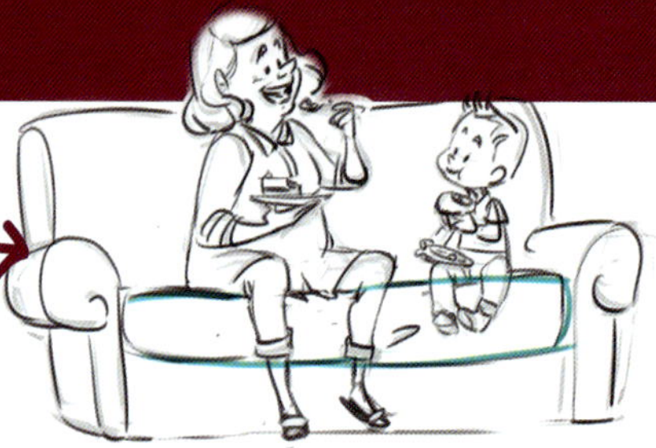

WEIGHT AND BALANCE

Just as people do in real life, characters affect things with their weight or are affected by weight. By considering weight, designs gain more believability.

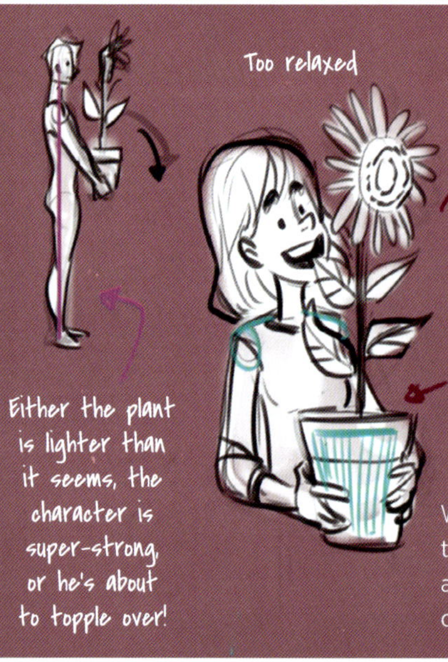

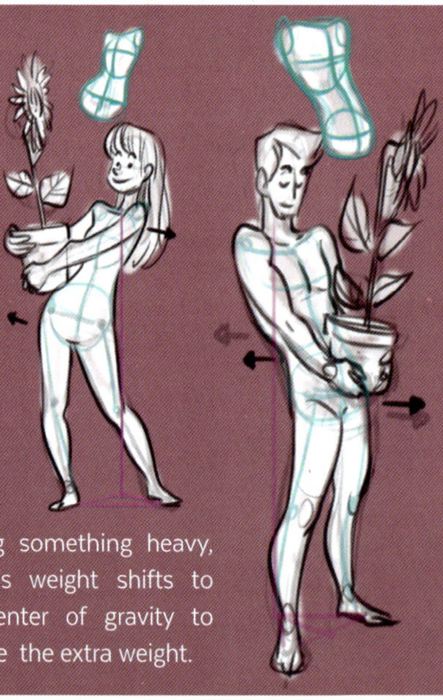

When carrying something heavy, the character's weight shifts to a different center of gravity to counterbalance the extra weight.

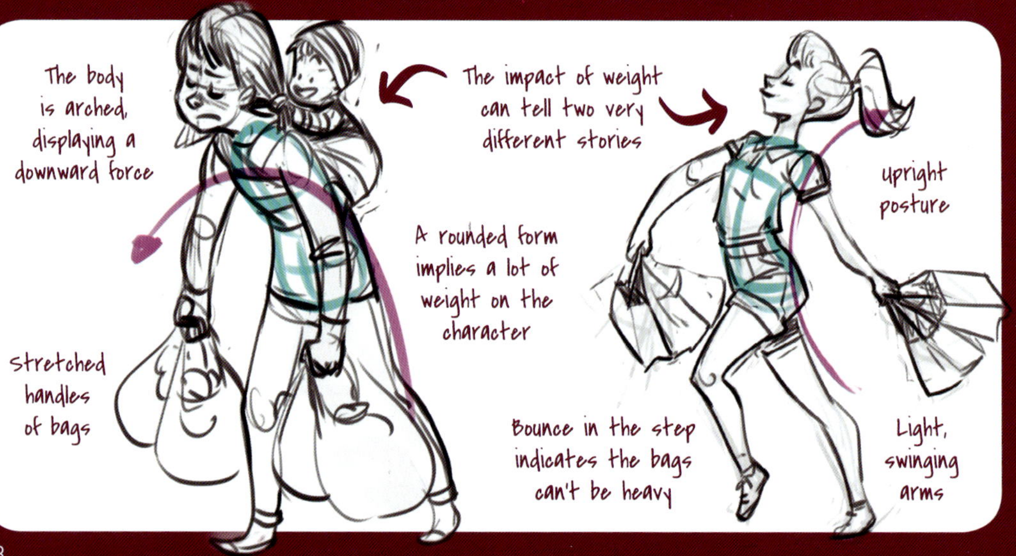

GO WITH THE FLOW: CREATING FLUID YOGA POSES

- Aim to achieve the best flow from the very first rough sketch
- Use long strokes
- Draw from the arm rather than the wrist
- Align all the body parts to follow the chosen action lines
- Draw the body as a whole and don't focus on any part in isolation

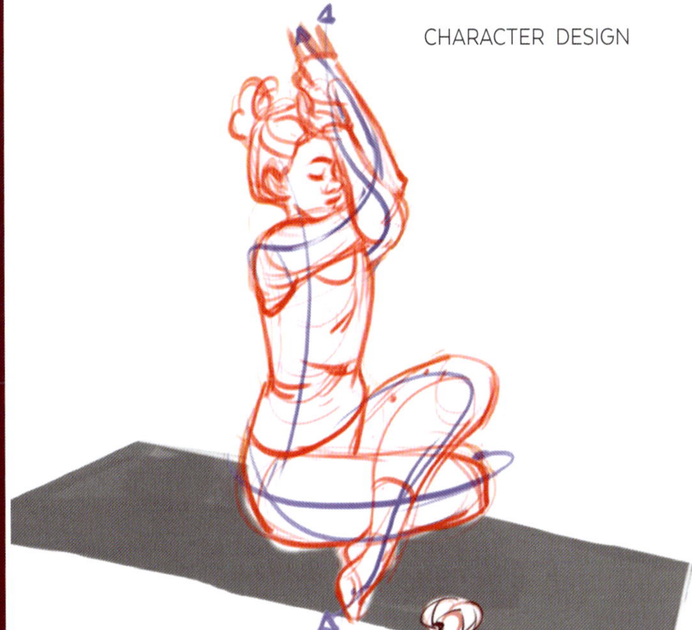

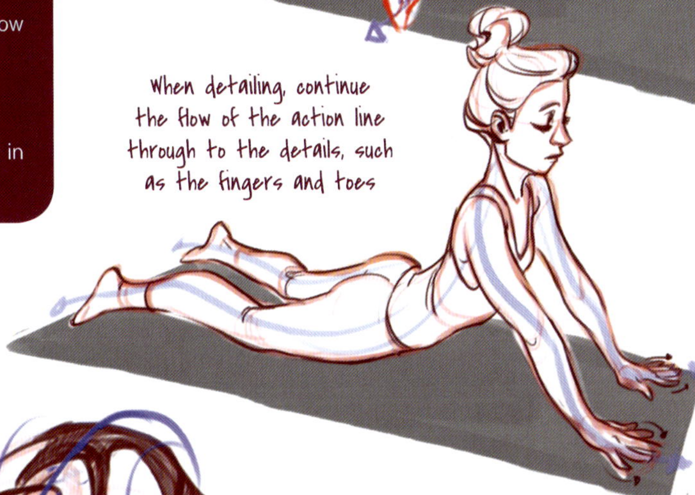

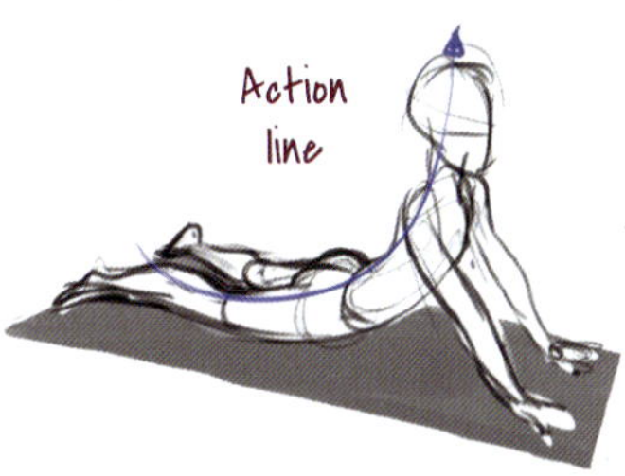

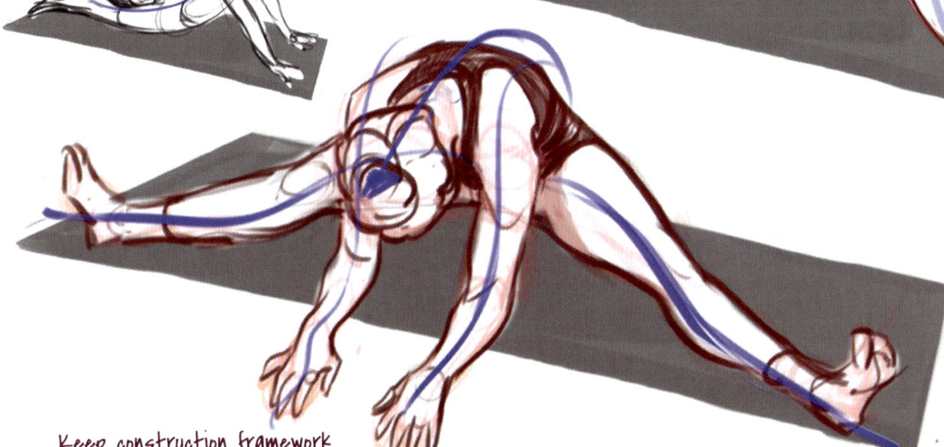

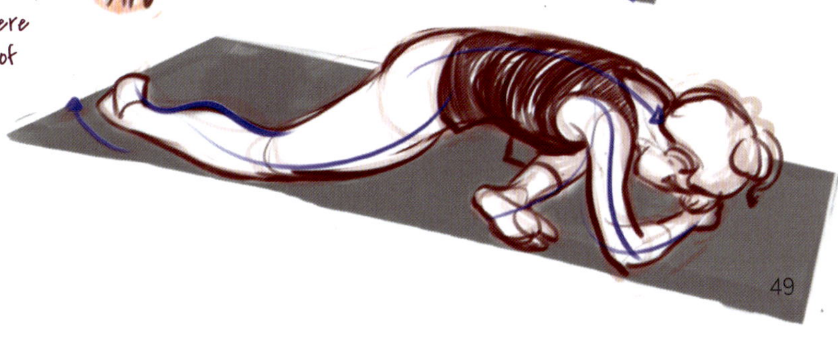

SITTING ON OBJECTS

We probably spend half our time sitting or lounging on things, so I think it is essential that we know how to pose our characters when doing so.

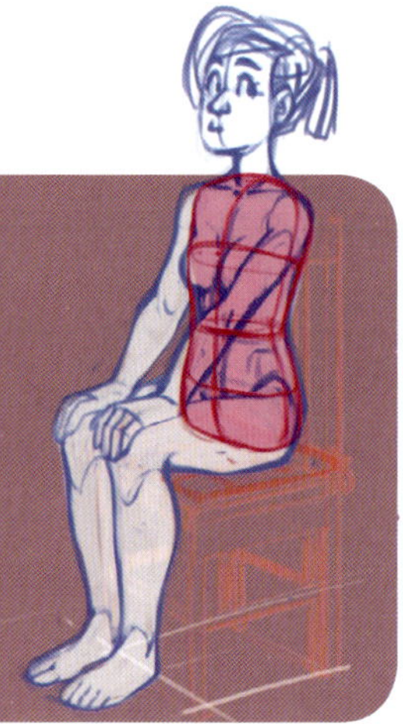

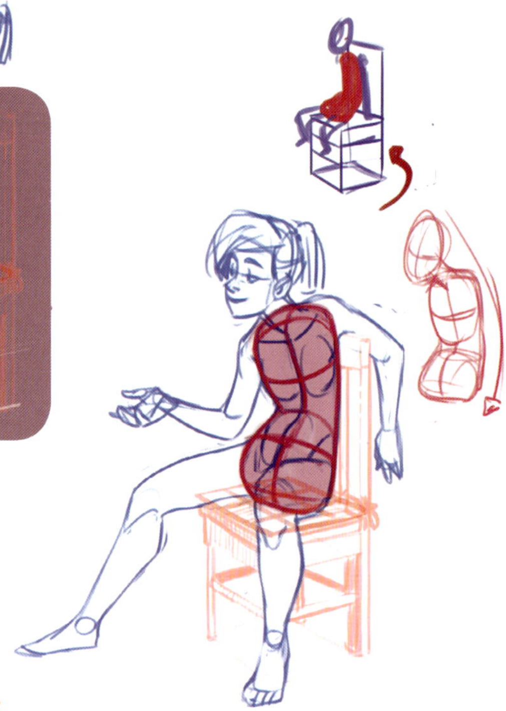

First, draw an object for the character to sit on, to help define their pose.

Once the object has been drawn, use it to play around with the poses that can be achieved. Start by posing the torso – this also defines the size of the character in proportion to the object.

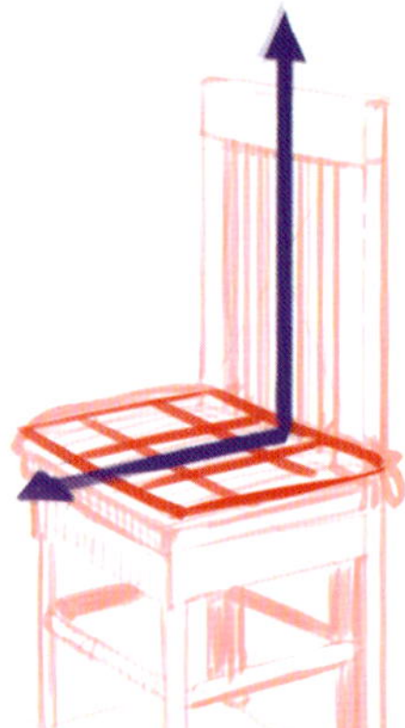

When drawing a character like this it can quickly become stiff if the structure is followed too closely

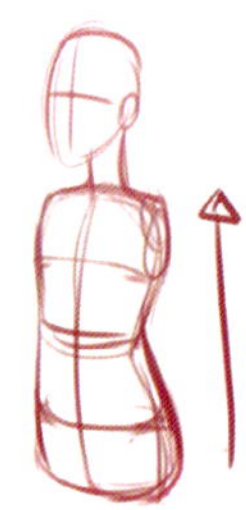

The position of the torso defines where the limbs go – if the arm hangs over the back of the chair, the torso will tilt in that direction

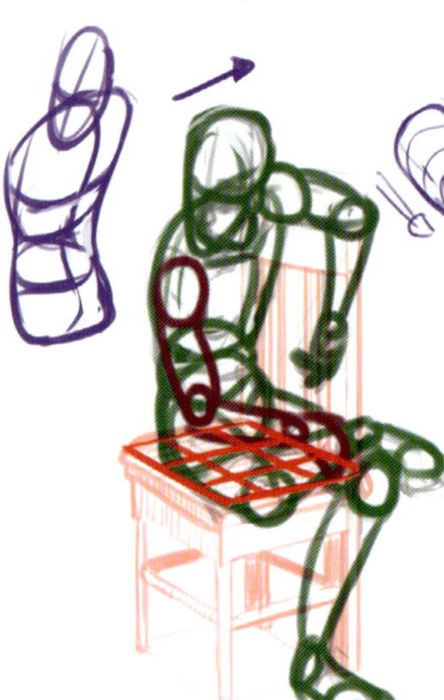

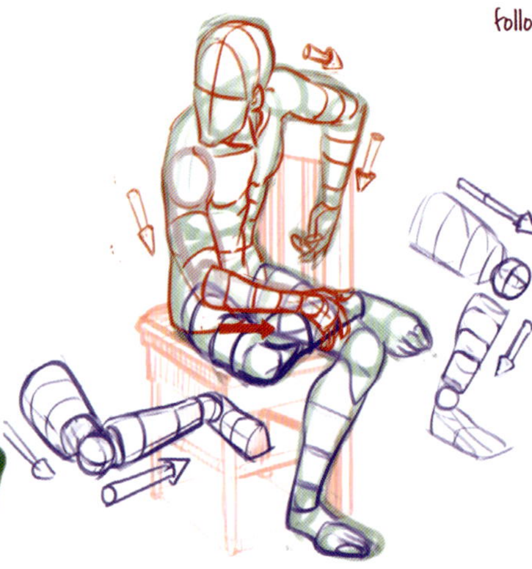

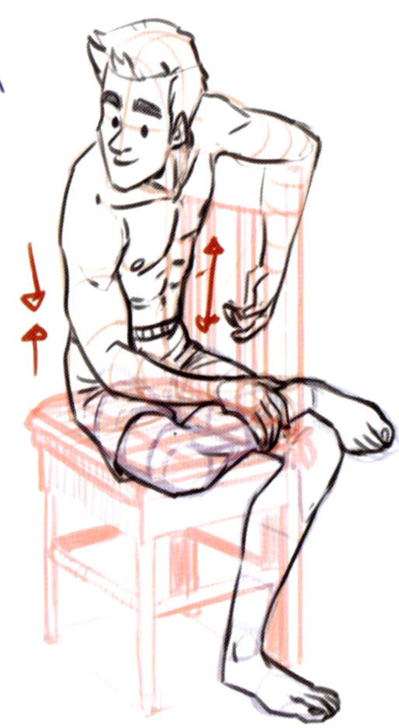

Continue to add limbs, while always keeping their direction in mind

Squash
stretch

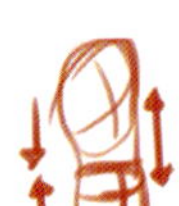

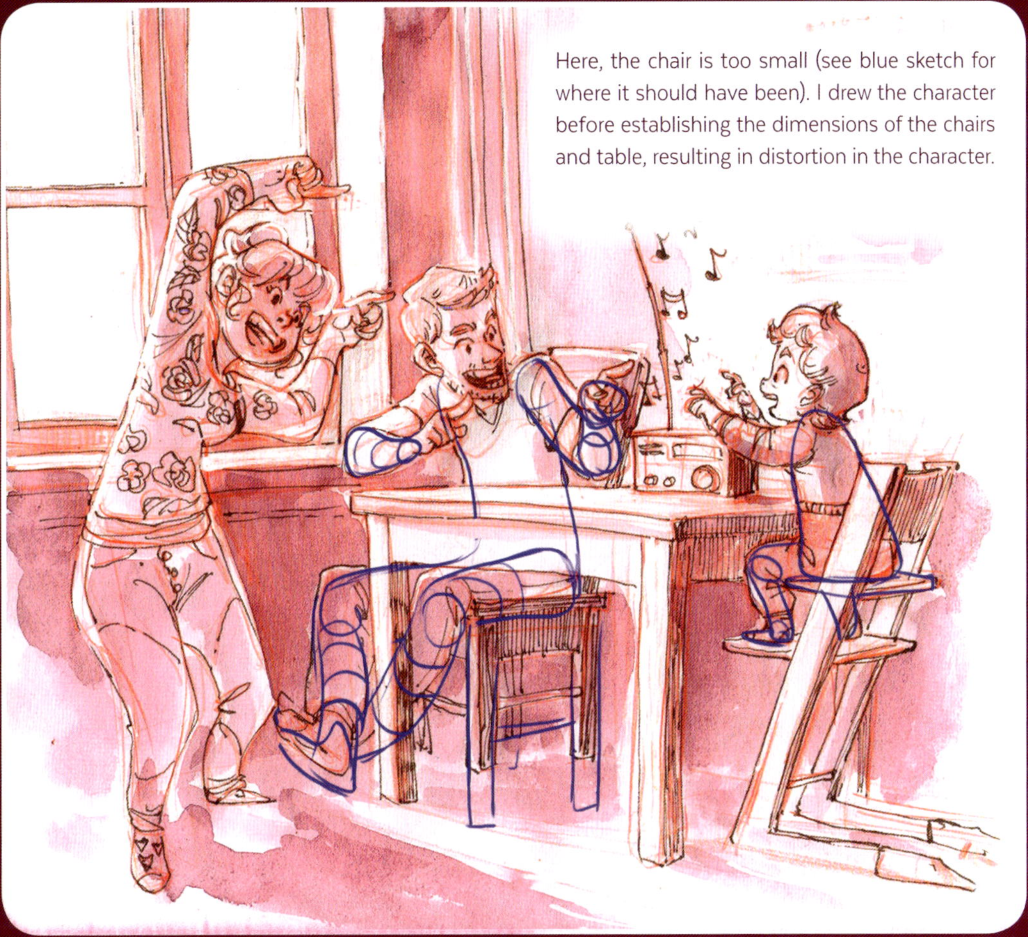

Here, the chair is too small (see blue sketch for where it should have been). I drew the character before establishing the dimensions of the chairs and table, resulting in distortion in the character.

In the example below, I sketched the rounding of the bridge before posing my characters in order to achieve the correct angle and seated positions.

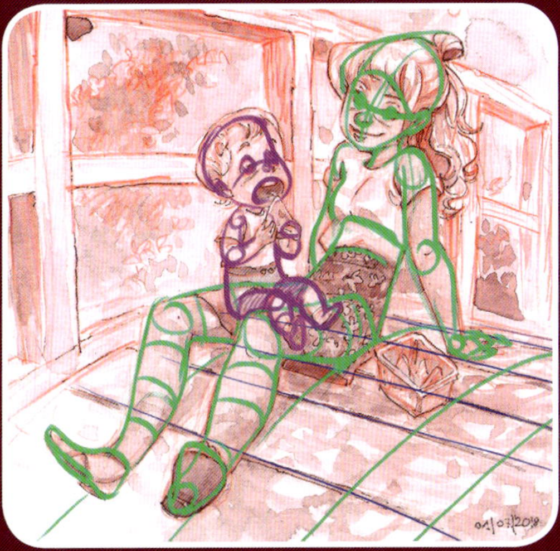

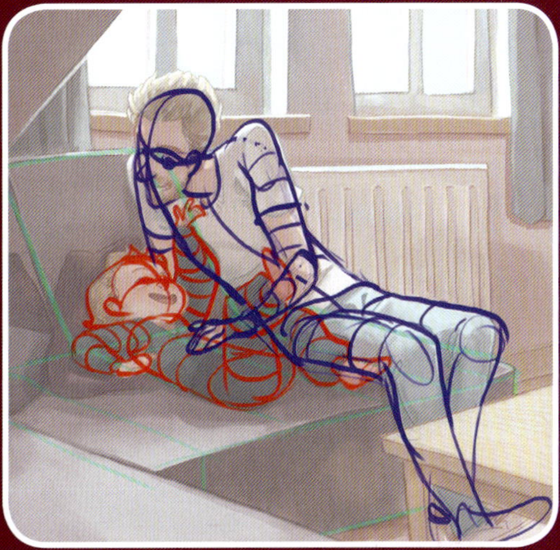

When designing the piece above, without having the sofa in place, it would have been really tricky to align these two characters and find the right angles.

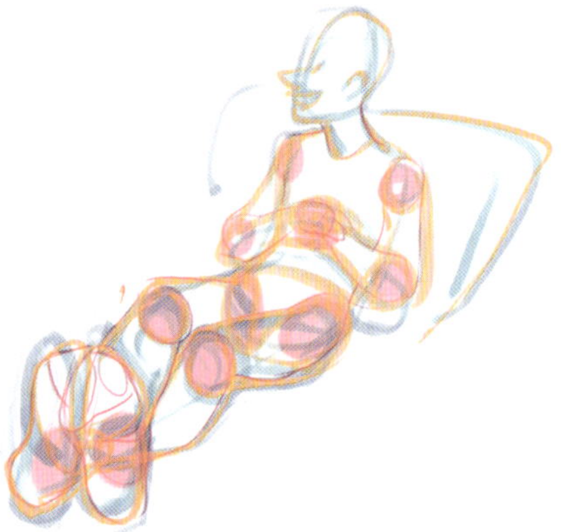

FORESHORTENING

Foreshortening happens in many different situations, in action and extreme scenes, but gentle foreshortening can also happen at any time when posing, depending on the point of view.

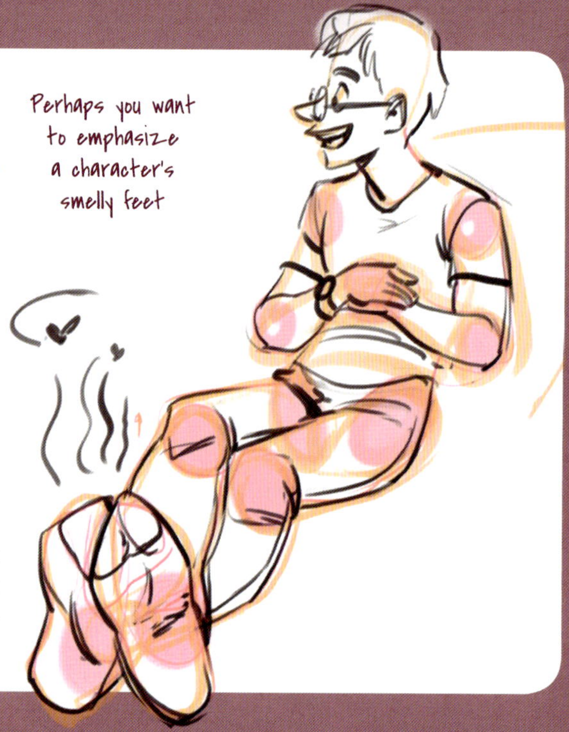

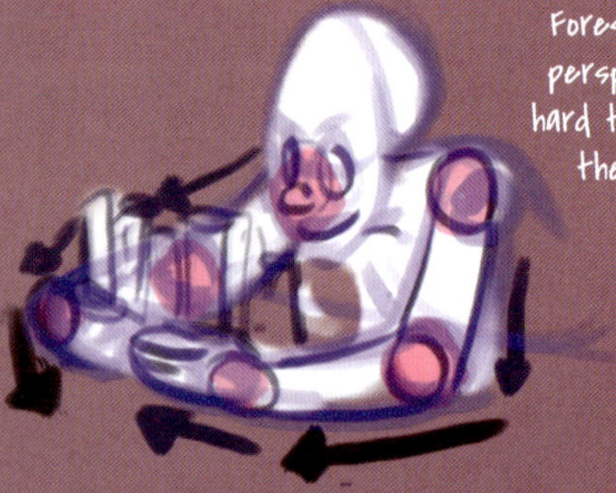

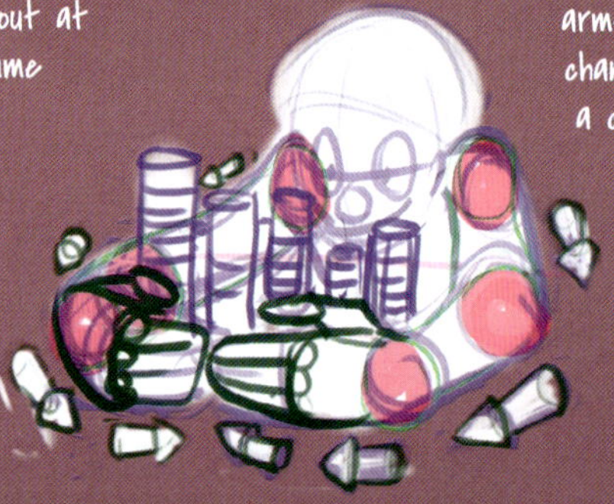

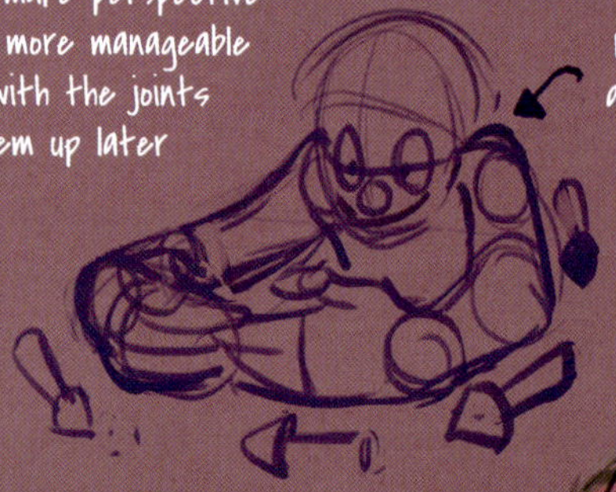

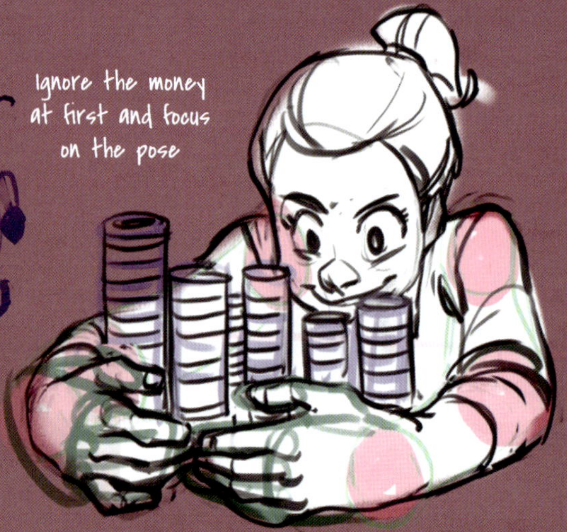

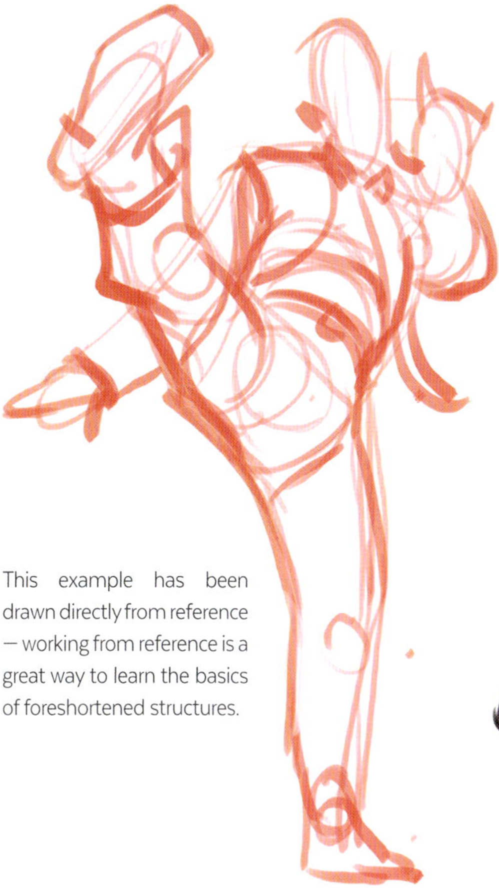

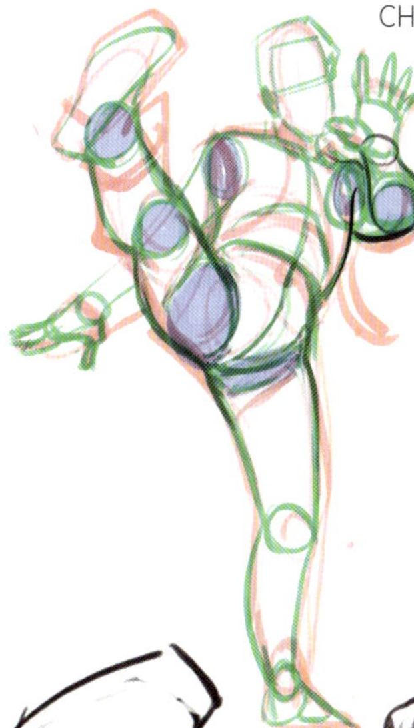

Overlapping volumes and marked joints

This example has been drawn directly from reference — working from reference is a great way to learn the basics of foreshortened structures.

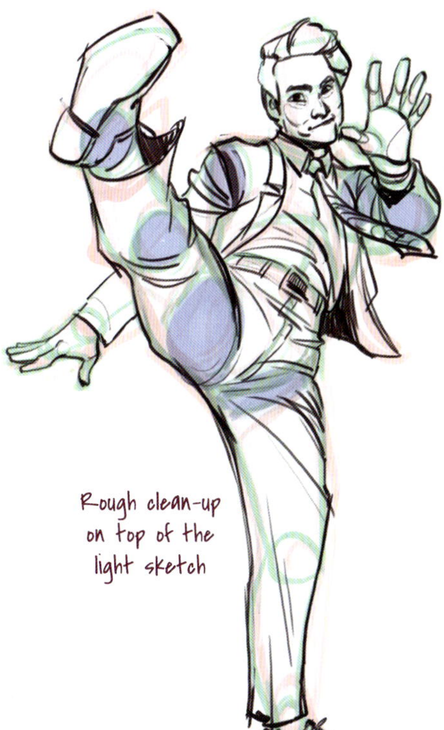

Rough clean-up on top of the light sketch

"START WITH THE JOINTS AND CONNECT THEM UP LATER"

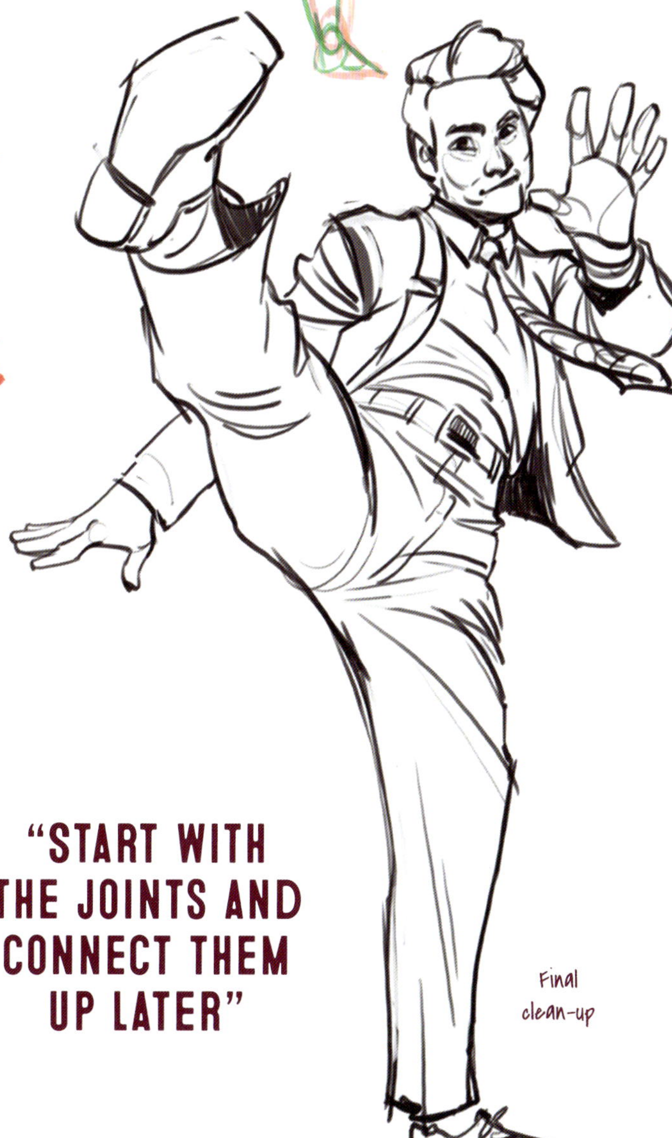

Final clean-up

FIGHT!

Action poses are challenging. Not only is it important to select the most effective perspective to depict the scene, but when working with two interacting characters it is also crucial to balance their poses against each other.

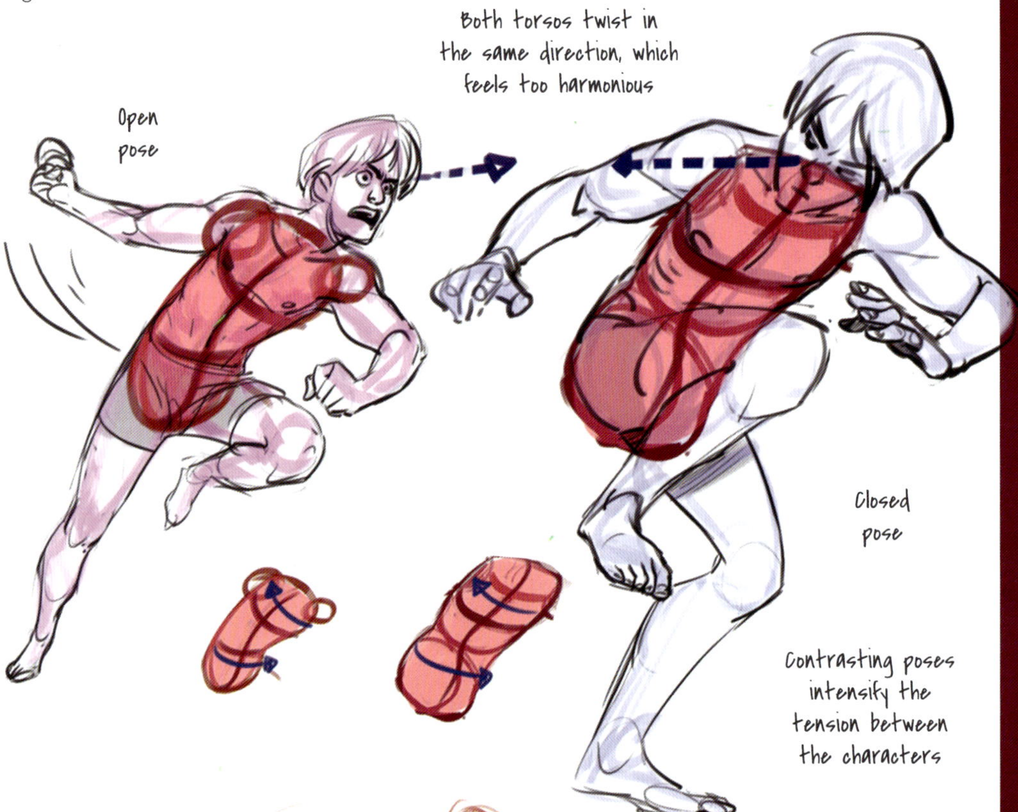

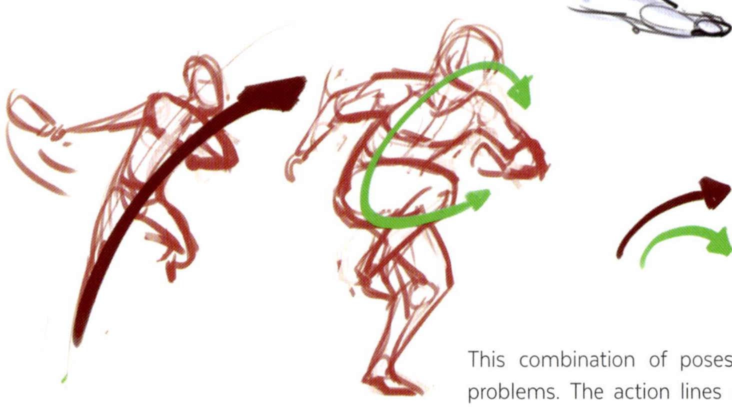

This combination of poses works, but has some problems. The action lines are curved in the same direction, which makes the poses flow into one another and feels like the characters are in sync and harmonious – the wrong mood for a conflict!

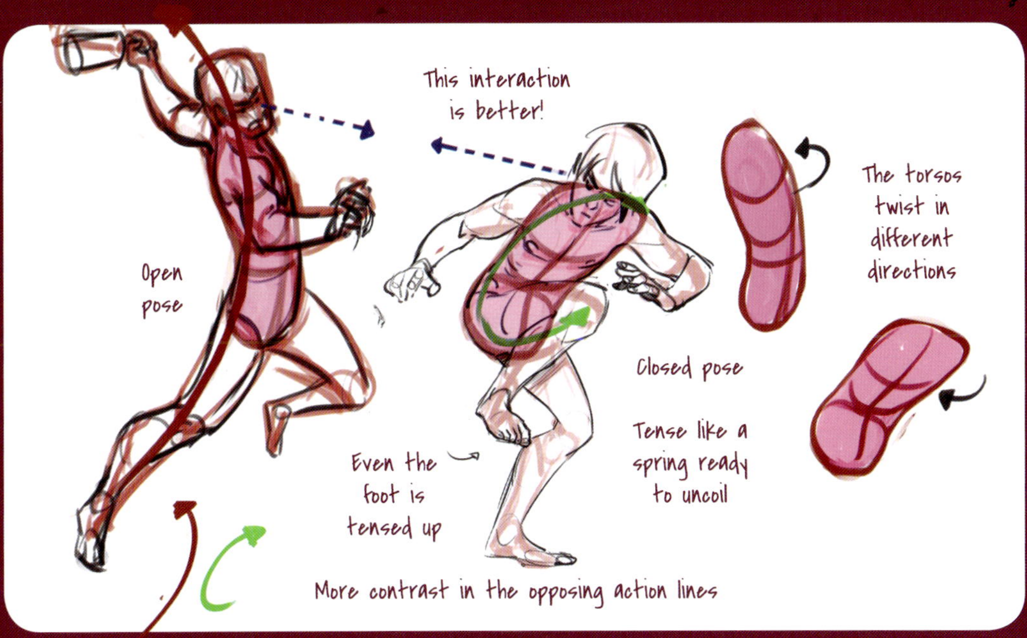
This interaction
is better!
The torsos
twist in
different
directions
Open
pose
Closed pose
Tense like a
spring ready
to uncoil
Even the
foot is
tensed up
More contrast in the opposing action lines

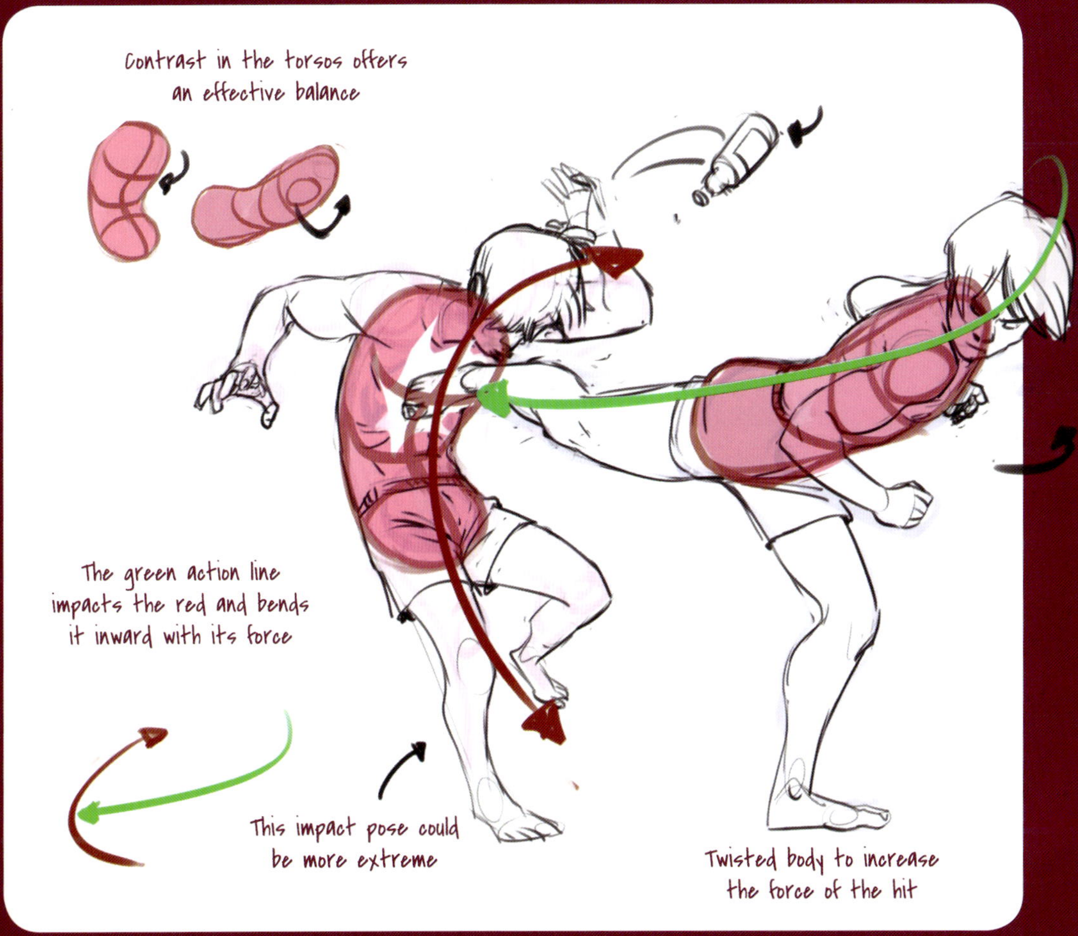
Contrast in the torsos offers
an effective balance
The green action line
impacts the red and bends
it inward with its force
This impact pose could
be more extreme
Twisted body to increase
the force of the hit

MERMAIDS

When posing a mermaid, think about a combination of human and creature. There are lots of possible combinations and I highly recommend doing some research and gathering references beforehand. You don't have to copy one single type of fish; in fact, having a reference board of aquatic creatures will help build an authentic fish-like fluidity in the motion of the character.

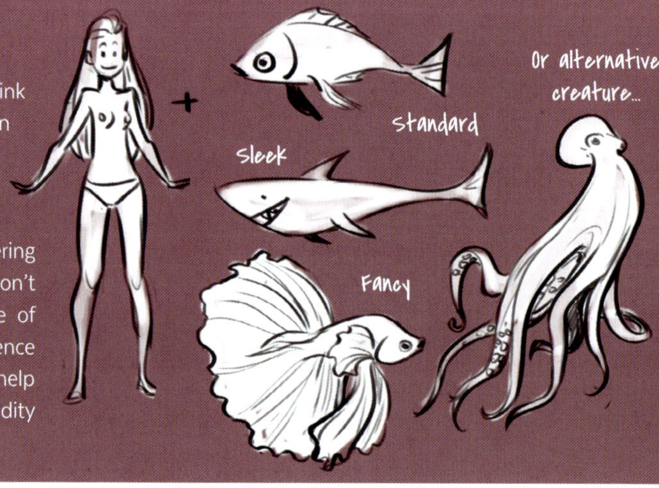

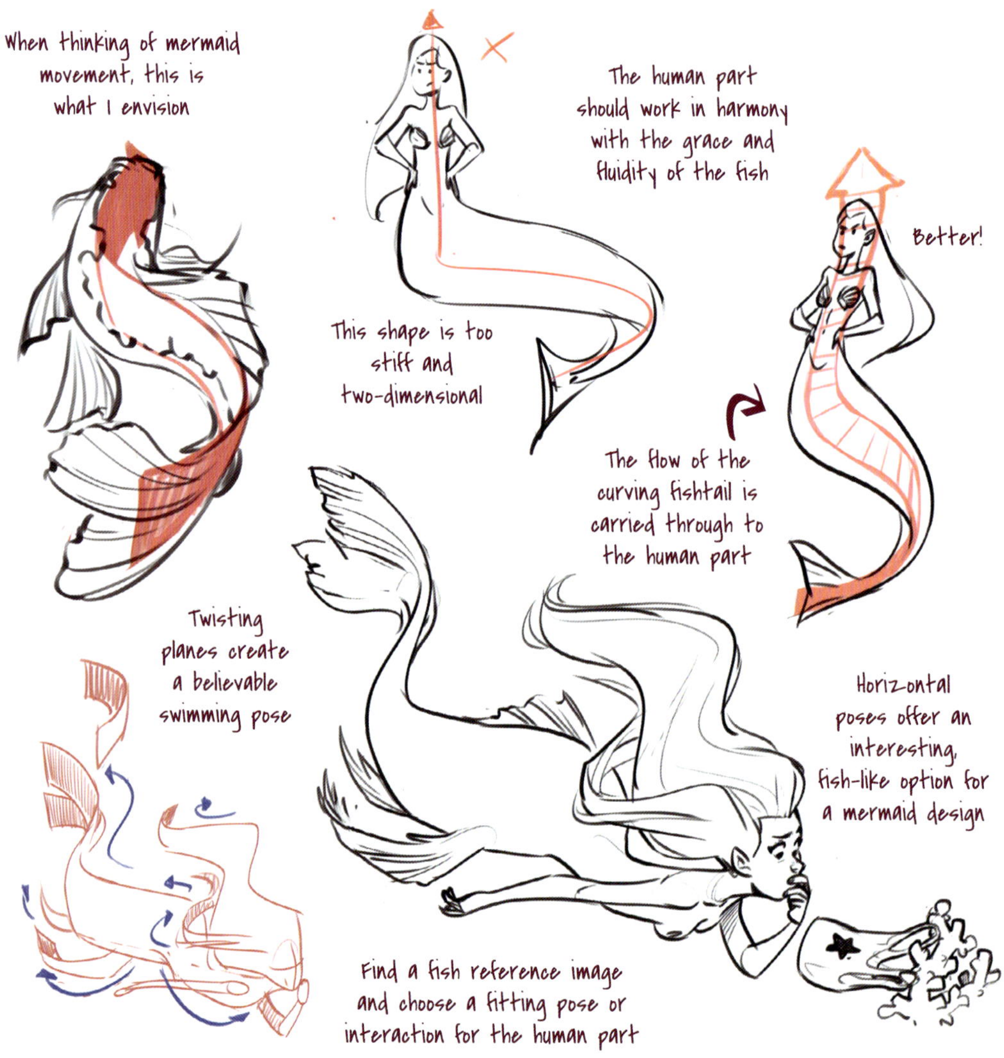

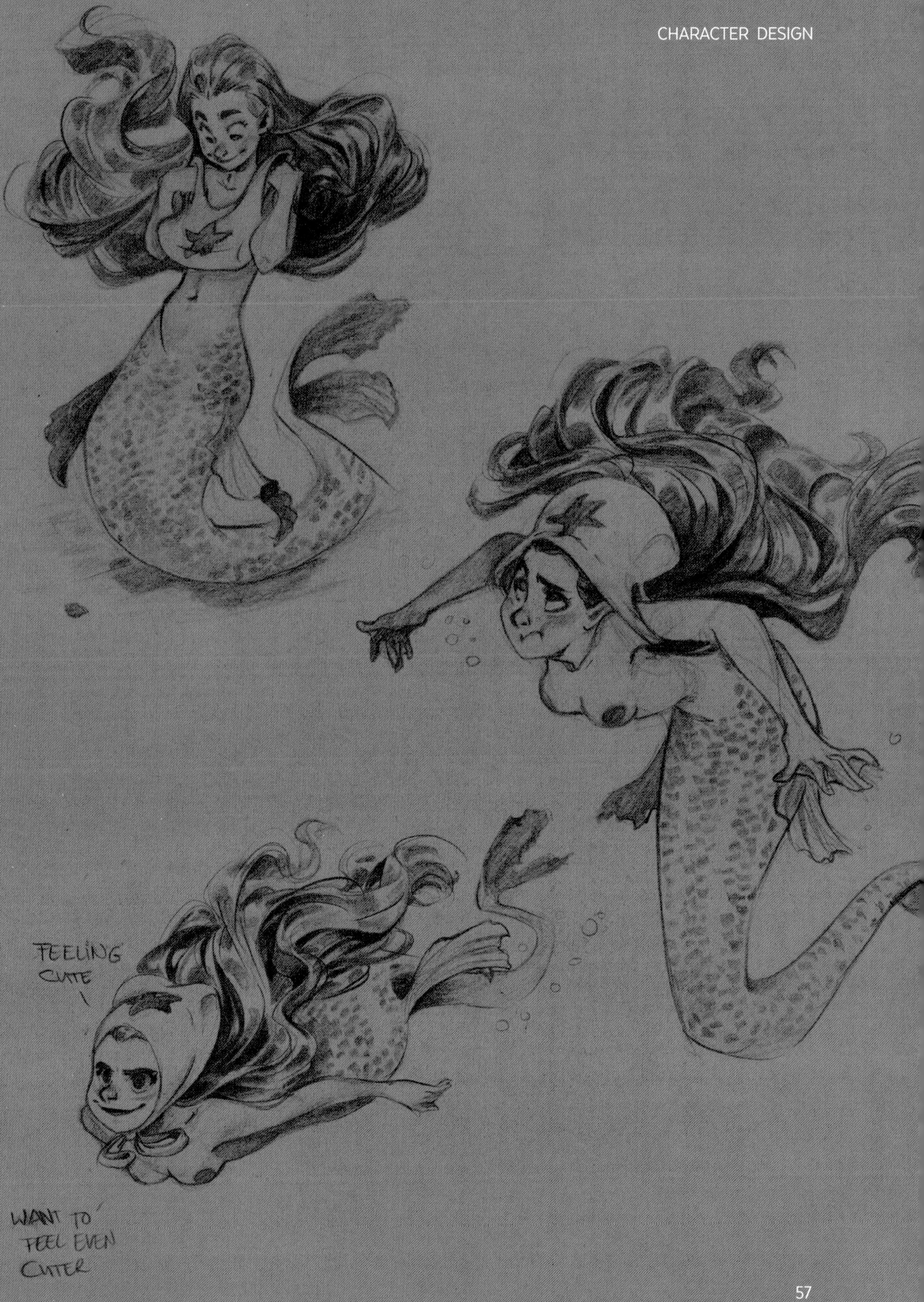
FEELING CUTE
WANT TO FEEL EVEN CUTER

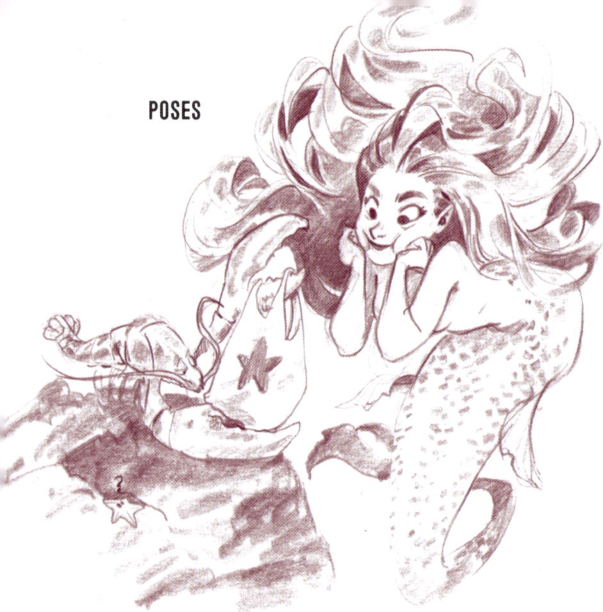

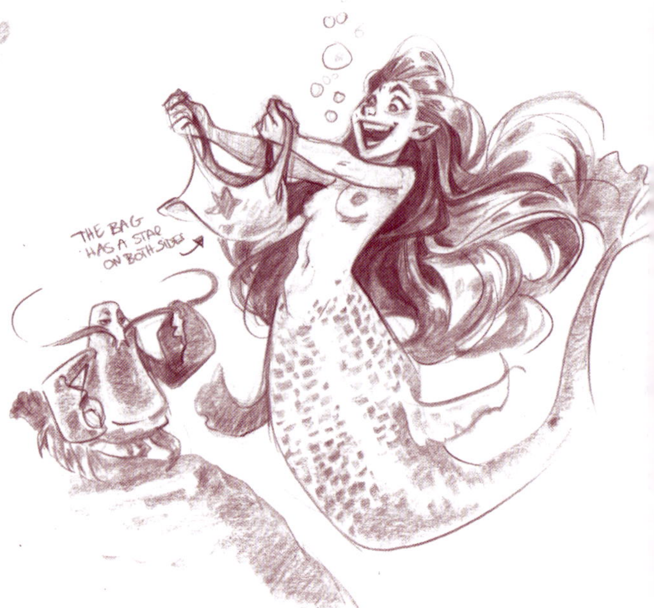

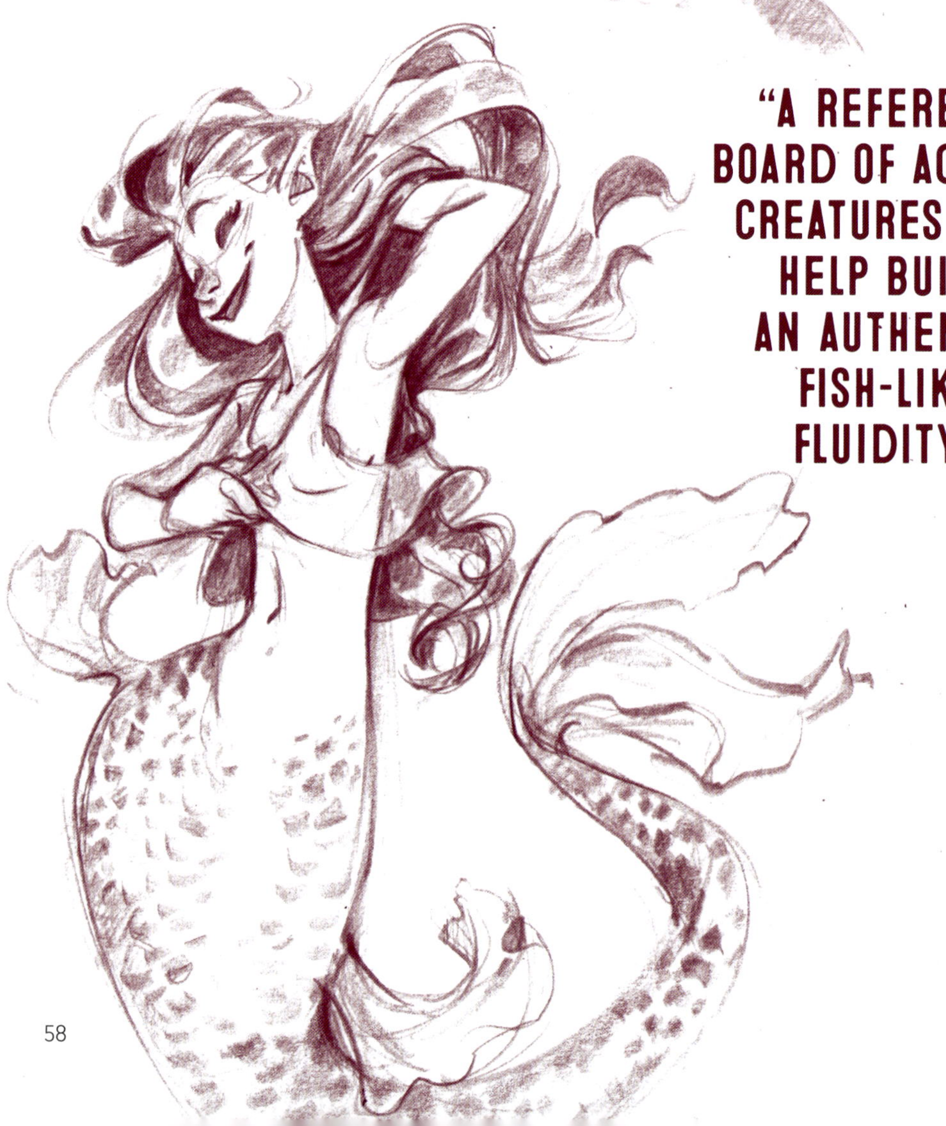

"A REFERENCE BOARD OF AQUATIC CREATURES WILL HELP BUILD AN AUTHENTIC FISH-LIKE FLUIDITY"

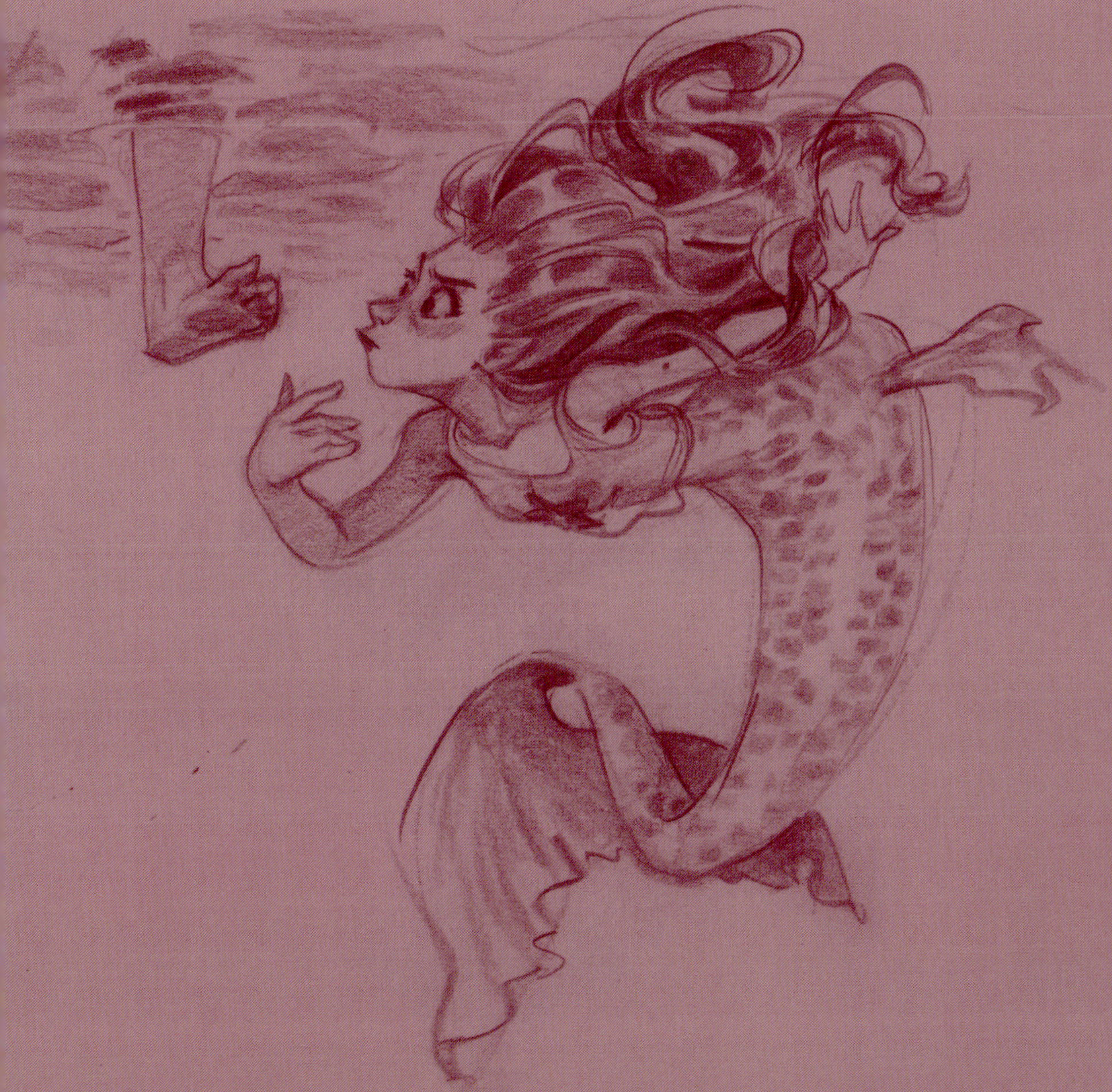

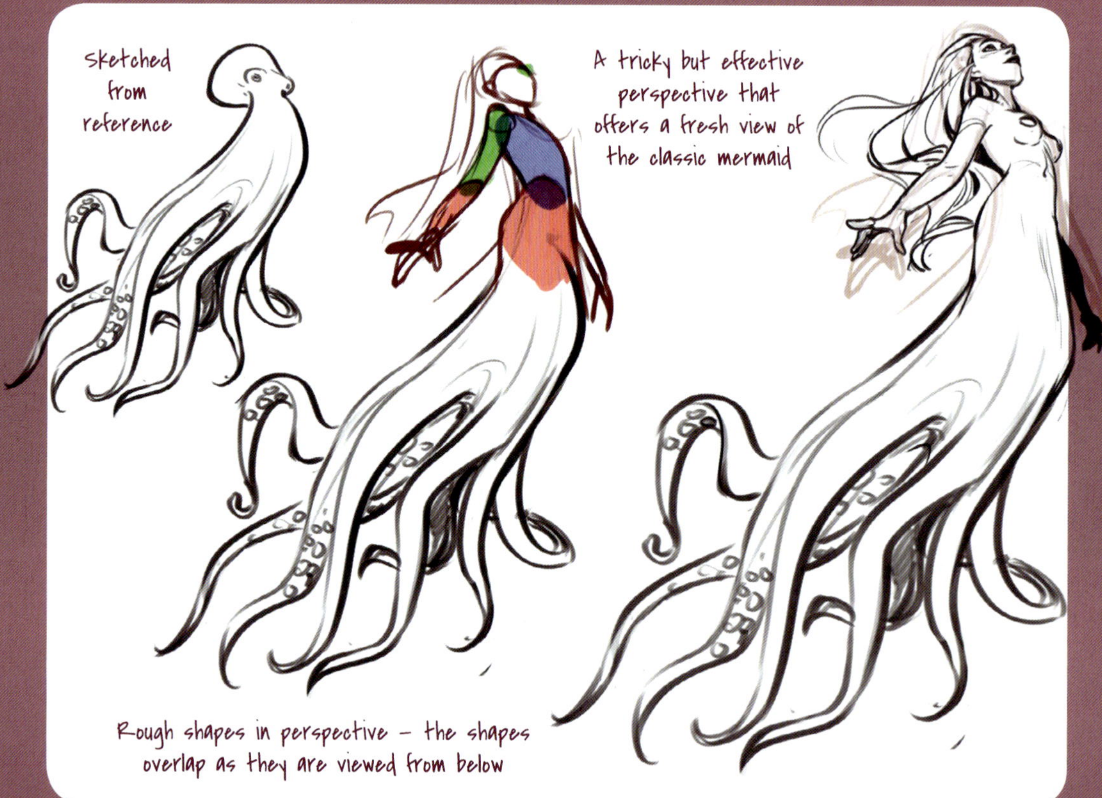
Sketched from reference
A tricky but effective perspective that offers a fresh view of the classic mermaid
Rough shapes in perspective – the shapes overlap as they are viewed from below

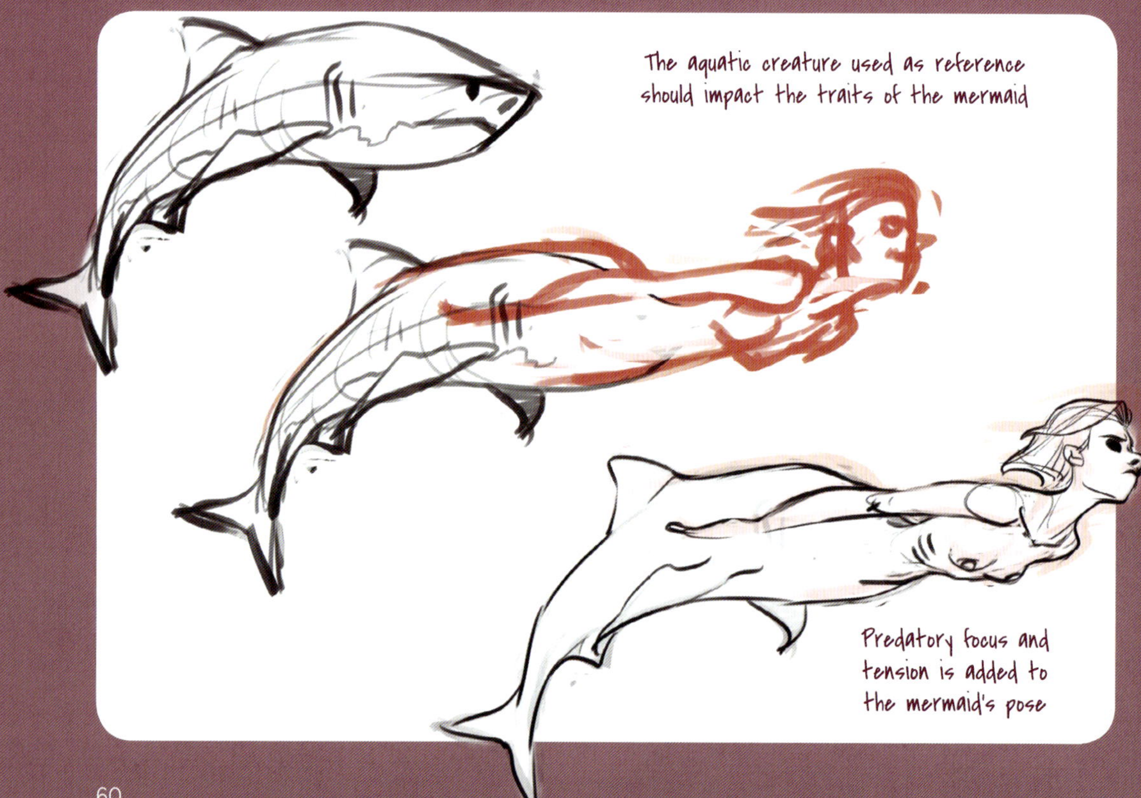
The aquatic creature used as reference should impact the traits of the mermaid
Predatory focus and tension is added to the mermaid's pose

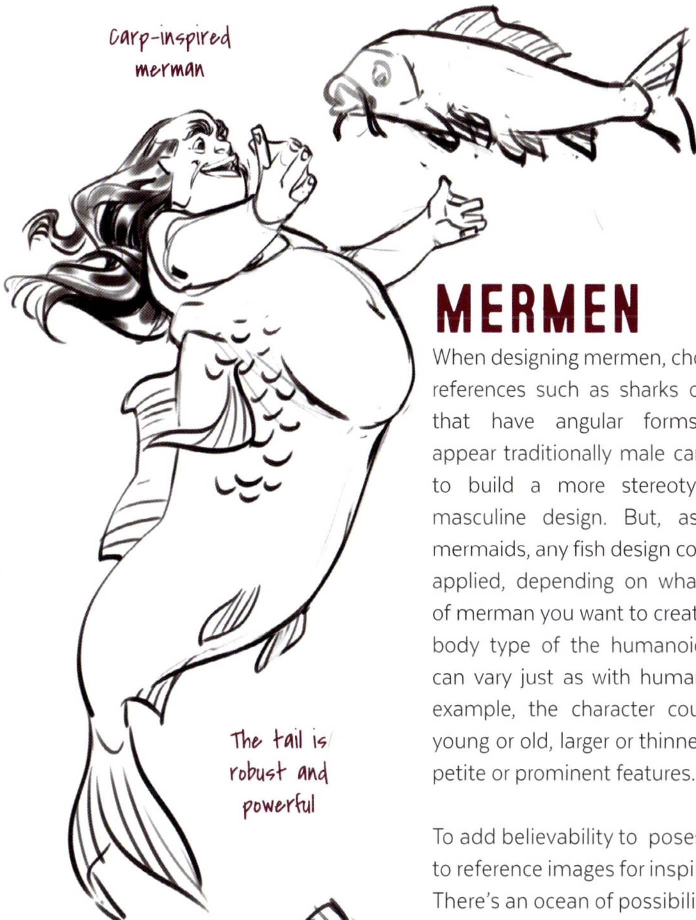

MERMEN

When designing mermen, choosing references such as sharks or rays that have angular forms and appear traditionally male can help to build a more stereotypically masculine design. But, as with mermaids, any fish design could be applied, depending on what kind of merman you want to create. The body type of the humanoid part can vary just as with humans, for example, the character could be young or old, larger or thinner, with petite or prominent features.

To add believability to poses, look to reference images for inspiration. There's an ocean of possibilities — they can be wonderfully alien!

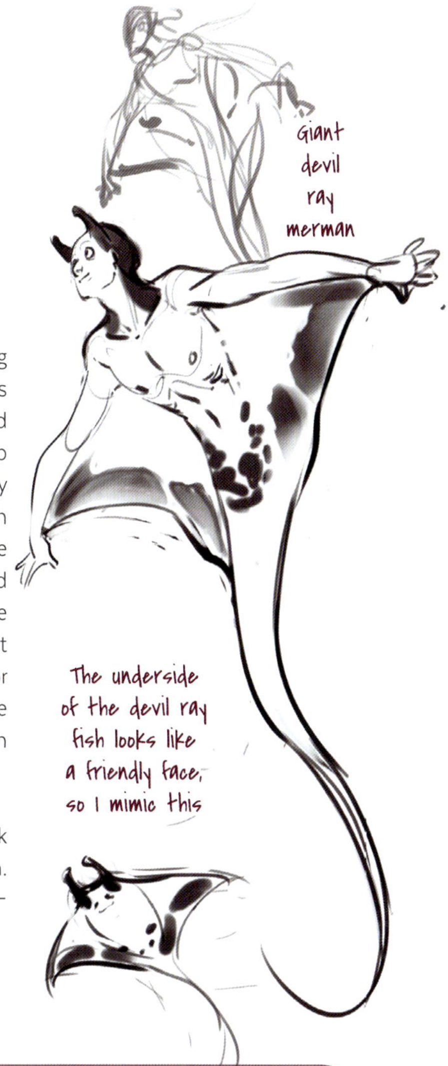

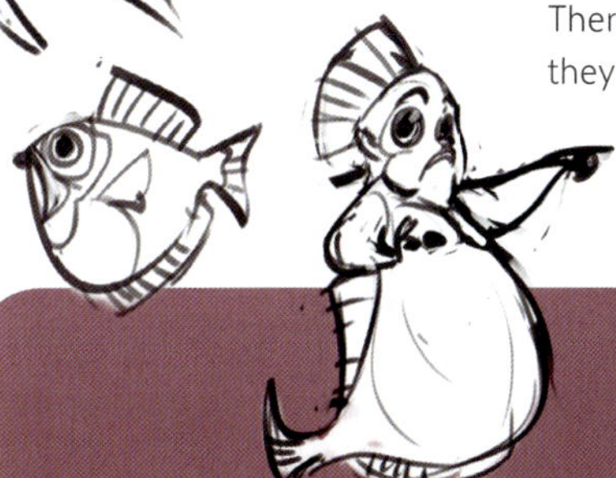

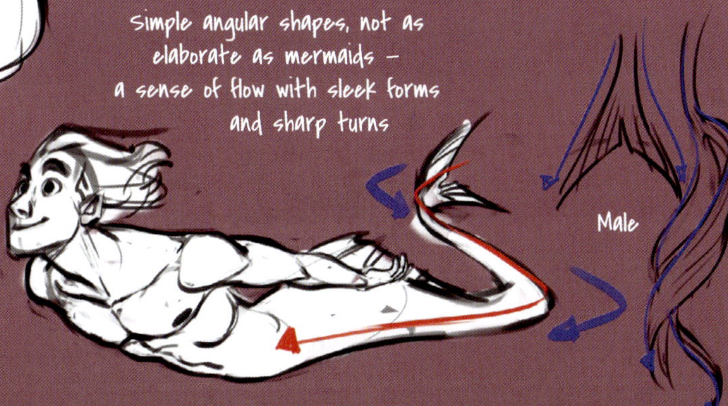

These creatures can move easily on many planes — a view from below achieves a sense of "flying" through the water.

CLOTHING

CLOTHING HACKS

When drawing simple everyday outfits there are a few quick tricks I use to add believability and detail.

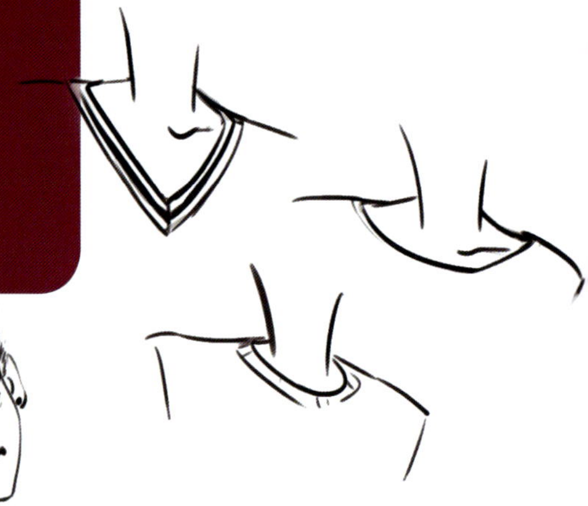

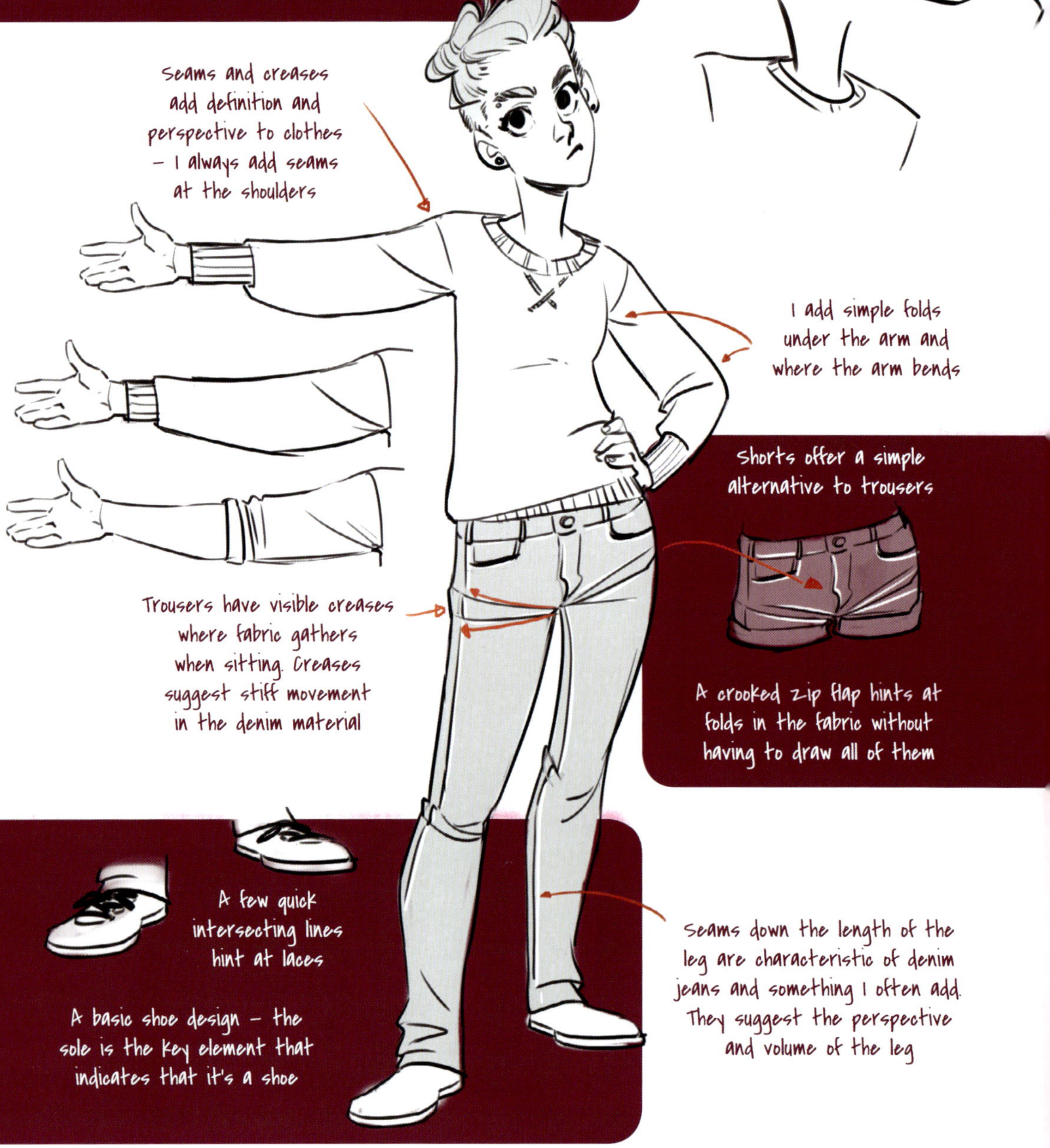

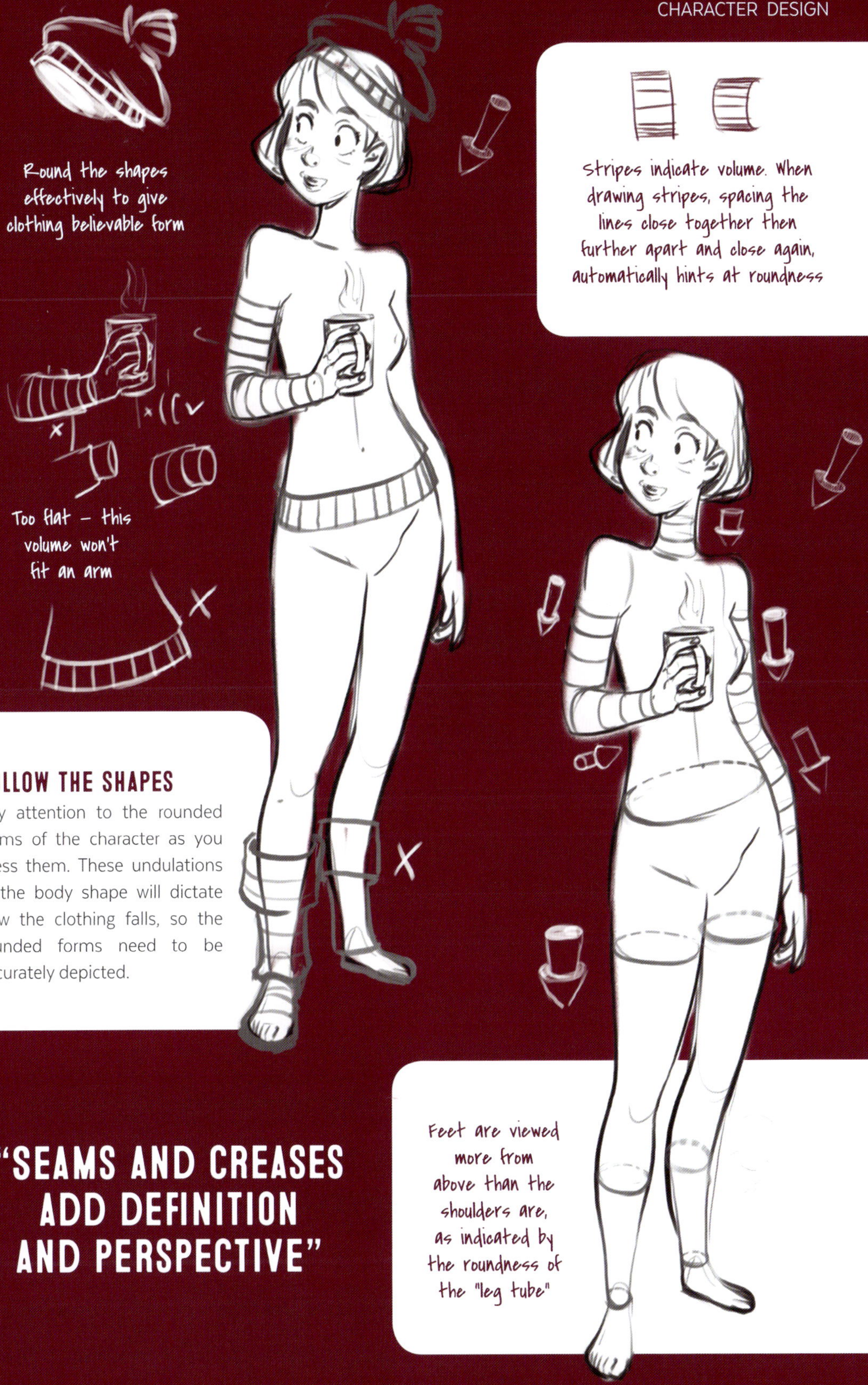

FOLLOW THE SHAPES

Pay attention to the rounded forms of the character as you dress them. These undulations in the body shape will dictate how the clothing falls, so the rounded forms need to be accurately depicted.

"SEAMS AND CREASES ADD DEFINITION AND PERSPECTIVE"

Thick materials create large folds, indicated by much thicker crease lines.

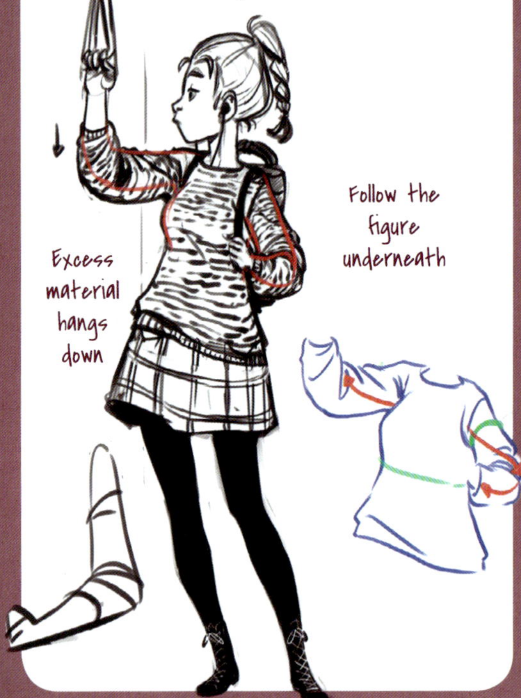

Thin materials create small folds, so creases can be indicated with finer lines.

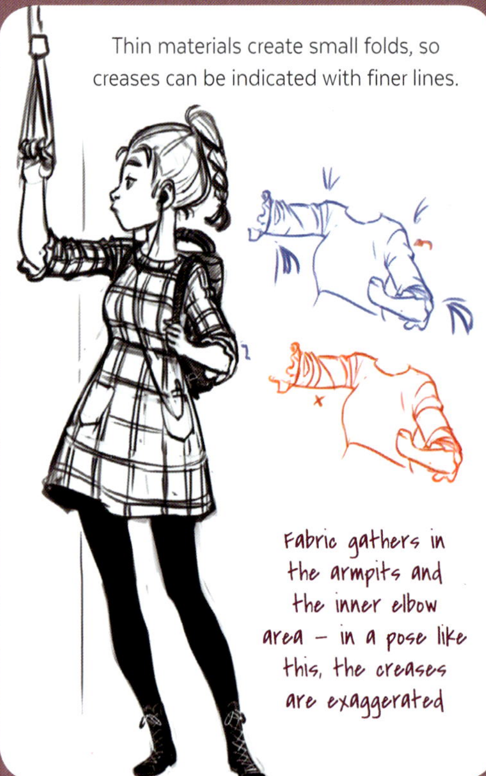

If fold lines continue unnaturally around the arm, the image can appear stiff, however, in more stylized designs it can effectively indicate creases.

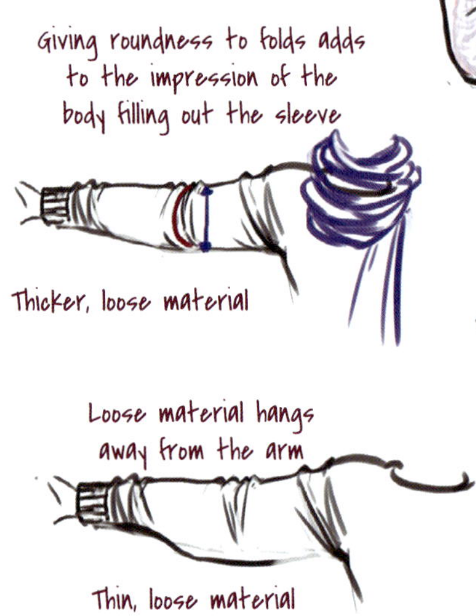

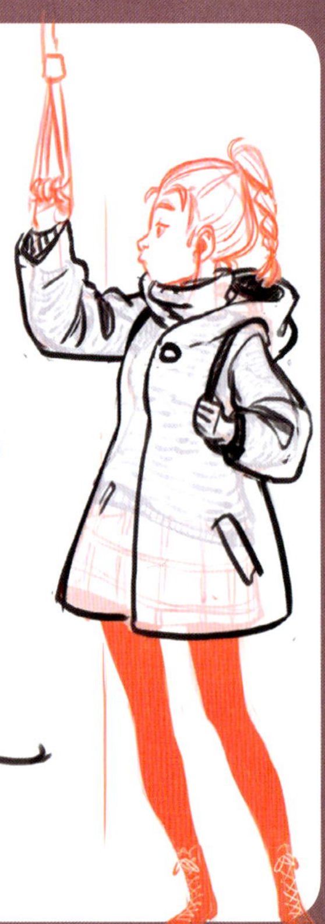

LAYERING

Whether the character is wearing loose or tight-fitting clothing, the folds and shapes of the materials on a body need to be taken into consideration.

Winter clothing is thick or layered up, with a looser fit, so will create large folds of fabric, often leading to the body shape of the character getting lost. Although tighter clothing has less excess material, many small creases indicate the shape of the body within.

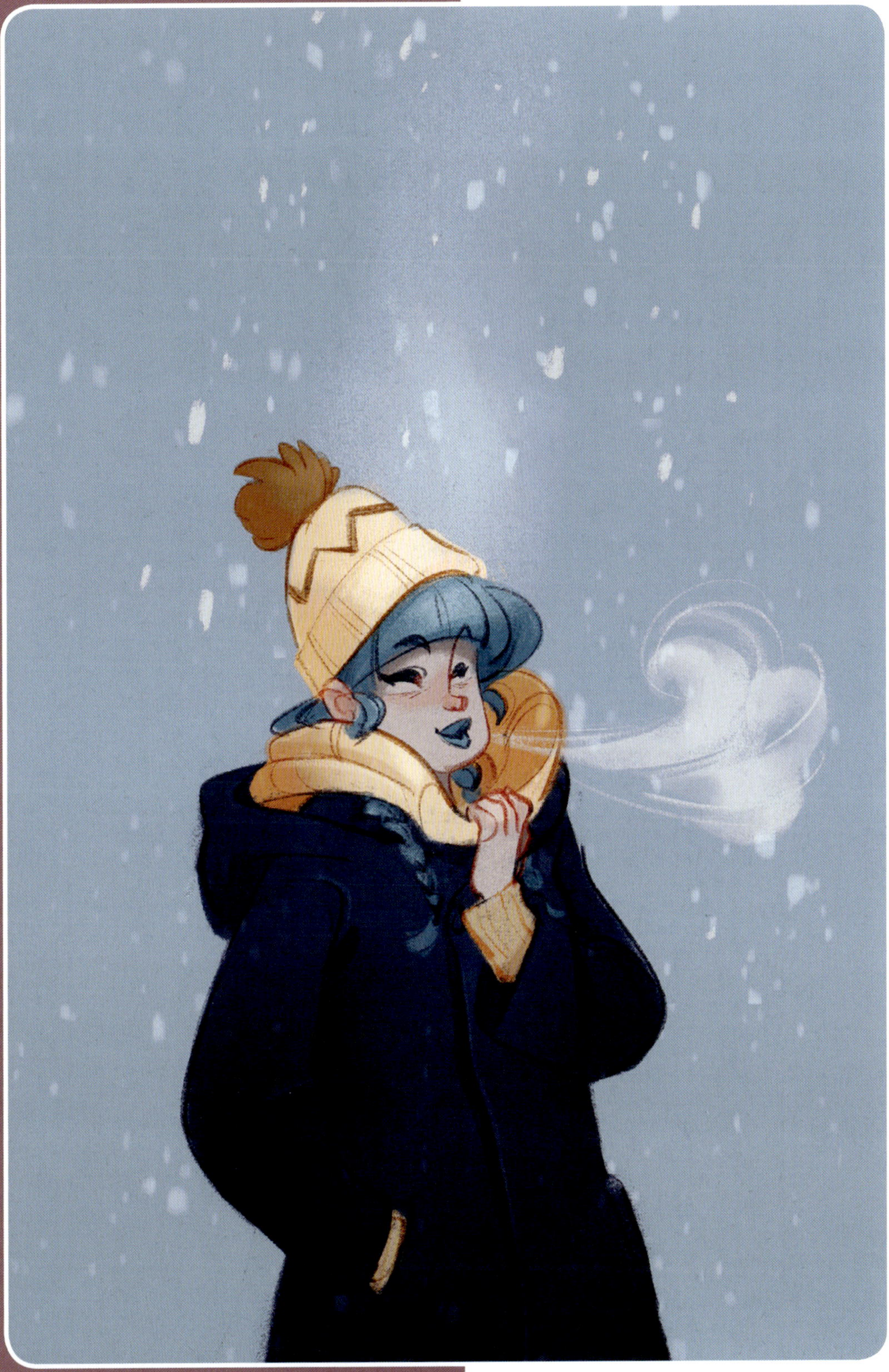

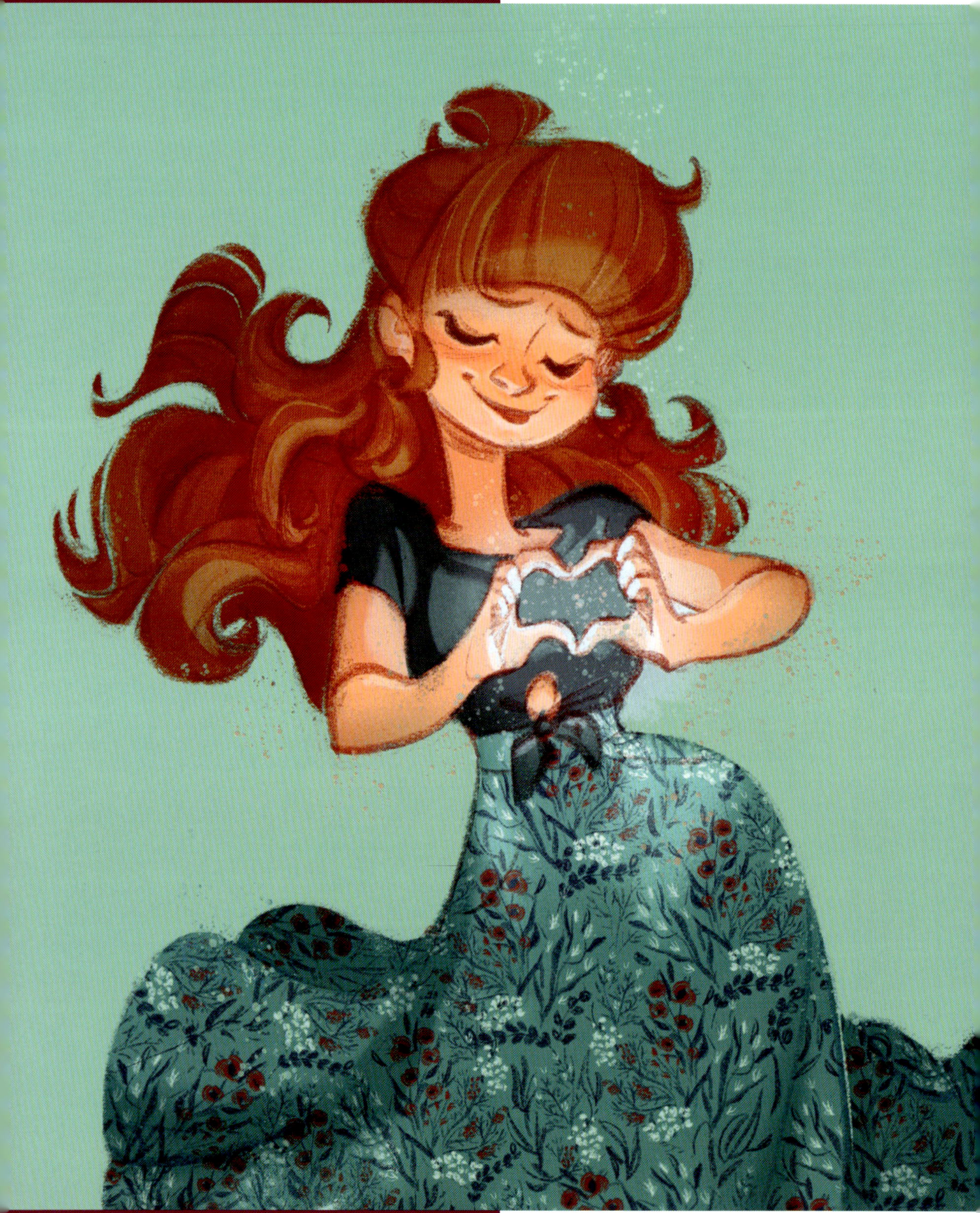

TEXTURE AND DRAPE

The drape of different items of clothing is determined by the cut and shape of the garment as well as the qualities of the material it's made from – its thickness, stiffness, or reflectability, for example.

As a rule, thin materials create fine folds and thick materials create big folds. Although thick materials don't produce small folds, thin materials can produce big folds. Stiff materials create angular folds, while soft materials create rounded folds.

LINEN

Stiff material, resulting in large folds with a matte finish that is not very reflective.

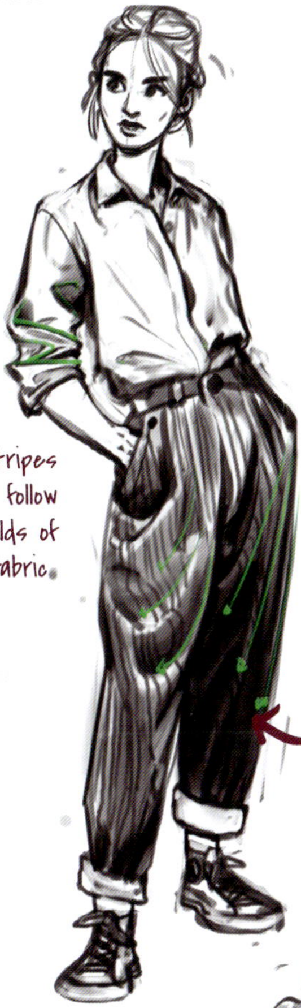

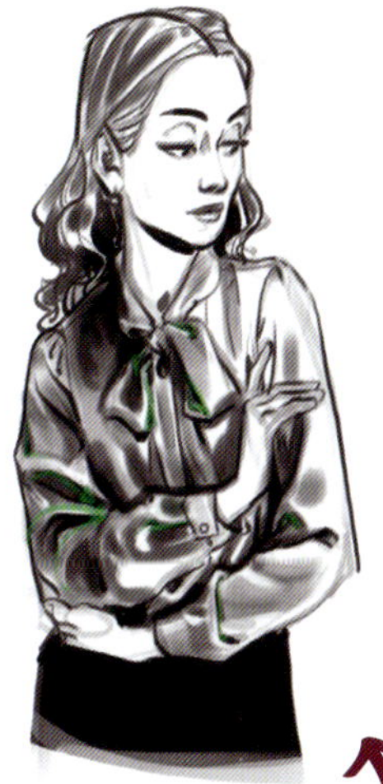

SILK OR SILK-LIKE MATERIAL

Usually highly reflective and creates soft, slightly angular billowing folds that flow with the cut of the garment and shape of the body.

CORDUROY

Comes in different thicknesses and can range from matte to reflective. As a soft material it flows into big, gentle folds. The cut of these trousers adds to the flowing nature of the material.

TRANSPARENT MATERIAL

is darker when it is layered on top of itself, such as when it creases and folds.

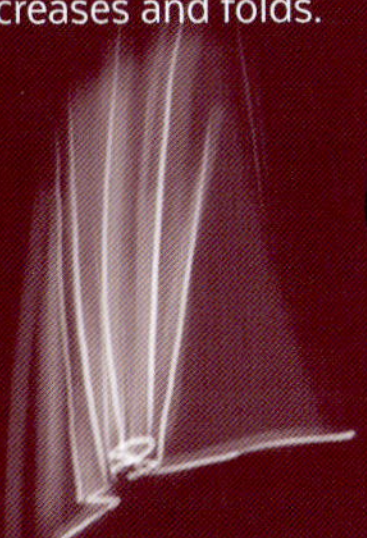

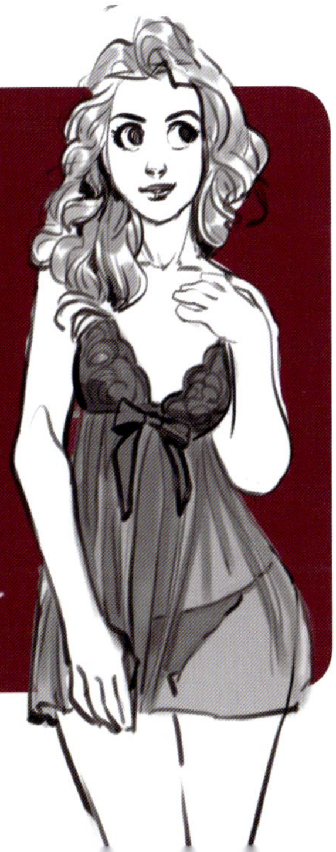

VELVET

Very reflective, soft, and flowing material with moderate elasticity.

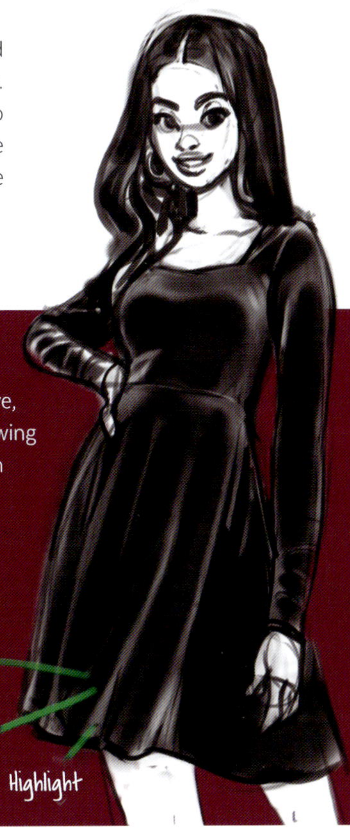

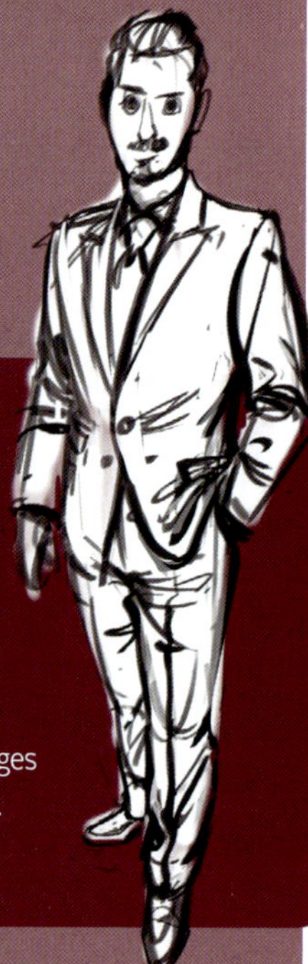

SUITS

When building a suit, especially when adding the creases, it's important to consider the body underneath. The forms can be exaggerated during the early stages of design and then finessed later.

Suits are cut with precision and often made from a stiff material

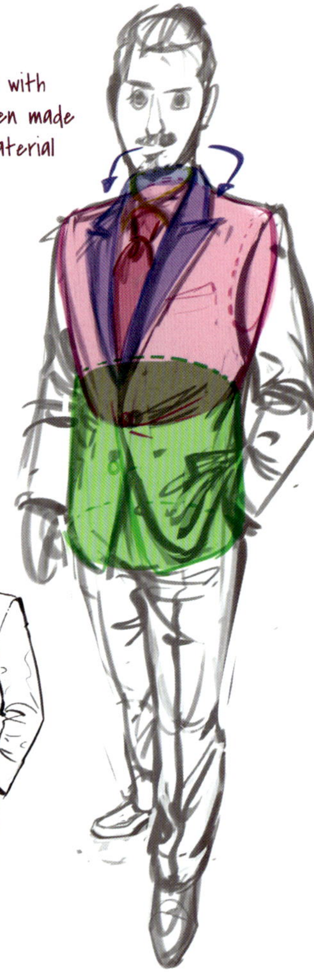

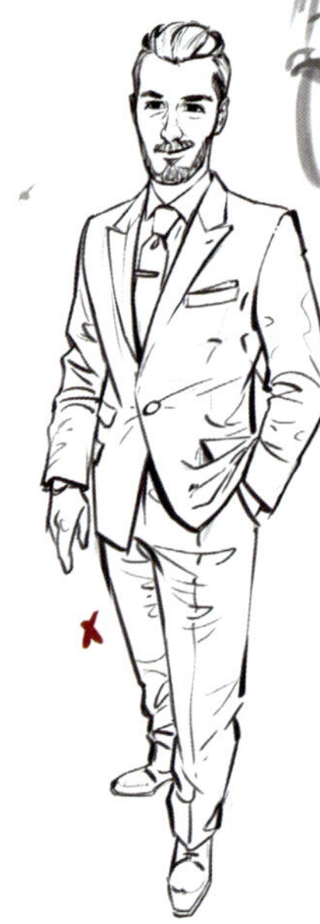

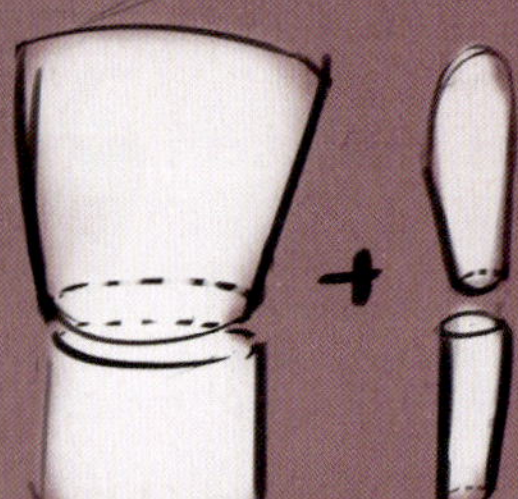

Think of the suit as being made from several shapes

Remember that characteristically, suits have distinctive angular shoulders

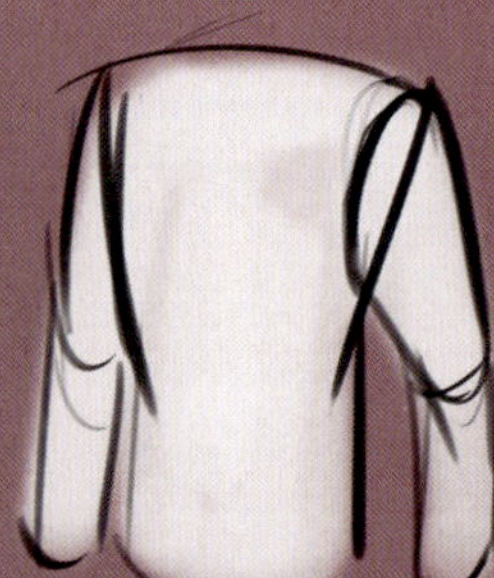

When cleaning up the design, it's easy to add too many creases and folds and make a suit look crumpled.

Less is more

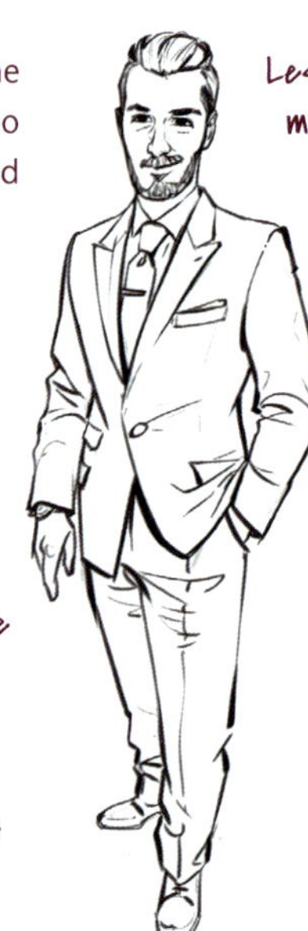

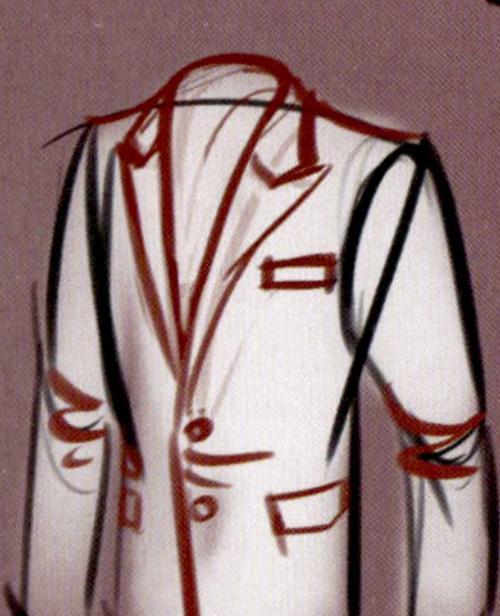

The collar needs to appear to wrap around the neck

Keep empty spaces to balance busy creased areas, such as where the material gathers at the joints

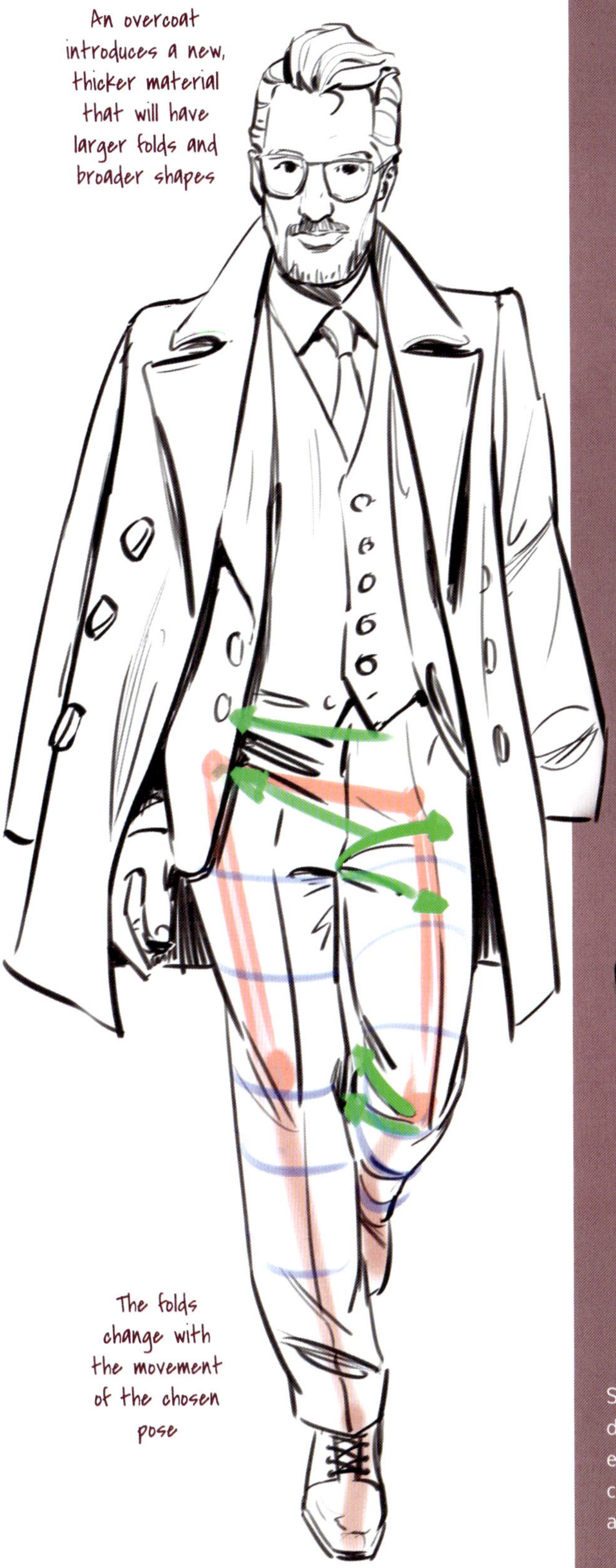

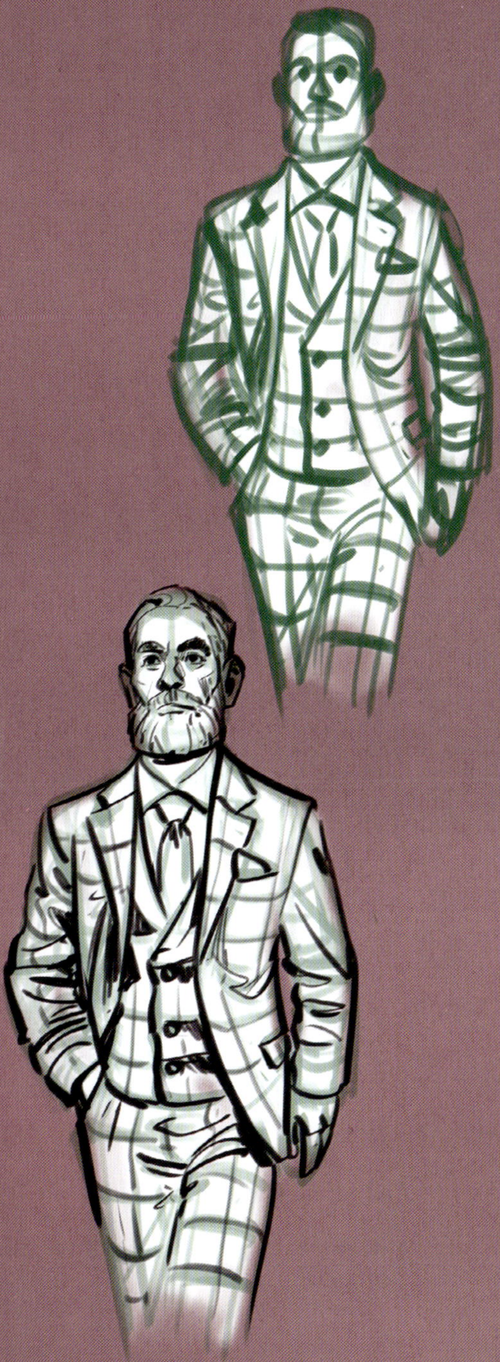

Suits come in many different materials. The differences in thickness and stiffness can create either softer or sharper folds. Patterns, such as check designs, can make a big difference visually and help to indicate form.

COSTUME DESIGN

When developing and drawing complex costumes, there are extra design considerations to take into account, such as historical accuracy, believability, and wearability.

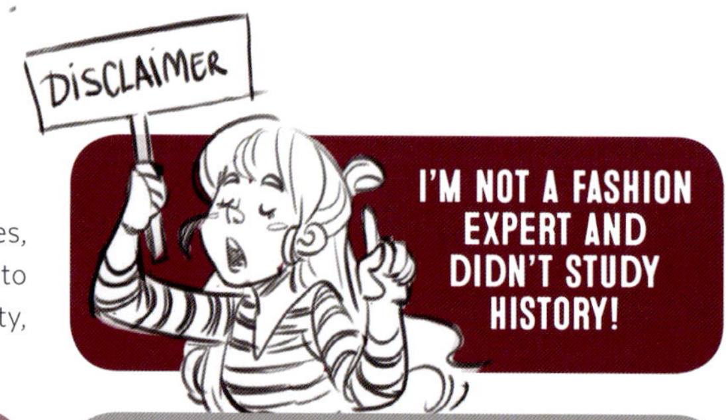

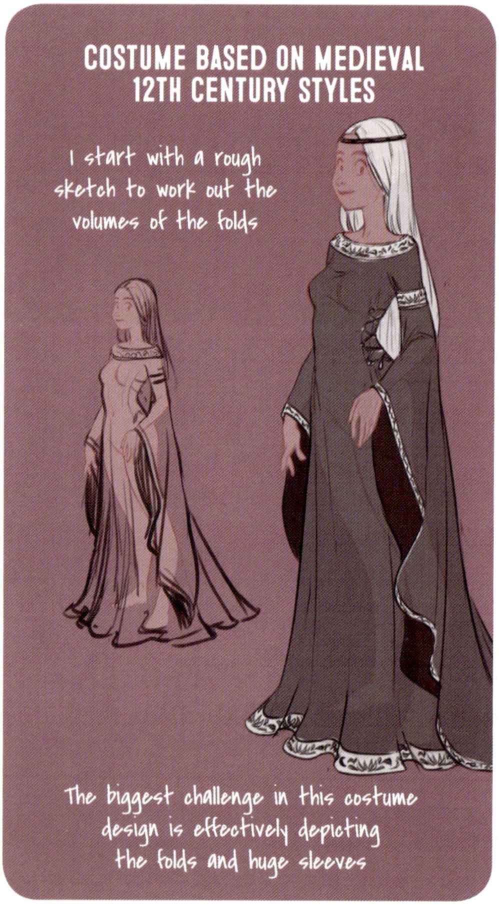

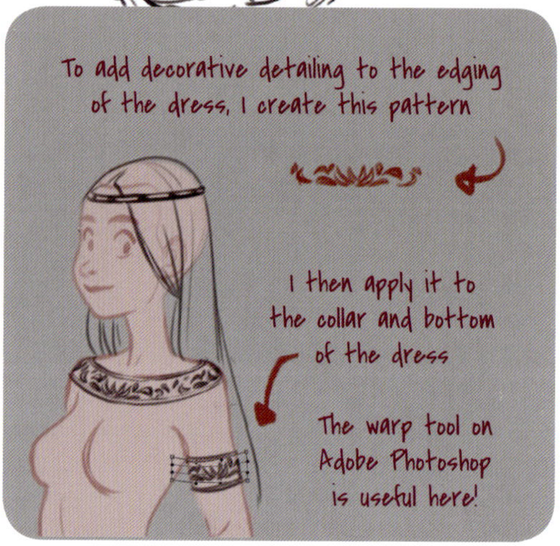

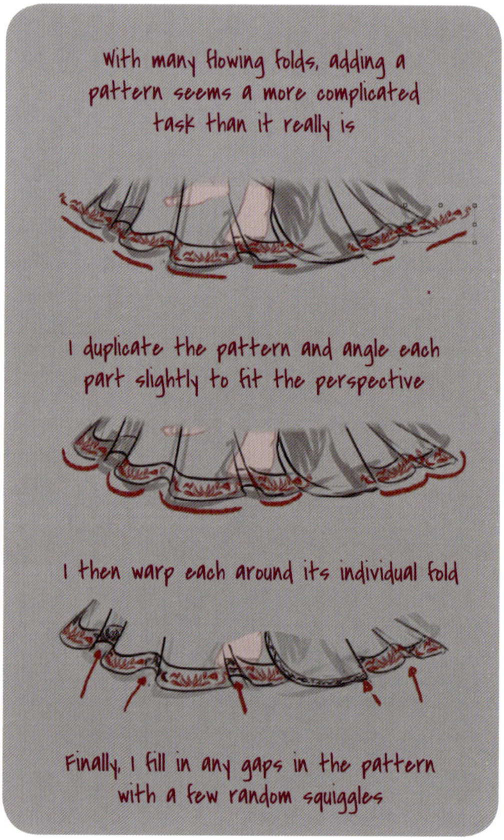

HISTORICAL CLOTHING

When drawing clothing from a specific historical era, it is very important to use accurate references to ensure the designs are authentic and don't just reflect everyday clothing.

For me, reference images are inspirational and help me to build a believable costume and character. I also sometimes like to mix styles that might be a century or so apart. This is a fun way to work, but it depends on what you want to achieve and how accurate you need to be.

COSTUME BASED ON 17TH-CENTURY STYLES

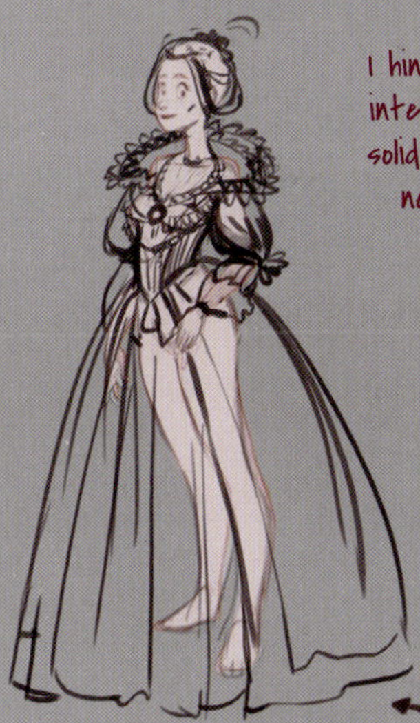

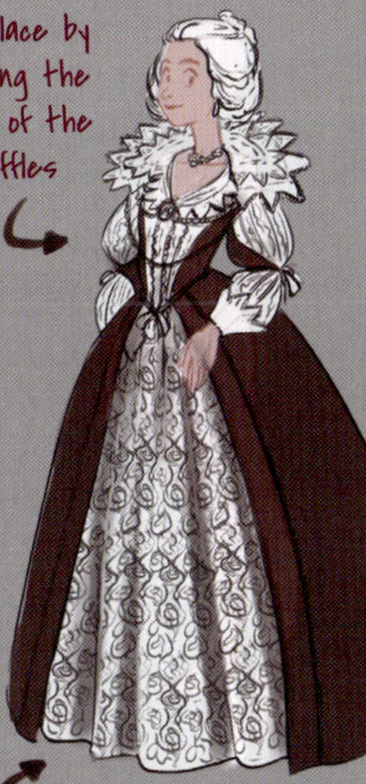

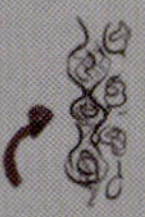

STEP 1

Pattern design. I produce the heavily patterned material for the skirt using a similar technique as the previous patterned edging.

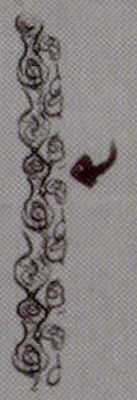

STEP 2

Repeat and make a stripe.

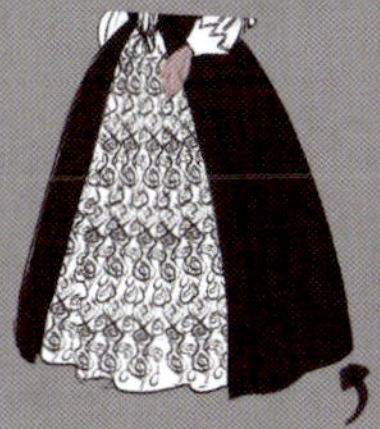

STEP 3

Duplicate stripe, line up and squash stripes slightly at the top to indicate the round shape of the skirt.

STEP 4

Reduce opacity and erase areas that disappear into the folds of the skirt.

COSTUME BASED ON 19TH CENTURY STYLES

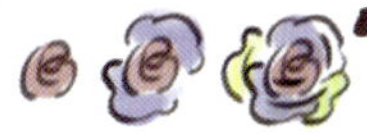

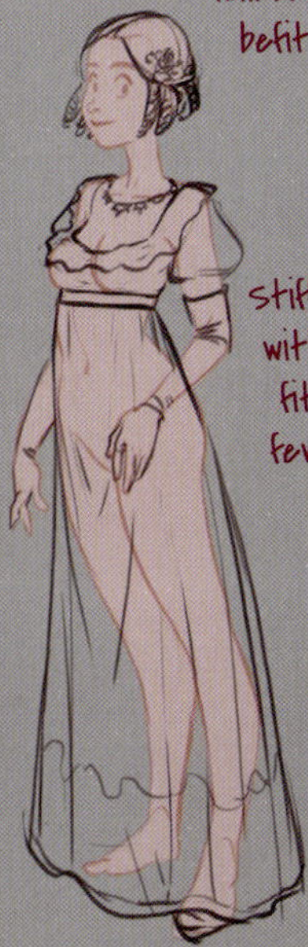

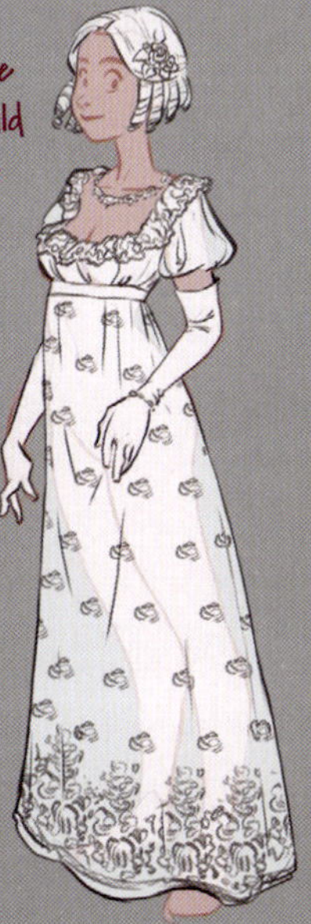

STEP 1

Draw a flower motif.

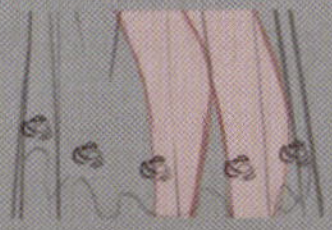

STEP 2

Duplicate and arrange flowers horizontally in a gentle curve around the shape of the dress.

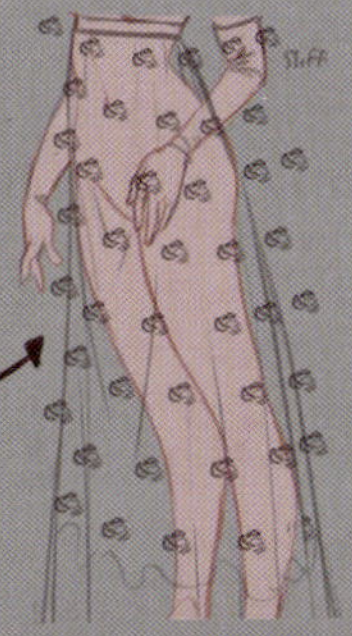

STEP 3

Merge the curved line of flowers, duplicate, and arrange the rows as required. I transform the pattern to be slightly narrower at the top.

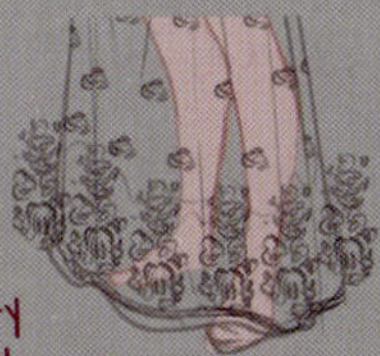

STEP 4

Tweak the placement of some flowers and erase where they disappear into creases.

INSPIRED COSTUME DESIGN

I find birds very interesting, so here I aim to incorporate bird-like elements into my costume design to create a form of modern shaman style. My concept is loose and has just enough detail to create a costume design for demonstration, but the clearer the story, the more successfully a believable design can be developed.

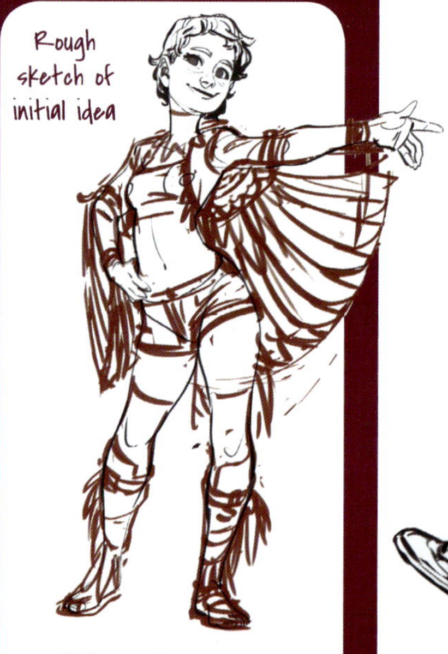

KEY REFERENCES USED TO DEVELOP THE DESIGN:

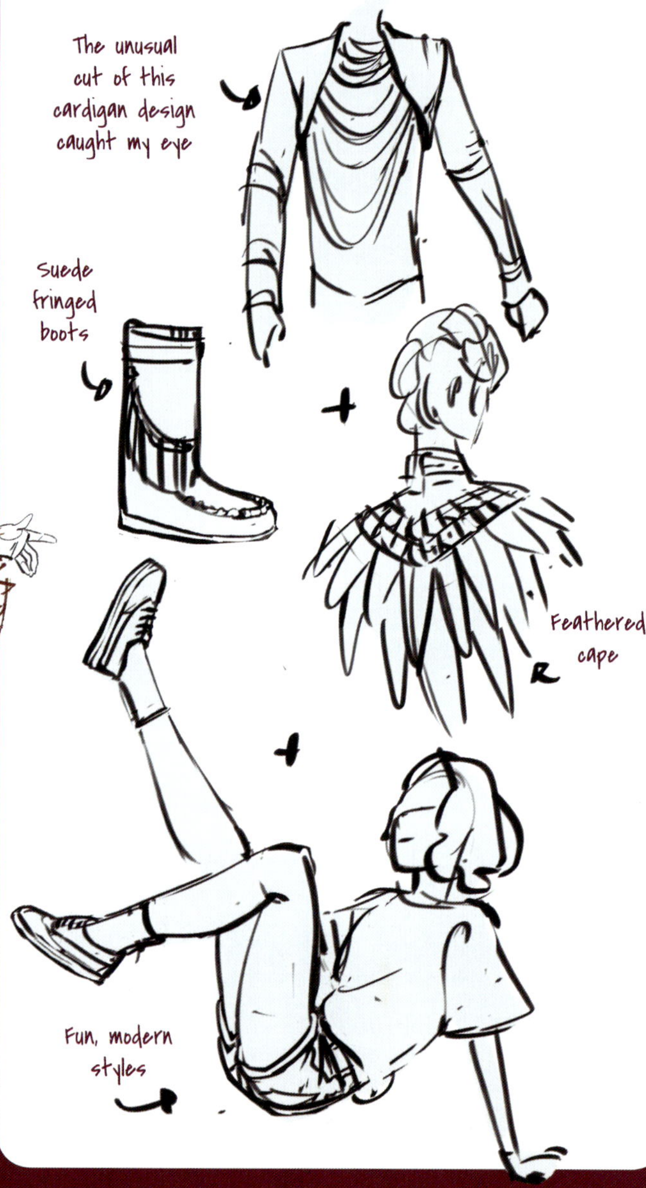

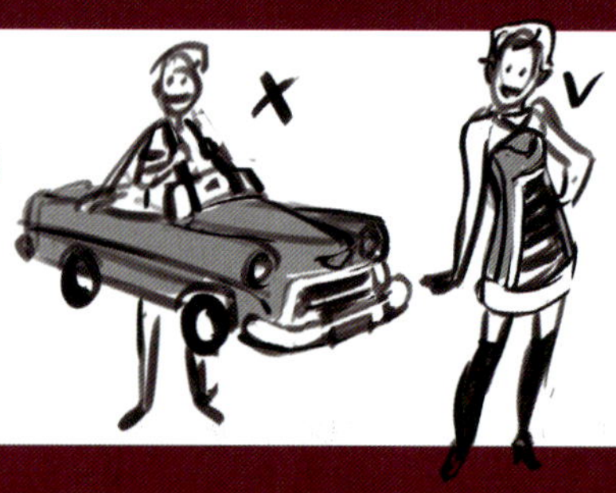

Depending on what you're designing, you can really experiment with your costumes. For example, you could use car parts for inspiration. Look for creative solutions for working interesting elements into your costume designs.

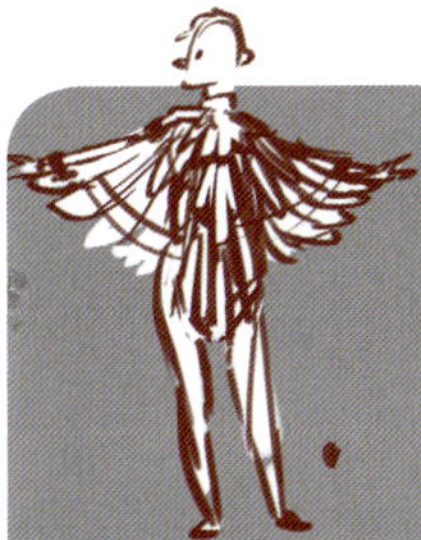

I sketch a rear view to understand how the feathered element would look from behind and how it might be attached.

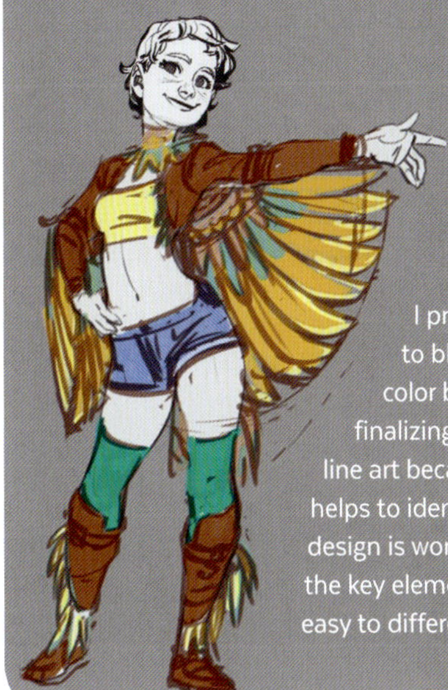

I prefer to block in color before finalizing the line art because it helps to identify if a design is working, as the key elements are easy to differentiate.

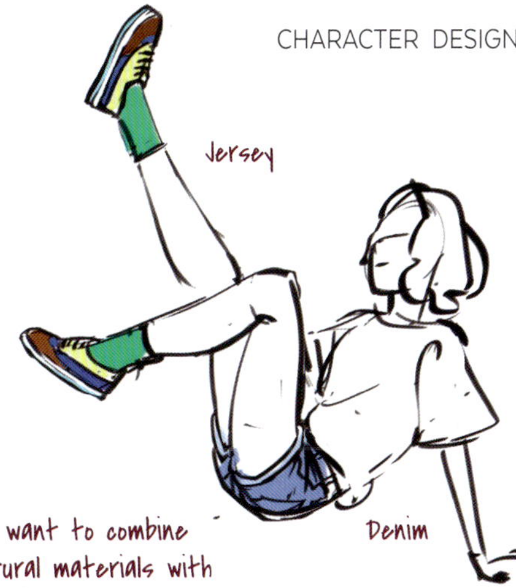

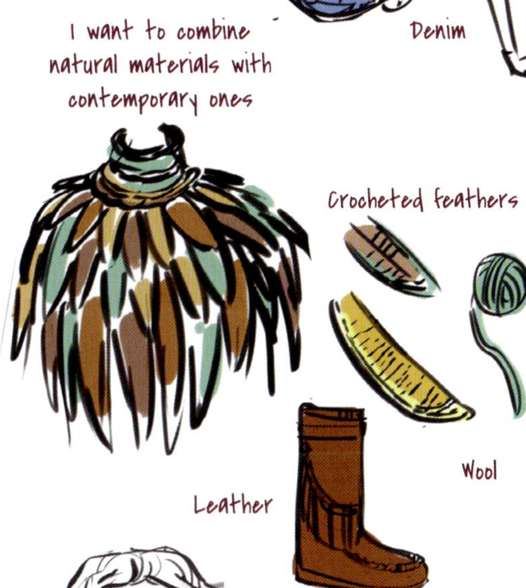

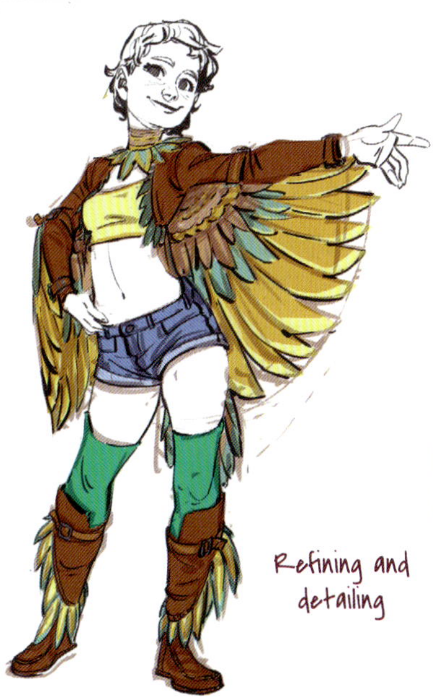

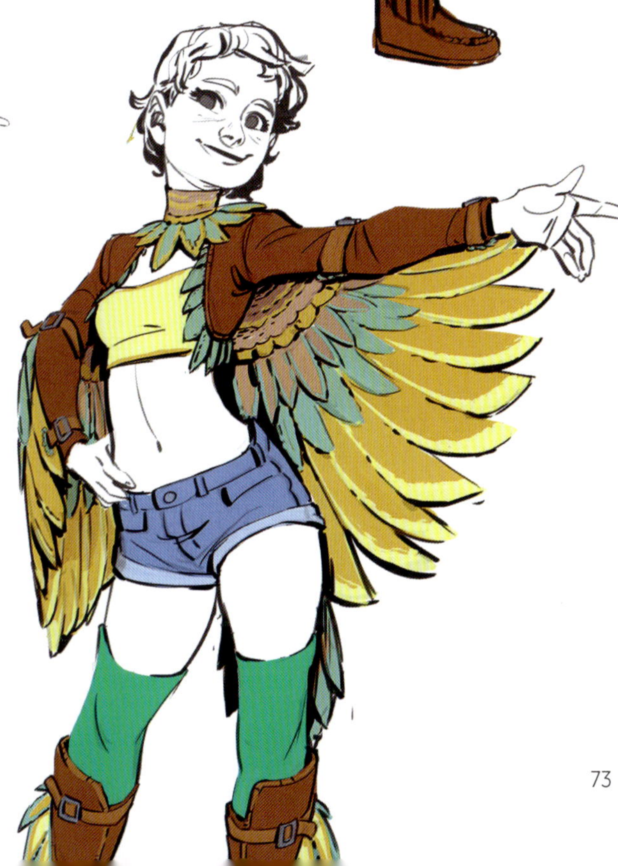

Final tweaks

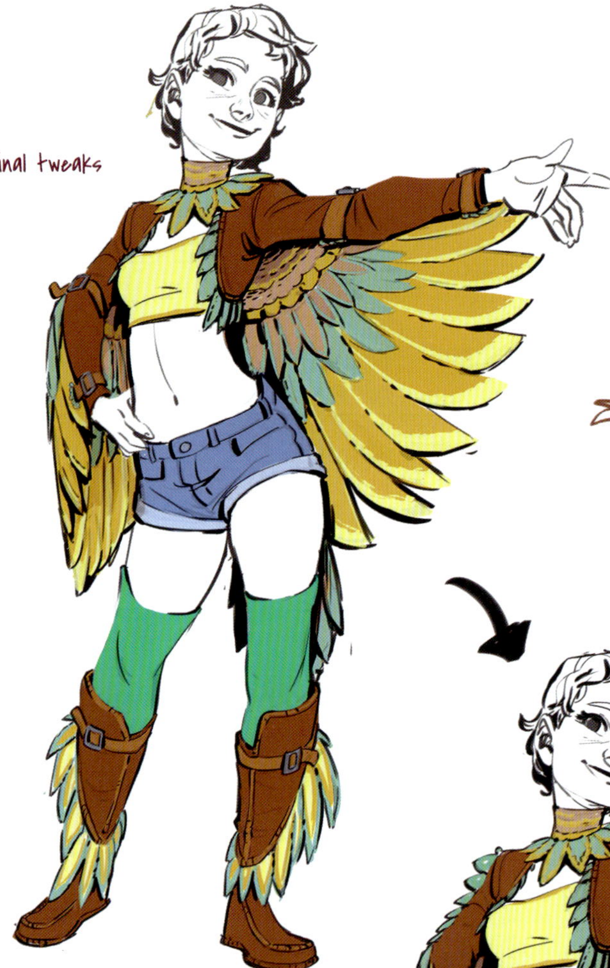

I decide to change the color of the socks from green to yellow, as I felt that the green brought too much unwanted attention to an unimportant part of the costume, when it's the wings that should pop out the most.

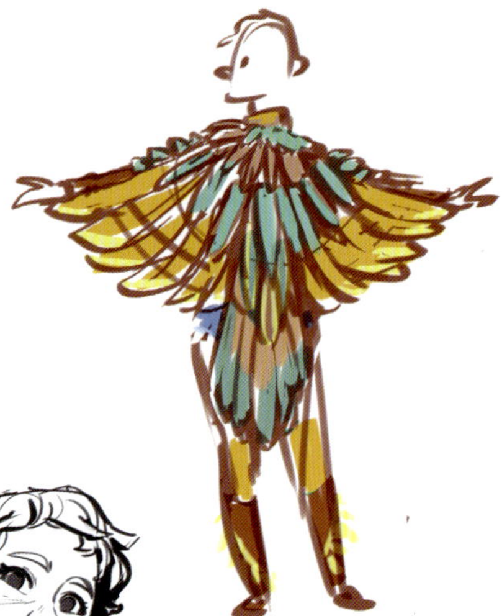

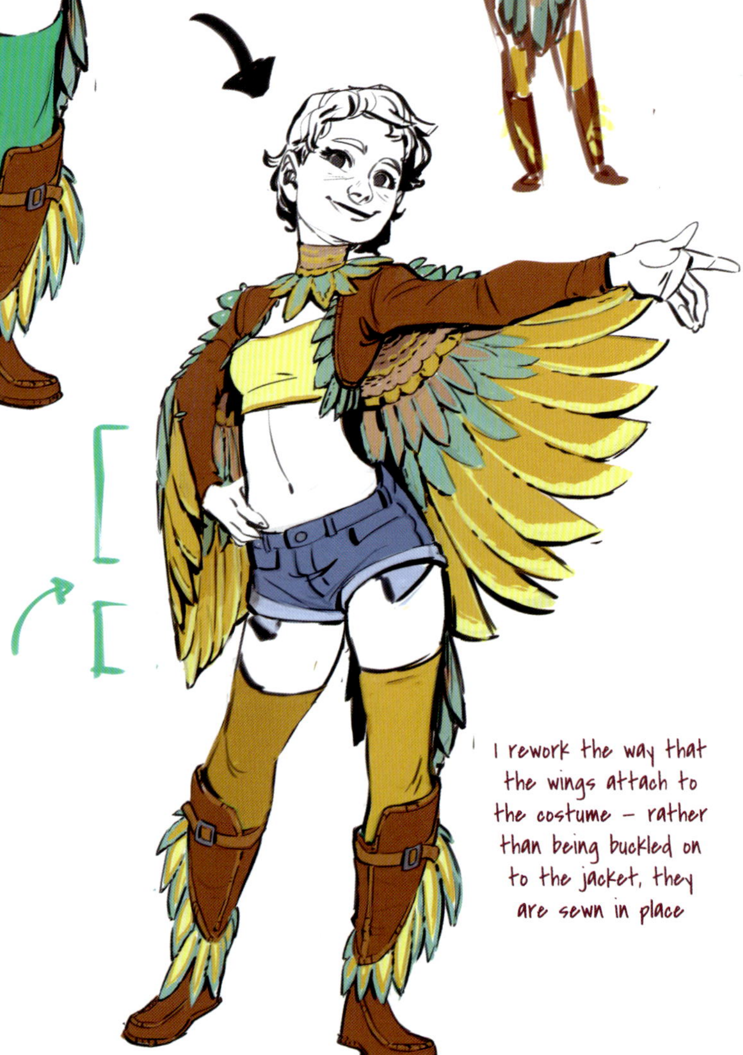

I extend the socks and add pockets hanging out of the bottom of the shorts, to make the portions of bare skin unevenly distributed and add interest

I rework the way that the wings attach to the costume – rather than being buckled on to the jacket, they are sewn in place

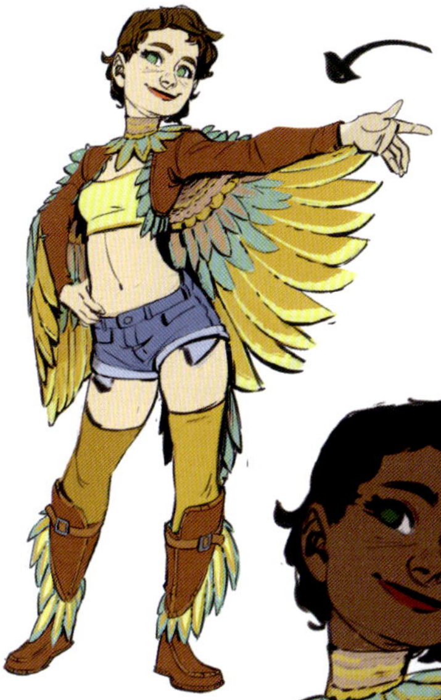

A fundamental mistake I made here was not considering the character's skin tone. As shaman are traditionally found in North America and northern Asia, the character would most likely have a darker skin tone.

By assuming the final character would have lighter coloring, the color palette could have been developed to work harmoniously with a lighter skin color. Fortunately, in this case the palette works for both a lighter and a darker skin tone, but it might have been even more successful if I had considered the darker skin tone from the beginning.

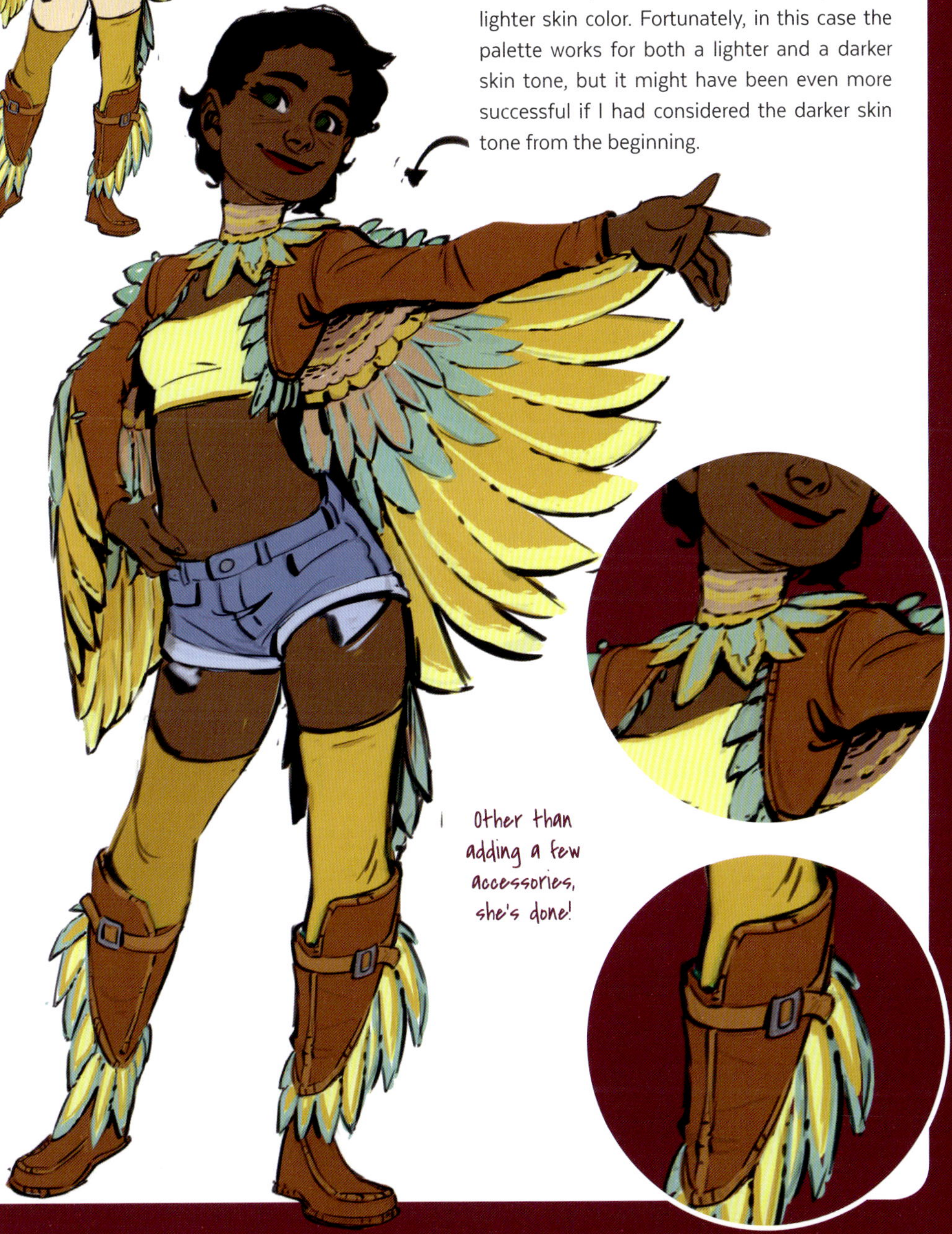

Other than adding a few accessories, she's done!

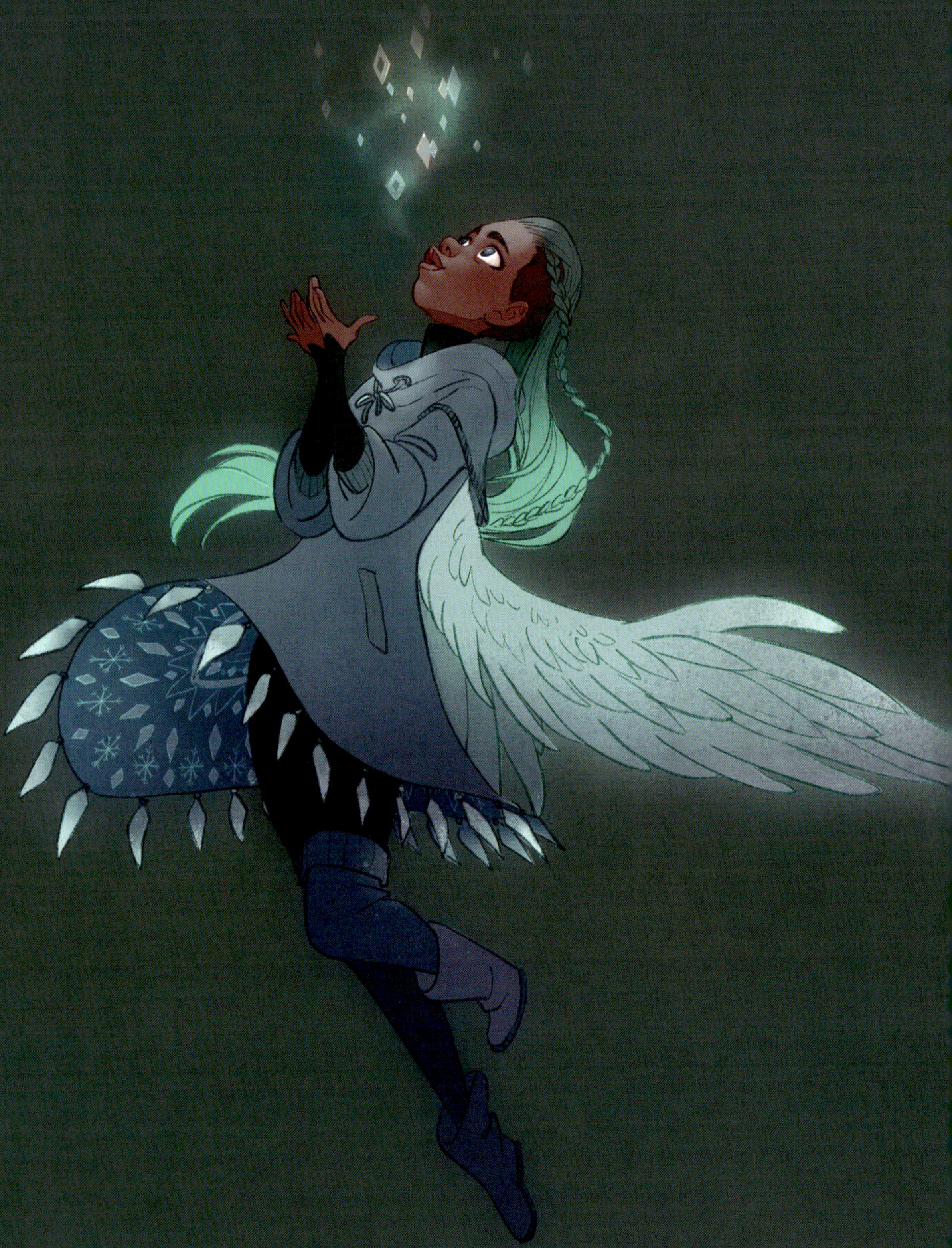

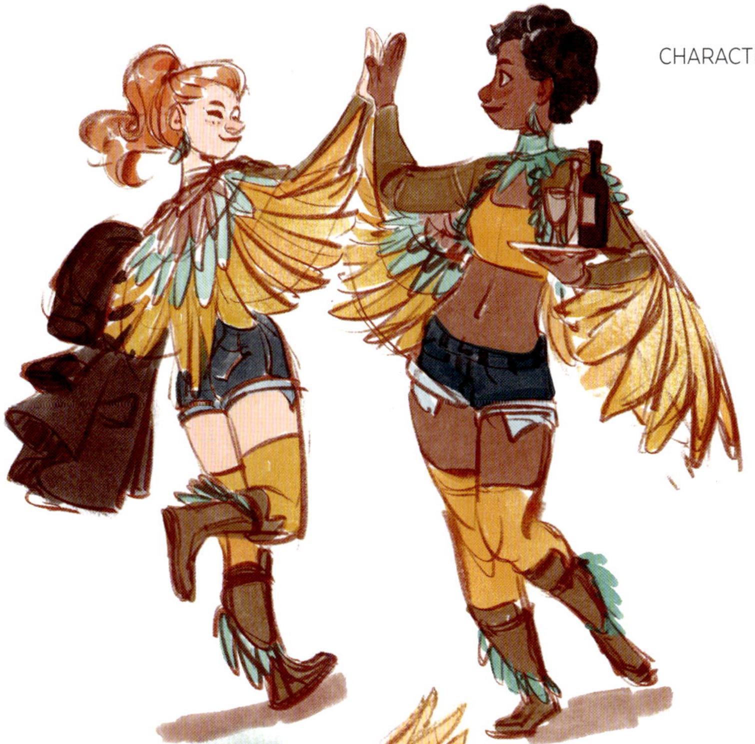

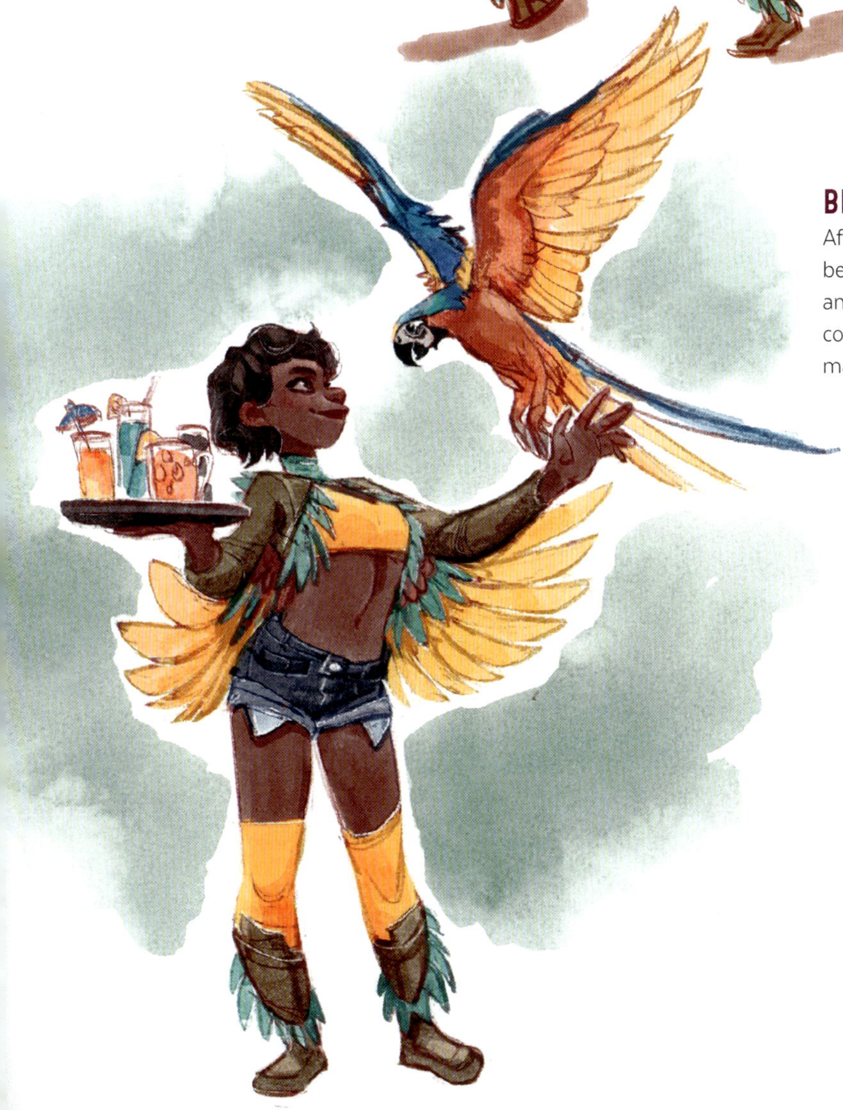

BIRDIES

After designing the costume, I began to develop the characters and their stories – strong costume design can lead you in many different directions.

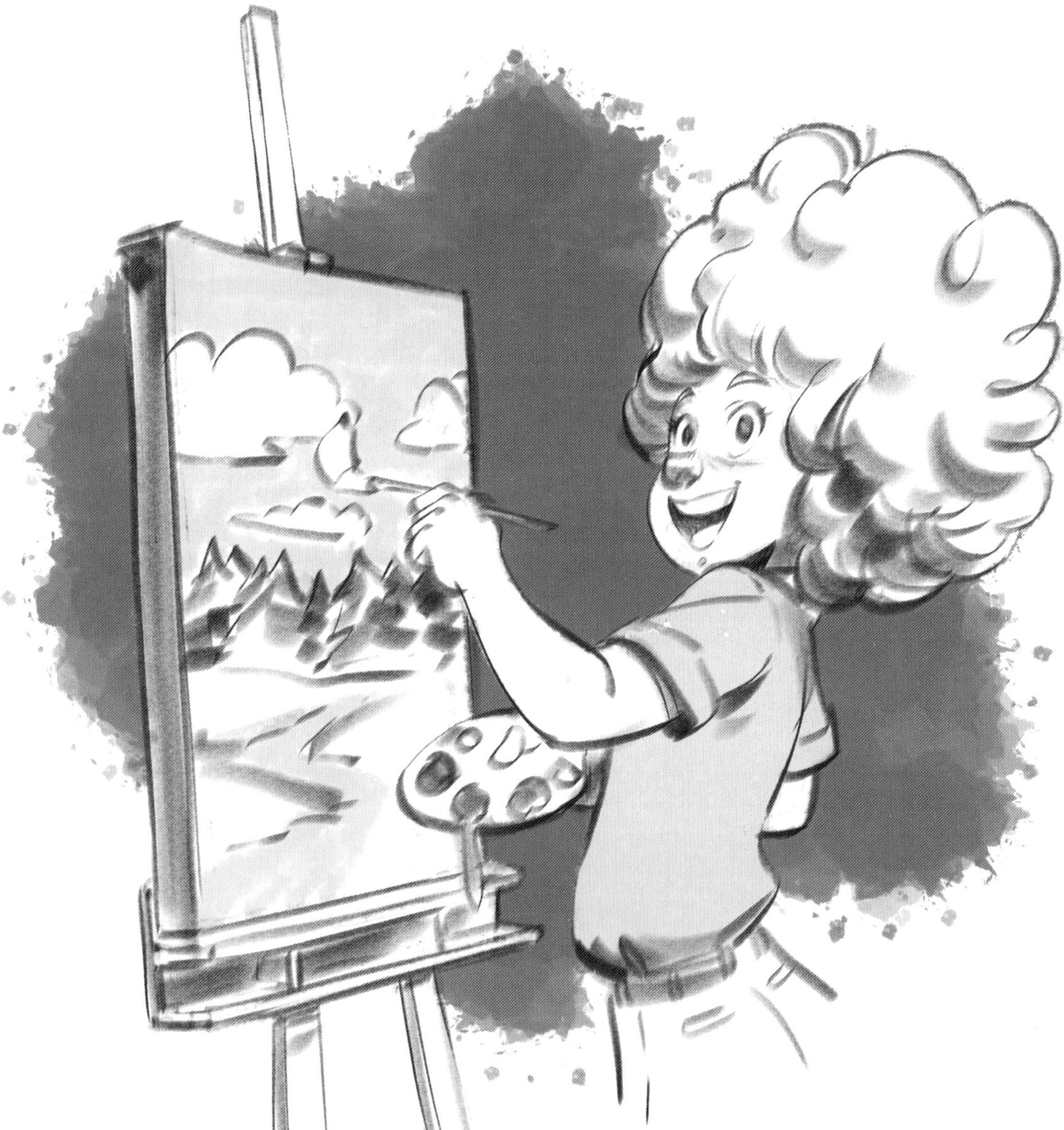

BACKGROUNDS

What I love even more than a character drawing, is a character in a believable environment. Background design is an area that many character designers find challenging and often neglect, but the invaluable richness achieved by adding an effective background makes it worth exploring and investing time in.

STUDIES

To develop my background drawing skills, I practice painting quick studies of references. It's a great way to build your understanding of scenic composition and the many different elements that are included in producing a strong background.

INSPIRED BY A PHOTOGRAPH BY@SAMANTHAMIAOU

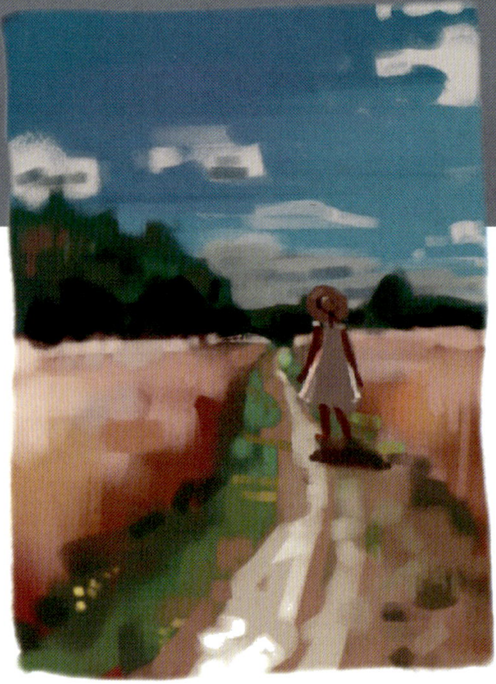

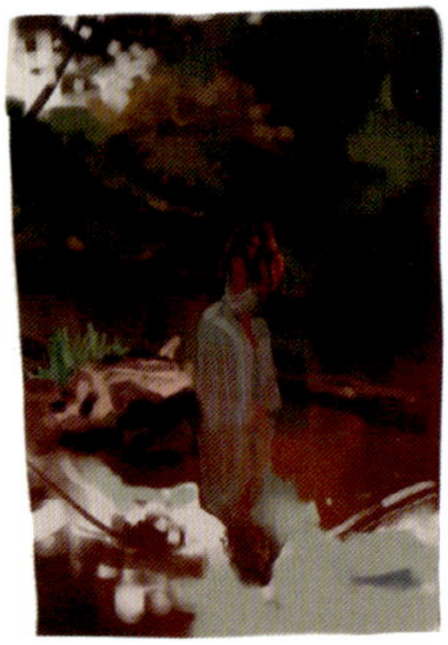

INSPIRED BY PHOTOGRAPHS BY @DEPECHESMODE

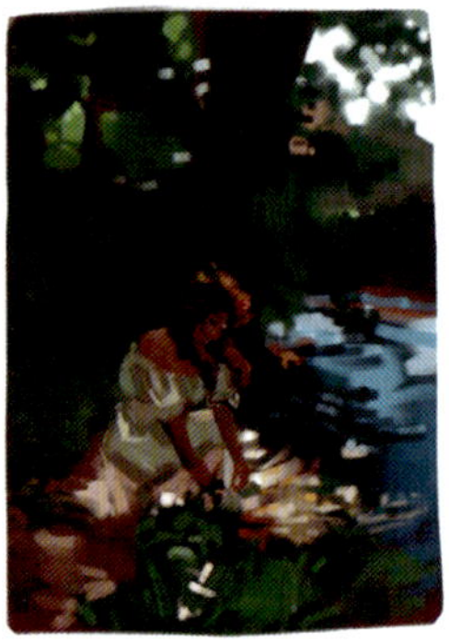

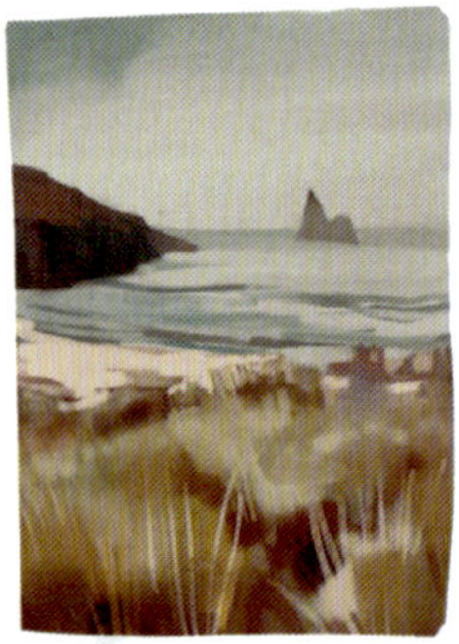

INSPIRED BY A PHOTOGRAPH BY KIM LEUENBERGER,@KIM.OU

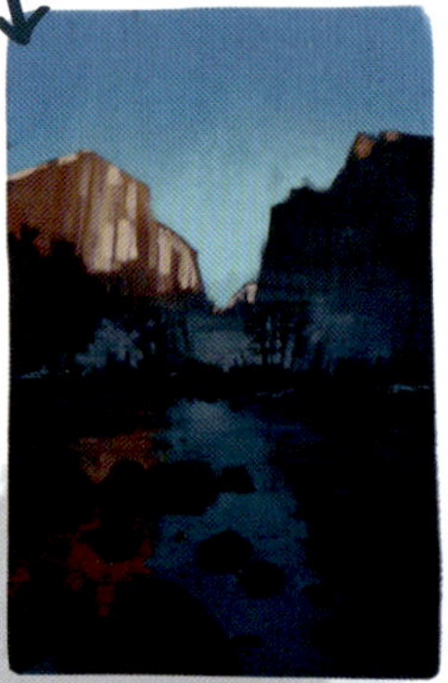

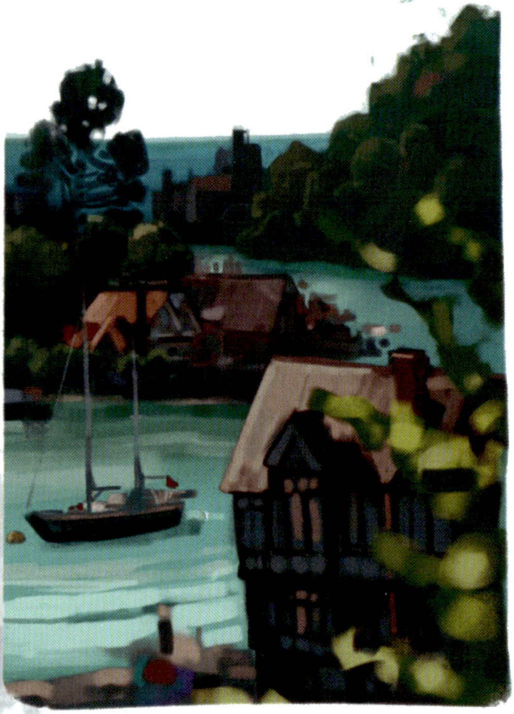

ROUND 1

After producing this set of studies, I decide I like the first design I created the most because it is the simplest (top right image). The idea behind these pieces was that they should only take 15-30 minutes each to create. I found that the shorter the time allowance, the sweeter the outcome! The hard part is not getting lost in the details and keeping an effective abstract finish.

ROUND 2

Again, here I prefer my first two studies (two top images) over the others, as I'm happier with how I captured the essence of each scene. When working on studies, I feel that I often start strong and then lose concentration as I near the end of the painting session.

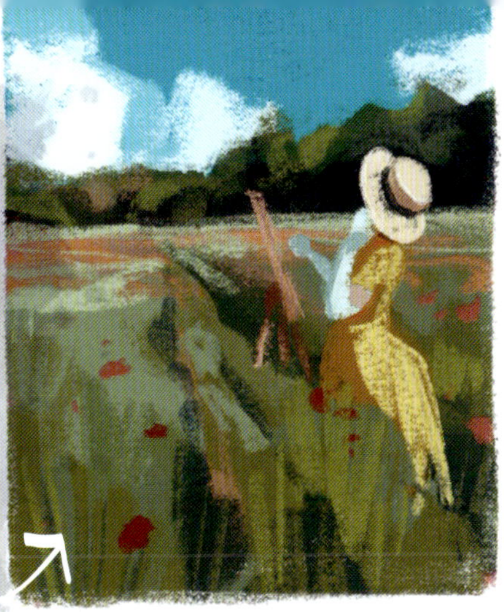

INSPIRED BY A PHOTOGRAPH TAKEN BY DOMINIQUE SADOUL. MODEL: CANDEUR TEXIER, @CANDORAS_BOX

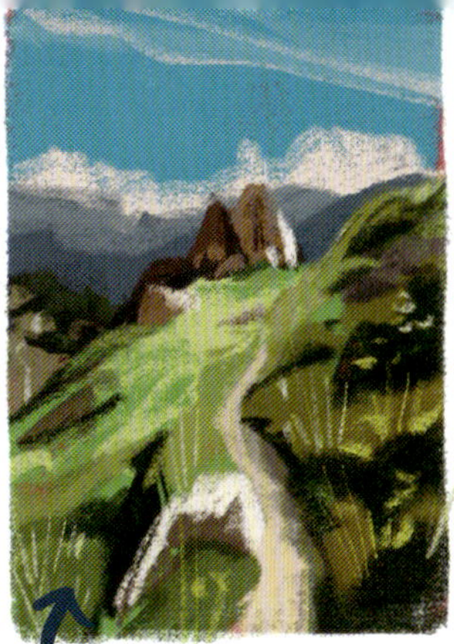

INSPIRED BY A PHOTOGRAPH BY KIM LEUENBERGER, @KIM.OU

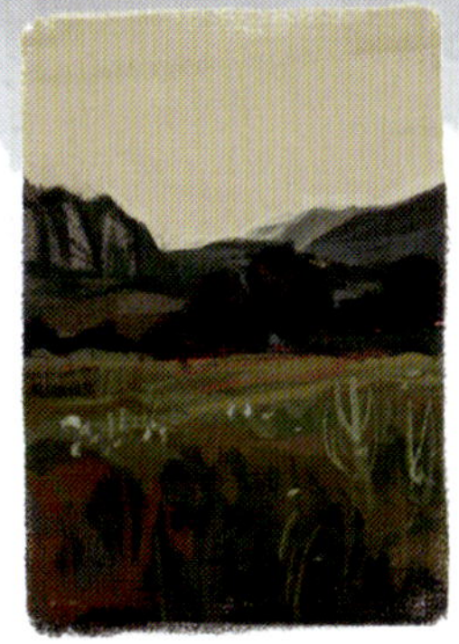

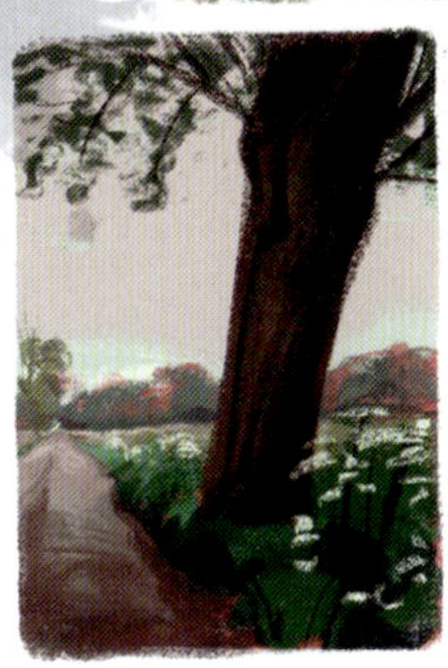

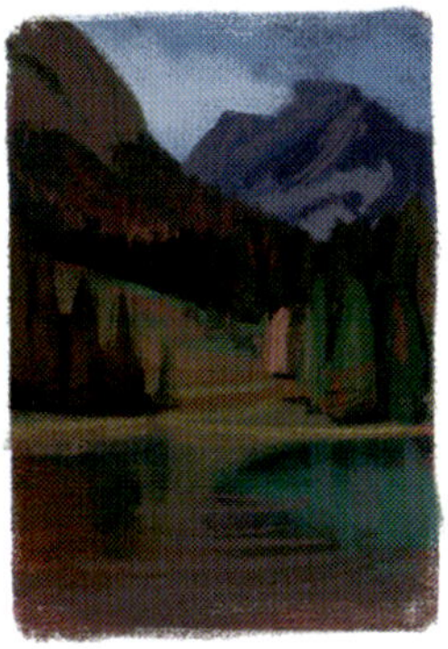

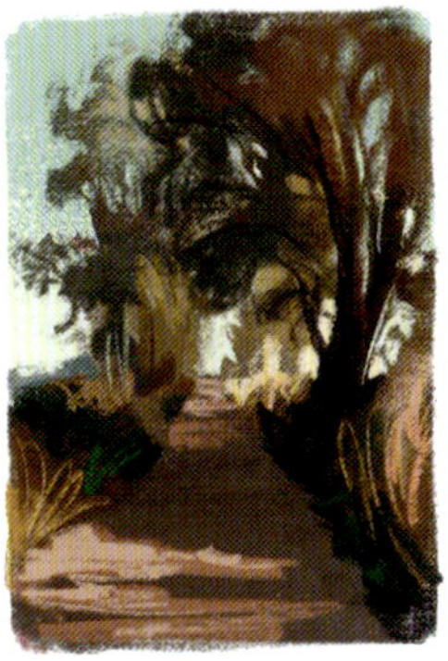

ROUND 3

I find reference scenes featuring buildings difficult to draw because I can't employ the same intuitive approach as used when drawing nature. As these studies are loose and organic, the style suits natural scenery better than angular modern architecture.

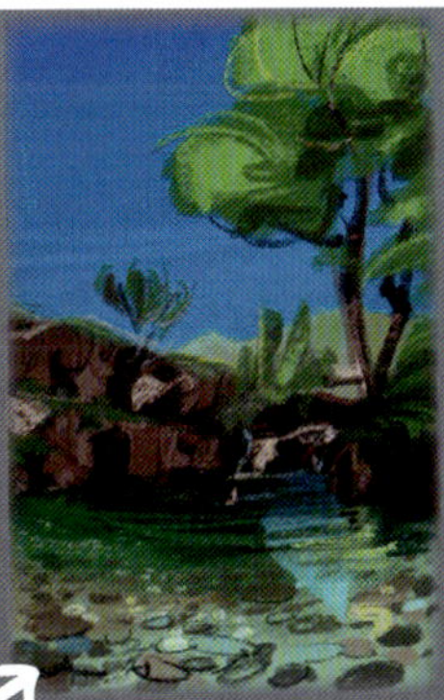

INSPIRED BY A PHOTOGRAPH TAKEN BY CLAIRE IVES, @CLAIREIVES

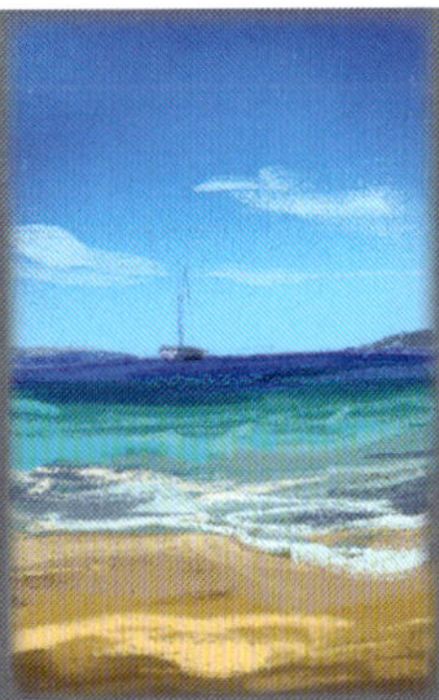

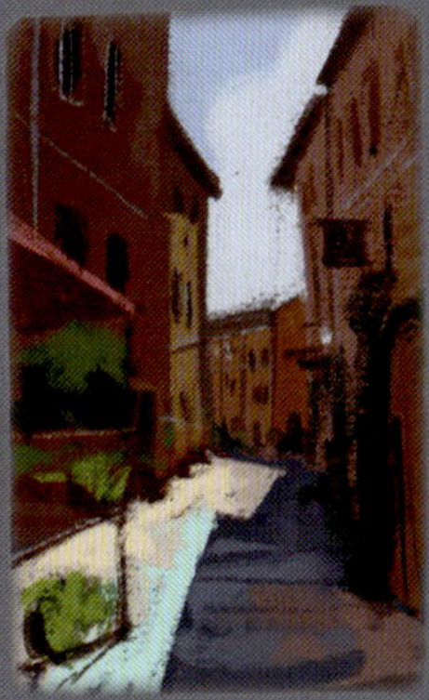

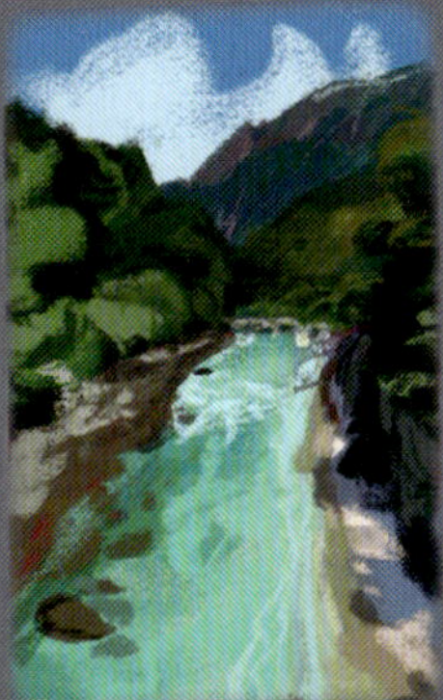

INSPIRED BY A PHOTOGRAPH TAKEN BY DOMAGOJ SEVER, @CROATIANNOMADS

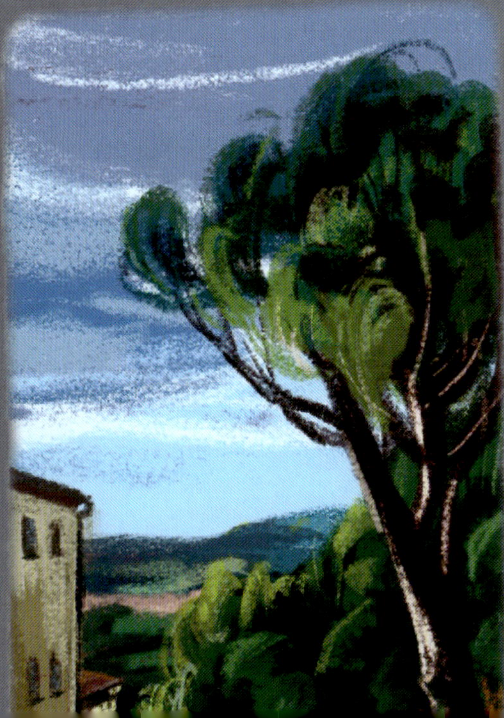

BACKGROUND HACKS

When adding a simple background to a character design, I avoid using solid straight lines, as they have little charm on their own.

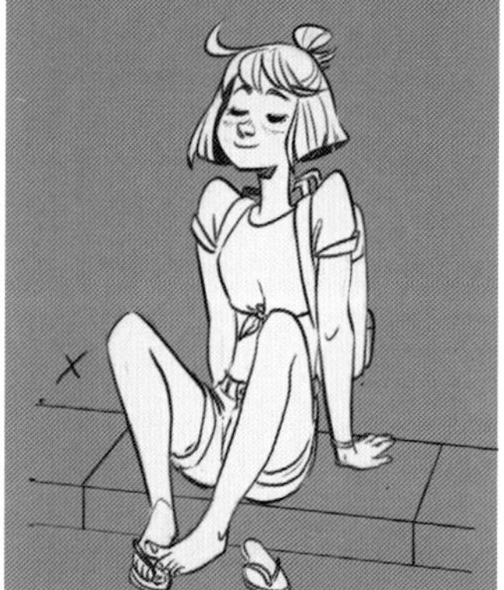

I add imperfections and fine textures to straight lines to give them a sense of realism.

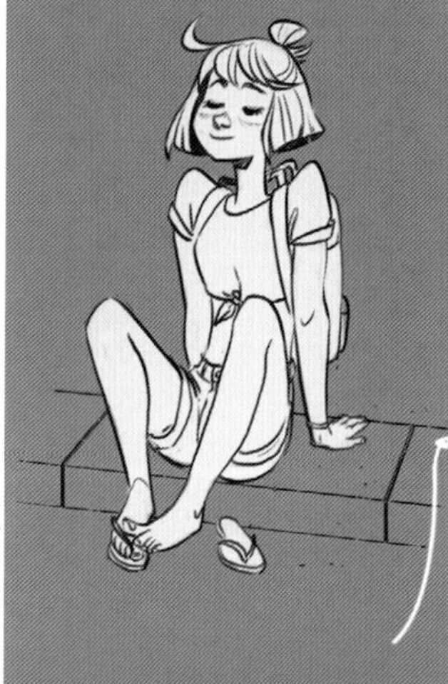

Erase small sections of the line to make it look less stiff

I like to draw over straight lines with slightly wobblier versions to add a slightly organic touch.

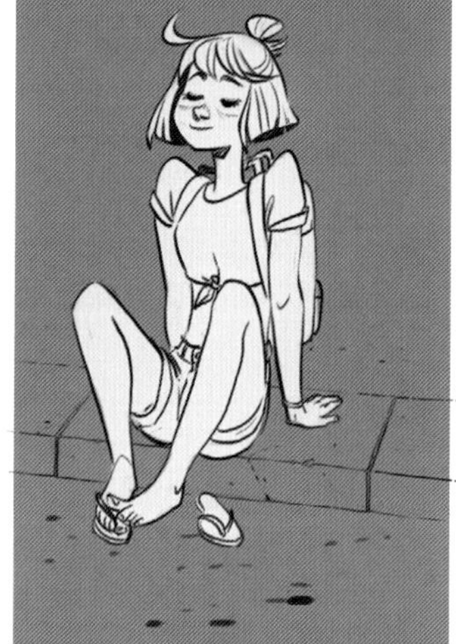

Featuring bigger textures in the foreground will suggest perspective with minimal effort

SKETCH

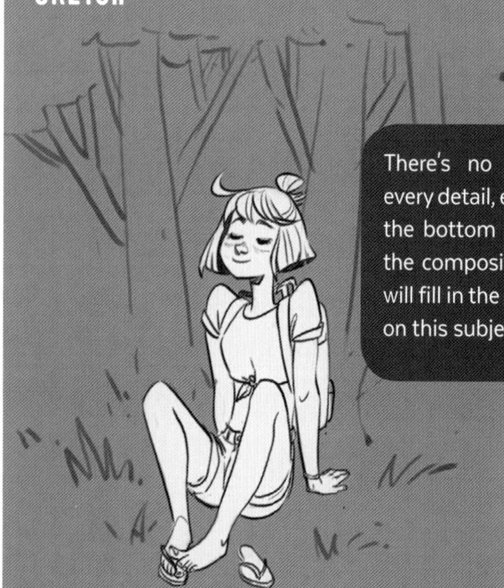

Super-simple sketch hinting at trees and foliage

FINISHED

There's no need to finish every detail, especially toward the bottom and the back of the composition — the brain will fill in the gaps itself (more on this subject later!).

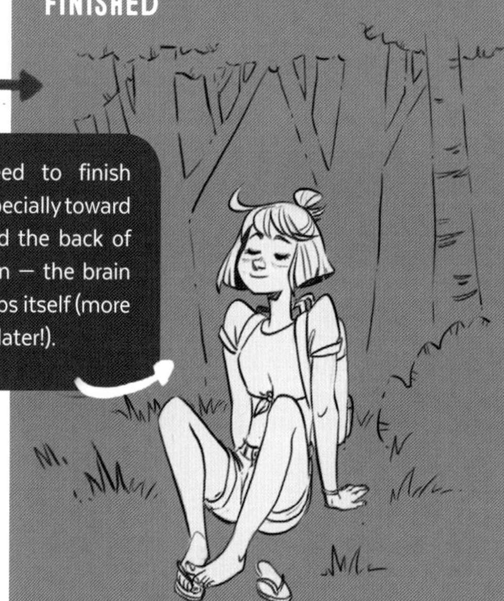

A cleaned-up version of the sketch, implying a stylized natural background

A basic path

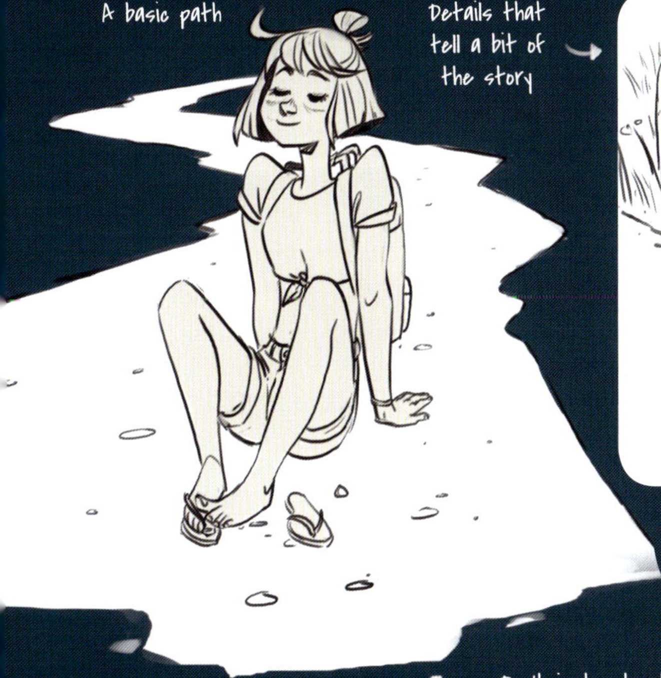

Details that tell a bit of the story

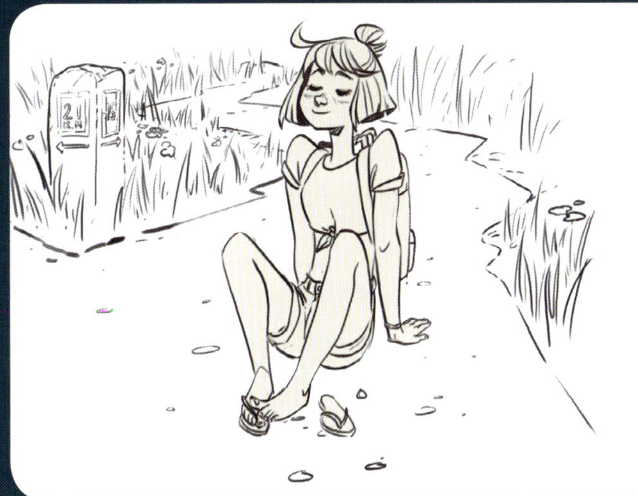

An irregular winding path can hint at a strong sense of perspective with very little effort

Don't just cut edges off – add small details to help the path to dissolve in an organic way that mimics the shapes of the stones

An open frame gives the composition more structure while allowing parts of the design space to breathe.

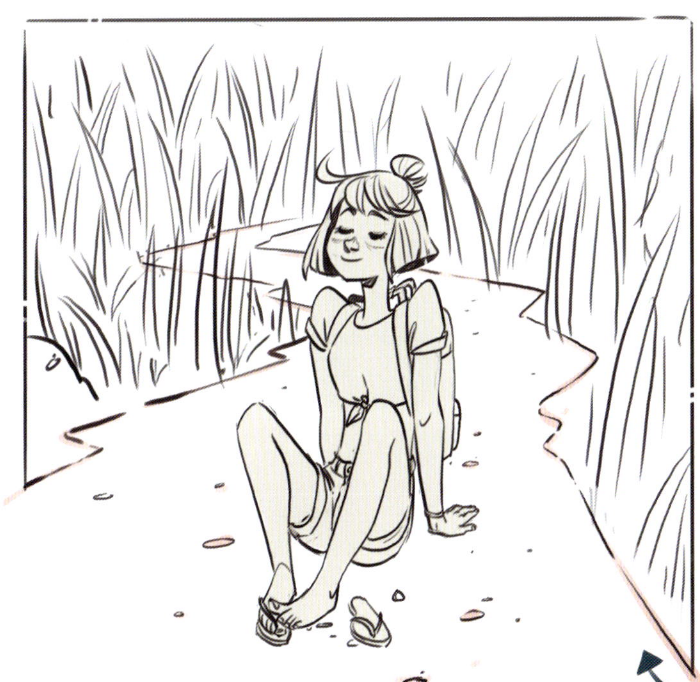

Draw open textures to help them feel more organic and loose

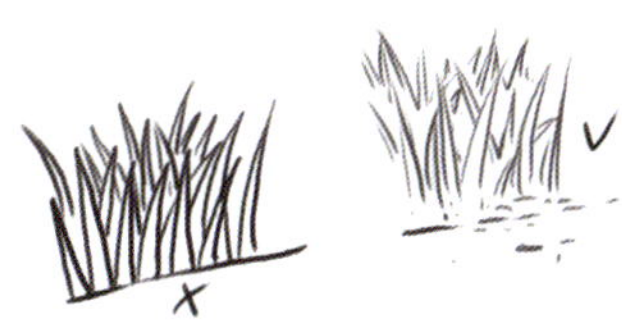

Close textures look too busy and are not necessary when it is clear what the object is when drawn with fewer lines

Busy

Balance busy textures with areas of calm

Calm

A gradient with some extra details

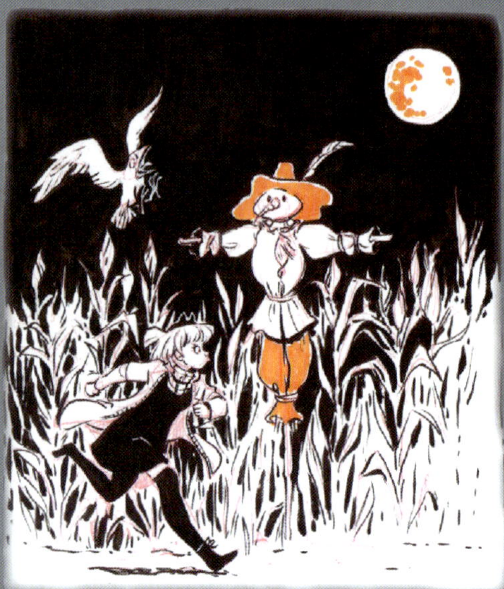

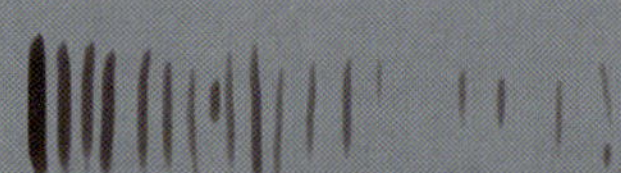

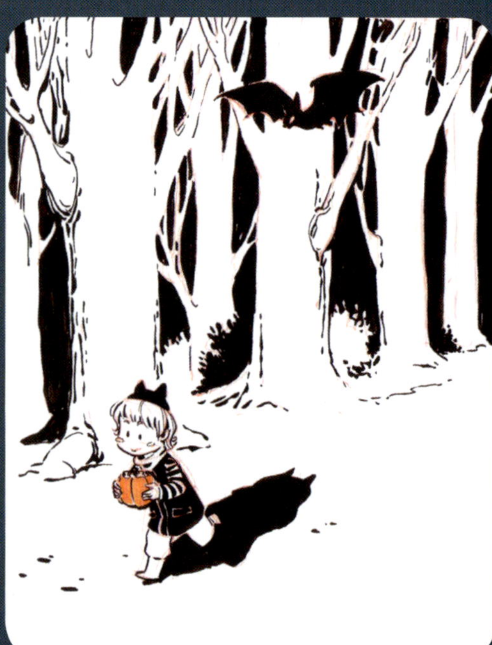

Here, I hint at trees and branches through the contrast achieved by areas of darkness.

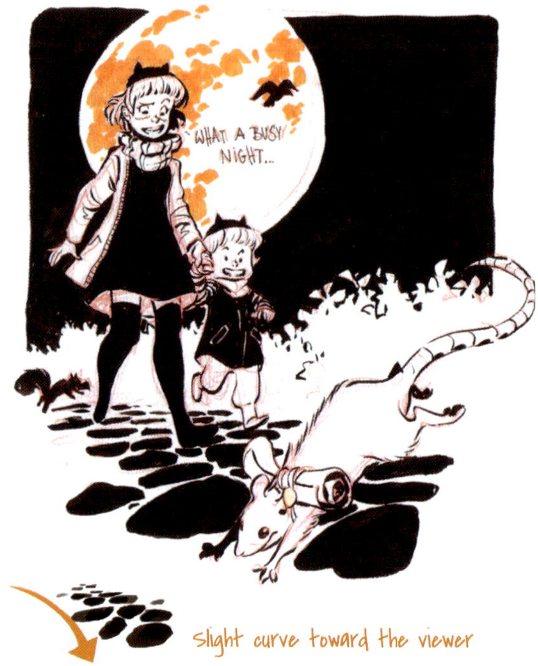

slight curve toward the viewer

To indicate direction and perspective in this path, I draw the stones that are furthest away as the smallest and most compressed and those in the foreground larger.

Using positive and negative space for the grass shapes gives the composition depth and adds interest to a background made of one element.

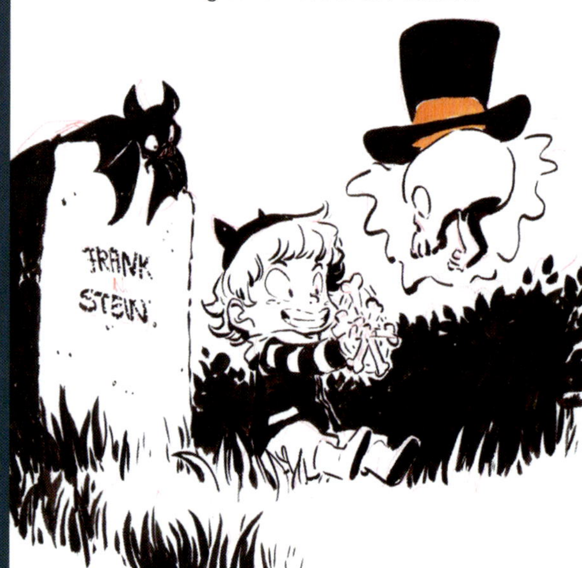

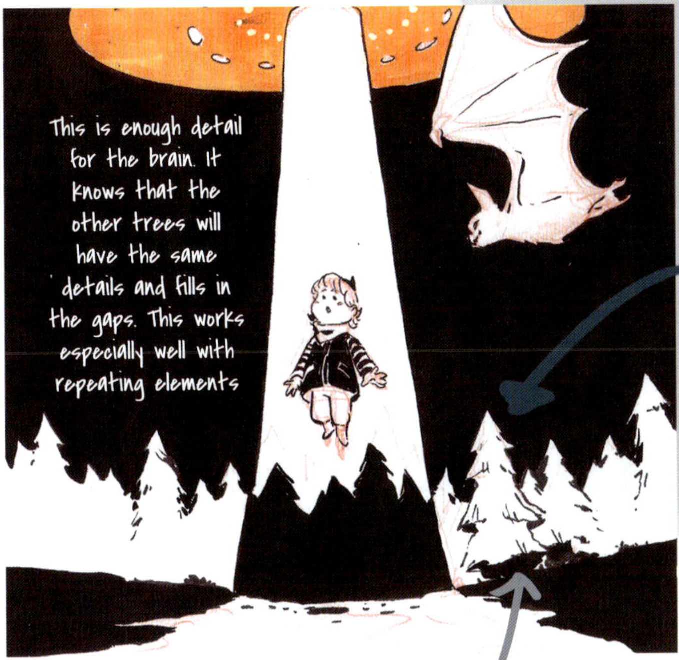

Here, I detailed one tree and hinted at details on a few more, while the rest are simple silhouettes.

LET THE BRAIN FILL IN THE GAPS!

As mentioned previously, when drawing a background, not every individual detail is required to accurately depict a scene. Indicating key features and silhouettes in the composition of a scene will often provide the viewer with enough information, and the brain will automatically make assumptions about the scene and fill in any small gaps.

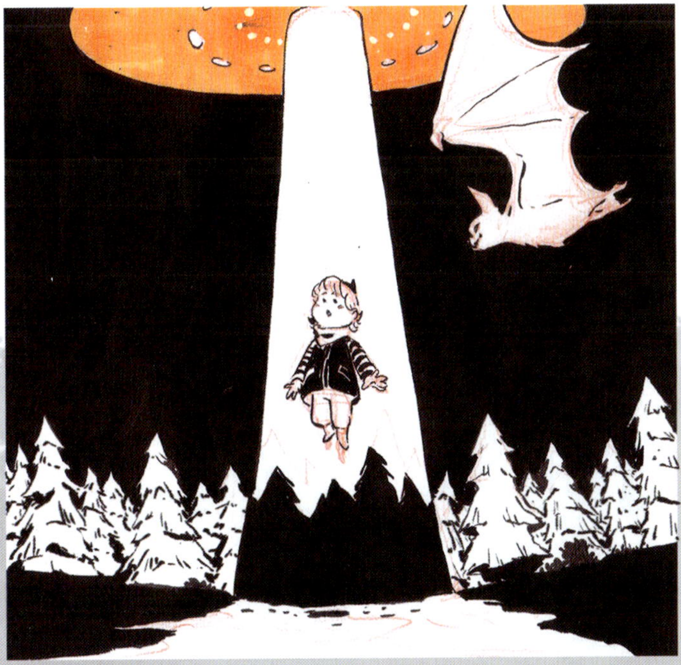

unless the finish is one of photo-realistic render, the brain will always assume some detail and add it in – but the more detail and realism you add, the less forgiving the brain is with mistakes!

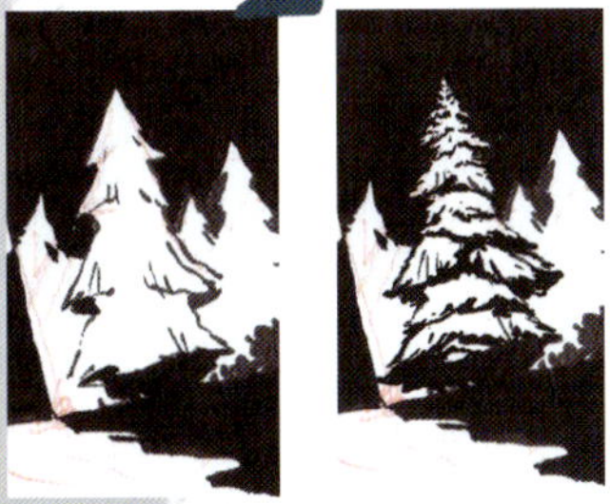

The detailed version isn't terrible, but I prefer it with less detail. This is purely a question of style and preference. But it's useful to know that you don't have to draw every tree in a forest!

LET THE BRAIN FILL IN THE GAPS

Areas of intense detail can be combined with minimal areas to hold focus on the focal point of the image. Here, I allow the bricks toward the top of the building to fade away to intensify the backlighting of the design.

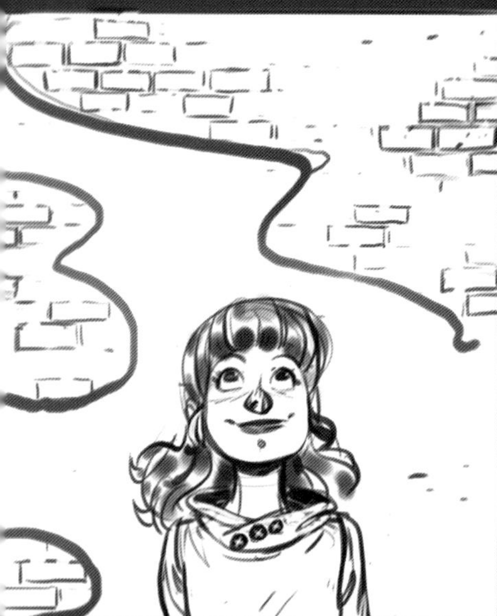

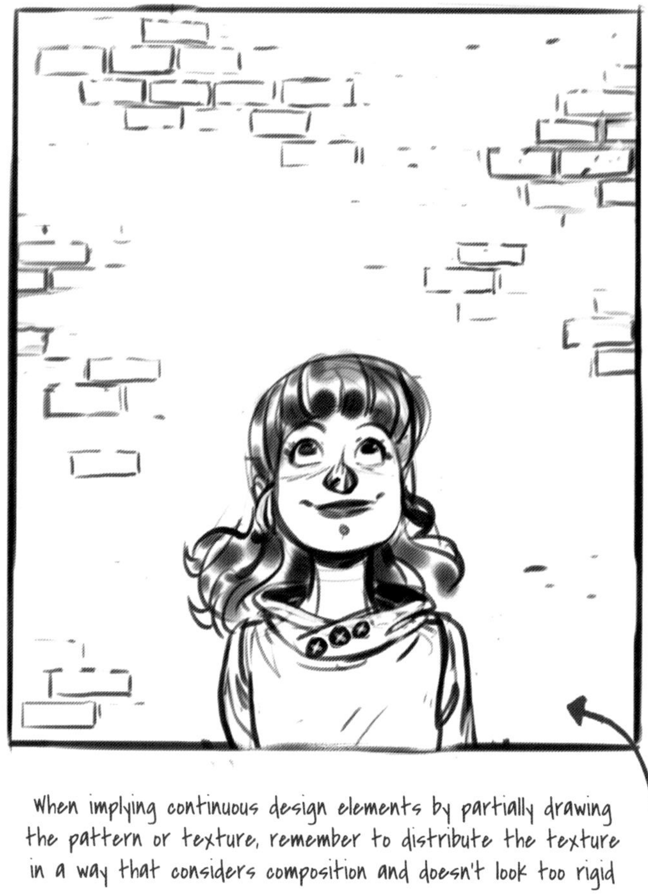

"INTENSE DETAIL CAN BE COMBINED WITH MINIMAL AREAS TO HOLD FOCUS ON THE FOCAL POINT"

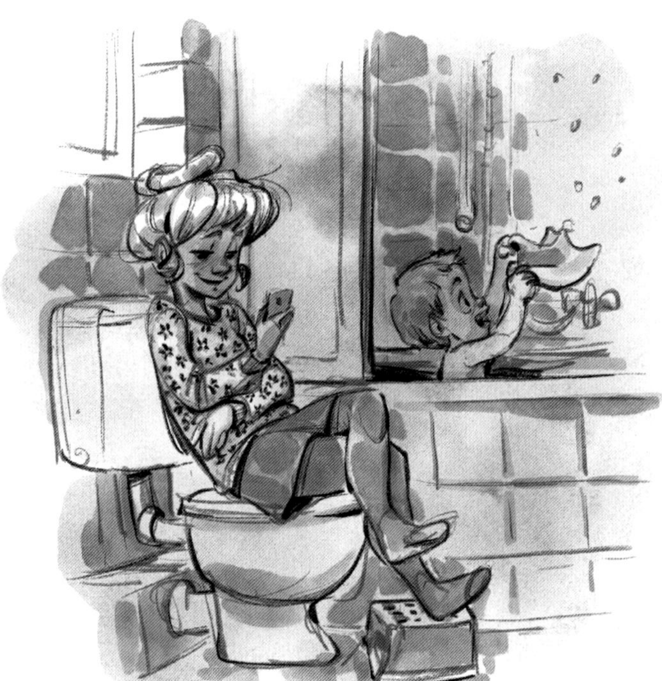

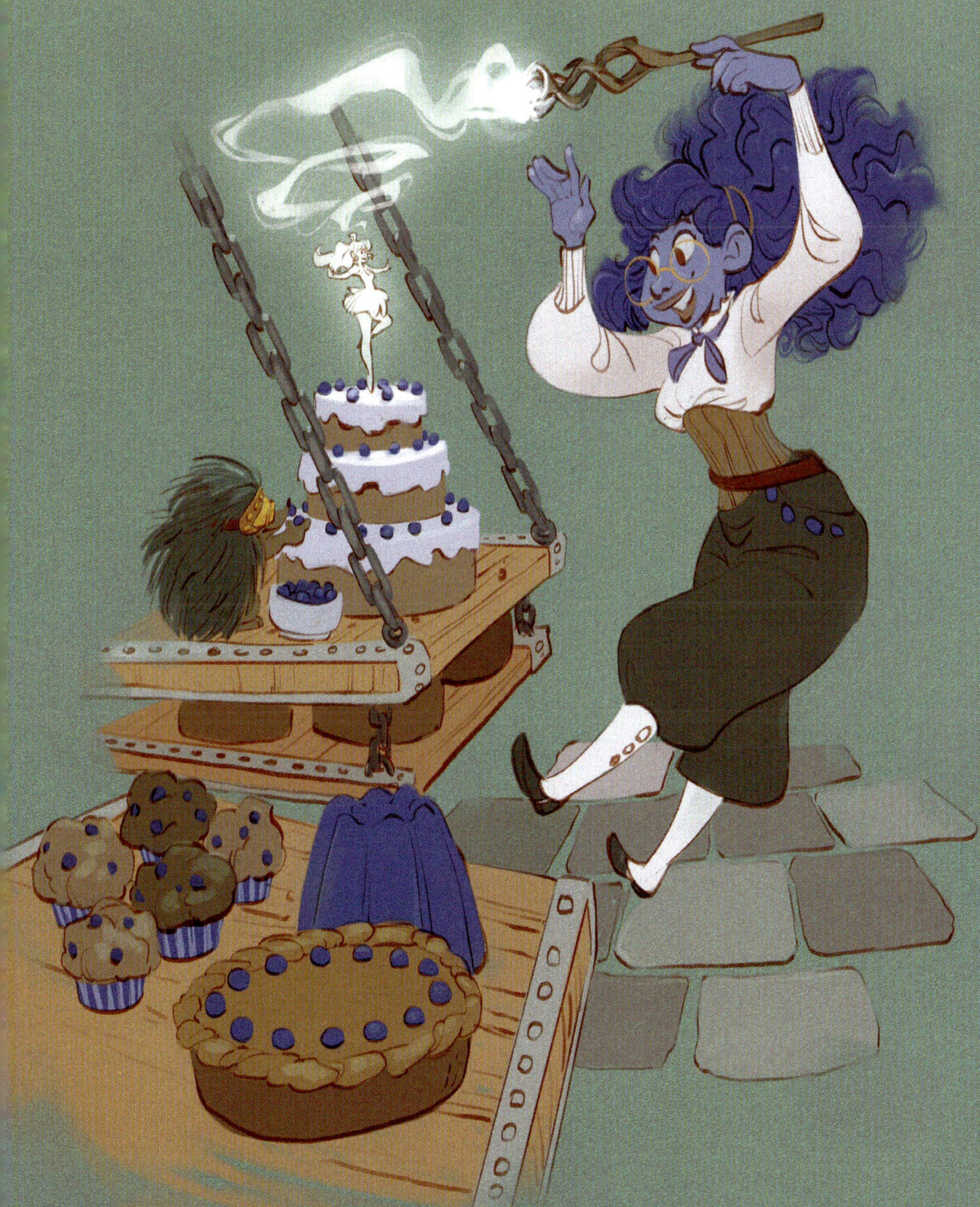

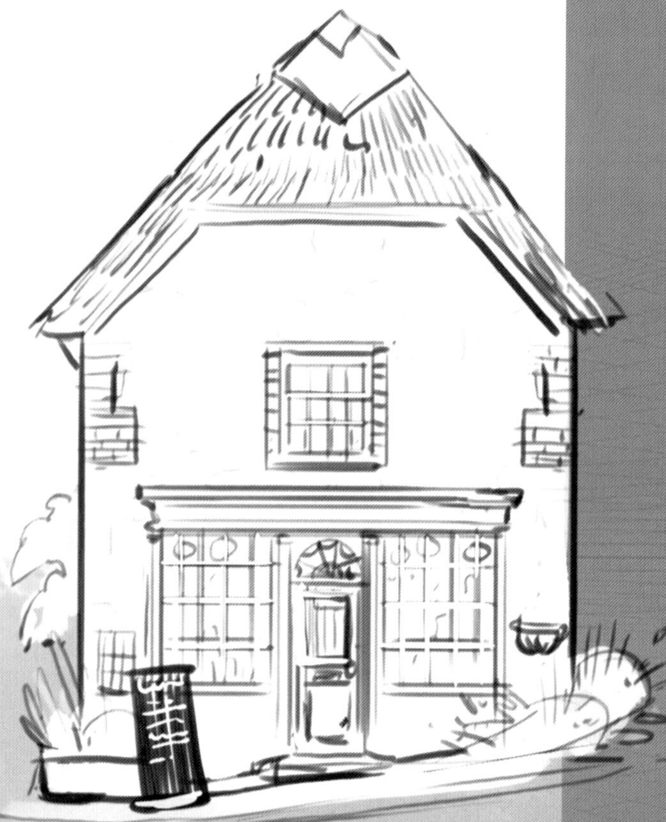

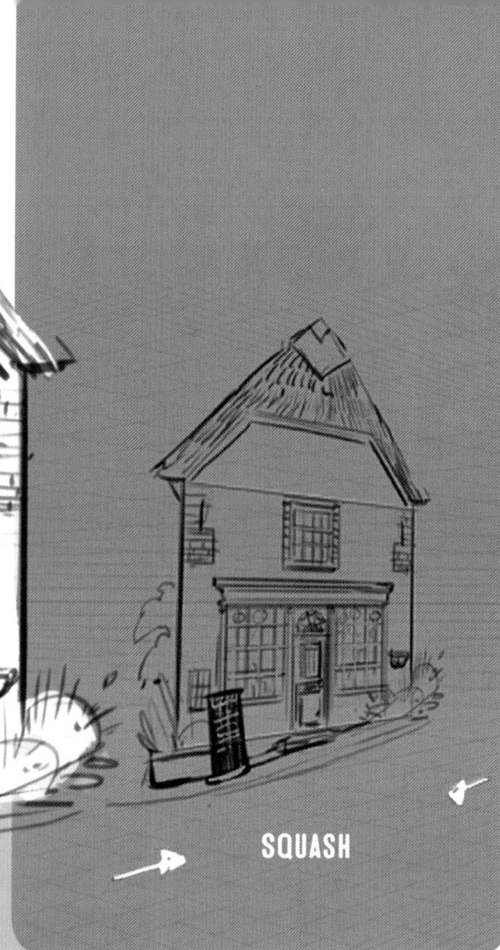

A FACADE IN PERSPECTIVE

You don't have to redraw a facade to add perspective! Drawing every individual element in perspective is time-consuming and much more tedious than simply using Adobe Photoshop to transform an existing sketch and add dimension. When developing a facade, for ease, simply draw the parts you want to add dimension to on an extra layer.

Simply place the facade on the perspective grid in the required orientation and transform it according to the grid using Ctrl+T.

As well as aligning the house with the perspective grid, I squash the sides of the house in a little to account for subtle foreshortening.

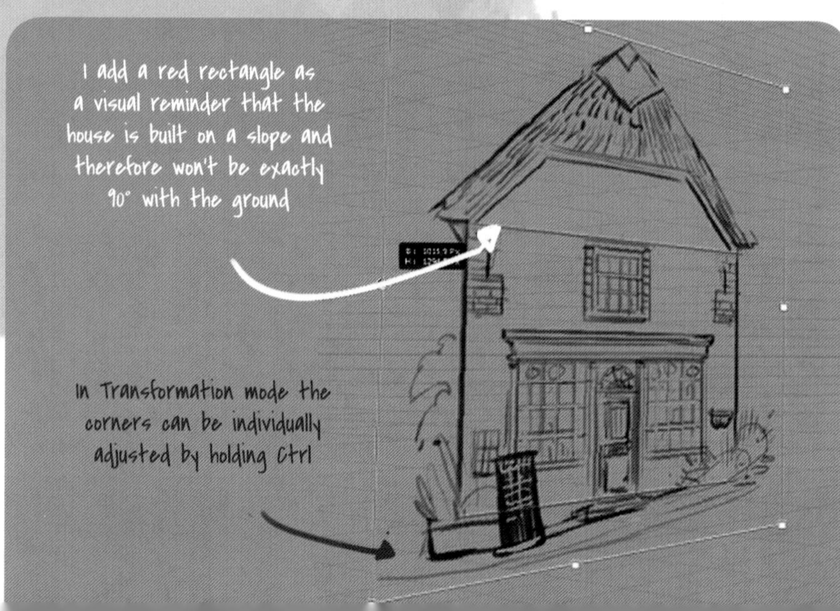

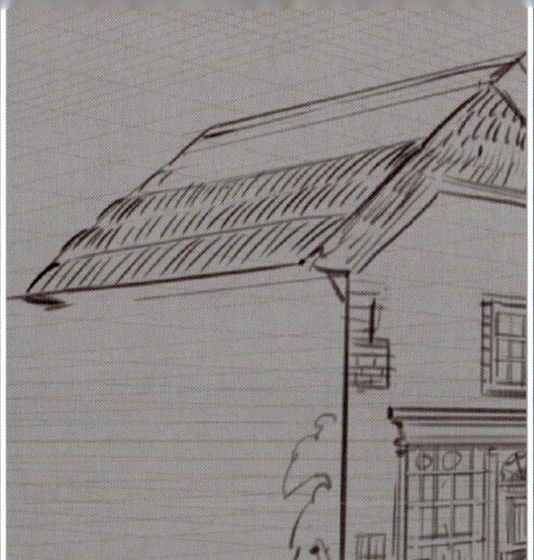

Next, I add a roof, also aligned to the perspective grid.

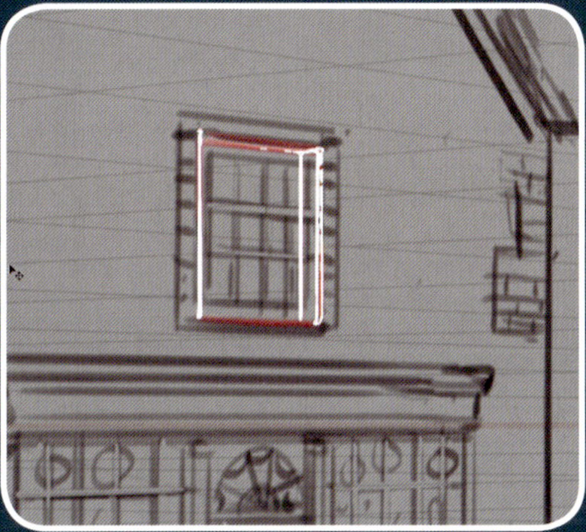

The window needs dimension. Select the window with the Polygon Lasso, right-click in the selection, and make a new layer via Cut.

Push the cut window back to add depth. I draw in the inside brick edge of the window opening as well as the window frame.

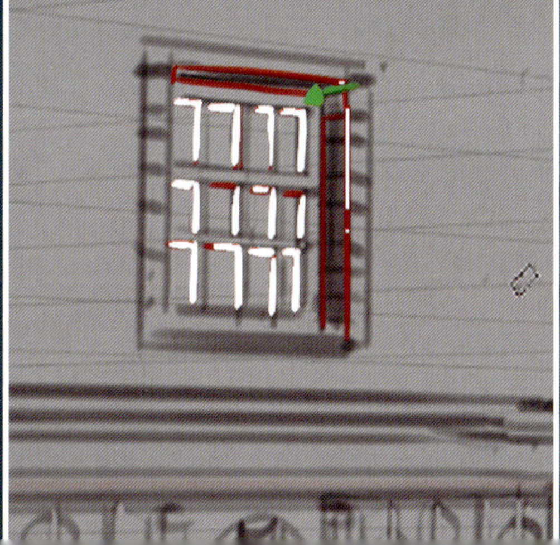

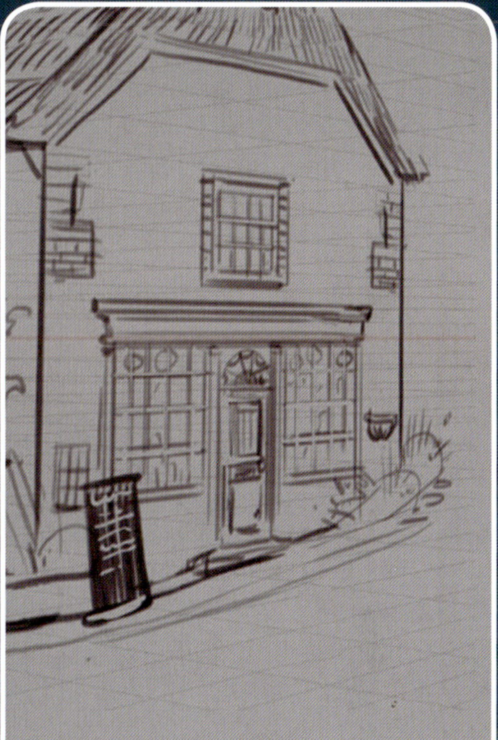

The frontage of the house looks a little flat, so the details need to be altered.

Continue the same process of adding dimension all over the house – the roof, for example, is selected and pulled away slightly from the original position to add thickness.

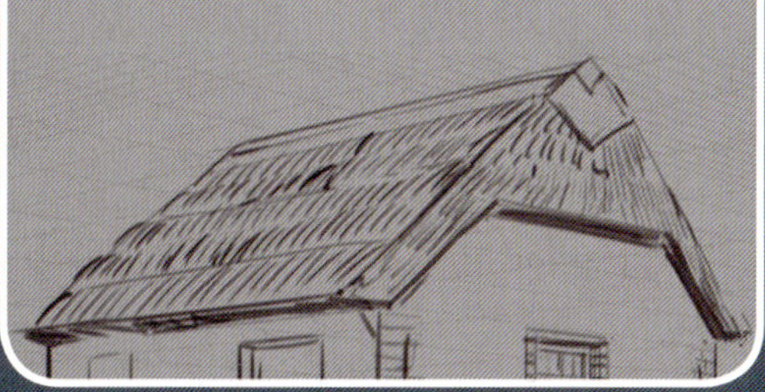

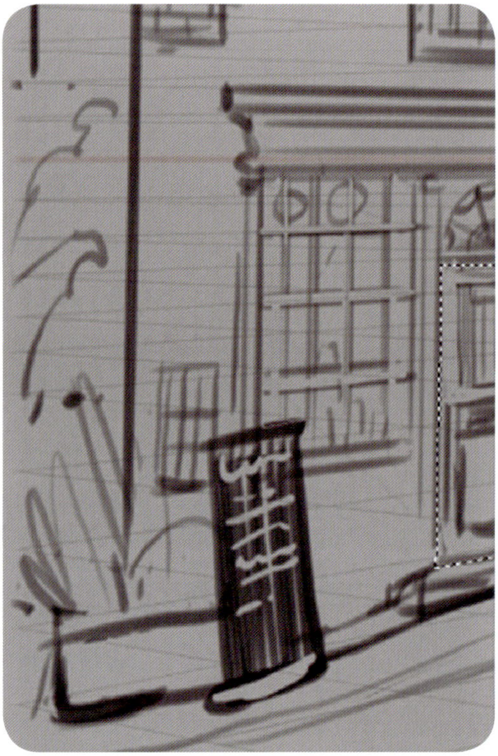

I continue to add dimension to the frontage. I can clean up this sketch later if I choose to, or work more precisely from the beginning, but I enjoy a bit of wonkiness!

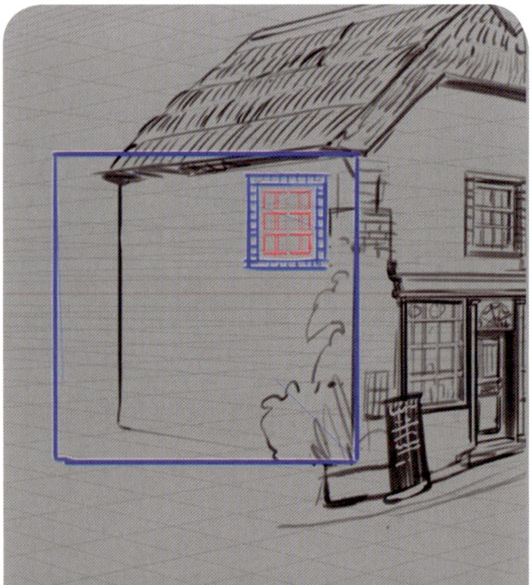

To add more detail to the side of the house, I simply add in another window and duplicate to create a set of windows.

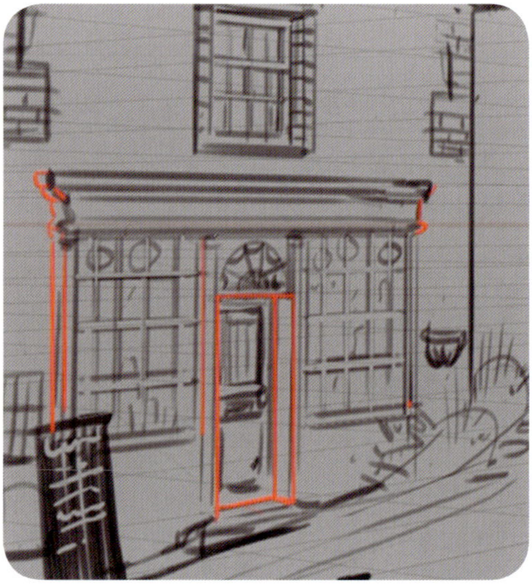

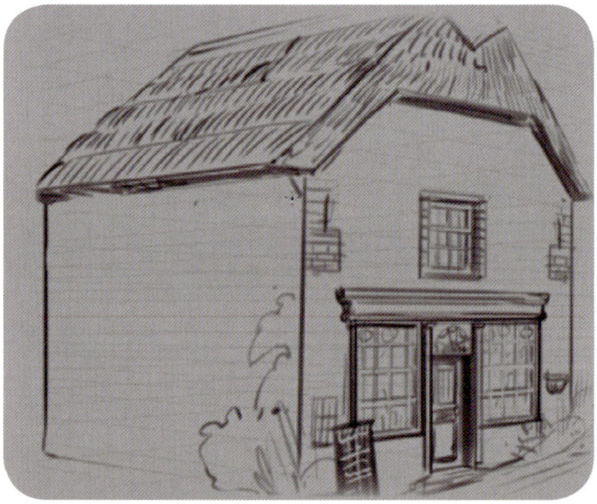

I draw the inside part of the window on an extra layer to make it easier to move later.

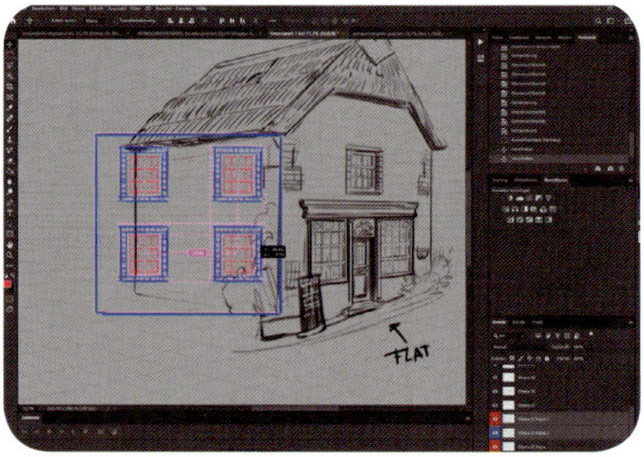

Select all layers of the new side facade and transform them to match up with the perspective of the front of the house.

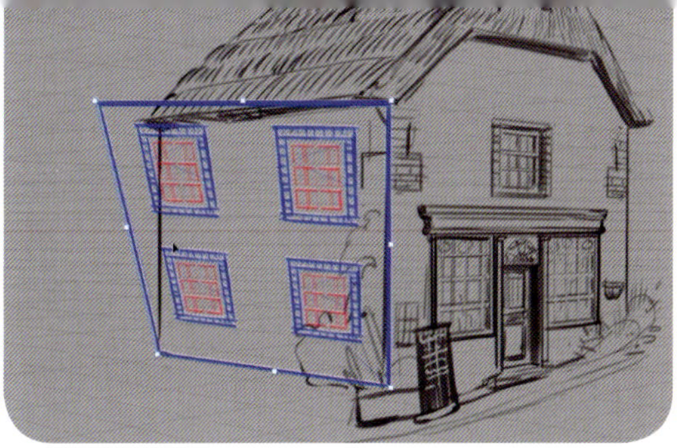

"YOU DON'T HAVE TO REDRAW A FACADE TO ADD PERSPECTIVE"

These windows also need some dimension. I move the top windows down and inward and the bottom windows up and inward, toward the horizon line.

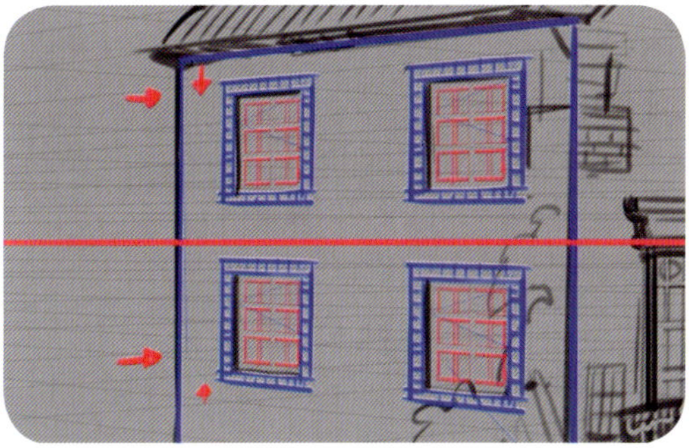

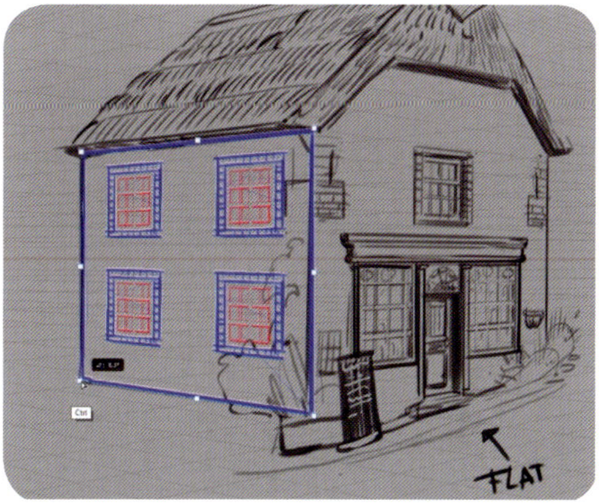

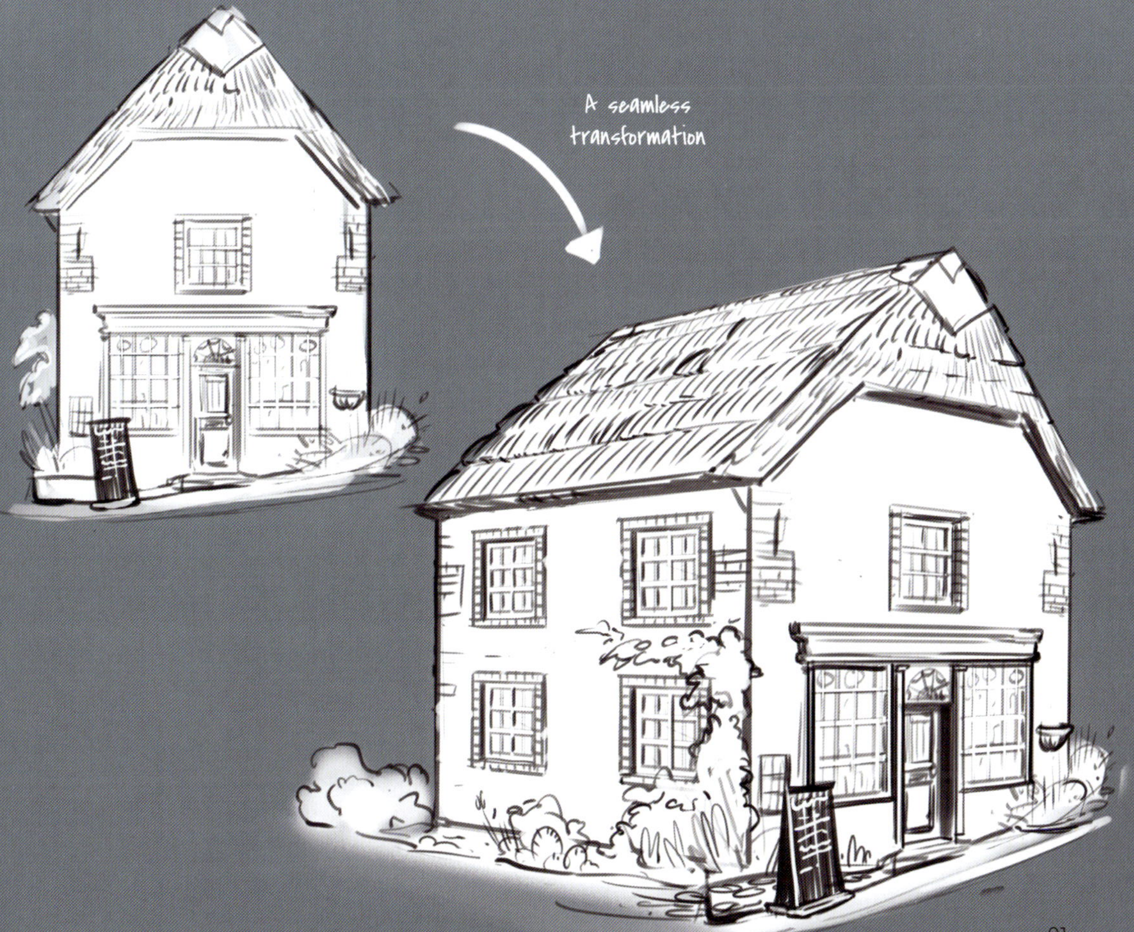

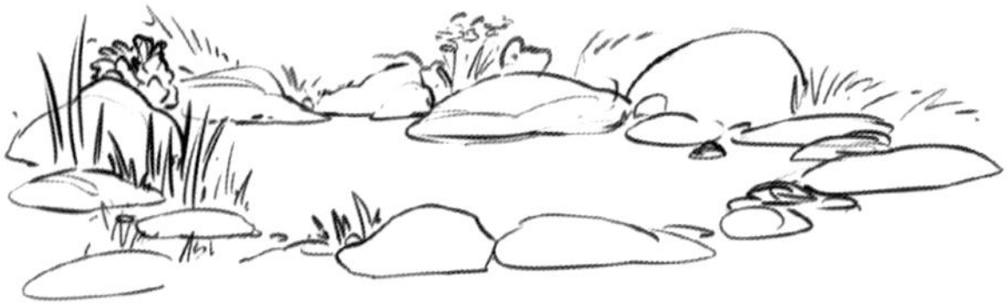

WATER

Drawing water can be very intimidating due to its many characteristic properties — it's reflective and translucent, and can be calm or fast-moving. It's best not to rush drawing it — water is best built by layering.

WATER IN A POND

To draw this pond, I used several pond image references.

Start with the reflections — the darkest reflections don't need detail and look more like shadows.

Once the reflection of the sky is applied to the surface of the water, the impression of a beautifully calm pond is instantly created.

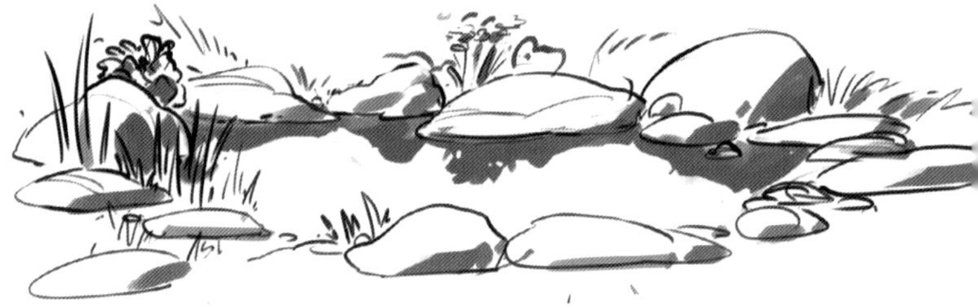

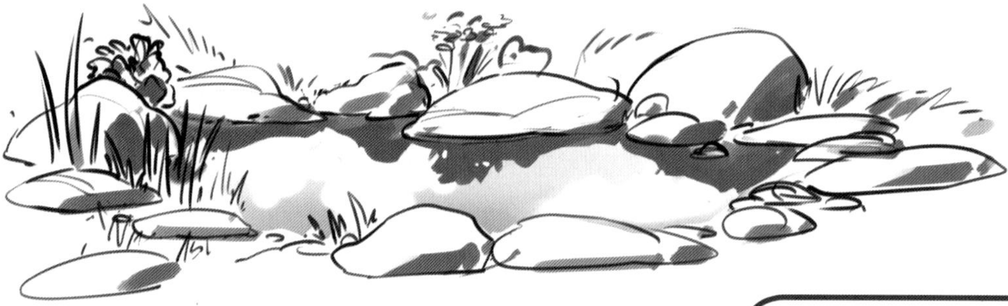

QUICK TIP!

When softening and fraying the edges of reflections to create ripples, remember that the light and dark should flow into each other evenly.

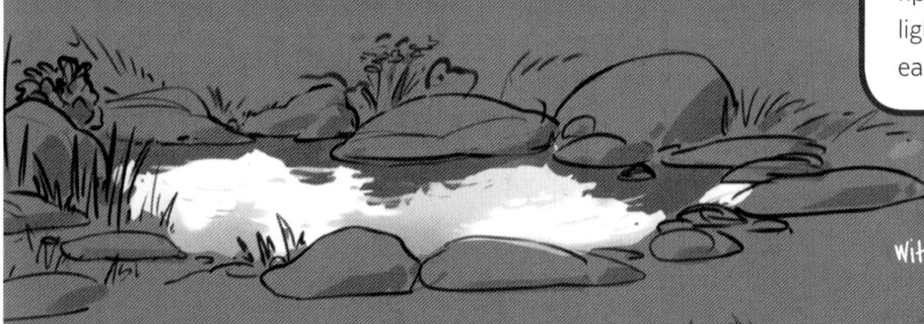

Select and paint with existing colors/values to fray the edges of the different reflections and add ripples. These ripples follow the perspective of the pond and have a collective direction, as they would in real life.

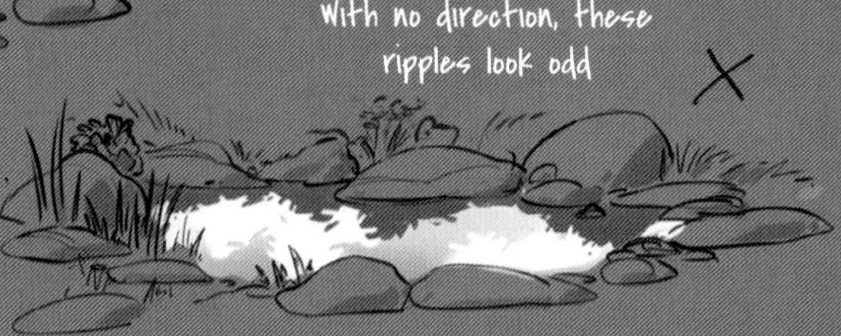

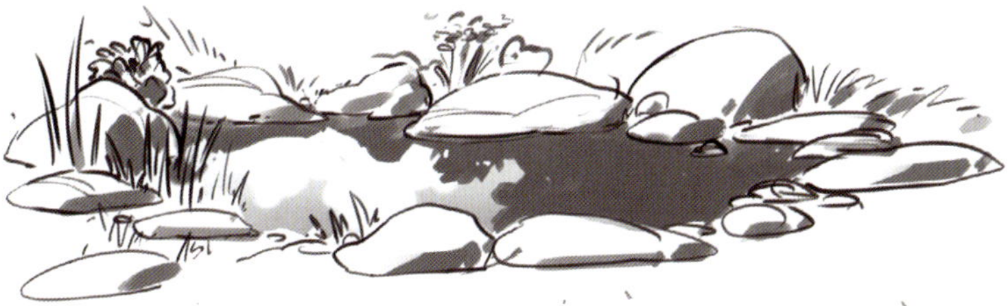

Consider the surroundings of the pond – this pond is being shaded by a nearby large tree, so I add areas of shadow, blocking out the reflections of the sky.

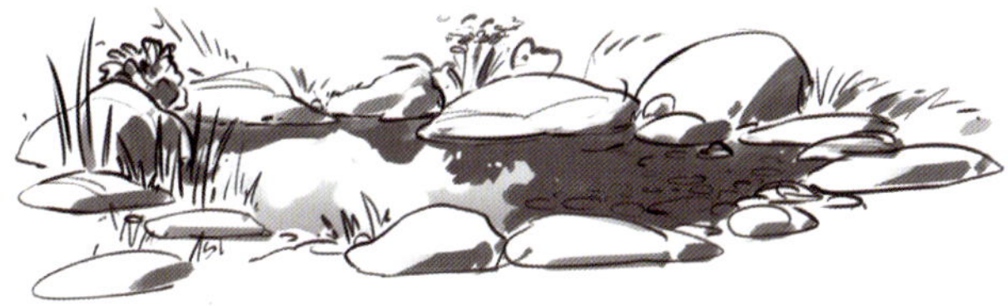

In the shaded part of the pond, it is possible to see into the water (this will depend on how clear or murky the water is).

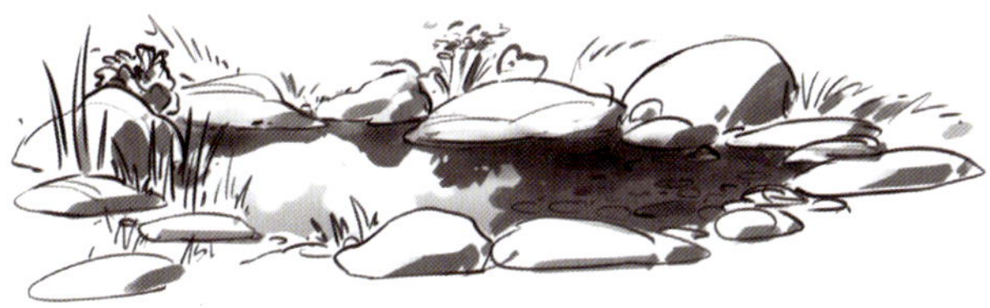

Next, I add darker shading to the deep areas and shade some of the stones to add realistic detail (they are rarely all the same value).

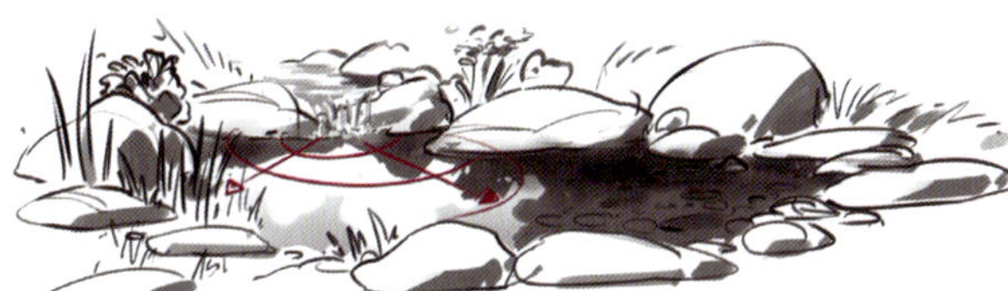

For further interest, I add a stream of running water – this has an effect on the calm water.

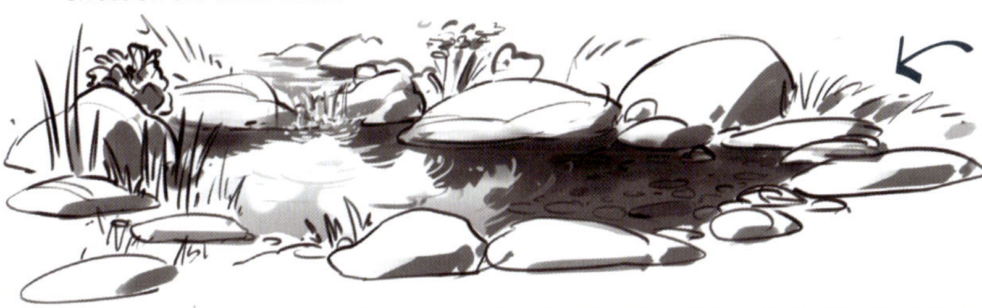

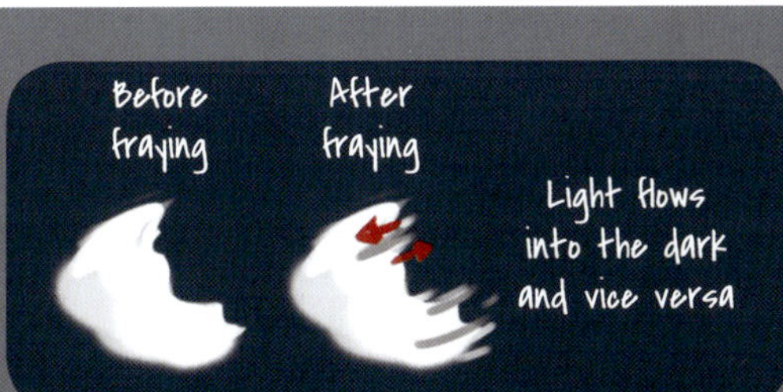

The surface of the water doesn't have to be in shadow for the bottom to be visible, but it will be more visible in the dark reflections of shadow, because it's not battling against the bright light of the sun and sky.

If the body of water is shallow enough, it is likely that the bottom will be visible, but it depends on the angle of the perspective – even a puddle can act like a bottomless mirror.

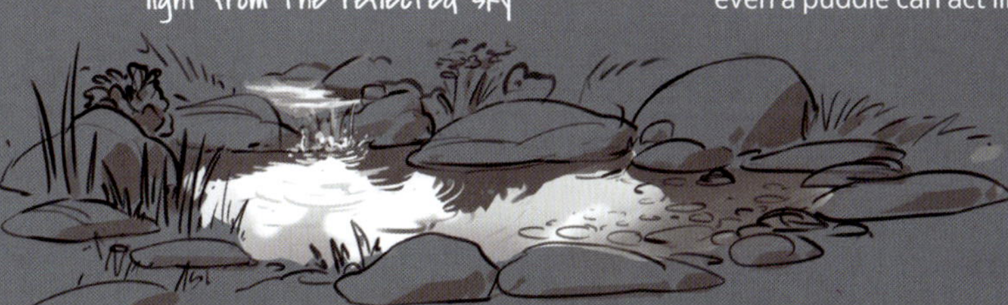

UNDERWATER

When submerged underwater, there are two aspects to consider – the surface of the water at the top of the frame, and the reflections on the ground surface at the bottom of the frame. This isn't a tutorial on how to paint every underwater scene, but I hope these principles and design considerations will provide the building blocks for a range of underwater settings. I will again be working in Photoshop.

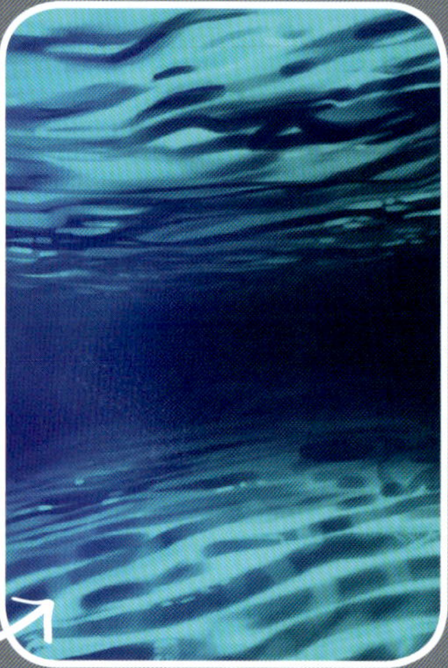

The final effect – this looks complicated to paint but when broken down cleverly it is easily achievable

Look at references and think about how the scene could be broken down into layers – it is often best to work from back to front.

Add variance in the background color, because if it is one solid shade of blue it will look artificial – this is important since this color will shine through under the ripples layer.

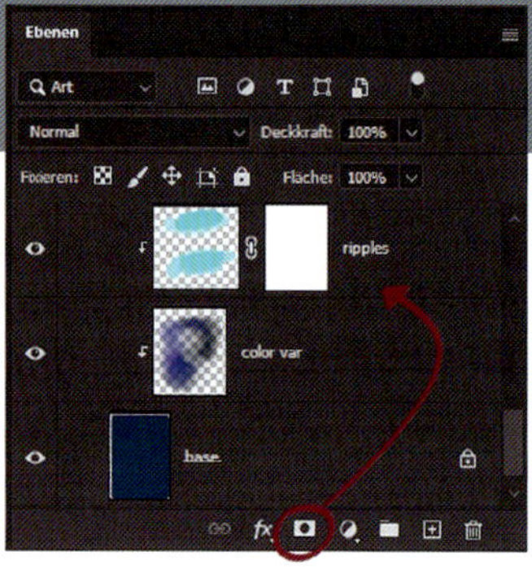

Select the ripples layer and add a mask – a white window will be added to the layer. Select the window by clicking on it and proceed to work onto the mask

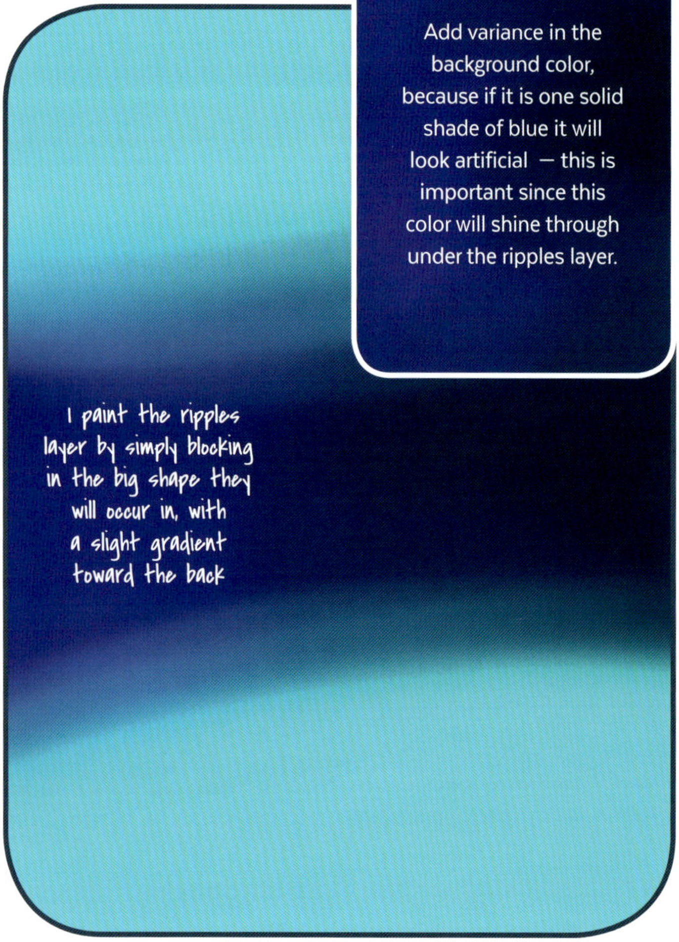

I paint the ripples layer by simply blocking in the big shape they will occur in, with a slight gradient toward the back

To introduce ripples, the Eraser tool could simply be used to erase sections of the light turquoise away to reveal the dark blue beneath. However, painting on the mask in grayscale values means the lines are not as permanent as erased lines. The beauty of using a mask is that you can correct the part you "erased" when painting black by painting white instead. Masks are best understood through experimentation, as they can feel quite alien to begin with. See pages 144-146 for further details on masks.

Even with something as abstract as water, it is beneficial to know the rough perspective grid of the landscape. In this case the grid determines the size of the ripples and identifies that the horizon is slightly tilted

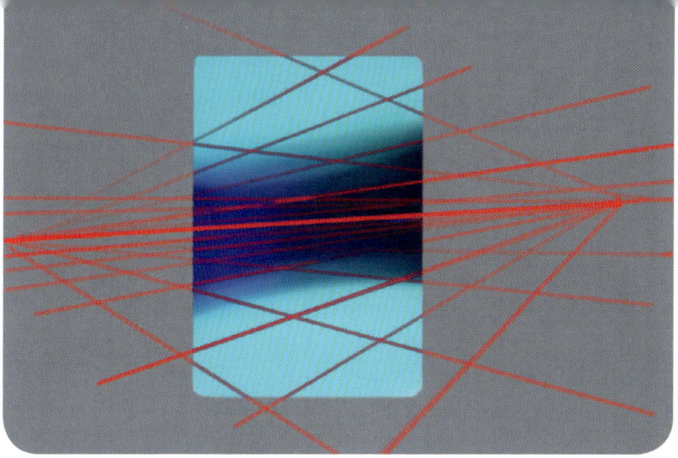

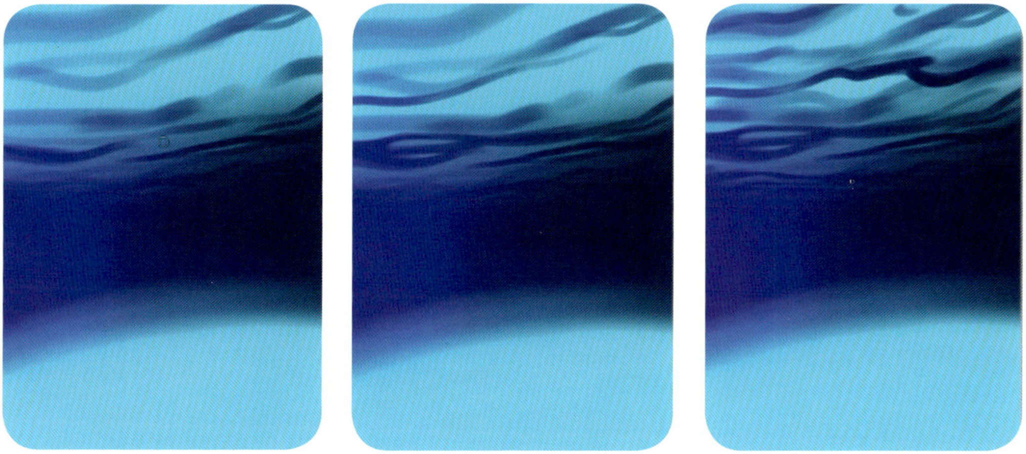

Next, I paint black on the mask, which looks like simple erasing of the base ripple layer — I mostly keep the strokes thicker in the foreground and a bit thinner toward the back.

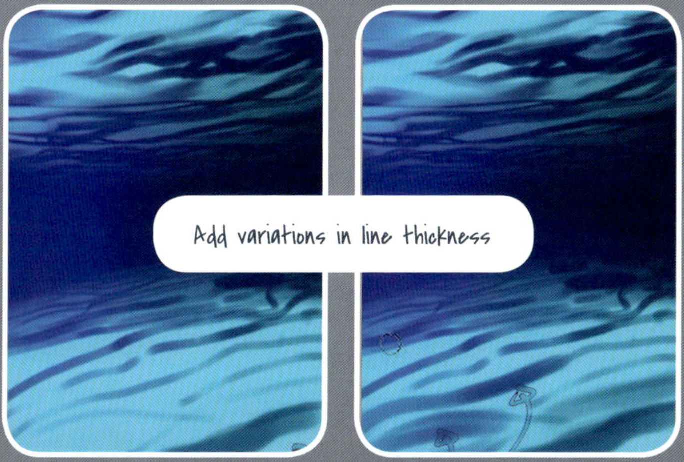

Paint with white on the mask to bring the turquoise back a little and layer the shades of blue

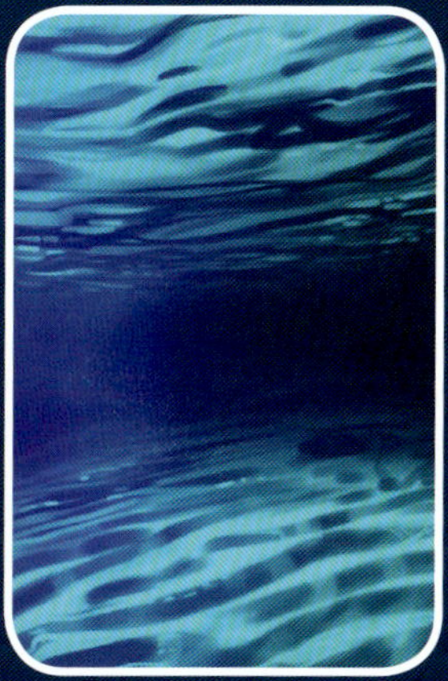

For the ground surface, I work in a very similar way as I did for the surface of the water. The structure is slightly different because the ground is made from sand, so I switch between black and white to correct strokes, or simply bring back some of the turquoise to add new ripple patterns.

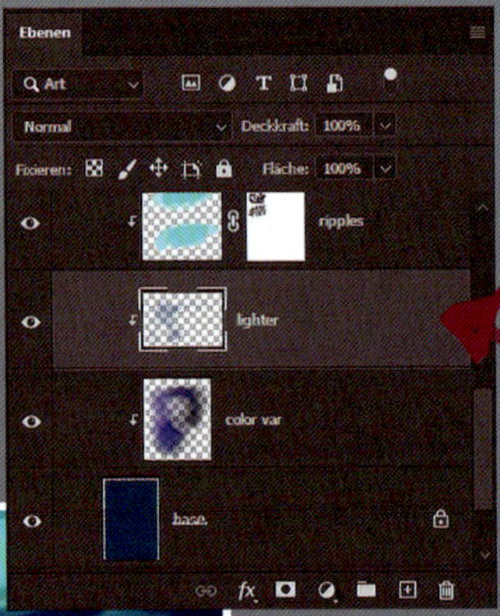

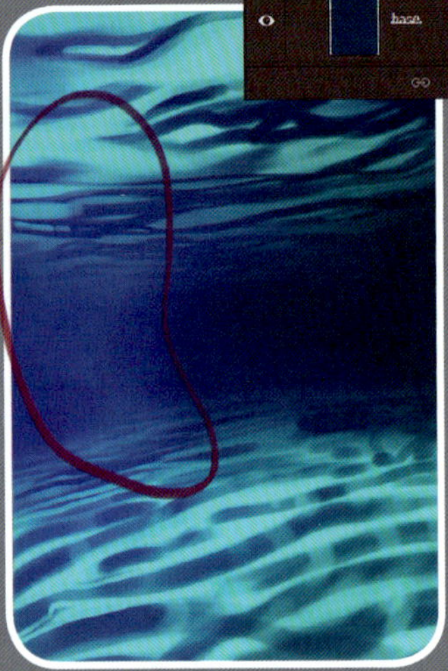

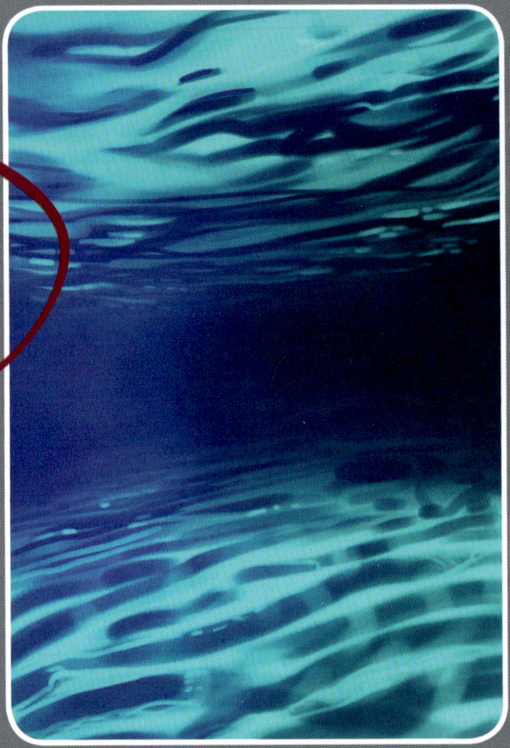

In order to add depth and a sense of translucent volume to the water, I lighten some of the background on a new layer

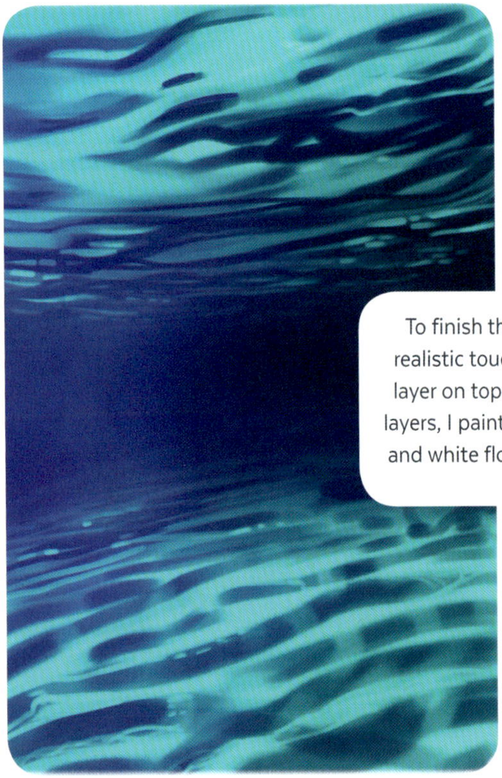

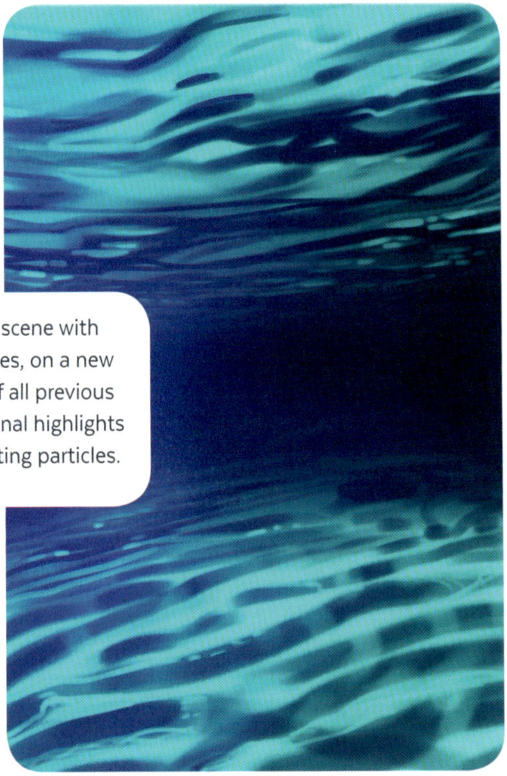

To finish the scene with realistic touches, on a new layer on top of all previous layers, I paint final highlights and white floating particles.

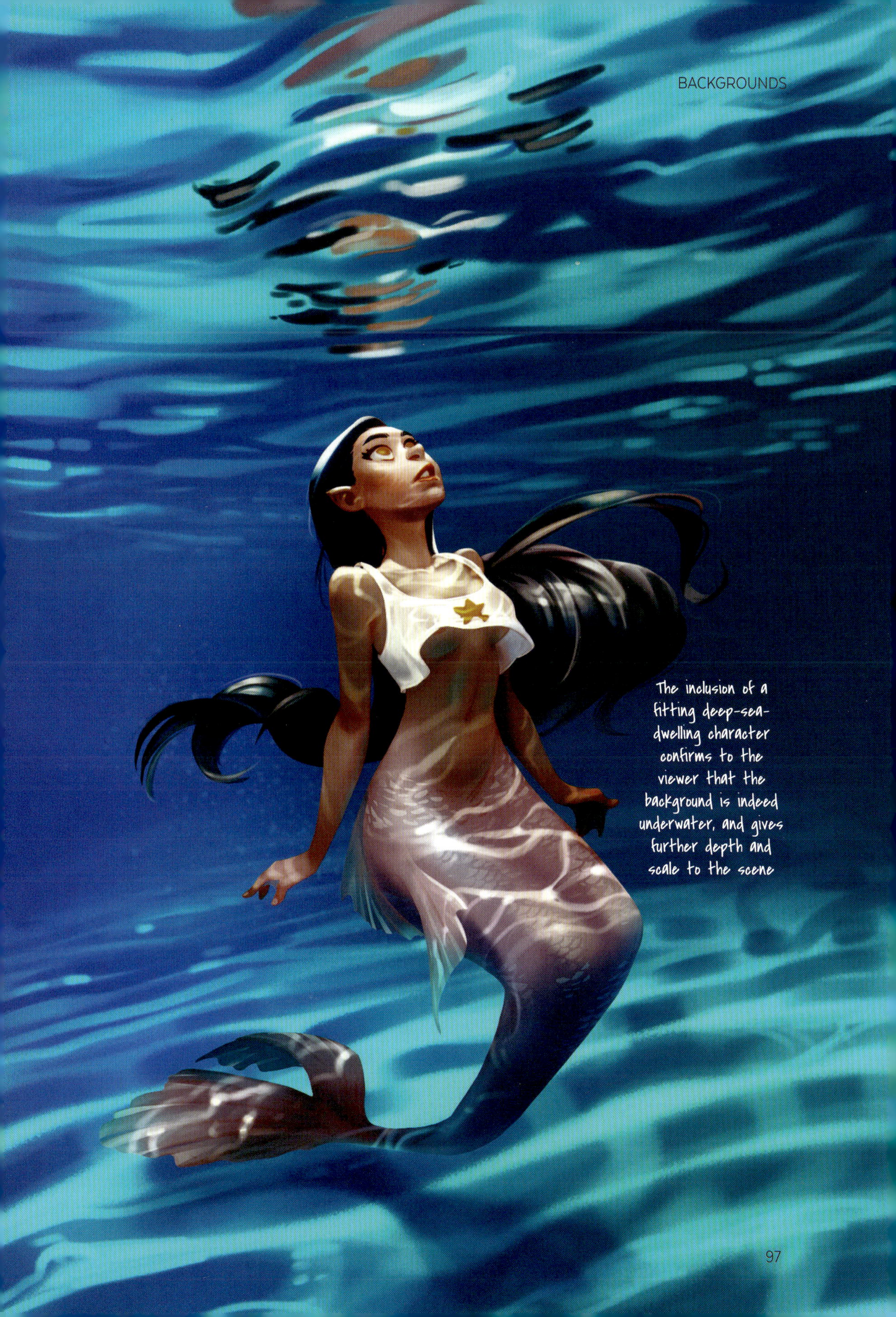

The inclusion of a fitting deep-sea-dwelling character confirms to the viewer that the background is indeed underwater, and gives further depth and scale to the scene

WORKING IN BLACK AND WHITE

Transforming a sketch into a black-and-white drawing can give it a strong graphic appearance. Working digitally or traditionally, the thought process is the same. Both media have advantages and disadvantages, for example, digital inking has an advantage in that mistakes can be easily corrected, but the fact that traditional inking cannot helps to train the mind to be more considerate when drawing.

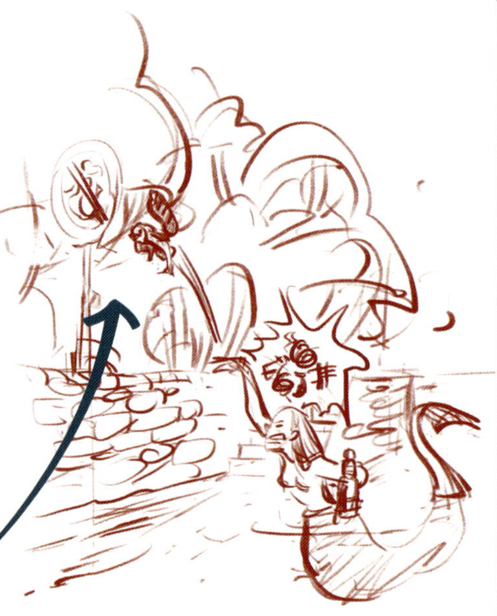

Start with a loose sketch – here the mermaid is vandalizing a sign.

It is very important to the readability of the image that any action is clear. This area seems a bit busy and unclear – I want it to be visible that she is throwing a fish sandwich

When refining the sketch, consider which elements should be darkest. Traditional shading rules do not apply here – think in terms of pattern, contrast, composition, and readability.

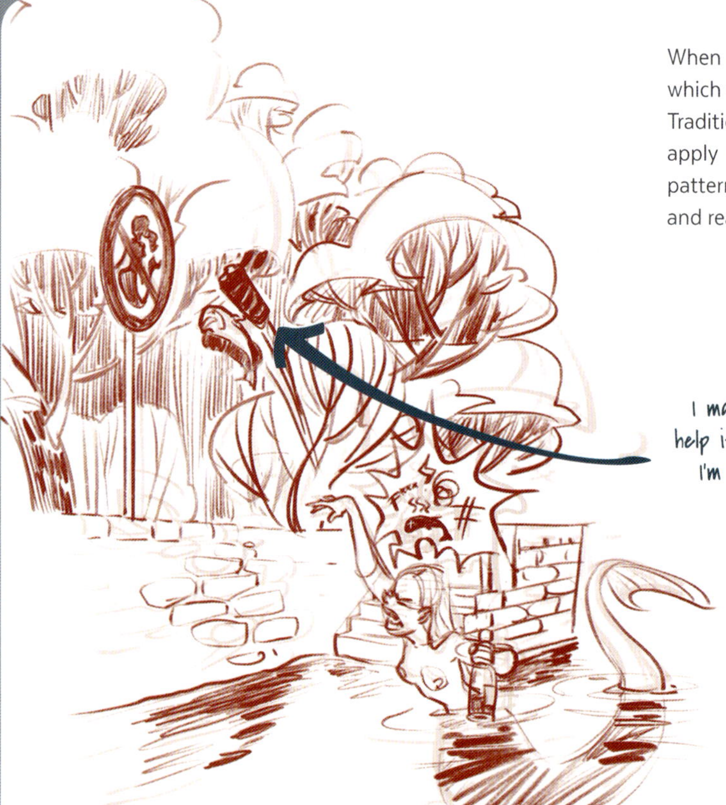

I make the sandwich dark to help it read a little clearer, but I'm not completely satisfied

Before inking, reduce the opacity of the sketch. When using traditional media, lightly trace your sketch with a light table or work directly on top of it. To me, inking is a controlled mess!

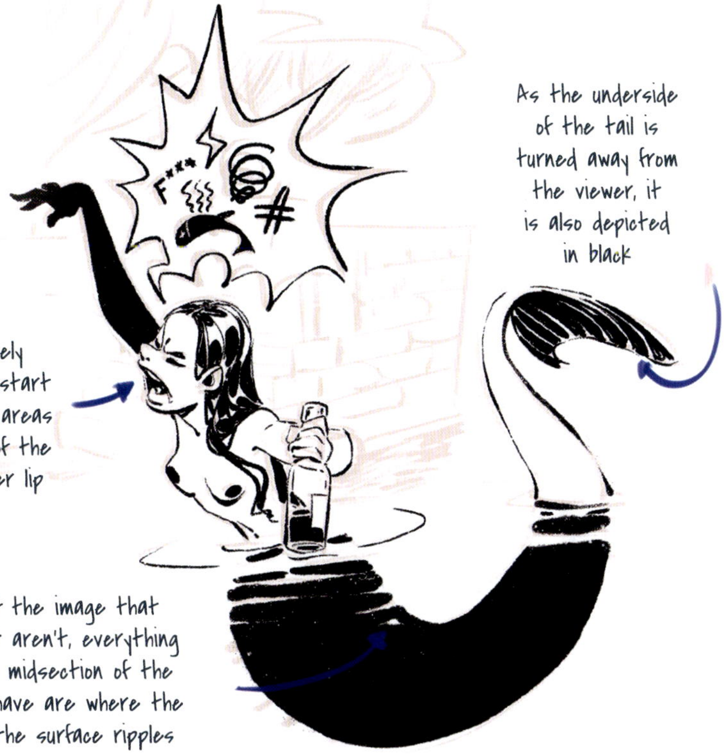

Although it doesn't always make sense in terms of lighting, I like to darken limbs that are toward the back of a composition to give a character depth.

To indicate the transparent quality of the glass bottle, draw what can be seen inside and immediately behind the bottle.

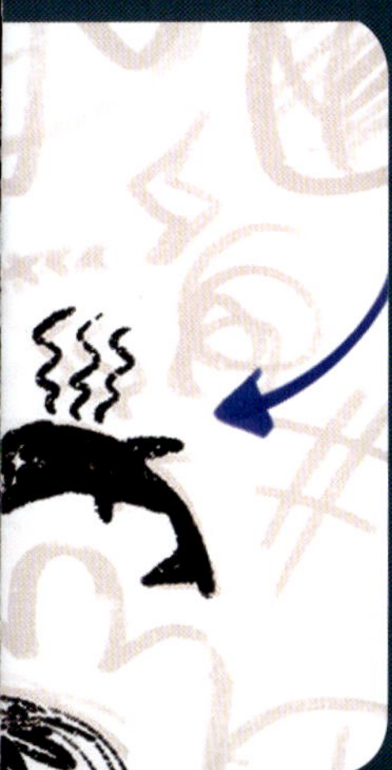

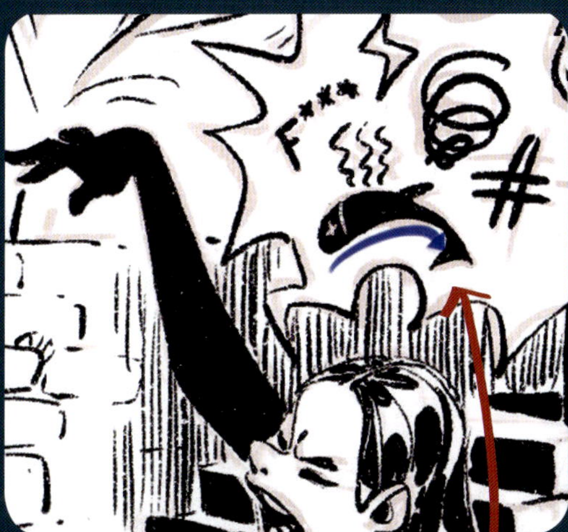

I clean up this wonky fish with a clean swipe of the eraser – another advantage of working digitally!

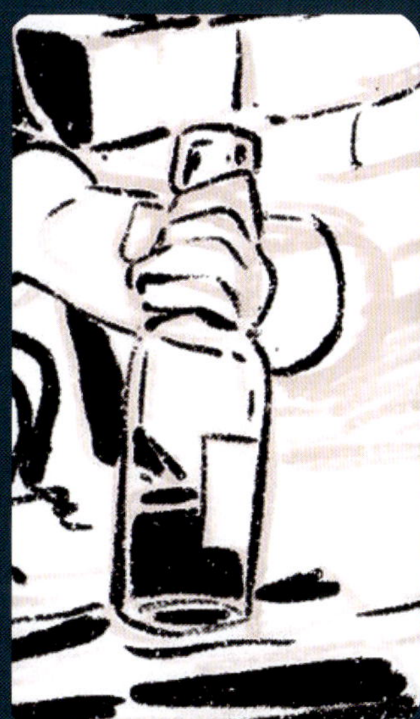

WORKING IN BLACK AND WHITE

I want the wall to appear to be made from old, uneven stones that have moss growing in the cracks. As mentioned previously, there's no need to detail every stone in the wall, so here I work loosely and intuitively, playing with varying pressure, but keeping the bottom lines thick.

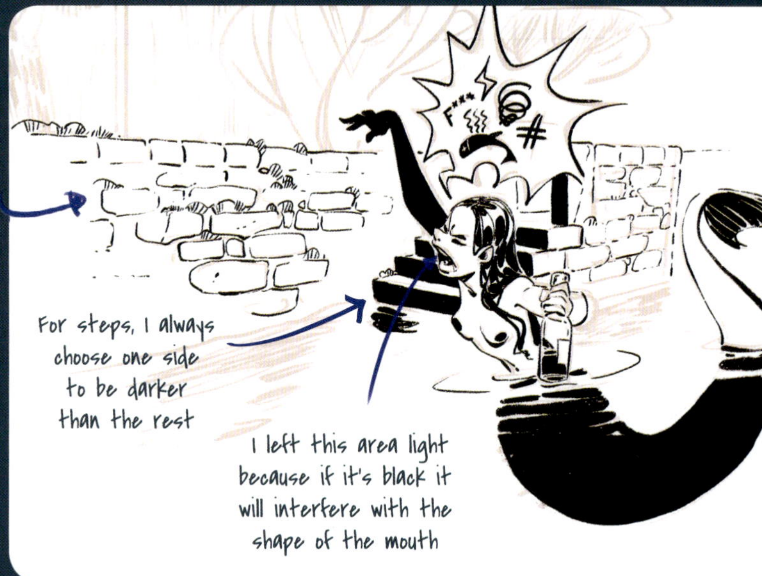

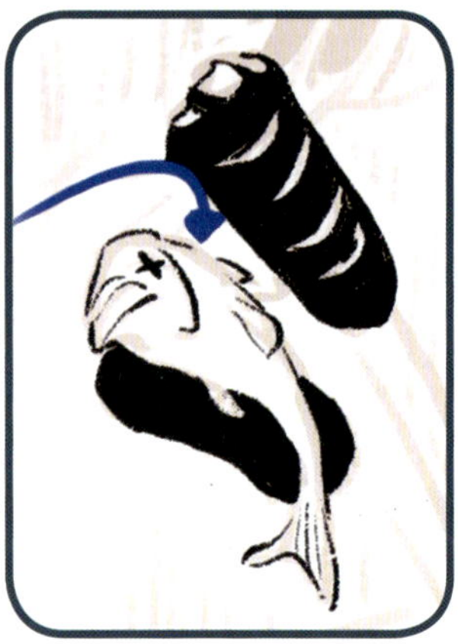

There's no need to close up all lines – leaving them open in places will add to the flow of the design

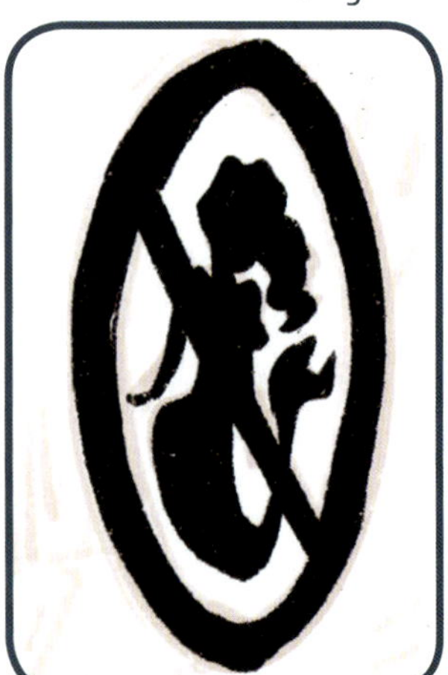

It is more visually comfortable if some elements are a little wonky – for example, this sign would stand out too much if it were perfectly oval

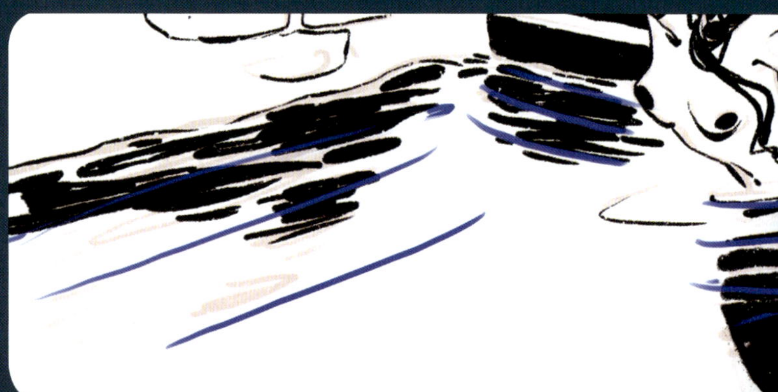

Although the design follows the original sketch, it feels a little stiff due to the abrupt change of direction of the ripples.

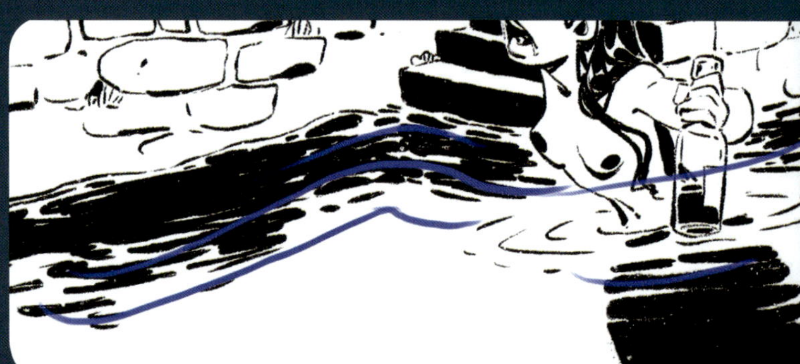

I correct the image by making the ripples more chaotic and organic, and by introducing a larger area of darkness that combines the shaded underwater areas of the wall and steps.

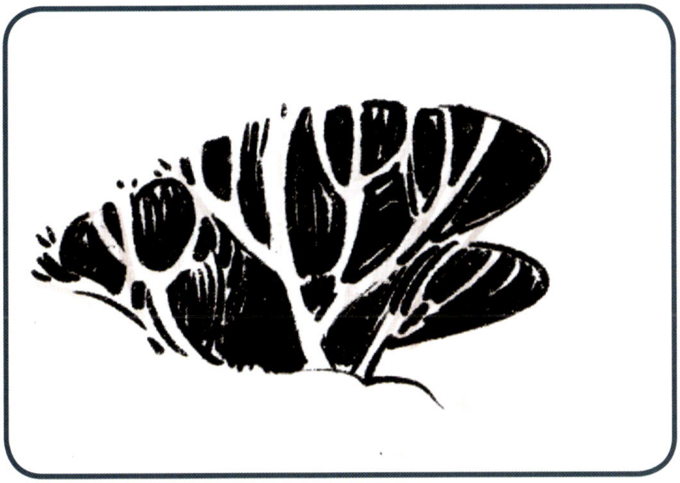

"ALWAYS FOLLOW THE UNDERLYING SHAPES AND VOLUMES CLOSELY"

When filling in darker areas with a slight texture, always follow the underlying shapes and volumes closely — there is no right or wrong way to do it, but it should fit in the context of the image.

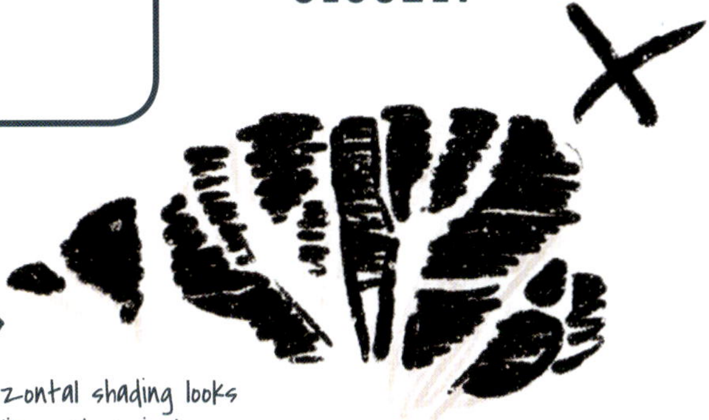

This horizontal shading looks more like water ripples

With the shading following the direction of the growth of the branches, these examples appear more organic

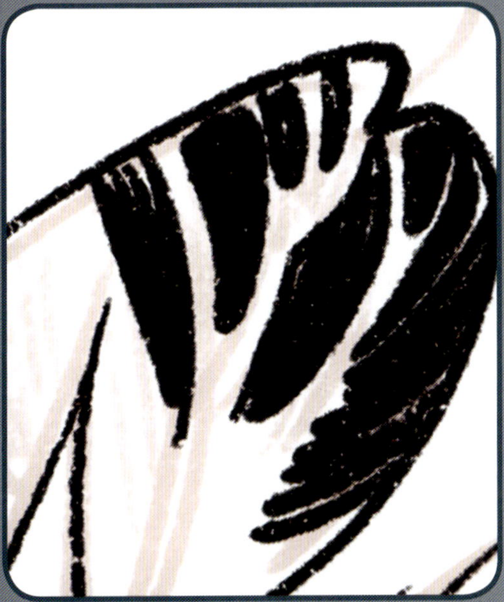

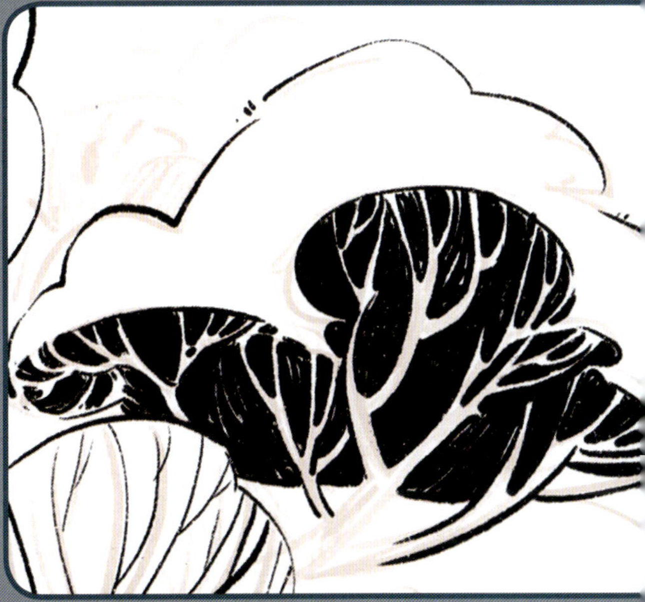

WORKING IN BLACK AND WHITE

At this stage, I review the composition, as it's not quite balanced and visually pleasing enough.

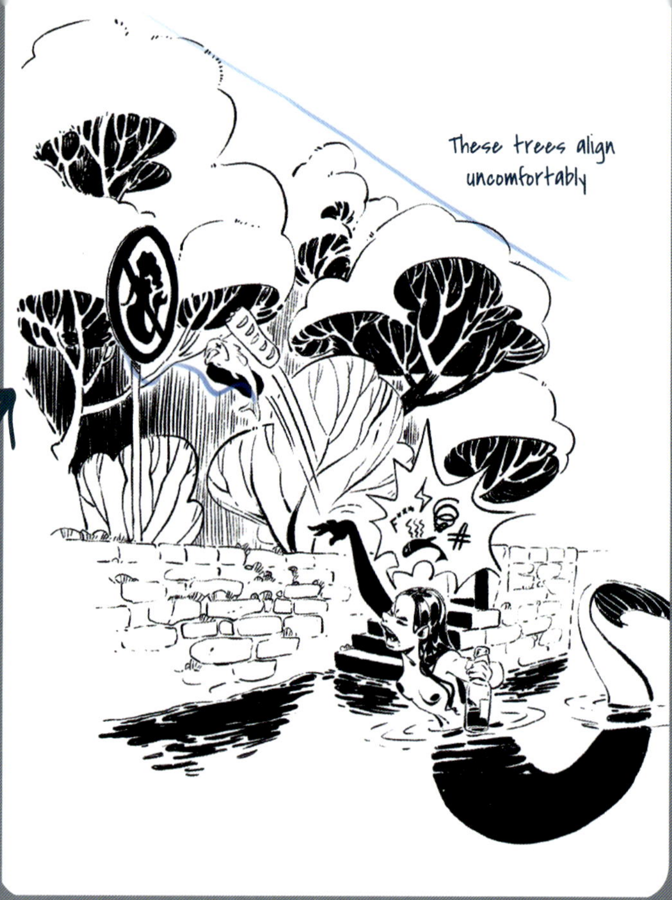

I add these vertical lines for shading, with closer strokes applied to the darker areas

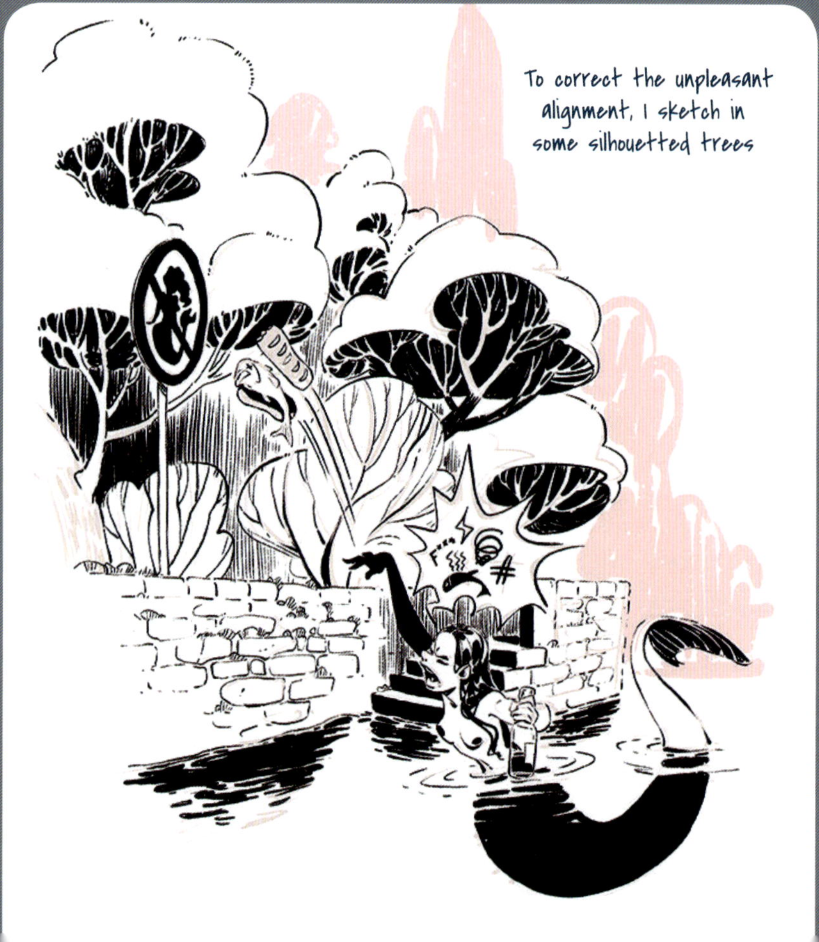

I like the overall image but feel that I could have made the sandwich more visible, as the surrounding area is a little too busy. I often say "if there's a problem in the initial sketch, there will most likely be a problem in the final result" and this piece is the perfect example!

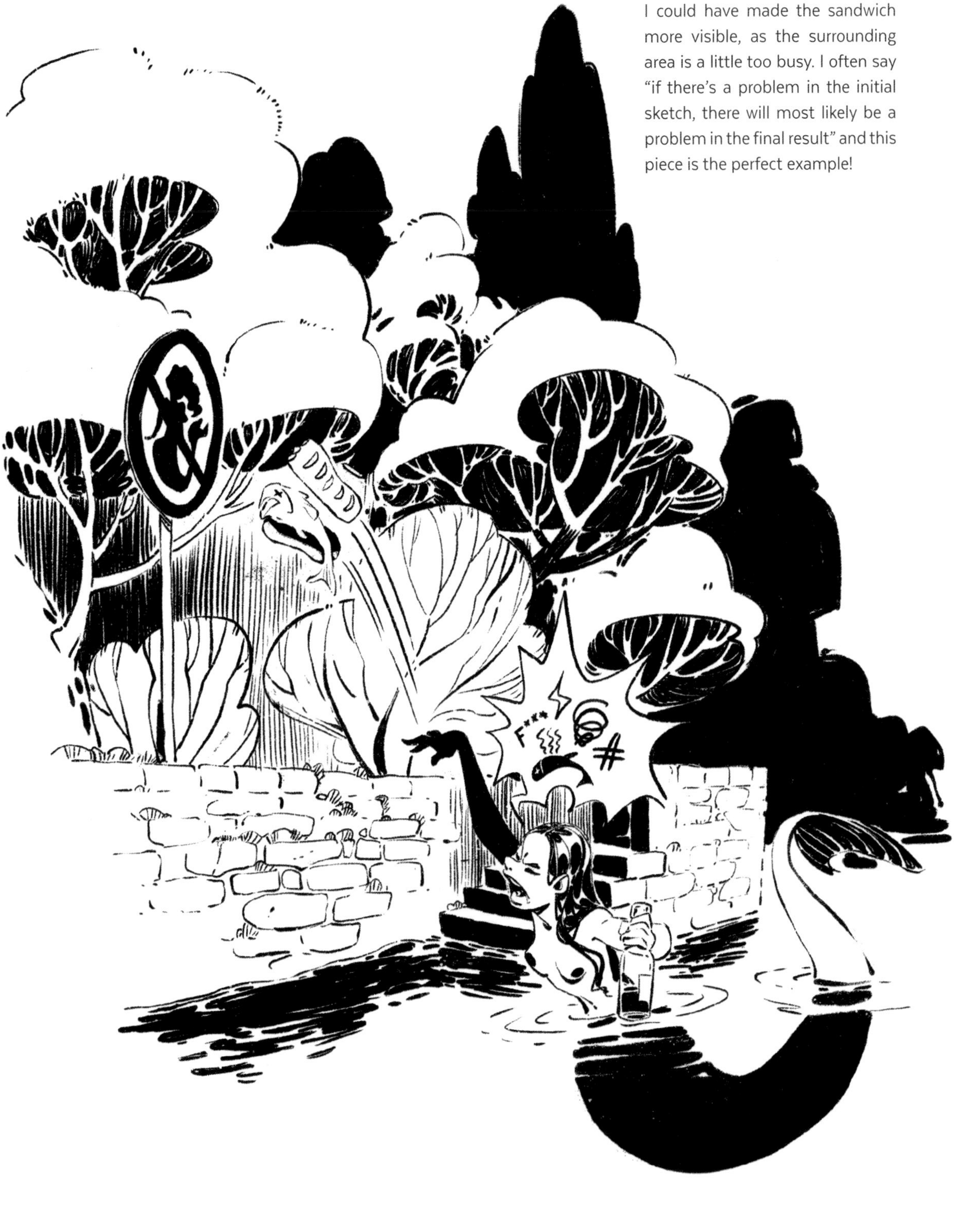

PAINTING A STYLIZED BACKGROUND FROM REFERENCE

START WITH THE SKETCH

A solid-colored background offers a less intimidating alternative to the usual white page, and this base color will shine through in places of the final image, creating a unique finish. Here I use a burnt orange, as I know I am going to paint a nature scene and the orange hue will complement any desaturated greens used. I use Procreate to create this image.

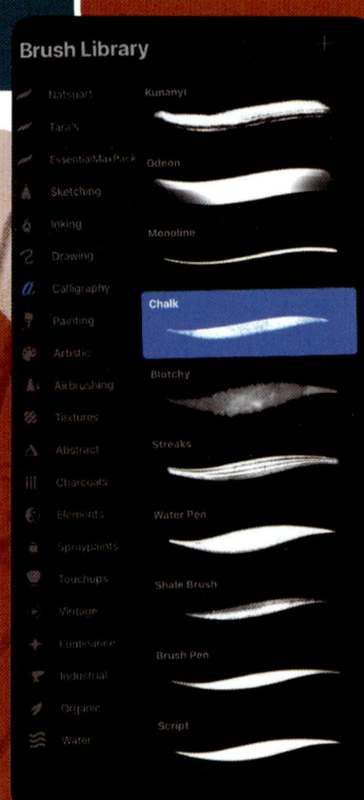

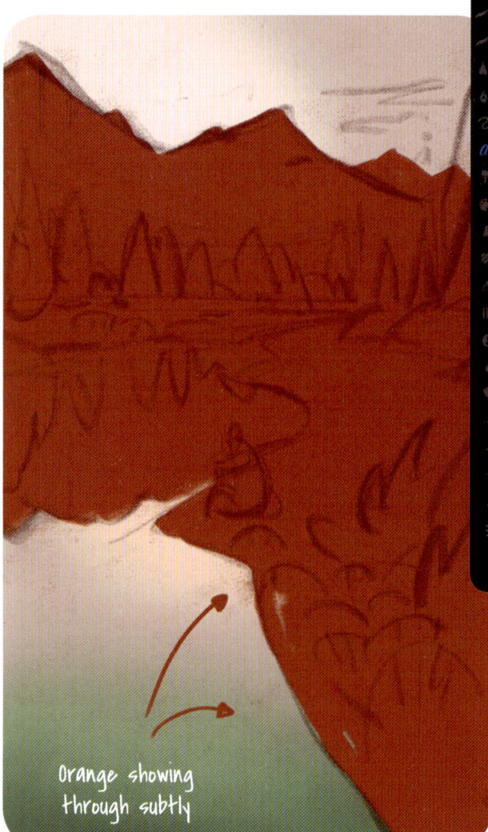

"HUE VARIATION GIVES THE IMAGE MORE LIFE"

DEFINE SHAPES

Block shapes out on a new layer, apply the Alpha Lock, and add some gradients. This approach helps to achieve clean edges. I always work from back to front. Here I use a chalk brush for the edges, which allows the underlying orange to shine through gently.

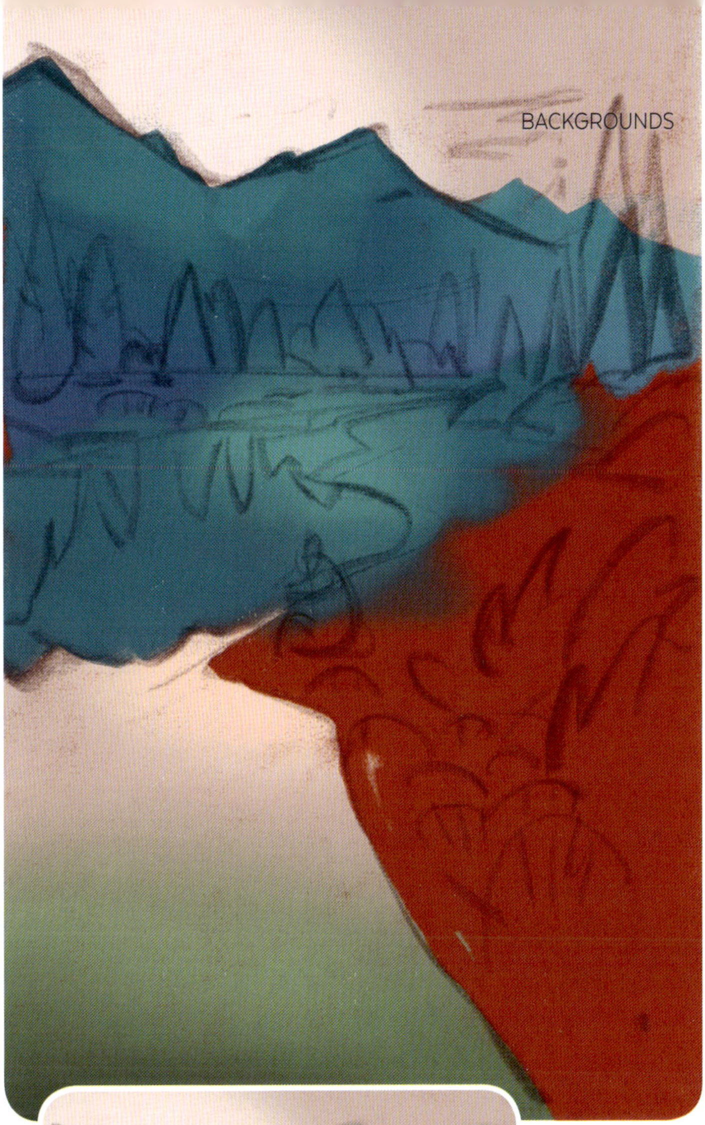

SOFT COLOR BLOCKING

On a layer under the sky layer, I roughly paint blue for the mountains. I apply patches of different blue hues with a soft brush. I use MaxU Shader Pastel (EssentialMaxPack brush set) but any soft brush will work.

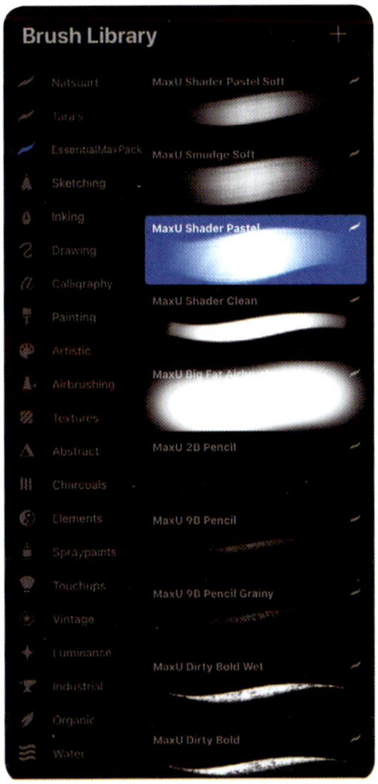

LAYERS USED:

SKETCH

SKY AND REFLECTION

MOUNTAINS AND REFLECTION

ORANGE BASE

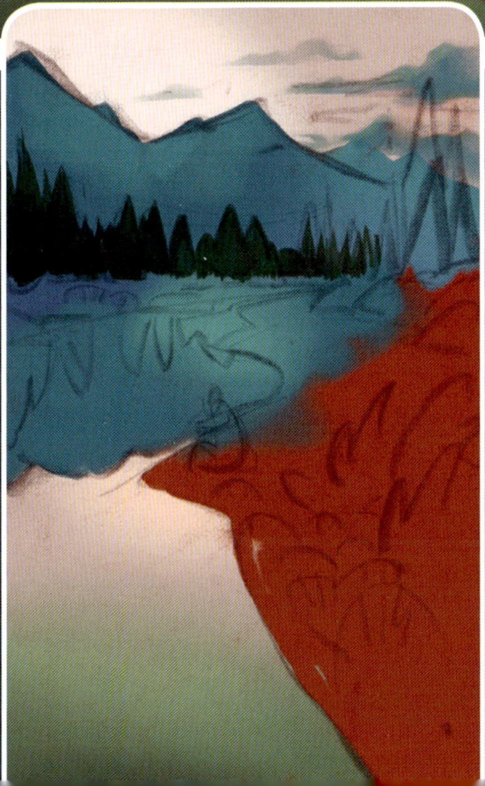

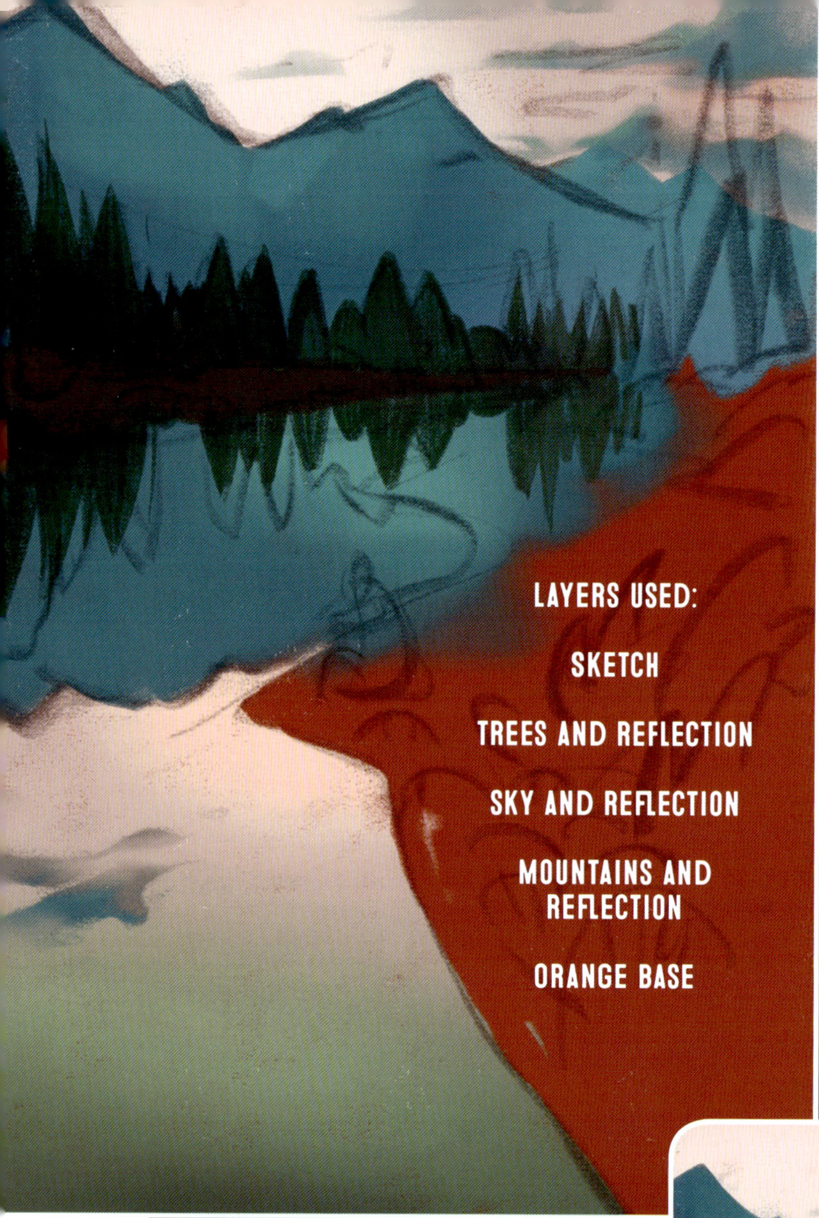

HUE VARIATION

On top of the mountains I block in simple cone-shaped trees. I start with the trees at the back, in a darker and slightly different hue to the other trees, and then paint the front trees on top, varying the hues slightly. This hue variation gives the image more life.

REFLECTIONS

To create the reflection of the line of trees in the lake at the base of the mountains, I simply duplicate and flip the trees. I then paint the edge of the lake on a new layer on top.

I then block in the bank. Again, I vary the shades of green used and allow the base orange to shine through and enhance the design.

LAYERS USED:

SKETCH

LAKE EDGE/BANK

TREES AND REFLECTION

SKY AND REFLECTION

MOUNTAINS AND REFLECTION

ORANGE BASE

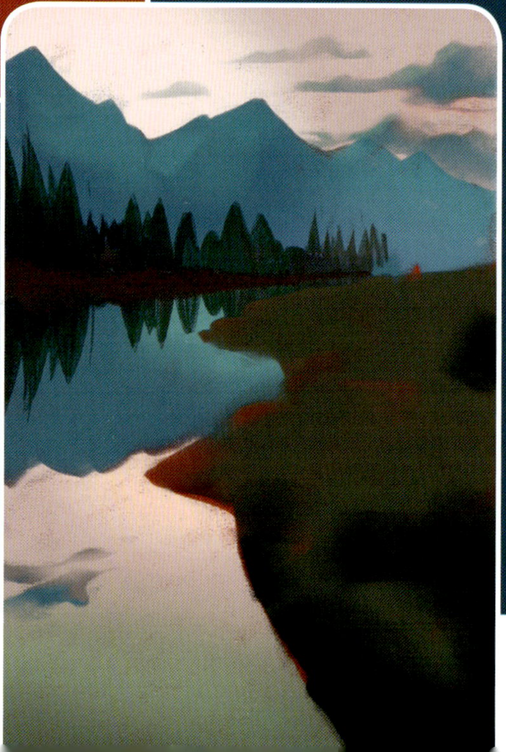

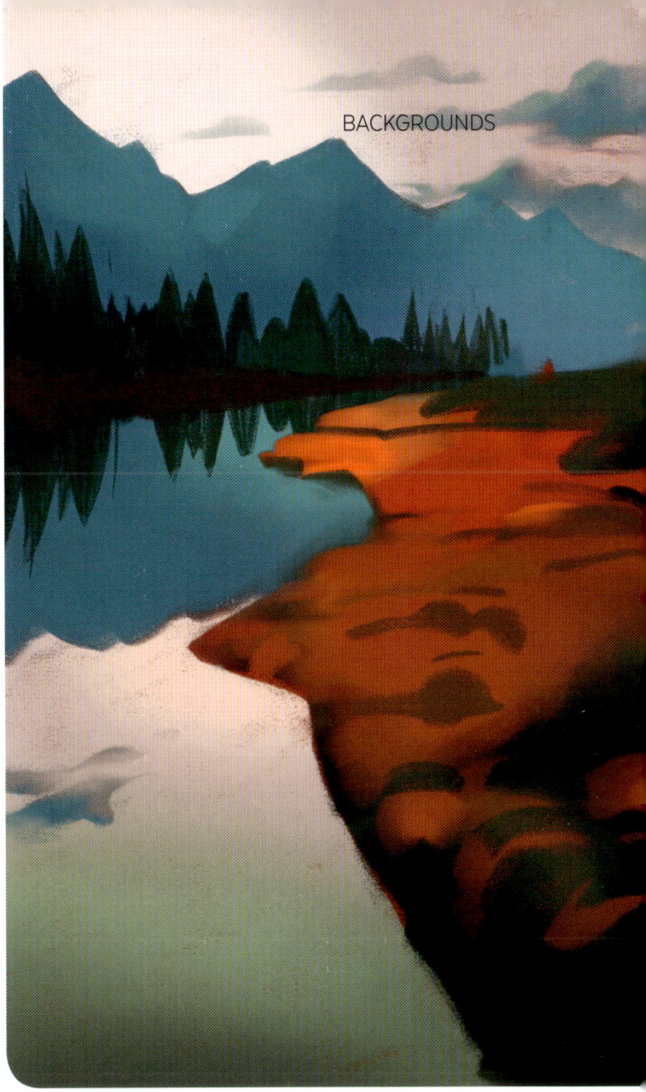

BUILDING GROUND

Using a clipping mask, I add orange grass on top of the grassy bank. I reintroduce green spots on the orange grass to create a more cohesive environment.

LAYERS USED:

SKETCH

LAKE EDGE/BANK 2

LAKE EDGE/BANK

TREES AND REFLECTION

SKY AND REFLECTION

MOUNTAINS AND REFLECTION

ORANGE BASE

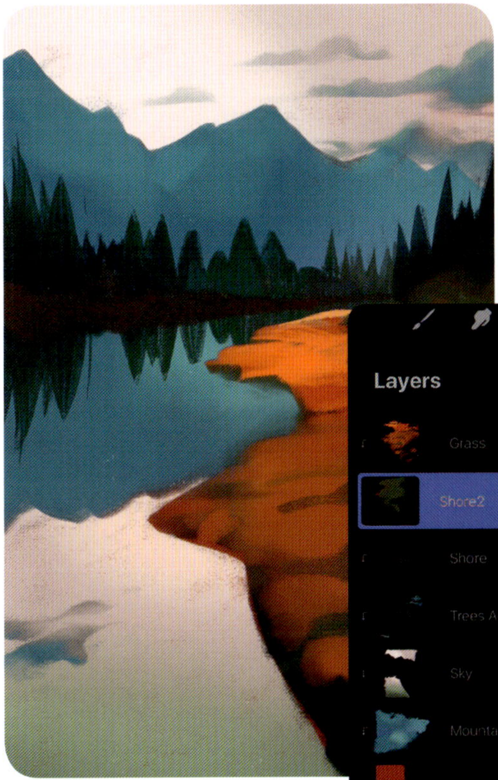

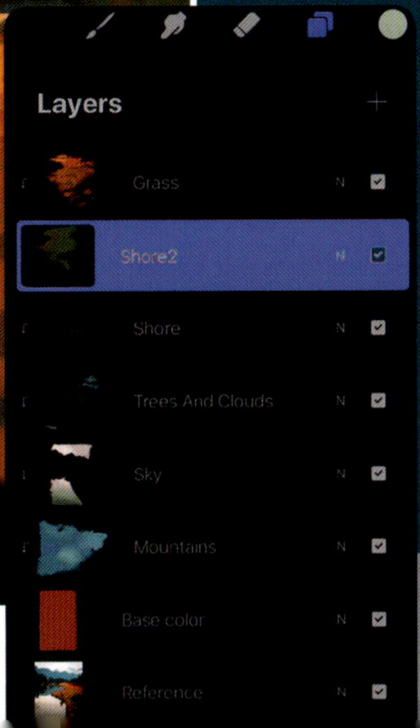

LAYERING

On a new layer, I add more trees. At this point you could flatten the layers. I like to keep the layers separate, but it's not necessary. When painting traditionally in oil paint, the approach would be similar – painting from back to front, layering details and colors on top of each other.

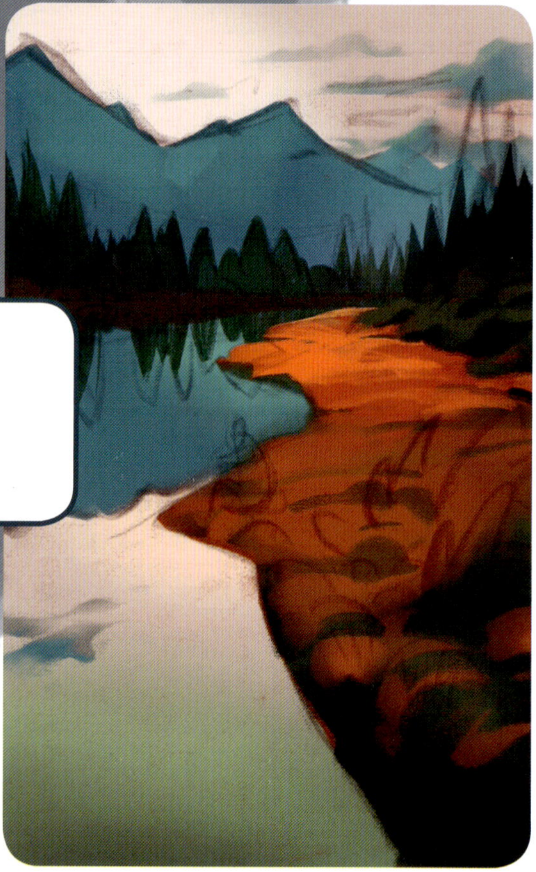

CHECK IN WITH THE SKETCH!

While painting, I keep turning the original sketch layer on and off to see how the painted version compares to the initial design.

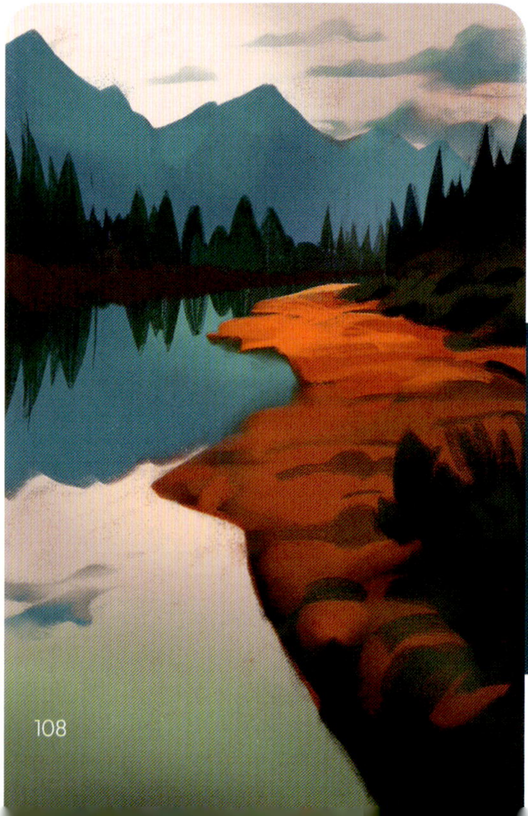

"IT'S IMPORTANT TO HAVE A SOLID BASE... OTHERWISE IT IS EASY TO LOSE DIRECTION"

FINAL FORMS

On a new layer, the last missing background element, bushes, are added. From this point it's all about detailing and cleaning up the image – the illustration won't change drastically. At this stage, it's important to have a solid base to add details to, otherwise it is easy to lose direction and end up with something that has nice details but fails to work as a whole.

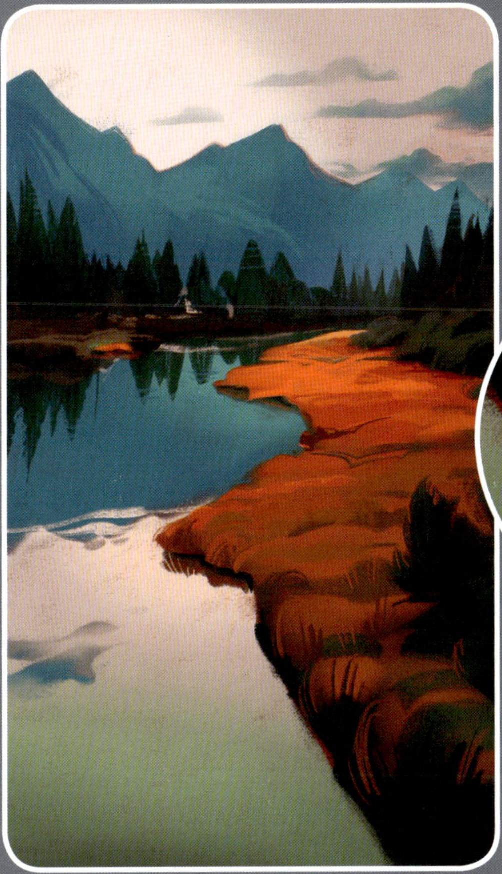

BLENDING AND DETAILING

Have fun blending and detailing the design. I work on new separate layers and keep layering the image up, but details could also be added straight on to the image. I use the chalk brush for details and a soft brush for blending.

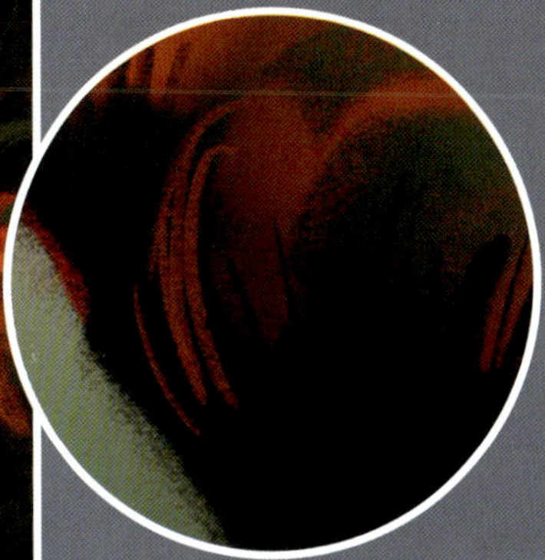

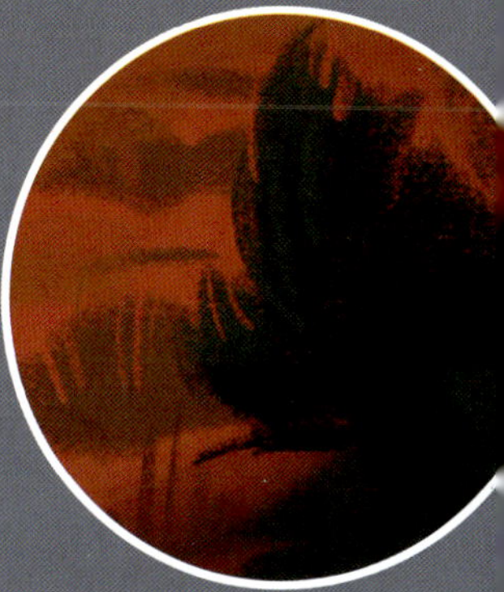

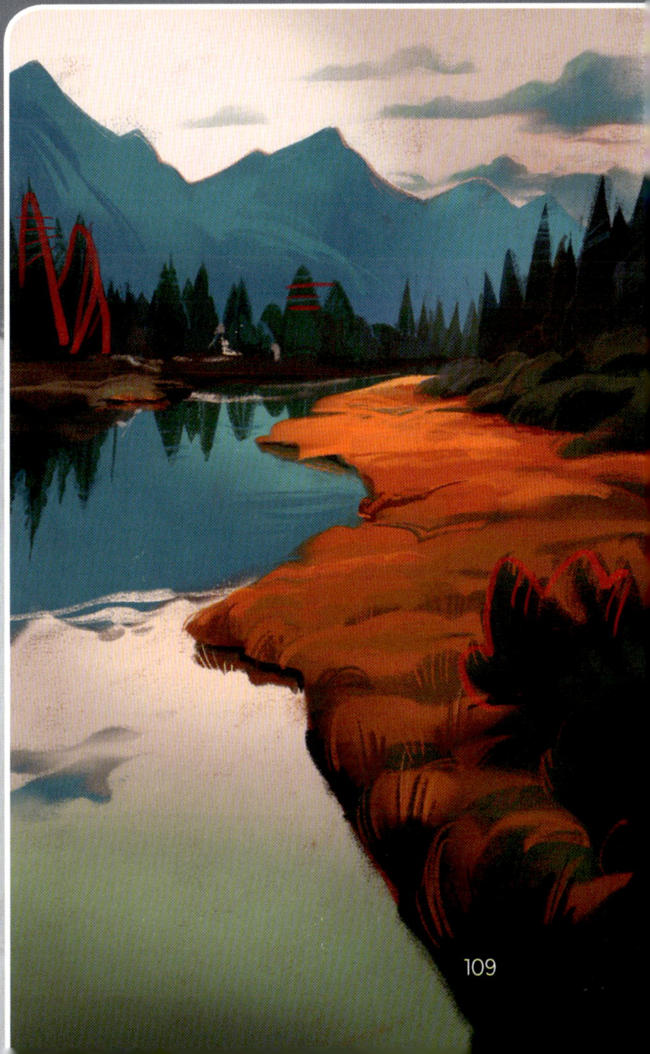

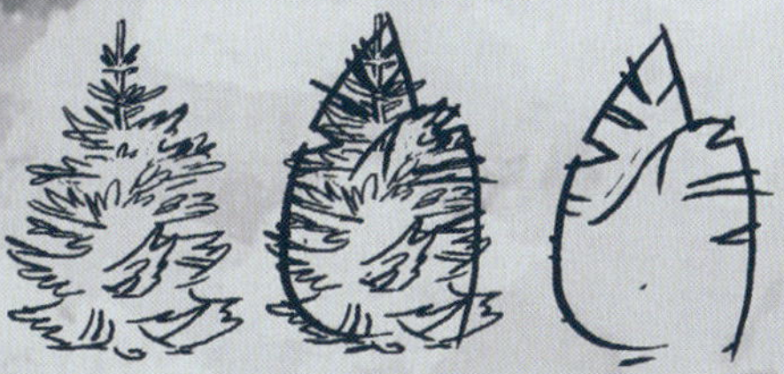

COMPOSITIONAL TWEAKS

I continue to tweak and add more details. I darken the trees using green on a new layer set to Multiply. On a large scene like this, try to keep foliage structures simple while still based on the original shapes of reference examples. Abstract forms hinting at realistic features provide the brain with enough information to decipher what the eye is seeing.

PAINTING A STYLIZED BACKGROUND FROM REFERENCE

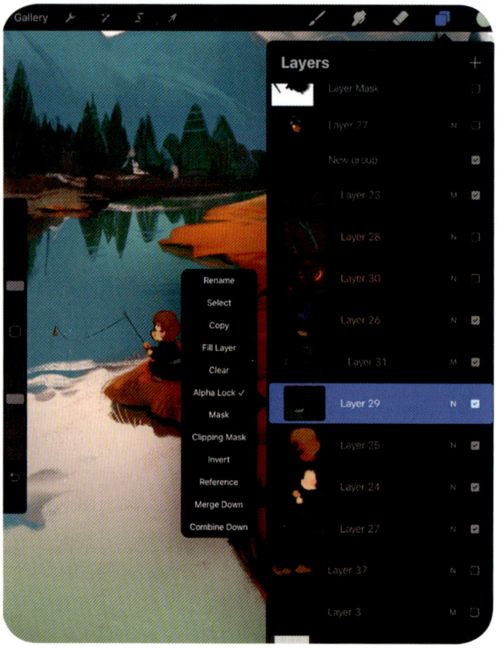

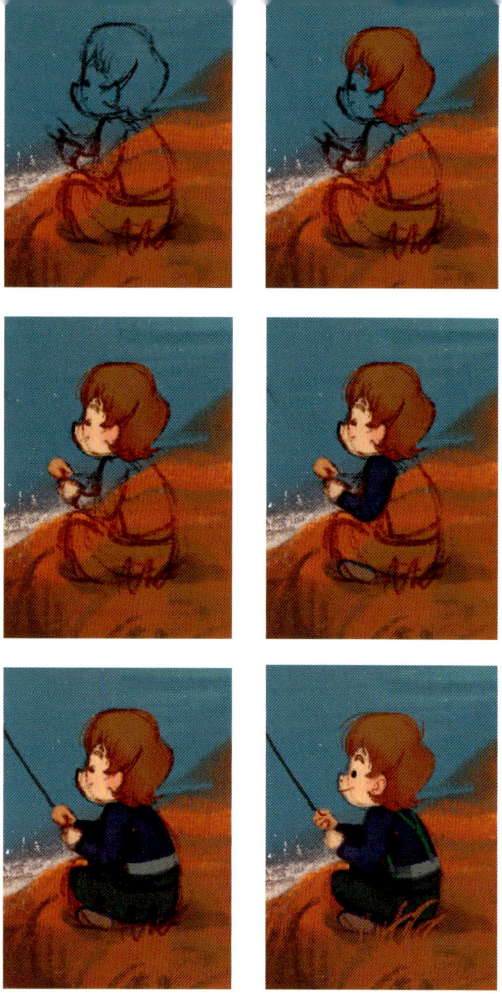

ADD THE CHARACTER

I sketch the character – a boy sat on the bank of the lake, fishing – into the scene. I use a new layer for each element of the character, apply Alpha Lock, and gently shade to complete.

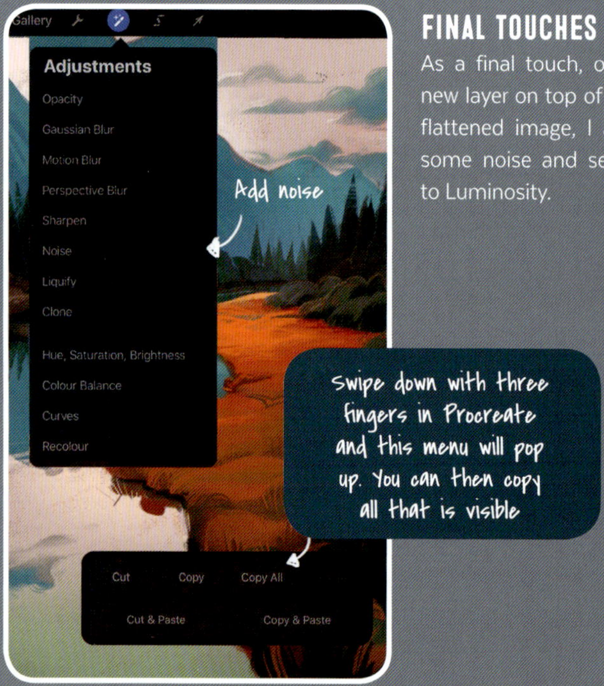

FINAL TOUCHES

As a final touch, on a new layer on top of the flattened image, I add some noise and set it to Luminosity.

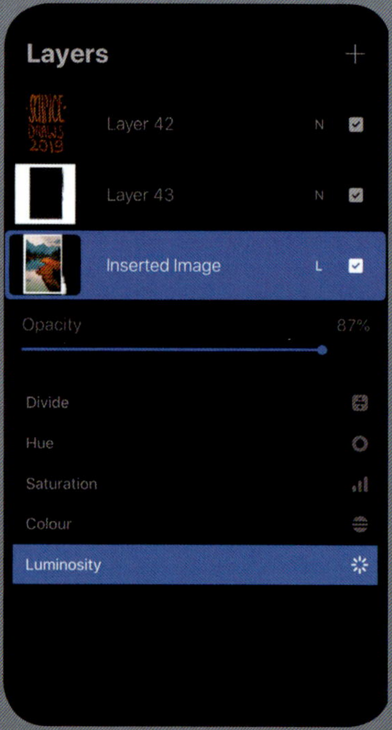

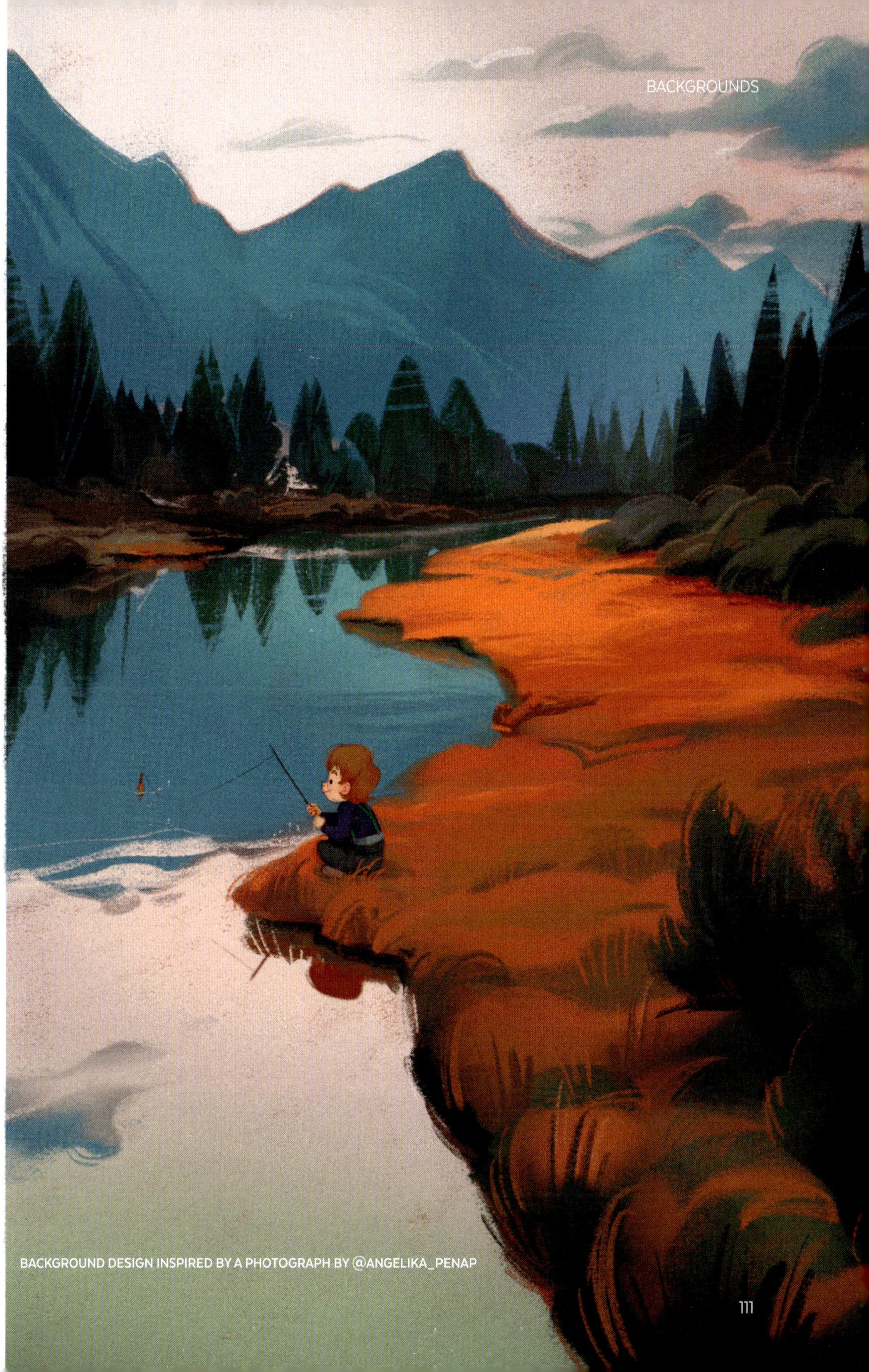

BACKGROUND DESIGN INSPIRED BY A PHOTOGRAPH BY @ANGELIKA_PENAP

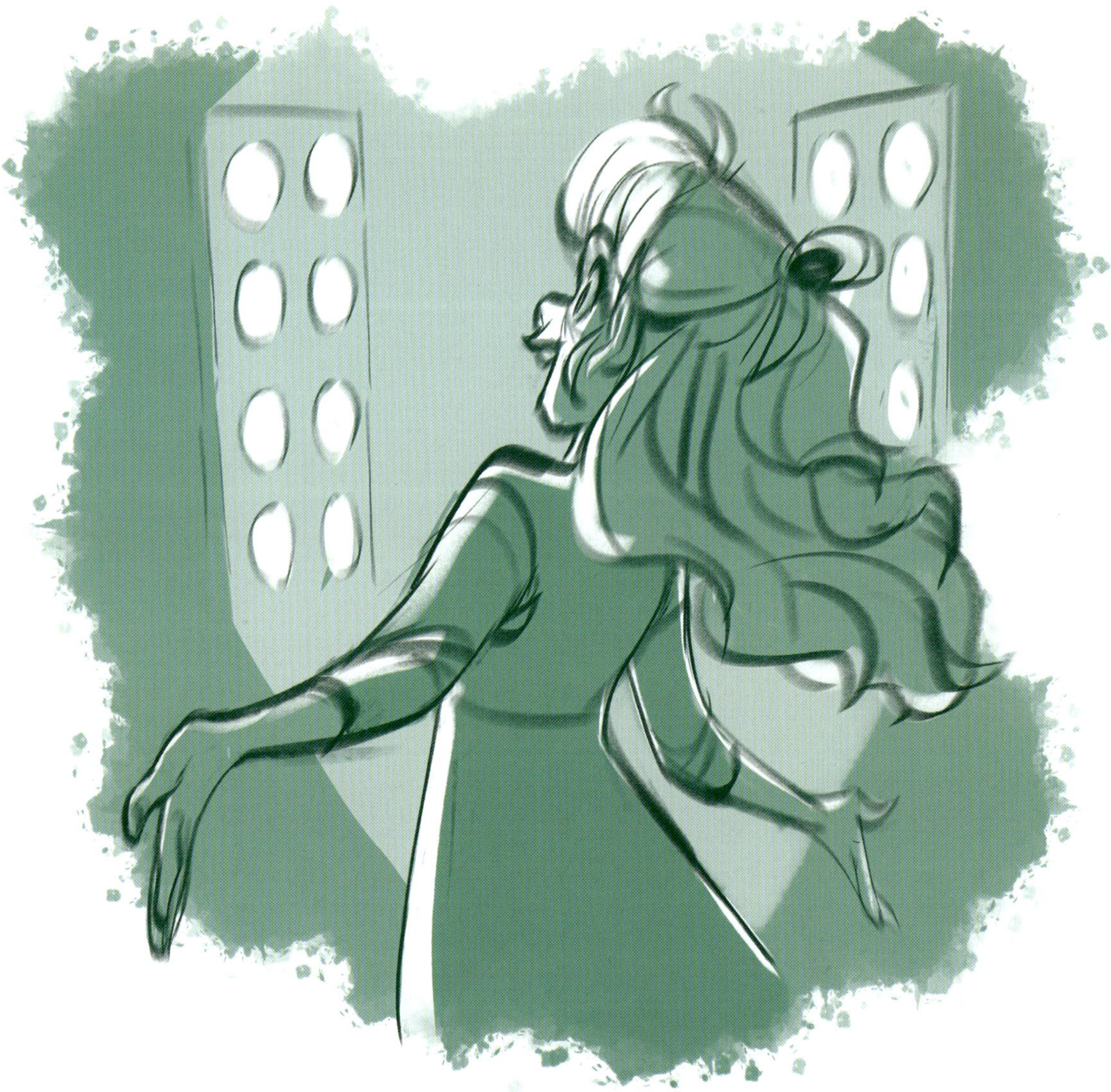

LIGHT

Color and light has always baffled and intrigued me. It's only recently that I have started to get a grip on the subject, but the more I delve into the topic, the more I enjoy the play and dimension it offers. So, here I would like to share what I've learned.

COLOR: HUE, SATURATION, AND VALUE

Light contains color, so understanding the basics of color theory is crucial when developing a believable light source and effective illumination. Color theory is a huge topic that can fill many books, but don't be intimidated, as there are just a few fundamental points, which I will explain here, that should offer a solid base on which to work from.

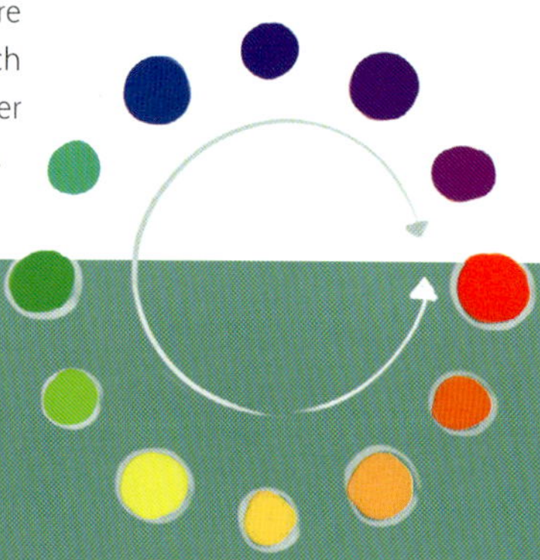

BASIC TERMS TO UNDERSTAND WHEN WORKING WITH COLOR:

HUE is simply the dominant color as seen on the color wheel

SATURATION refers to the spectrum of grayscale to dominant color

DESATURATION occurs when some of the color is removed from the original hue, bringing it closer to gray

VALUE of the hue can be adjusted by adding either white or black

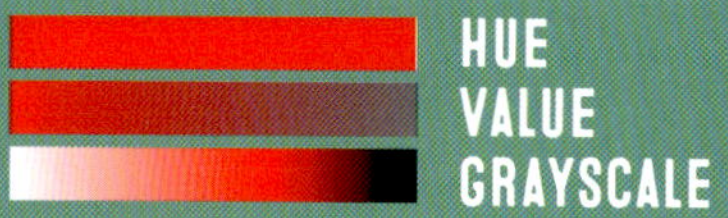

Some artists start in grayscale values and then add color. In this way of working, it is important to understand how values work. Colors have different value properties and shine brightest at different values!

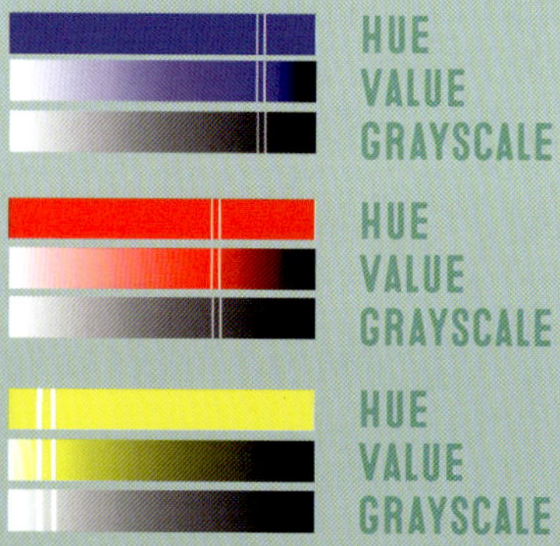

BLUE IS BRIGHTEST AT A DARK VALUE

RED IS BRIGHTEST AT A MID TO DARK VALUE

YELLOW IS BRIGHTEST AT A LIGHT VALUE

Hue, saturation, and value levels need to be balanced to make an image visually appealing. I often forget about value and experiment with just hue and saturation, only to wonder why my painting doesn't look quite right. Check how a painting looks in grayscale and adjust the values to achieve the best level of contrast for the design.

Knowing the exact value of a color is not necessary to achieve an effective finish – a rough idea of the value of each color is enough to improve overall application of value

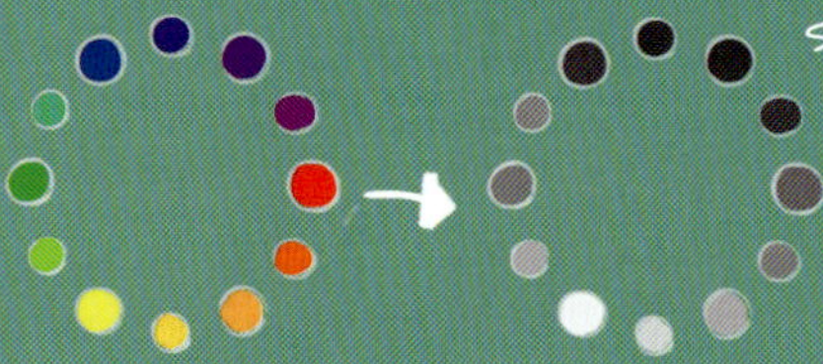

Simply reducing the saturation with an adjustment layer will not achieve a true grayscale effect; applying the grayscale mode will create the closest finish

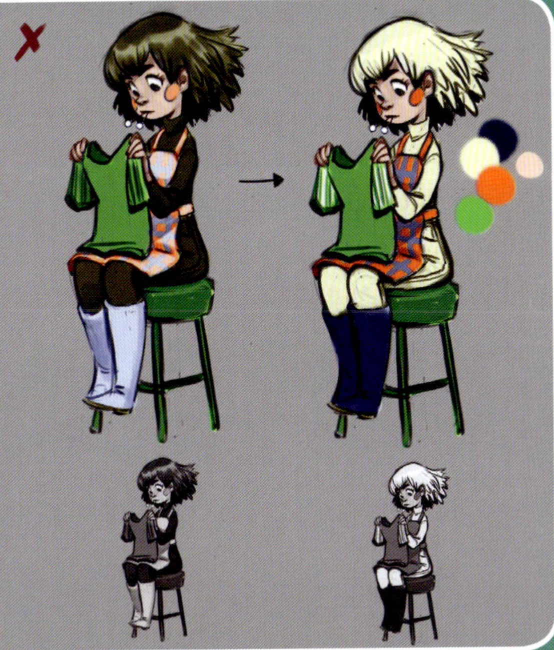

The same set of colors applied on top of base layers with different values

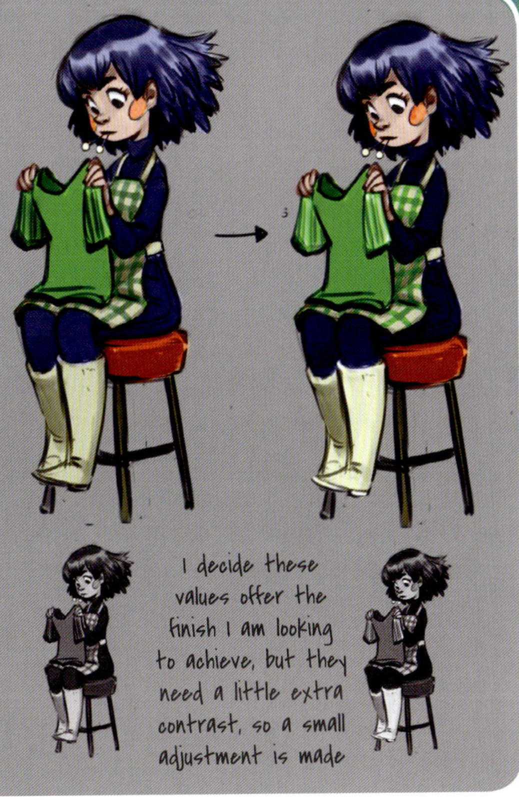

THE FINAL PAINTING

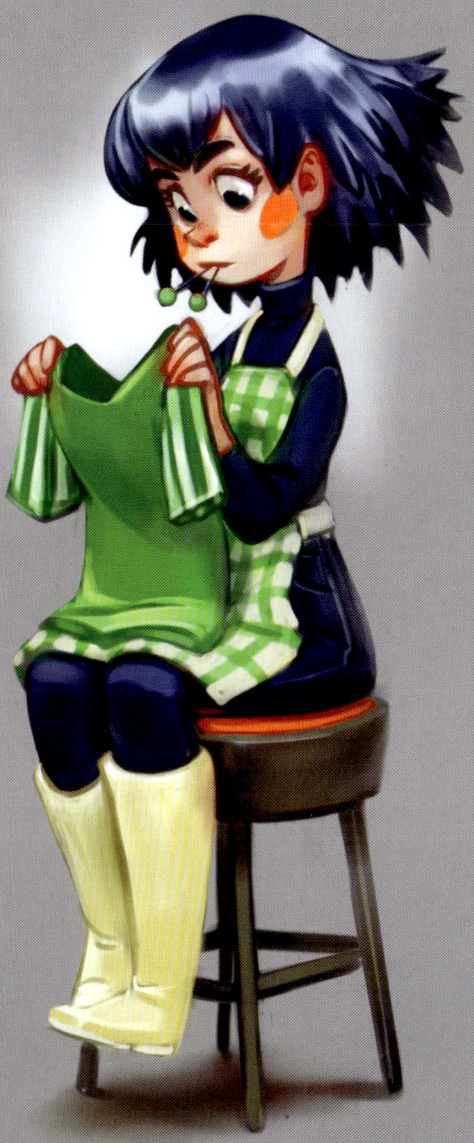

Once the blocked-in colors are visually appealing, the final painting can begin

Color blocking a design after adding a base layer of black-and-white values is a great way to quickly identify if a color scheme will work for a final piece. Altering the values of a design can make drastic or subtle changes to its overall feel.

HIGHLIGHTS

Basic lighting of a character or scene comes in the form of highlights, so I'm going to start by introducing my approach to drawing highlights.

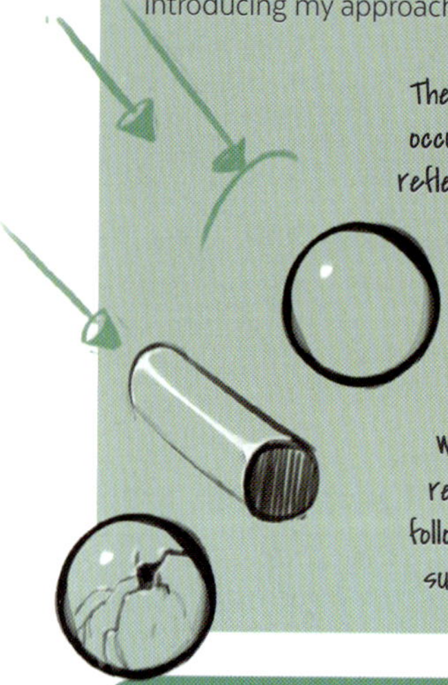

The brightest highlights occur where light hits a reflective surface directly

When light hits the reflective surface, it follows the edge of the surface of the object

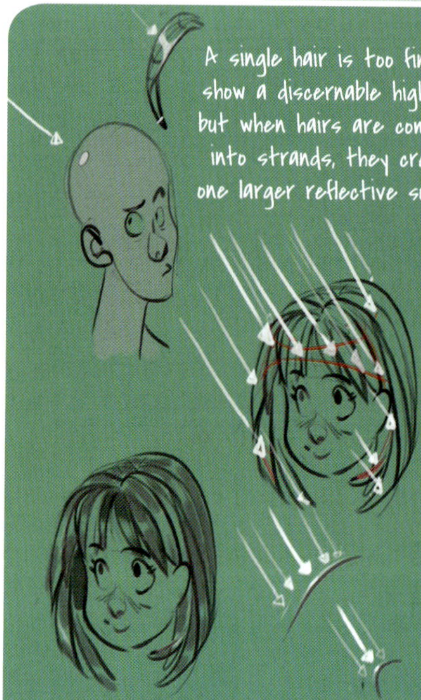

A single hair is too fine to show a discernable highlight, but when hairs are combined into strands, they create one larger reflective surface

A gentle curve will have a longer, softer highlight, whereas a sharp curve will have a shorter, sharper highlight

When painting a head of hair, I think of how the highlights should follow the shape underneath, but instead of painting the highlights, I find it easier to simply paint the dark hues, leaving white space for the highlights themselves.

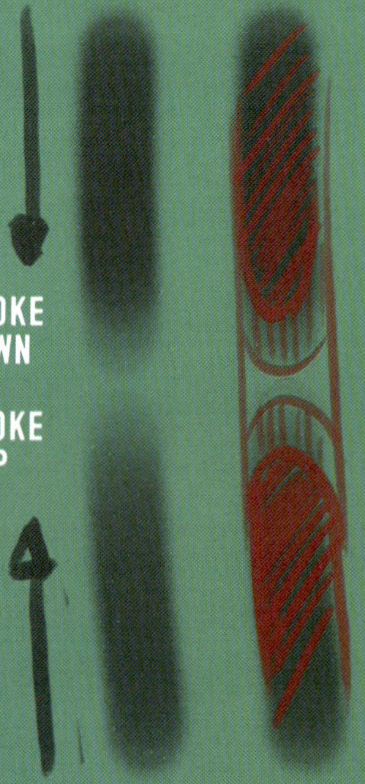

By simply painting the strand of hair using brushstrokes from the top and bottom, a natural-looking highlight can be created, which also features gentle gradients

I approach all highlights in this way...

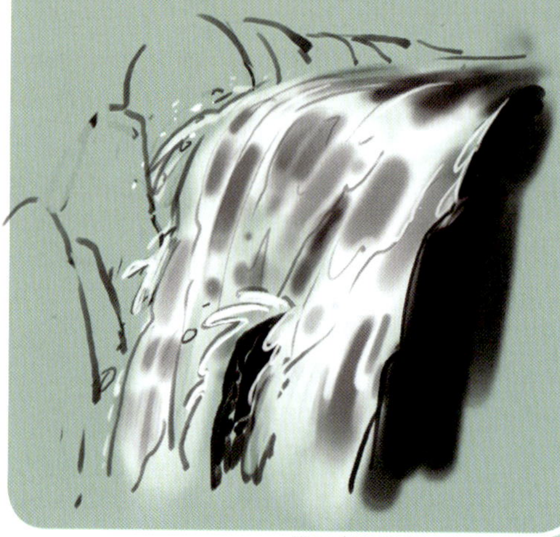

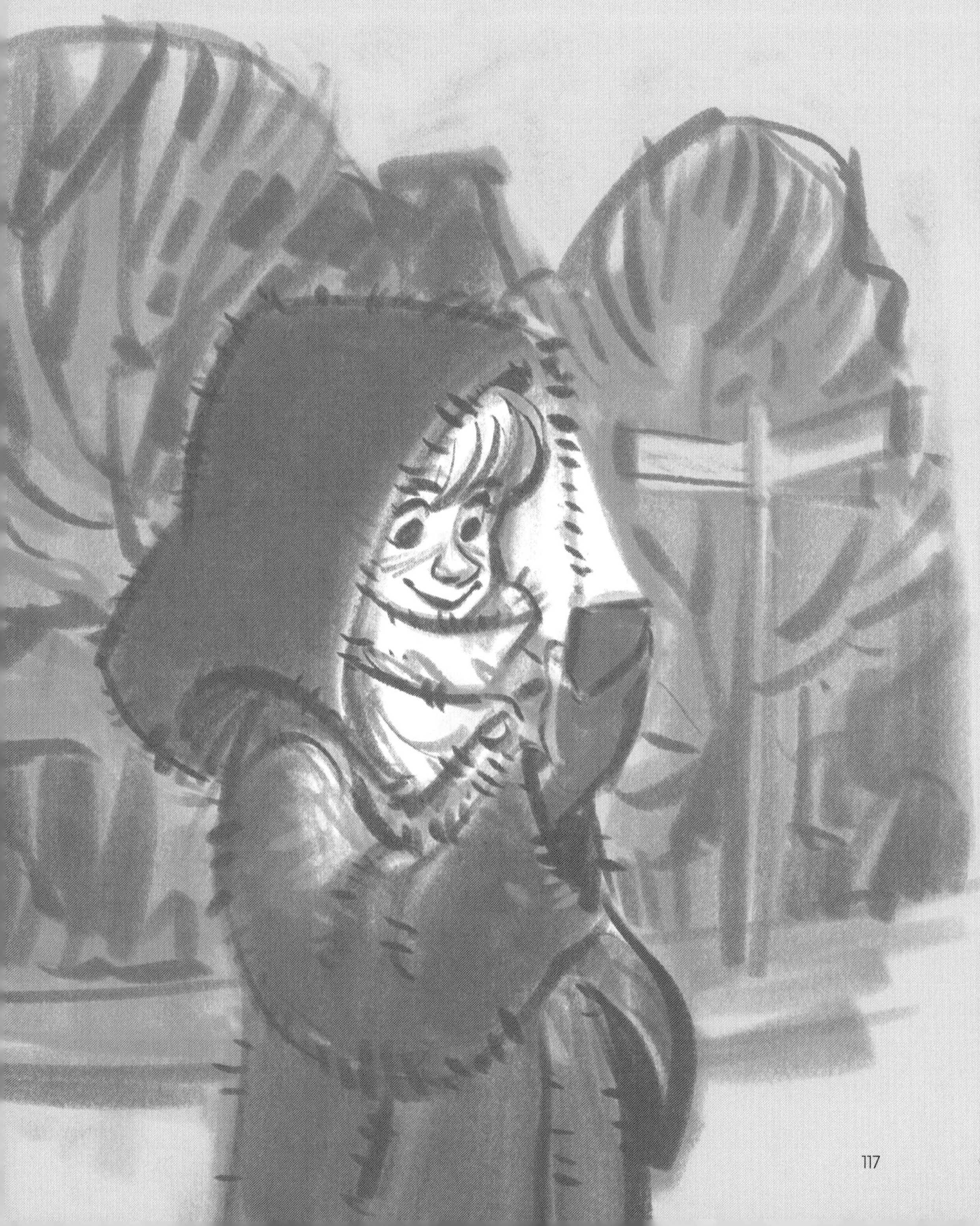

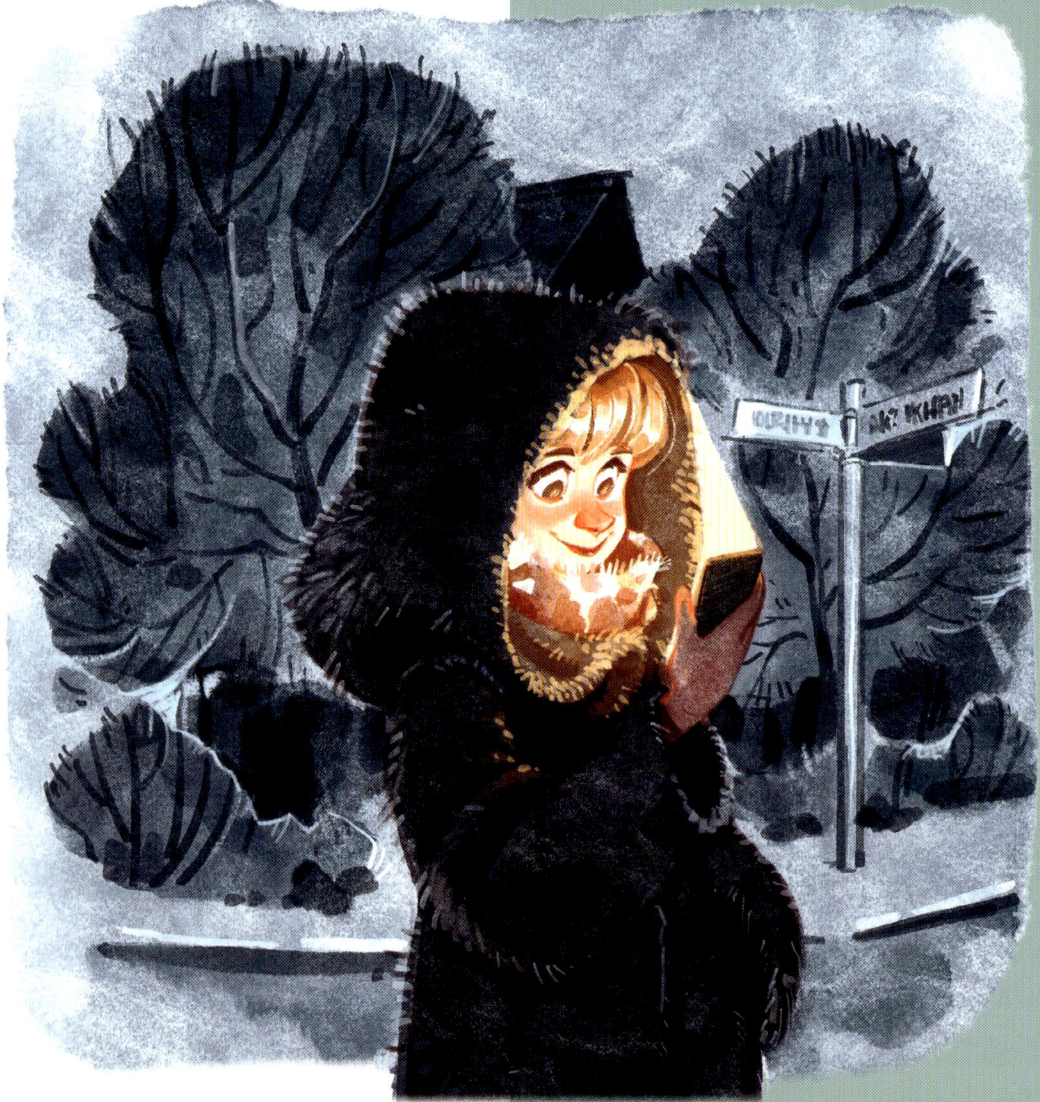

PHONE LIGHT

Nighttime walk to the studio of a friend, illuminated by phone light.

LIGHTING THE FACE

Here is a quick explanation of how light falls on the face in various lighting situations. Remember to follow the facial grid and volumes of the head.

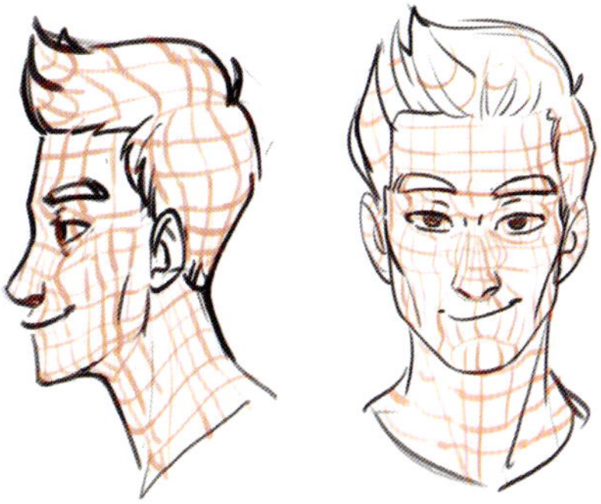

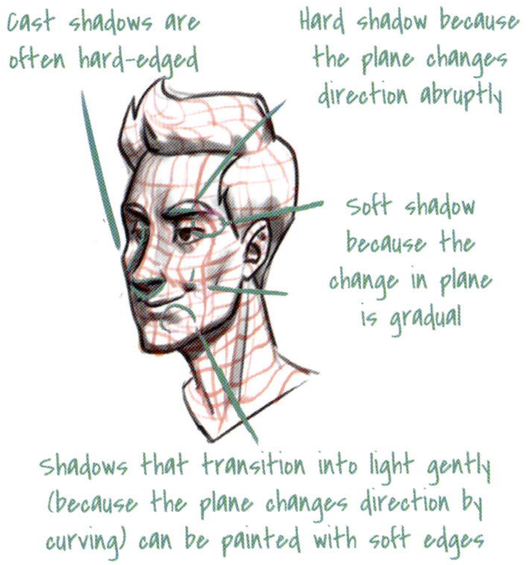

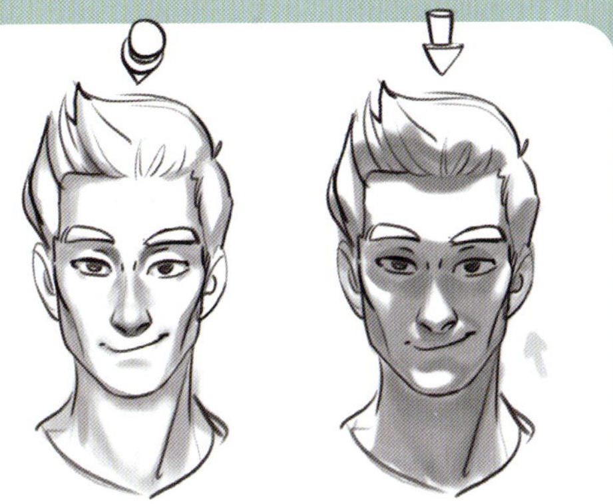

LIT FROM THE FRONT

LIT FROM ABOVE

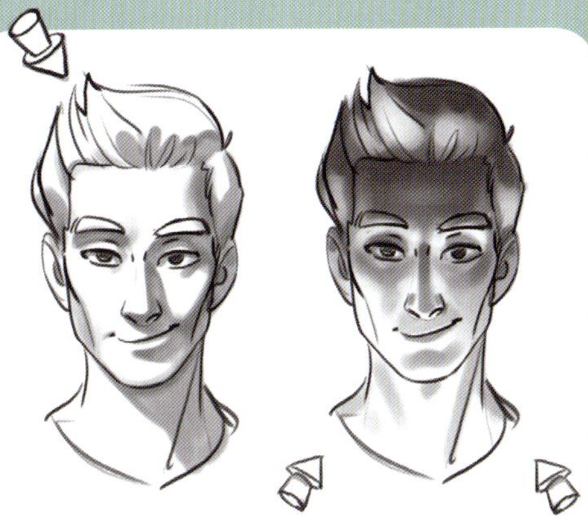

LIT FROM TOP LEFT

LIT FROM BELOW

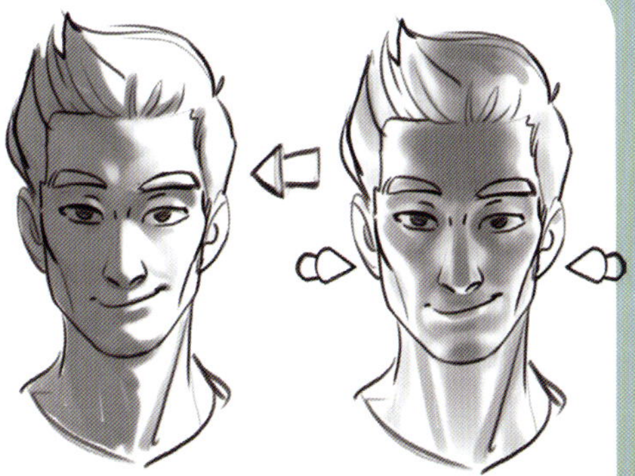

LIT FROM THE RIGHT SIDE

BACK LIT

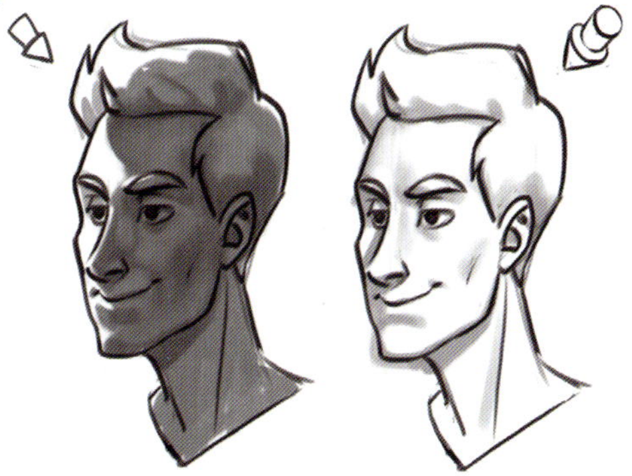

RIM LIGHT

LIT FROM TOP RIGHT

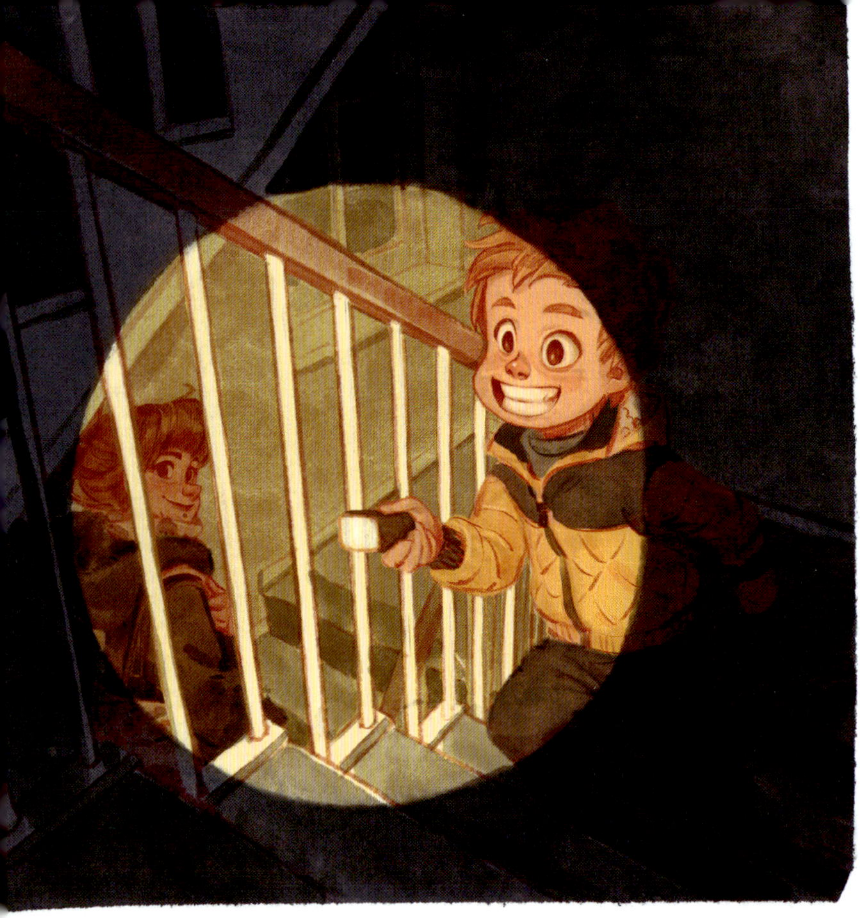

FLASHLIGHT

My son loves to go up the stairs to our apartment in the dark with his flashlight...

DISAPPOINTMENT

...so I always pray no-one turns on the lights that stay on automatically for a couple of minutes

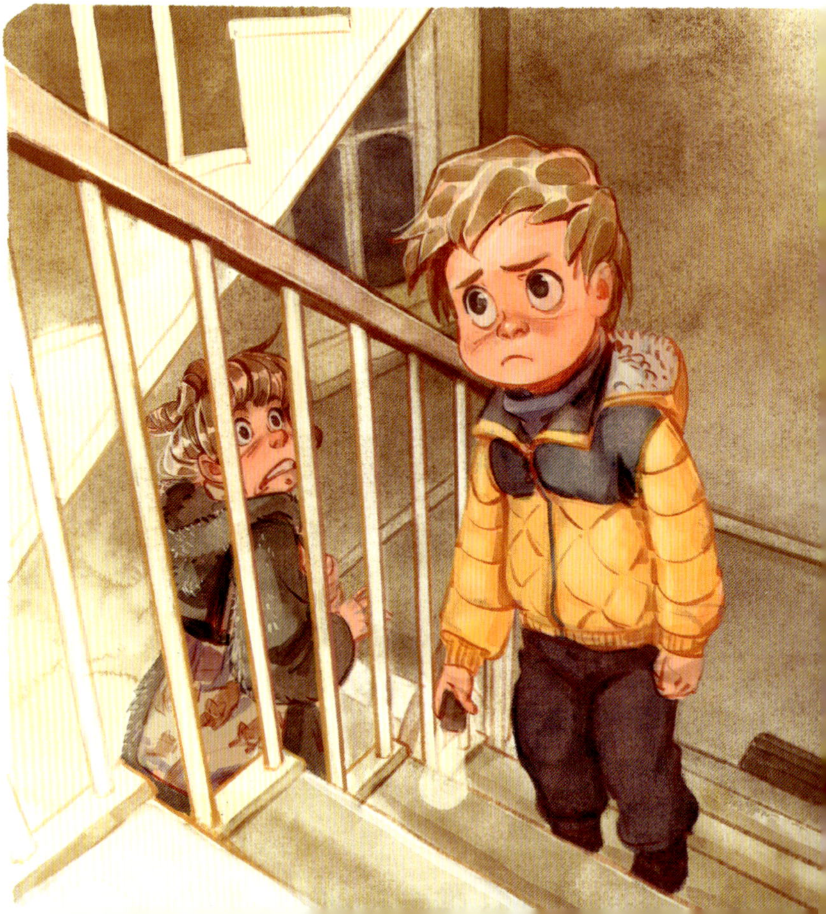

INDIRECT LIGHTING

Indirect (reflected) lighting may seem as though it is just a small area within the subject of lighting, but it's an incredibly fun and powerful aspect of shading.

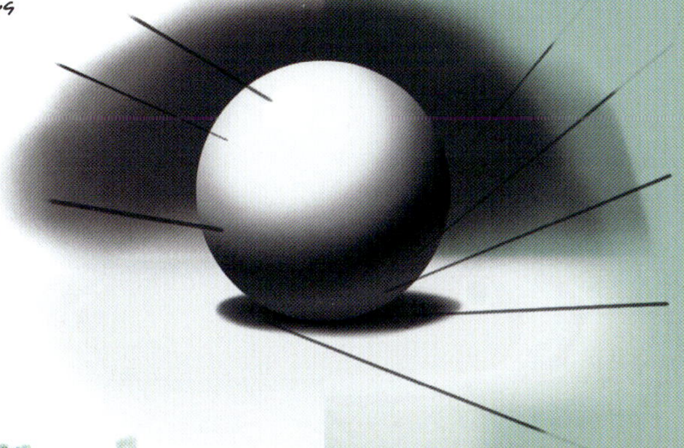

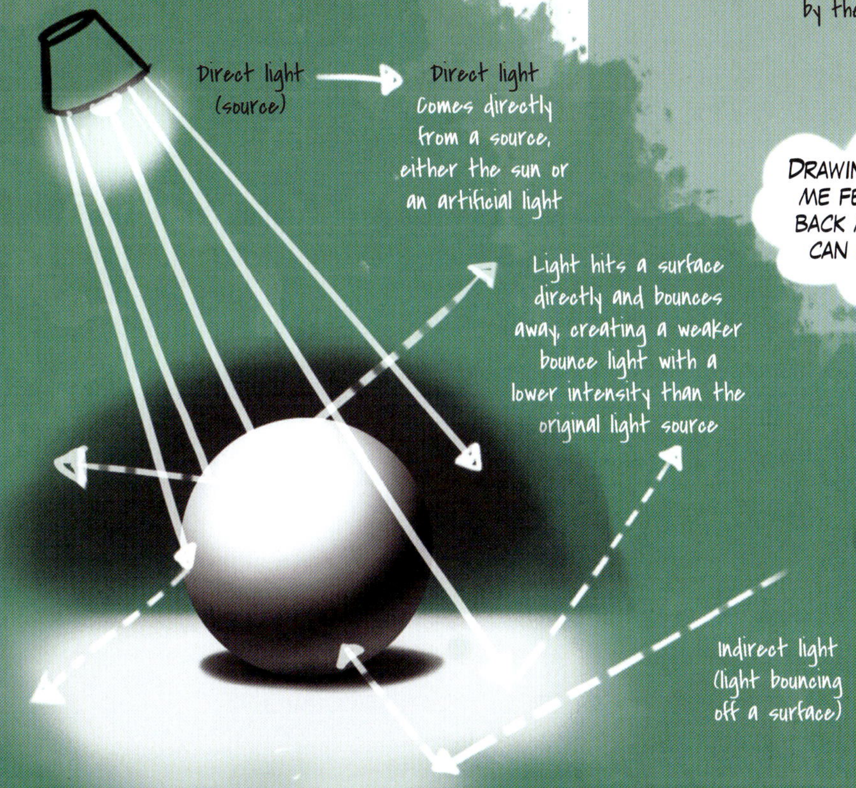

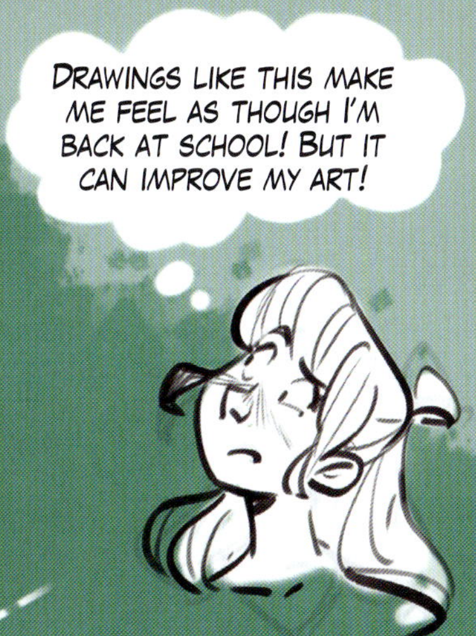

APPLYING INDIRECT LIGHT

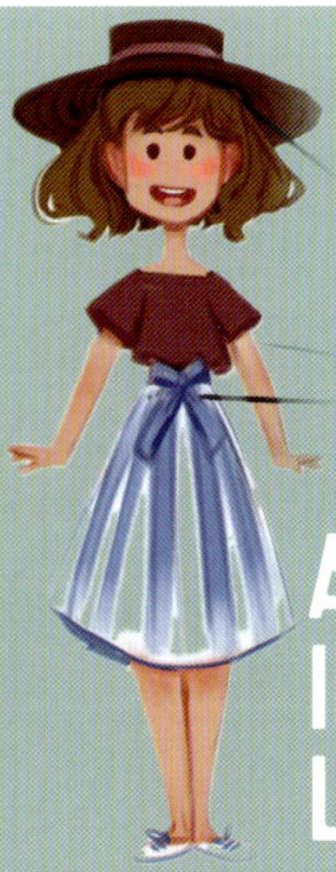

Start with a character painted in local colors on a white canvas.

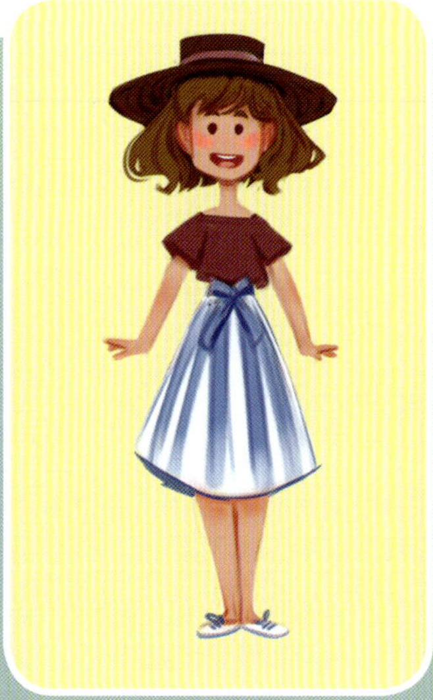

Apply a colored background. This works fine for certain projects...

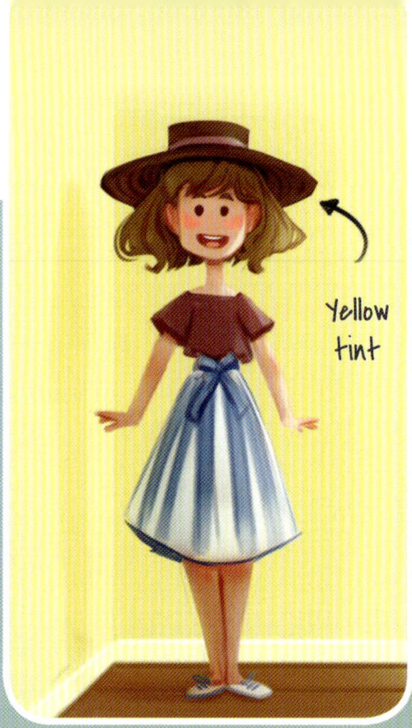

...but place the character in an environment and it will need to be slightly reflected in your character, as though realistically lit.

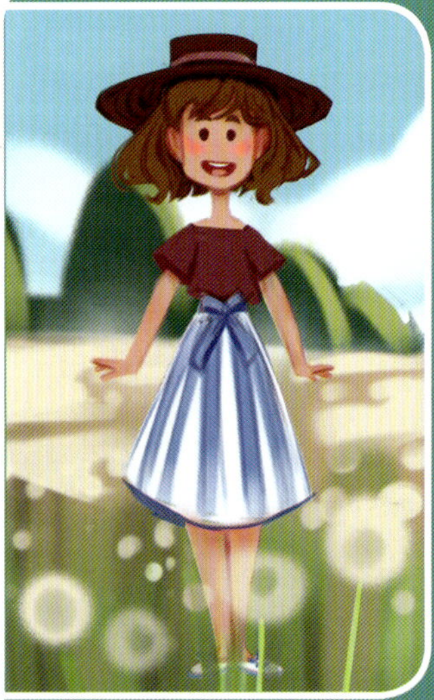

LOCAL COLORS ONLY

GREEN TONES REFLECTED ONTO THE CHARACTER

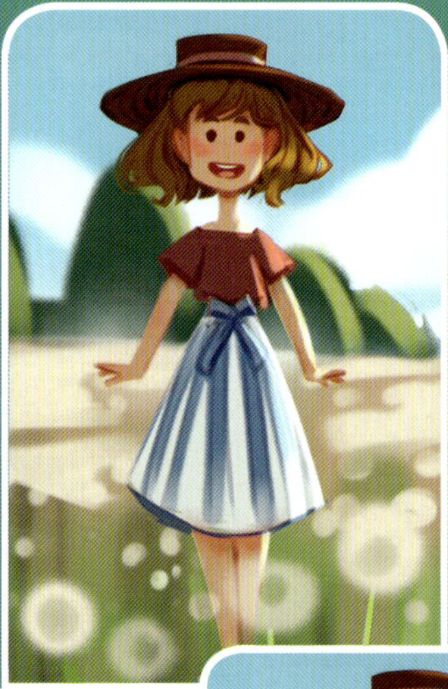

The character is facing away from the greatest source of light, but is lit by lots of reflected green light bouncing around. So, the character will become ever so slightly tinted with green light and blend into the scene harmoniously.

Green 30% opacity set to Soft Light to add overall green light

Green 20% opacity set to Multiply to darken the character a bit as she is in shadow with her back to the light

Blue reflected from the sky (color picked from sky, layer set to normal and opacity 30%)

The legs appear even greener due to being so close to the light-flooded green grass

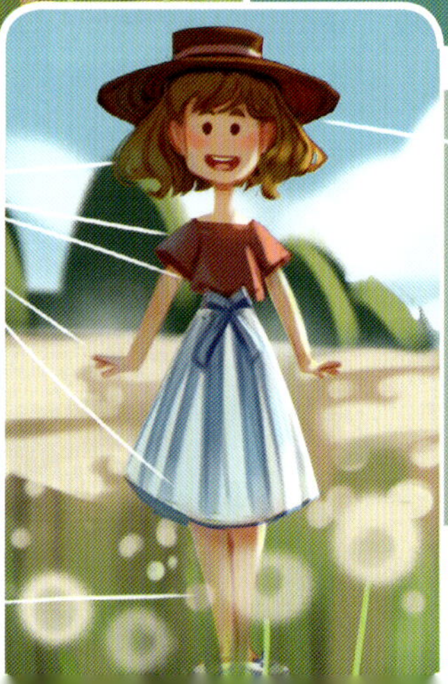

Orange light of the hair bouncing off the inner hat (color picked from hair, layer set to Soft Light, and opacity 30%)

RIM LIGHT

Rim light is one of my favorite types of lighting because when used in abstraction it creates appealing results quickly. When used in character design work, rim light provides a wonderful contrast and helps to emphasize the character, helping them stand out from their surroundings.

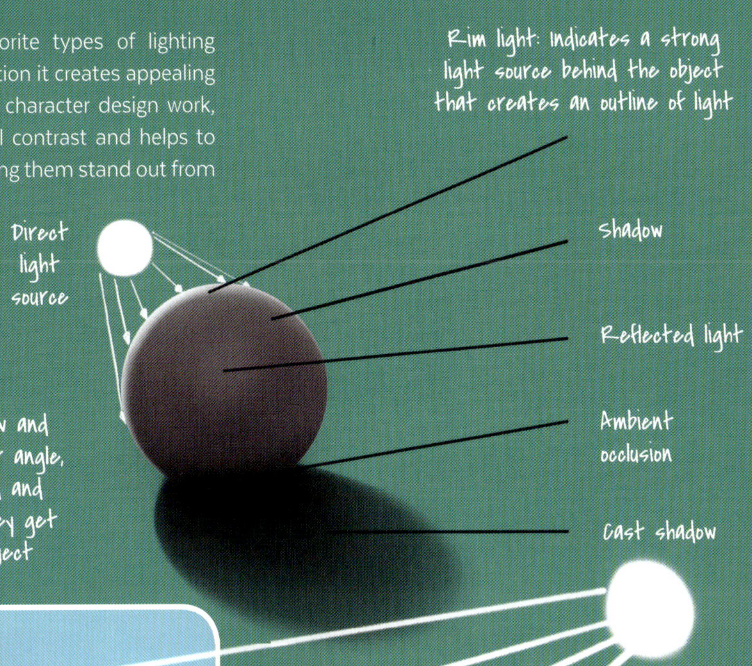

When the light source is low and hitting the object at a lower angle, the shadows are elongated and become more diffused as they get further away from the object

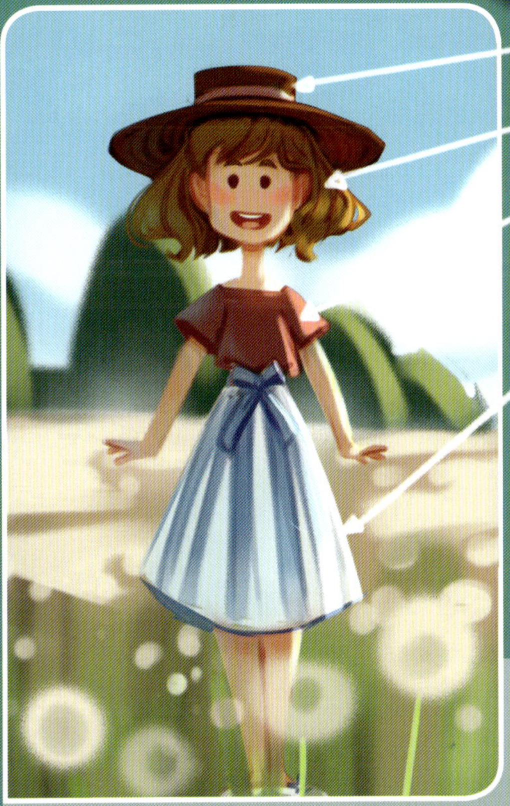

Rounded forms such as the skirt catch more light because more of it is facing the light source

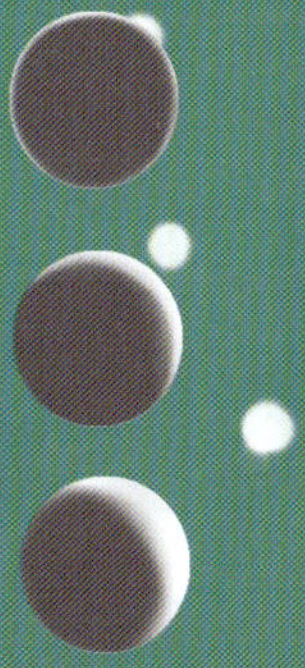

Light source almost directly behind the object

Light source behind and above the object

Light source nearly parallel to and above the object

In this example, although the lighting is mostly created by bounce light, some direct light causes subtle rim light. As the direct light hits the side of the character, the rim light is broader than an average rim light from immediately behind the character, and so lights up more of the side of the character.

APPLYING RIM LIGHT

ORIGINAL

There was no rim light in the original as I wanted to keep this illustration well-lit and quick and simple.

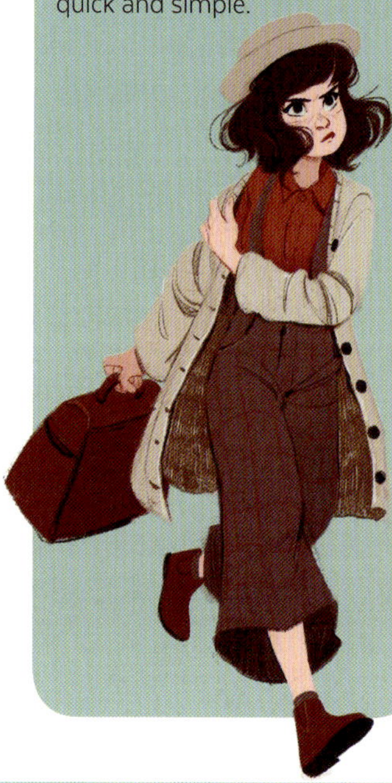

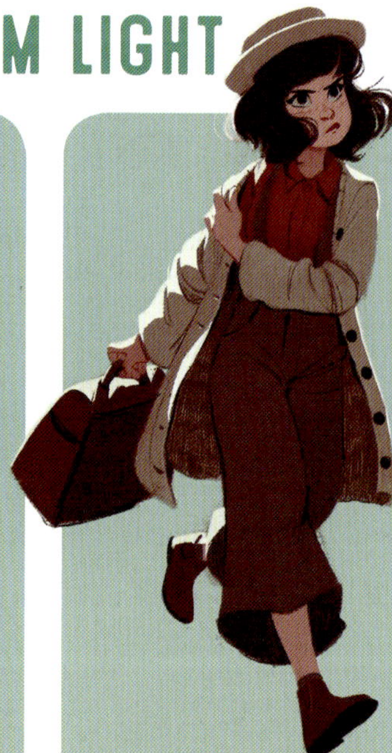

HARD-EDGED RIM LIGHT

By darkening the figure and adding a rim light, I introduce some drama and quick refinement to the character.

DIFFUSED RIM LIGHT

Depending on the style I want to achieve, I sometimes soften the rim light a bit. This is best done with a mask after defining it properly, but here I simply erased some of the light with a soft brush.

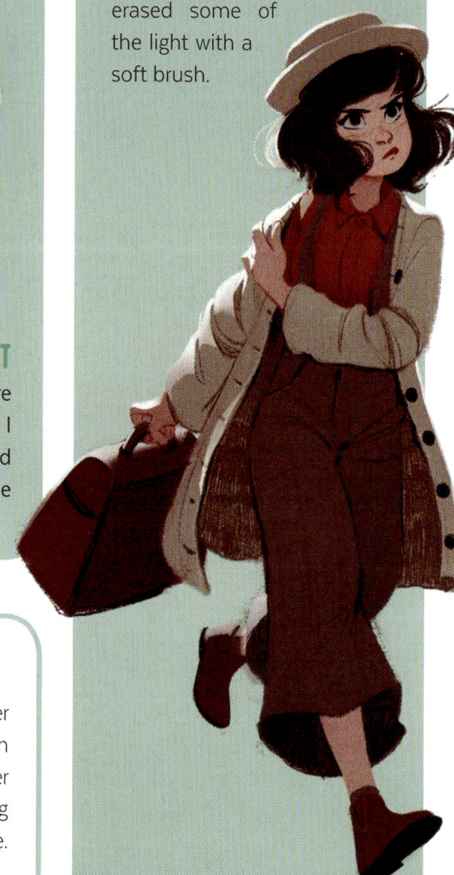

ADVICE AND PITFALLS:

Understand where your light source is coming from and keep the light consistent, following the behavior of real light sources.

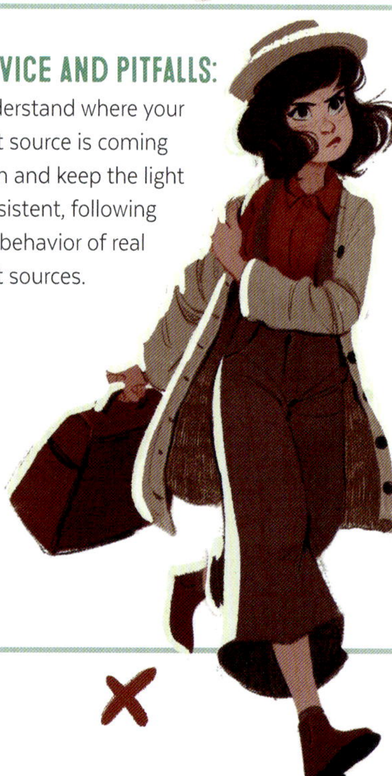

Don't follow the outer shape completely with the rim lighting, consider which planes are facing the light source.

For a more organic and realistic finish, choose a side for the rim light to appear on — only when the light source is exactly behind the character will the rim light be equally visible on both sides.

"BY DARKENING THE FIGURE AND ADDING A RIM LIGHT, I INTRODUCE SOME DRAMA"

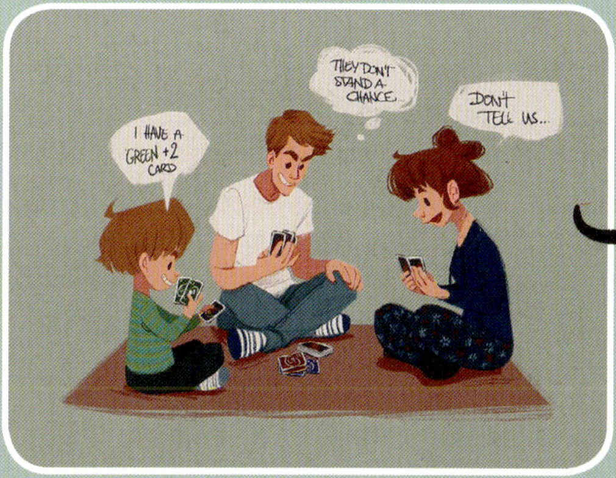

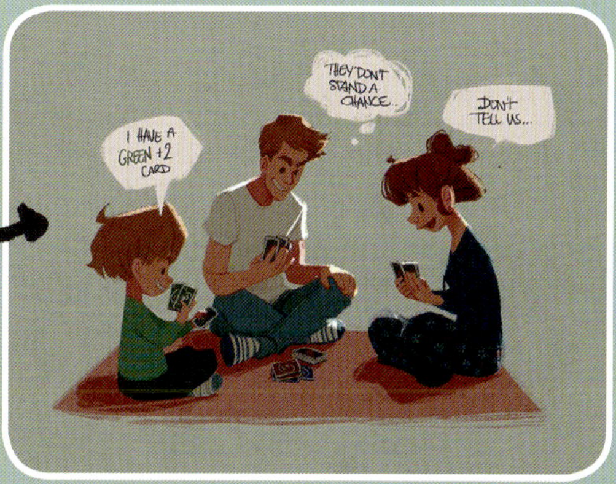

This piece was initially painted with flat colors and detailed with a few outlines

After darkening the characters and adding a subtle rim light, the design feels more complete

Gentle shading with bounce light with hard-edged rim light give this design a wonderful contrast

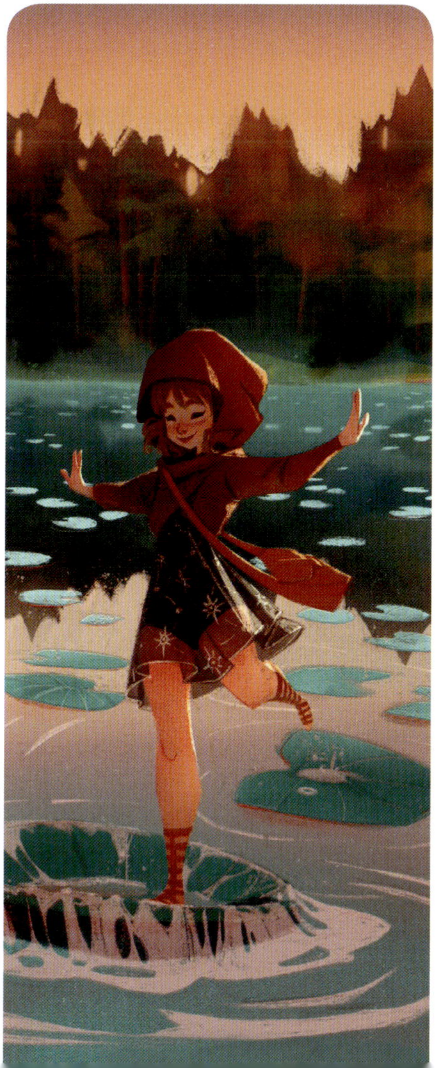

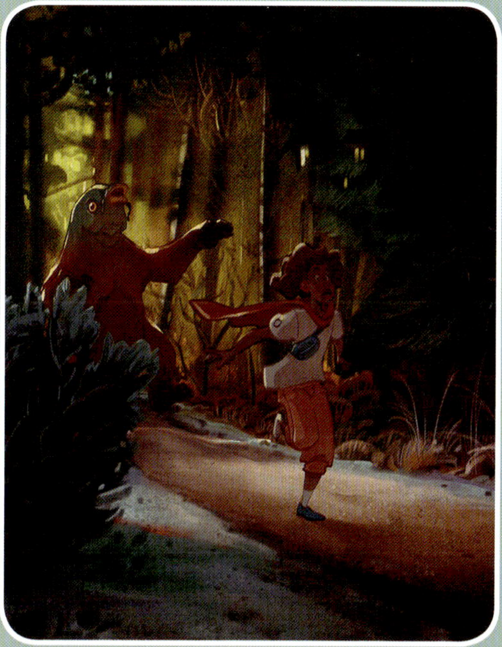

The background of this design indicates a strong light at the back, so rim lighting is appropriate. Here, it also helps to separate the characters from the background

I like to use rim lighting in pieces with very abstract styles too. Extensive shading is unnecessary, so a rim light gives this piece some finesse

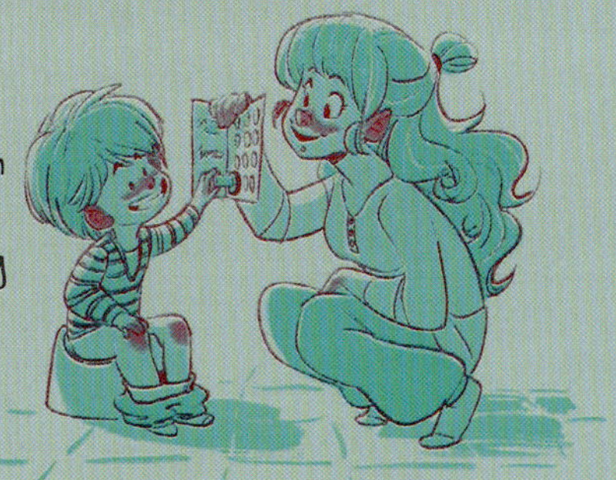

TWO LIGHT SOURCES

When is it best to introduce a second light source? A second light source could be seen on a moon-lit street with glowing street signs, or perhaps in a room with additional light coming from a computer, which changes the color of the light. The situations and possibilities are endless and always create interesting and challenging lighting situations.

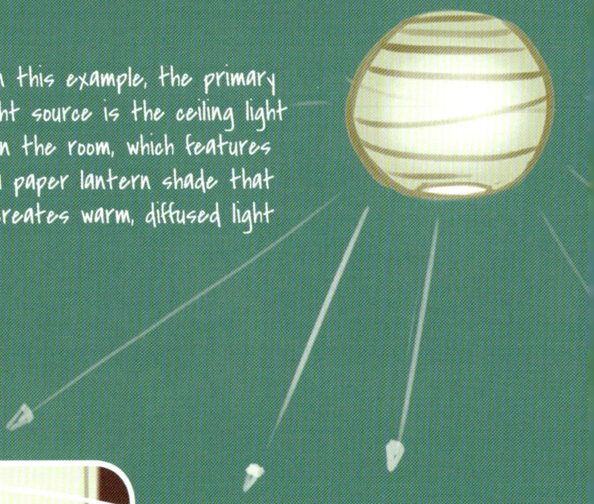

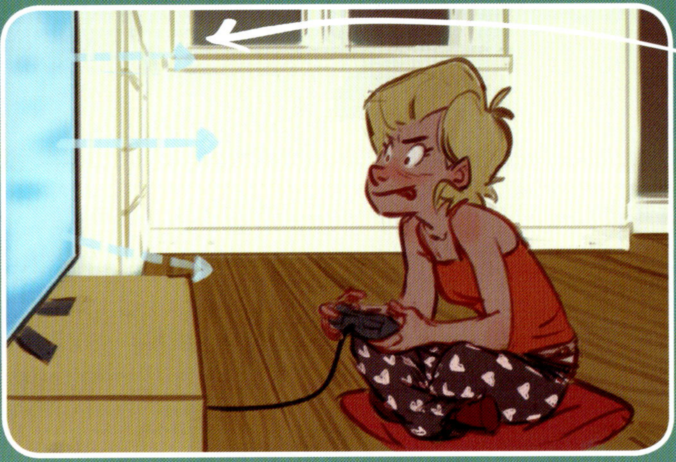

As always, I start with local colors for the character and background. Overall, I choose a warm color palette punctuated by a blue light for the television, to create greater contrast.

When including two light sources, it helps the clarity of the design if one source is greater than the other, so that one light source becomes the primary and the other, the secondary source. Here, the primary source of light here is the ceiling light, which bathes the whole room in soft, warm light. So, I begin by adding shading as though the ceiling light is the only light source.

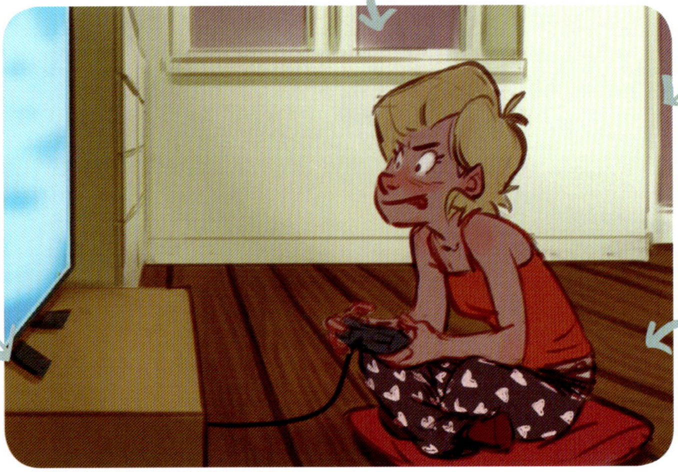

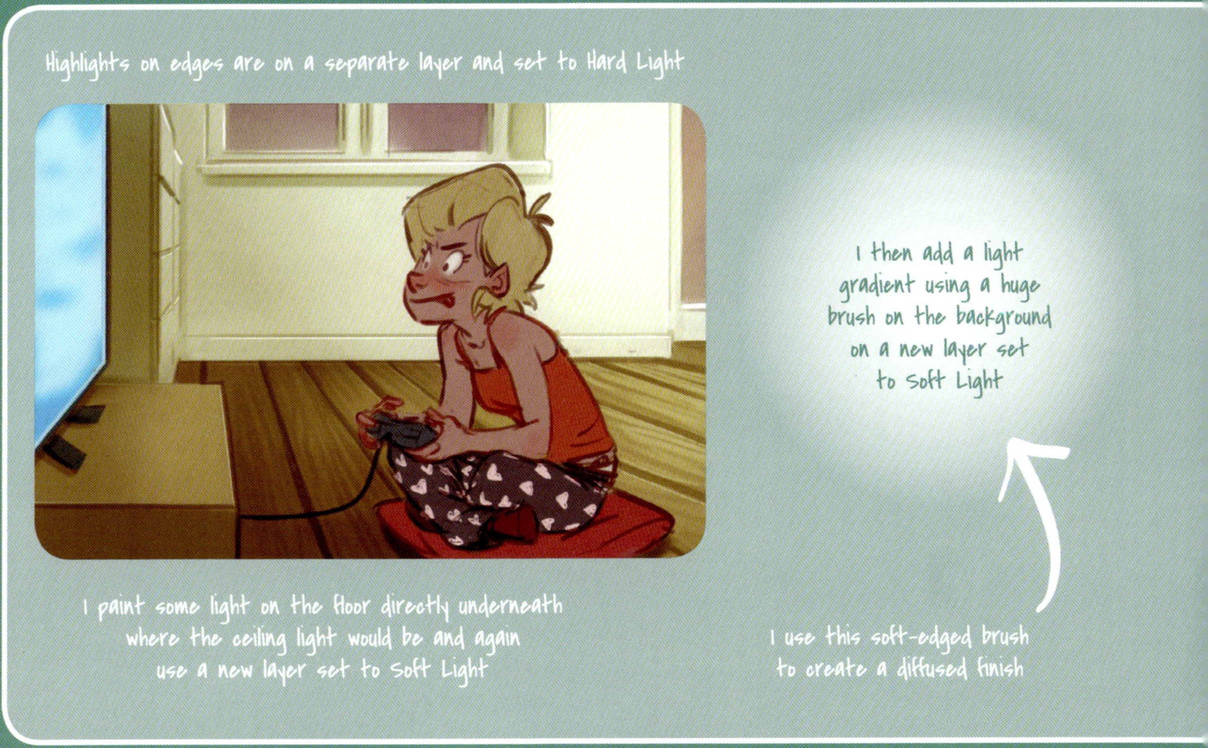

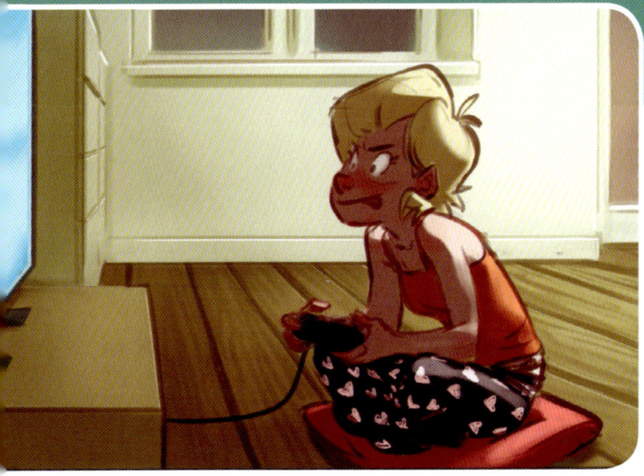

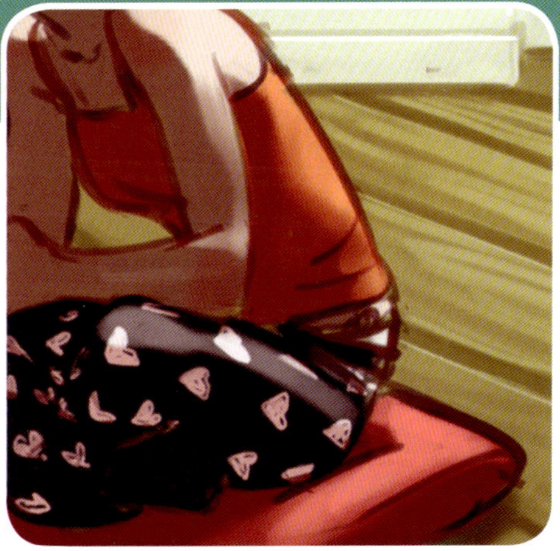

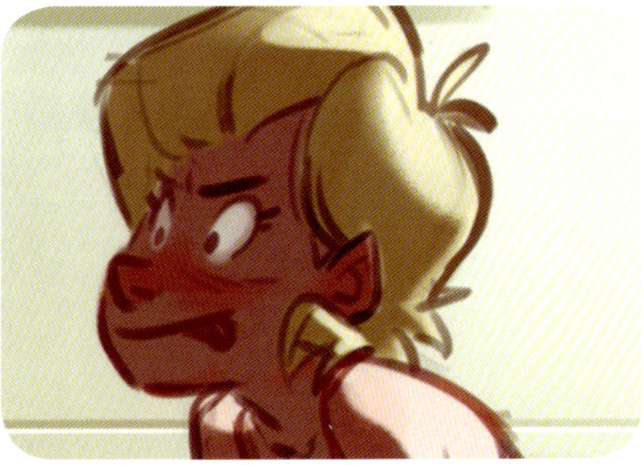

Next, I try a new method of shading the character I saw @iruse use on Instagram. I add a curves adjustment layer to the character group with a clipping mask. I pull up the curve to lighten the character and then fill the mask with black. I paint the light with white within the mask. The shadow is created by reversing the selection and pulling the curve down. I like the light and shadow colors this effect produces.

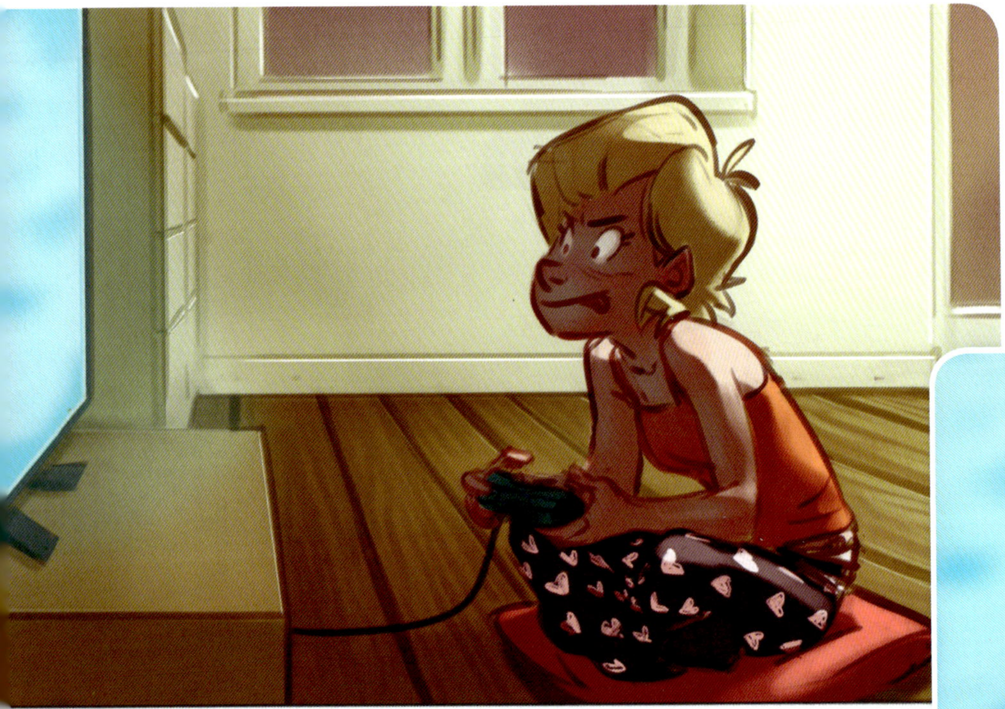

I also add a glow to the TV screen (turquoise, with low opacity)

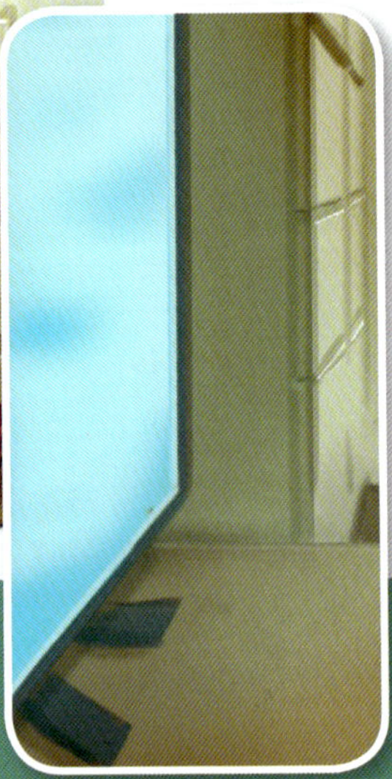

Finally, to add the second light source, I use the speckled brush to gently paint some turquoise light on the face

On a new layer, using the same setting, I paint in some details and highlights

I also paint a subtle cold light on the floor

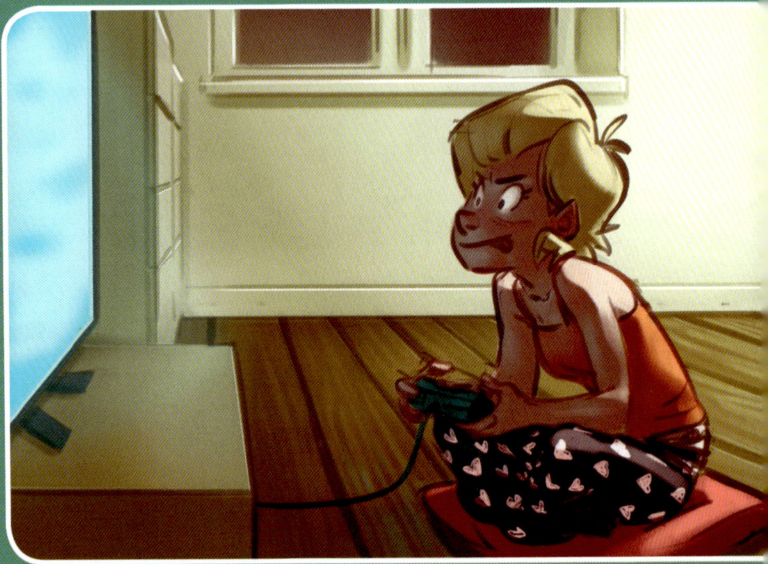

Color used for all the cold light painting

I believe two light sources work best when they are not fighting for attention and one only slightly brightens the shadow area, much like with bounce light but a bit more direct and orderly.

CHILDHOOD FORT

Who didn't love cozying up and reading in a self-made fort?!

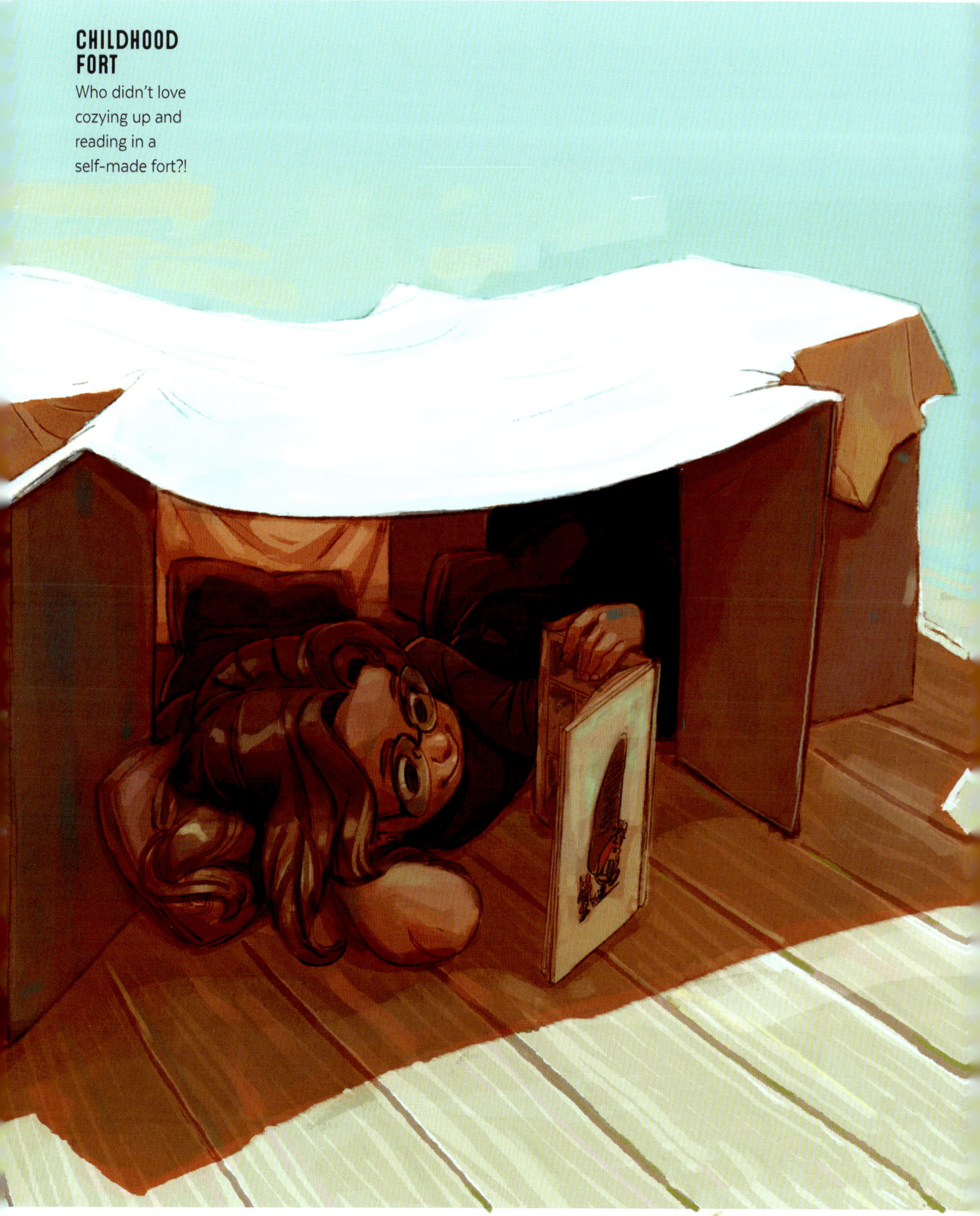

CHARACTER AS LIGHT SOURCE

In unusual situations and fantastical narratives, the light source can originate from the character themselves! Here, my character discovers a light emanating from their hand.

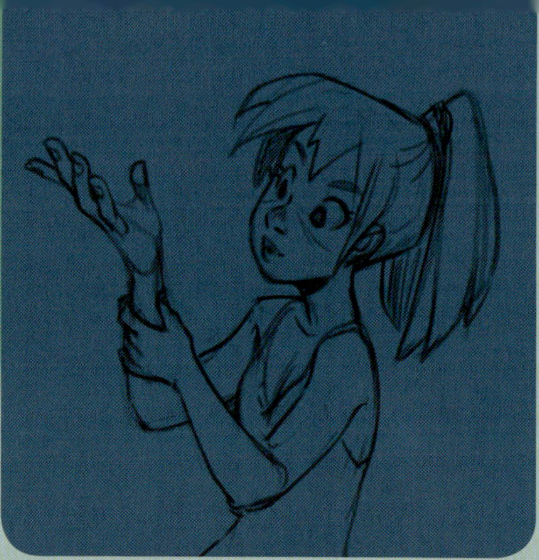

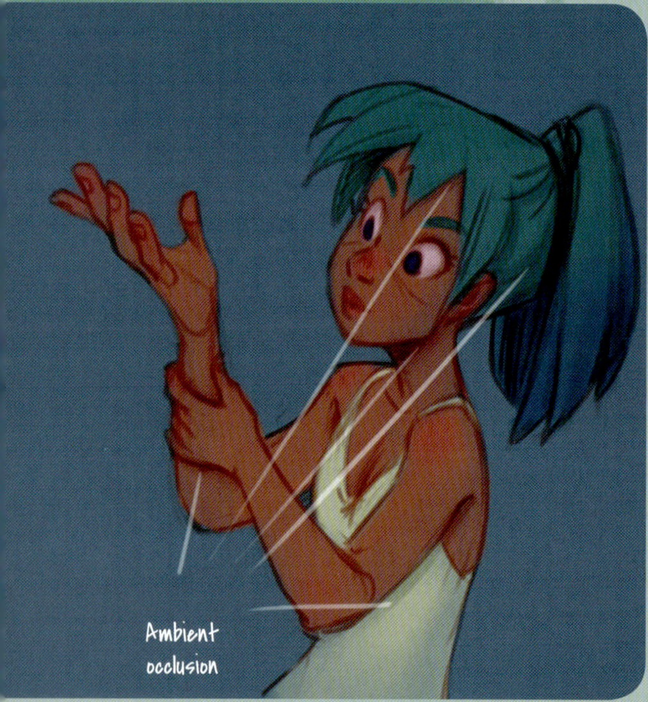

I always add shadow/subtle ambient occlusion in the crevices where light doesn't reach as much.

I roughly apply flat colors with a slightly textured brush, to allow some of the background color to show through. I also add some blush to the cheeks.

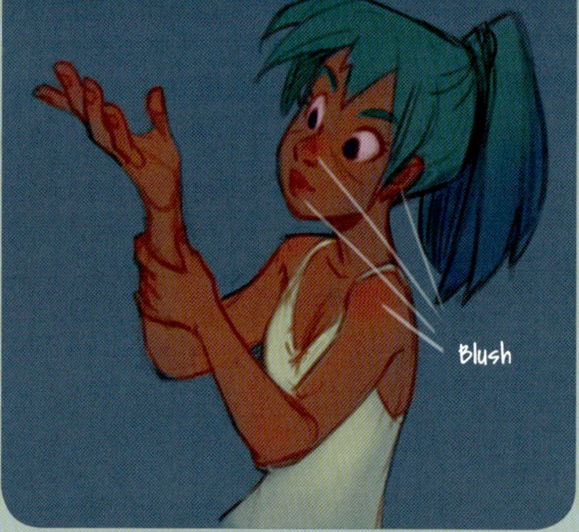

To develop the color of the glowing hand, I use the layer effect Vivid Light with a pale pink hue and build up the glow slowly on new layers, starting with a big brush to add a gentle glow.

Next, using the diffused light of night lights as reference, I continue building color with the brush, making the brush smaller to paint the details.

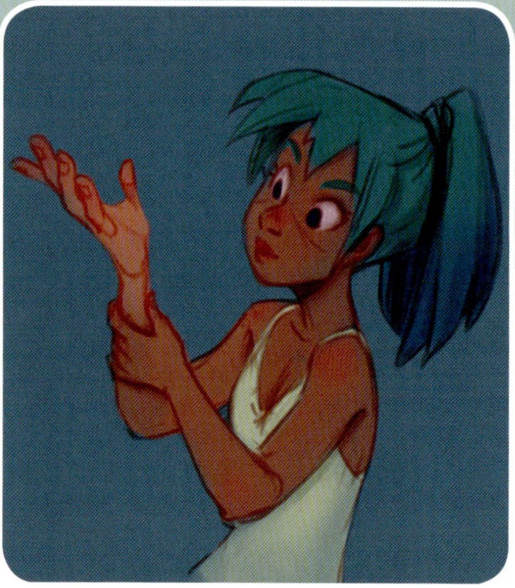

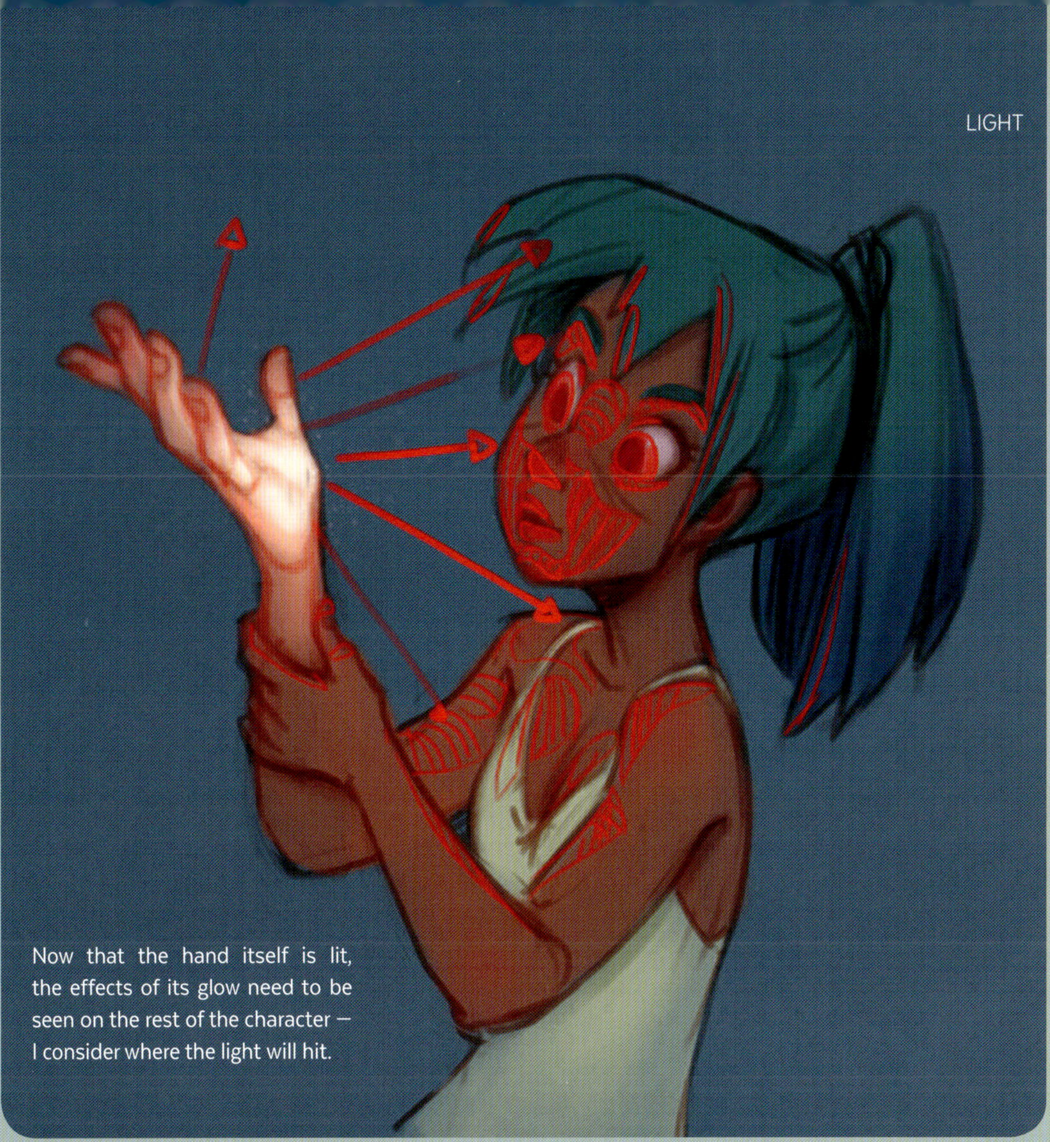

Now that the hand itself is lit, the effects of its glow need to be seen on the rest of the character – I consider where the light will hit.

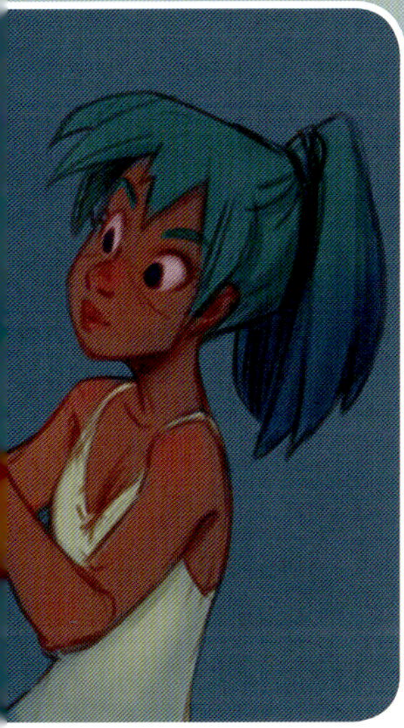

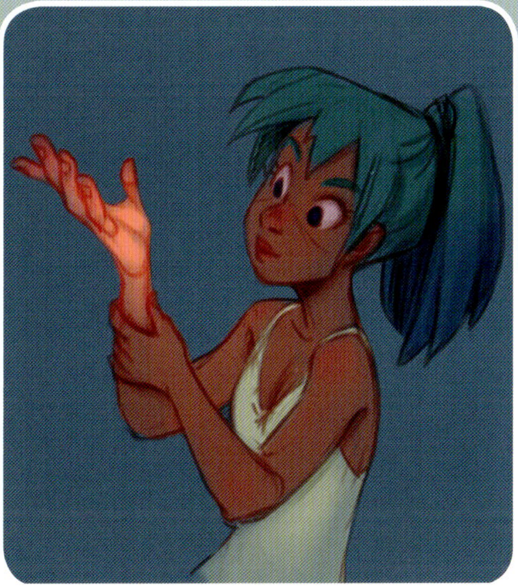

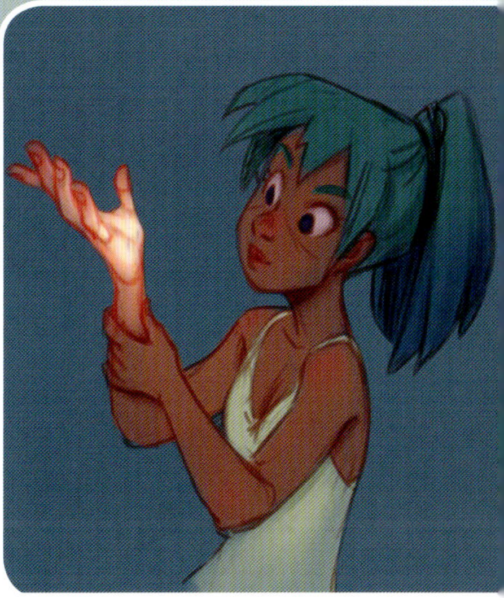

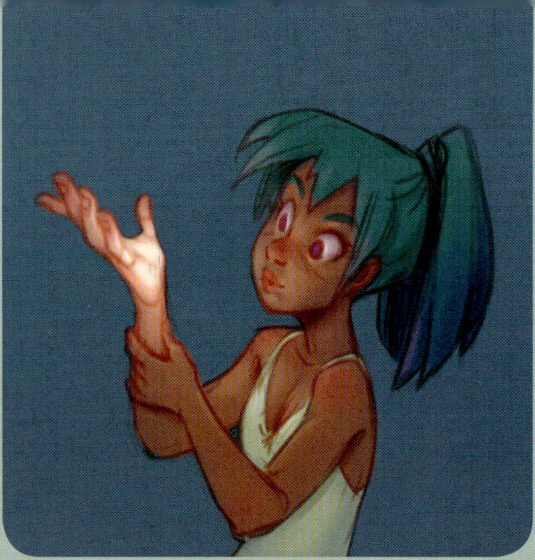

I gently build the reflected glow on the face. When painting realistic lighting on a stylized character it can take some time to find the right shading style to suit.

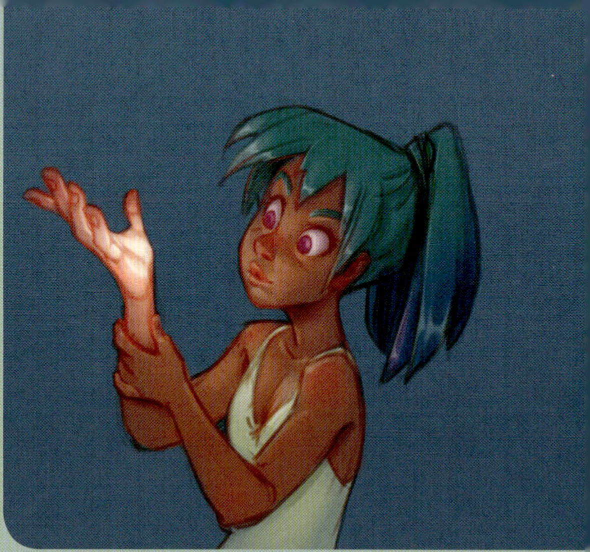

After deciding on the overall shading direction, I begin detailing – I highlight the appropriate edges and smooth out others.

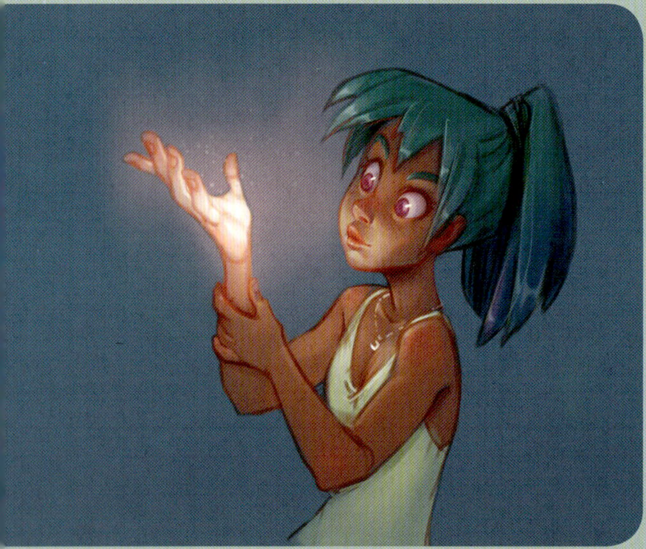

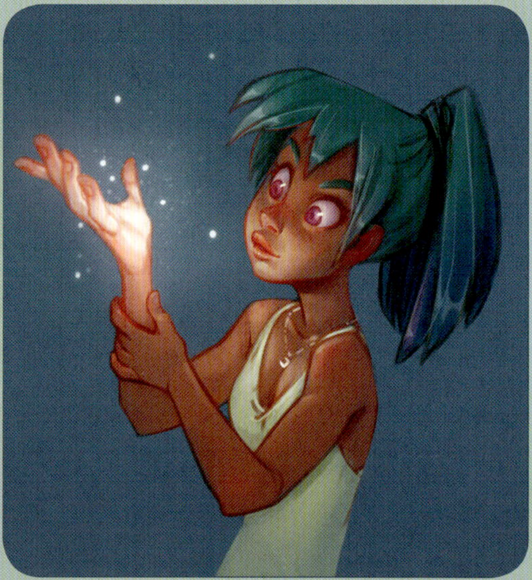

In the final stages, I flatten the character and duplicate it. I then add layer effects to enhance the lighting and contrast.

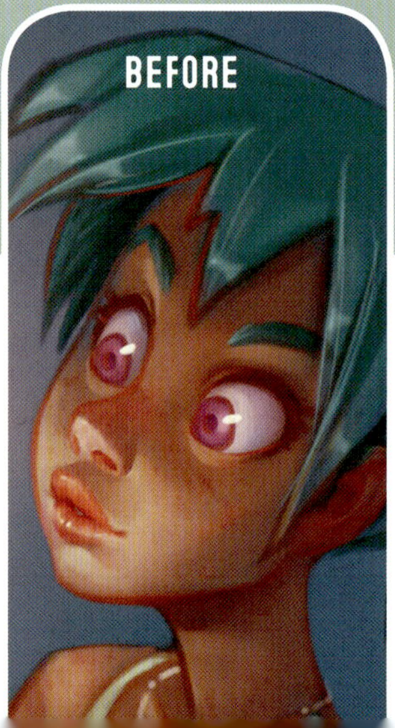

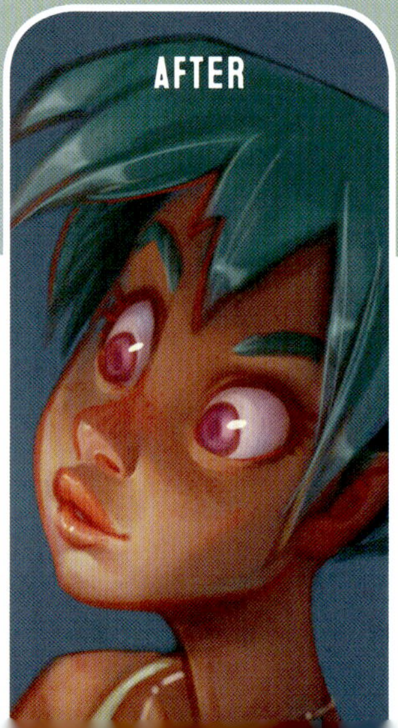

I continue to paint the face but find that I don't like the effect, so I alter the facial area once more and finally add a loose magical particle effect.

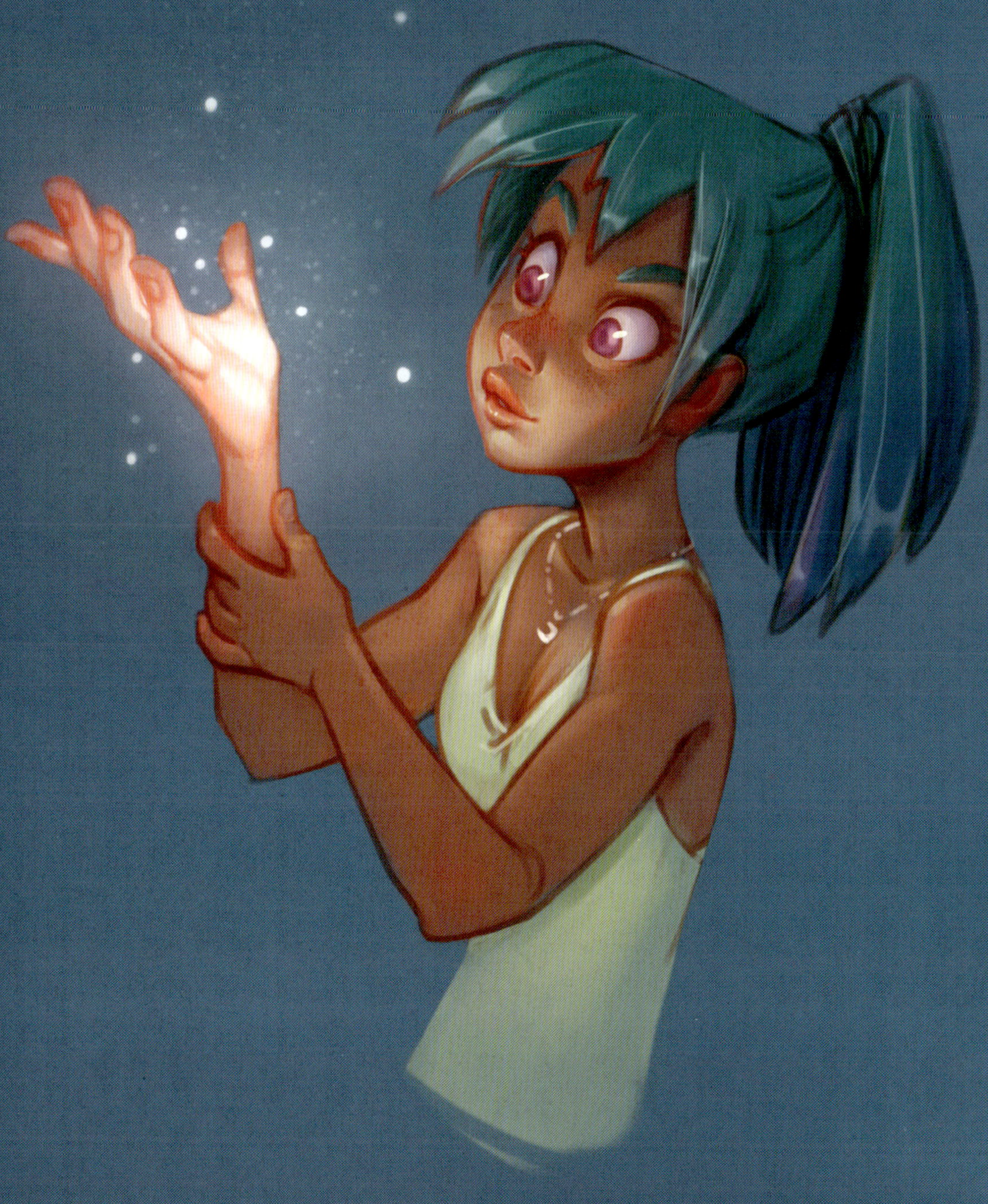

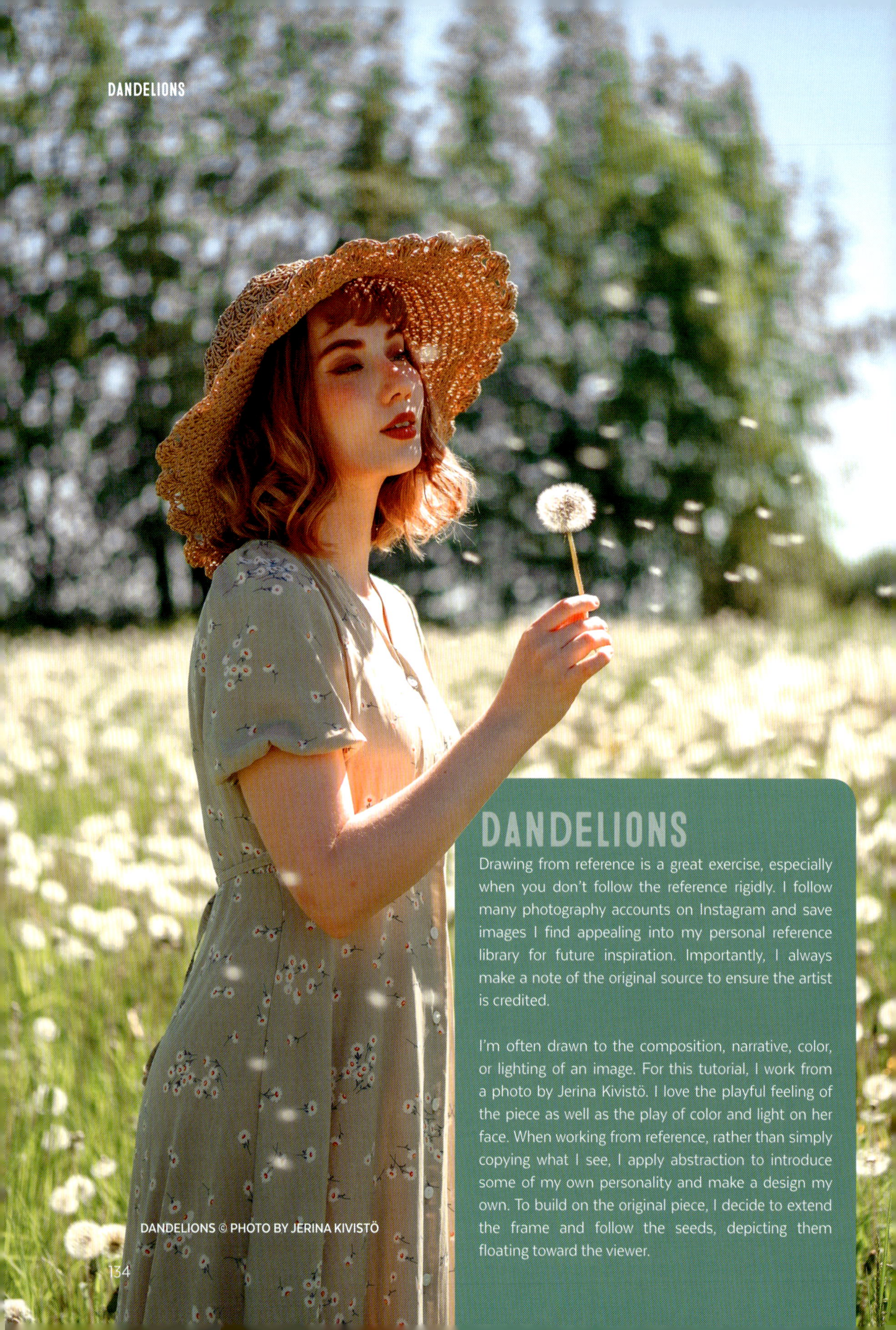

DANDELIONS © PHOTO BY JERINA KIVISTÖ

DANDELIONS

Drawing from reference is a great exercise, especially when you don't follow the reference rigidly. I follow many photography accounts on Instagram and save images I find appealing into my personal reference library for future inspiration. Importantly, I always make a note of the original source to ensure the artist is credited.

I'm often drawn to the composition, narrative, color, or lighting of an image. For this tutorial, I work from a photo by Jerina Kivistö. I love the playful feeling of the piece as well as the play of color and light on her face. When working from reference, rather than simply copying what I see, I apply abstraction to introduce some of my own personality and make a design my own. To build on the original piece, I decide to extend the frame and follow the seeds, depicting them floating toward the viewer.

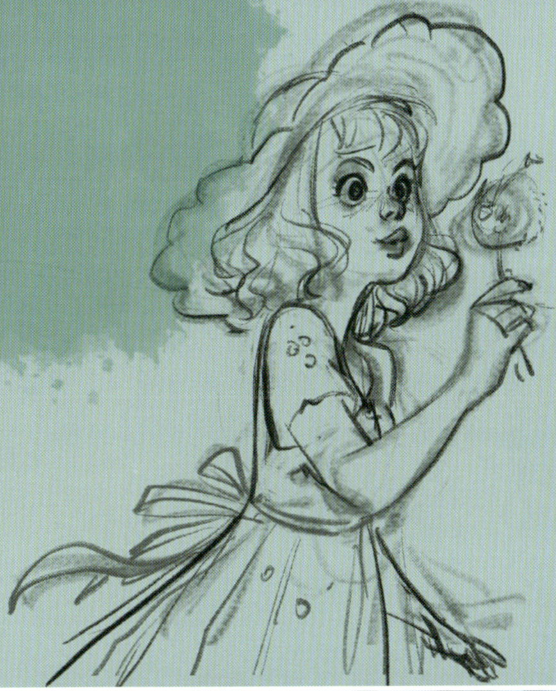

FIRST SKETCH

To enhance the movement in the blowing action shown in the reference, I depict the character leaning toward the dandelion. I also change the portrait format to landscape to give the floating seeds and background some space. The new landscape orientation also allows room for displaying more of the field in the background, to which I intend to introduce a slope in order to add dynamism.

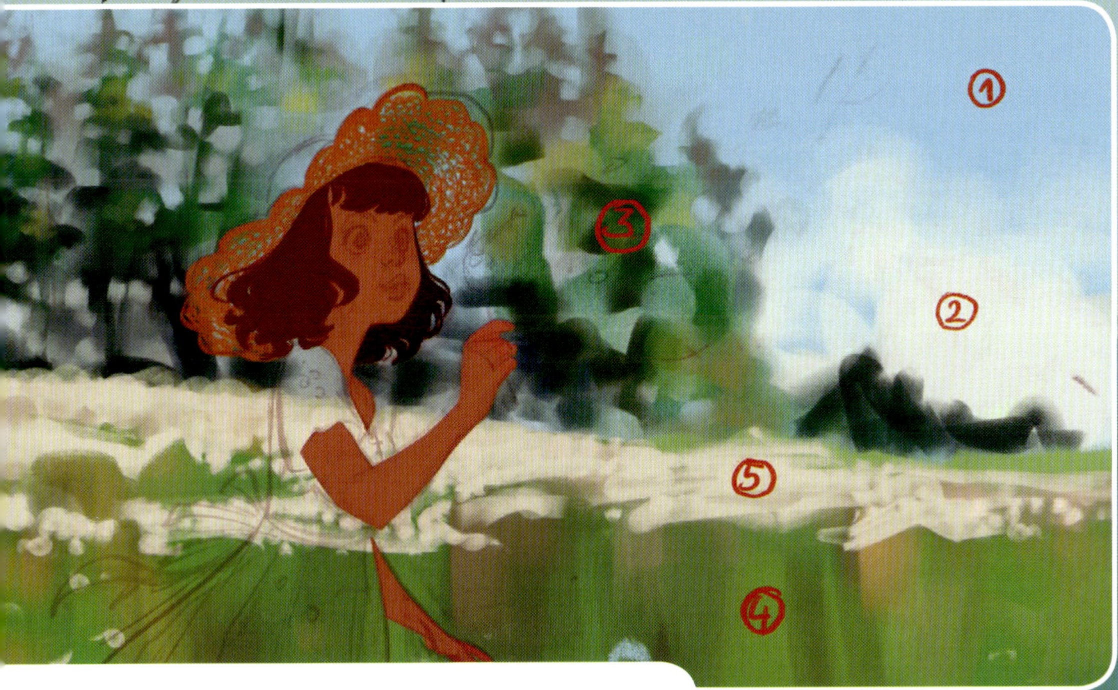

BETTER TO BE SAFE THAN SORRY!

When working on a commercial job, make sure to either get the rights from the image owner to use the reference, or change it enough for the new design to stand on its own. I recommend using several different references to mix styles and avoid replicating any key elements.

WORKING BACK TO FRONT

The next step is layering! Starting with the sky, I add each new background element on its own layer. I roughly paint in the colors I can see in the reference image.

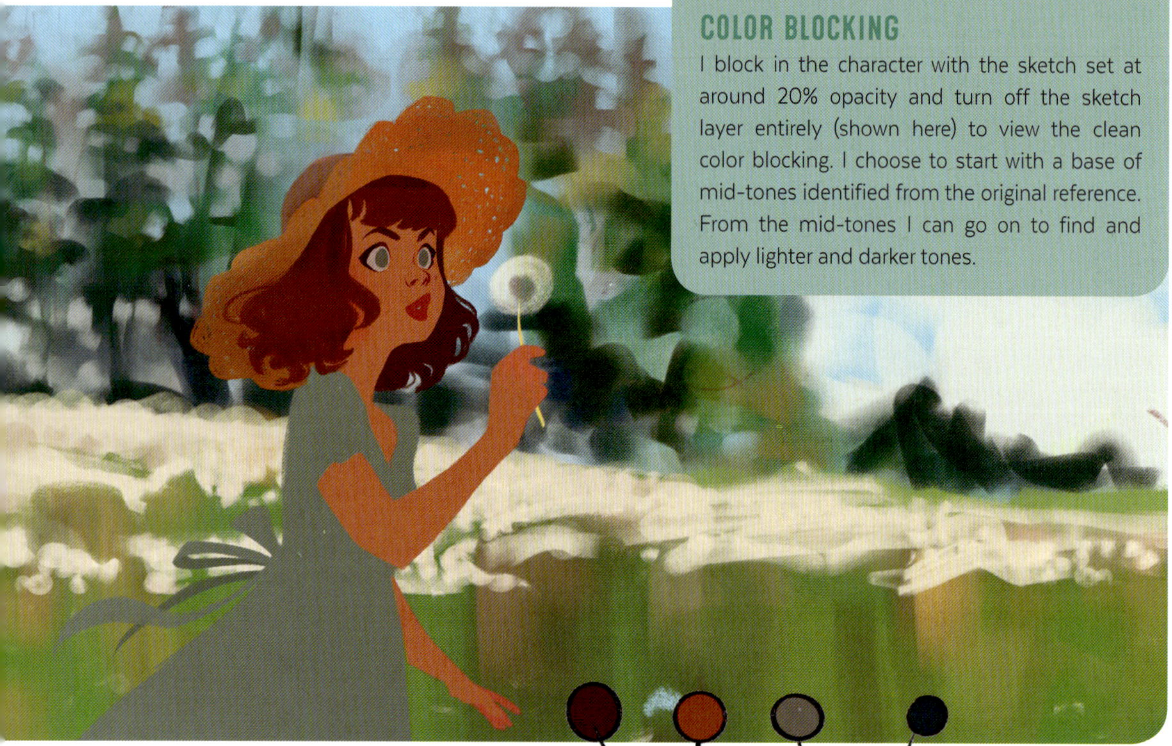

COLOR BLOCKING

I block in the character with the sketch set at around 20% opacity and turn off the sketch layer entirely (shown here) to view the clean color blocking. I choose to start with a base of mid-tones identified from the original reference. From the mid-tones I can go on to find and apply lighter and darker tones.

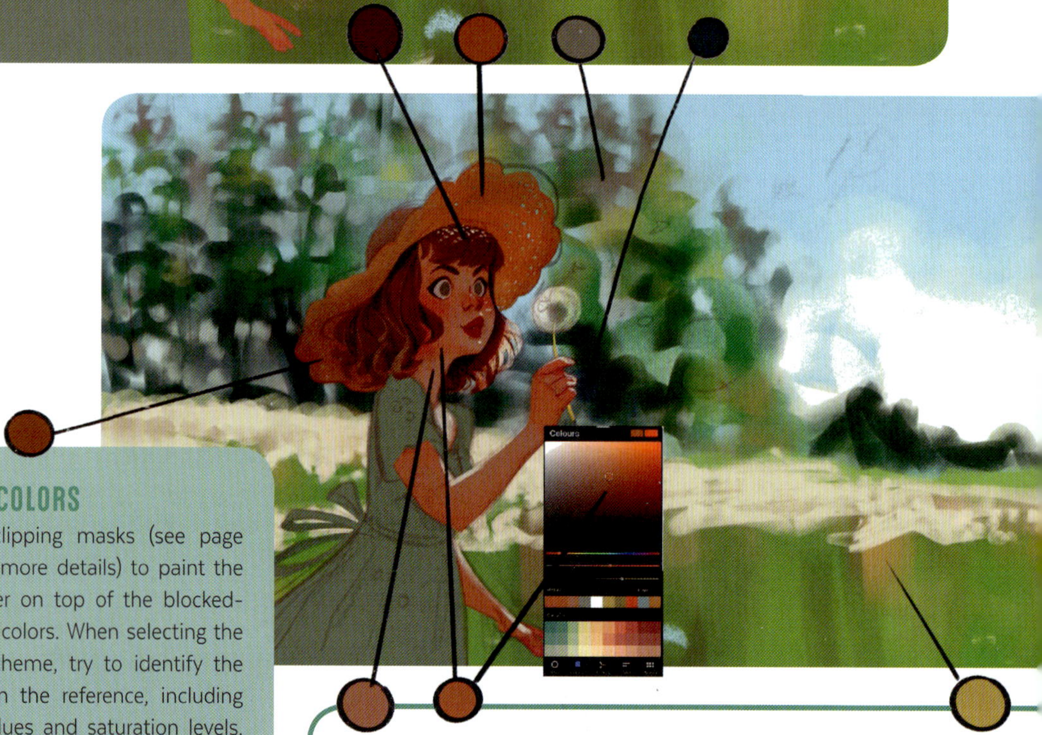

TRUE COLORS

I use clipping masks (see page 146 for more details) to paint the character on top of the blocked-in base colors. When selecting the color scheme, try to identify the colors in the reference, including their values and saturation levels. Colors can act unexpectedly when combined – for example, a desaturated rose-pink color next to a more orange tone can look almost blue!

PRACTICE MAKES PERFECT!

After years of practice and experience, I can identify and match colors without the use of the Color Picker tool. It takes time, but selecting colors without additional tools will train the eye to identify the nuances of colors and understand color relationships.

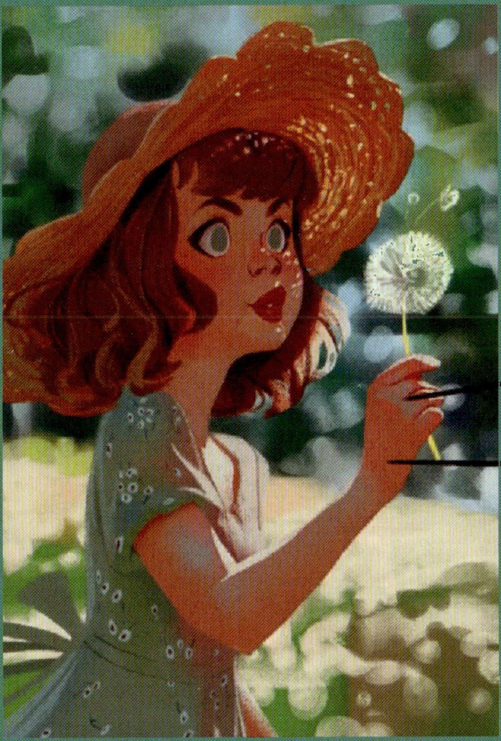

PRIMARY LIGHT

I start to add details to the character and consider the lighting of the piece. The reference is helpful as it demonstrates the natural lighting situation clearly. I introduce bounce light – a green tone on her dress reflected from the grass, and blue reflected from the sky – as well as a strong light from the side and back from the sun.

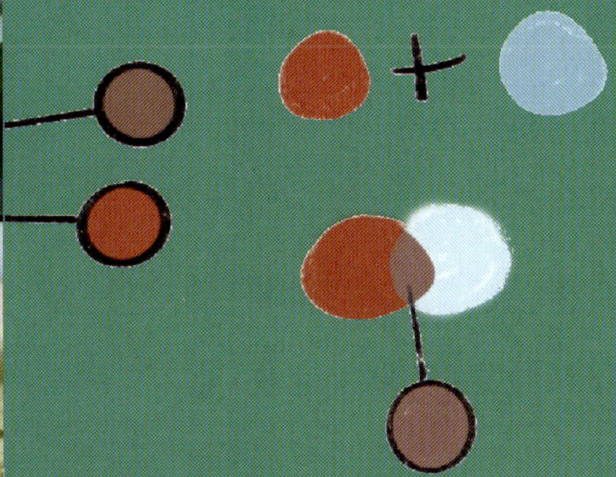

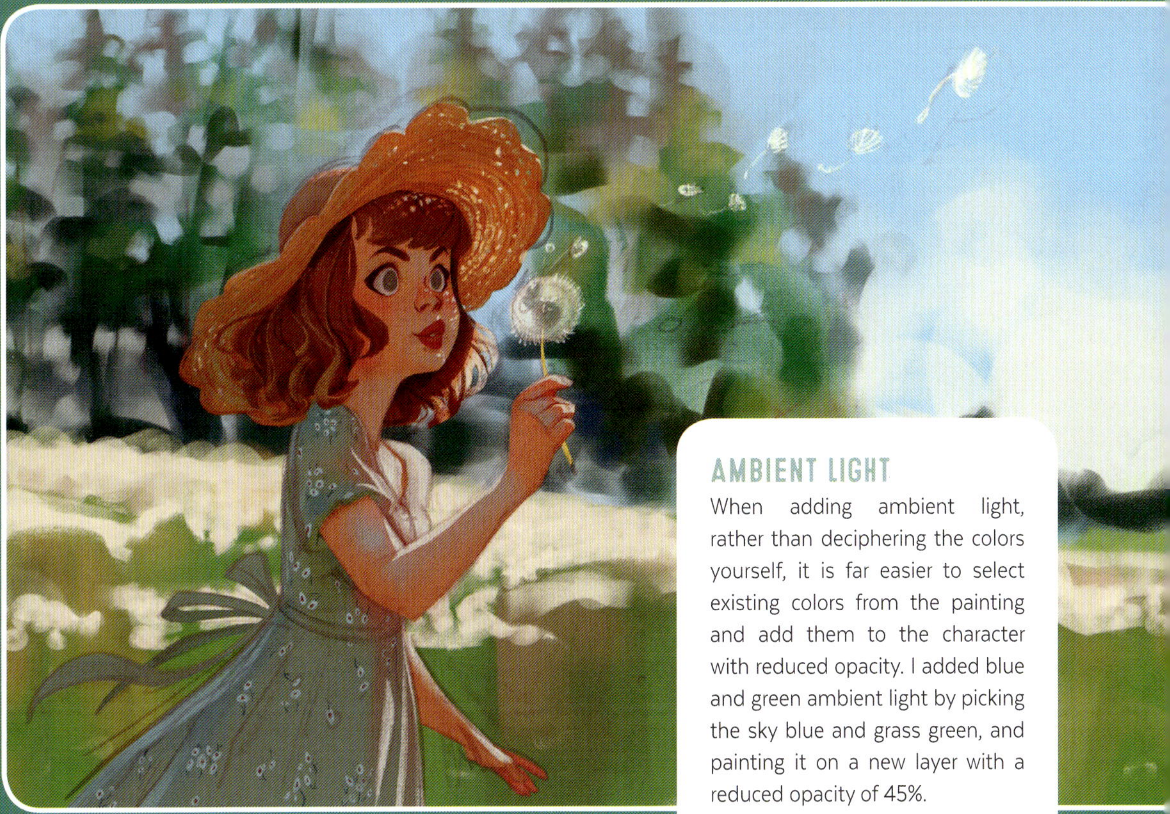

AMBIENT LIGHT

When adding ambient light, rather than deciphering the colors yourself, it is far easier to select existing colors from the painting and add them to the character with reduced opacity. I added blue and green ambient light by picking the sky blue and grass green, and painting it on a new layer with a reduced opacity of 45%.

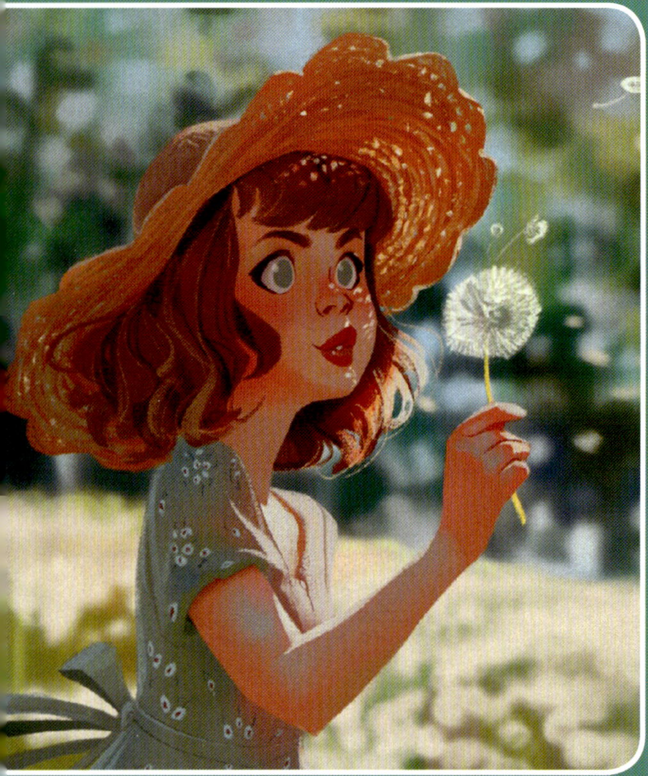

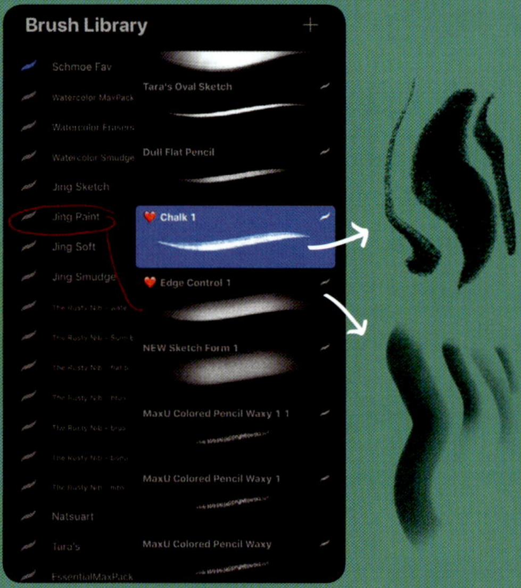

BRUSHES

I paint the whole piece using just two brushes. Both brushes are great for adding a textured finish. The chalk brush comes with Procreate and the "Jing Paint" brush is part of a free set of brushes the artist Jimmy Jing Xia, also known as "Jingsketch", offers on Gumroad (visit gumroad.com/jingsketch to get yours!).

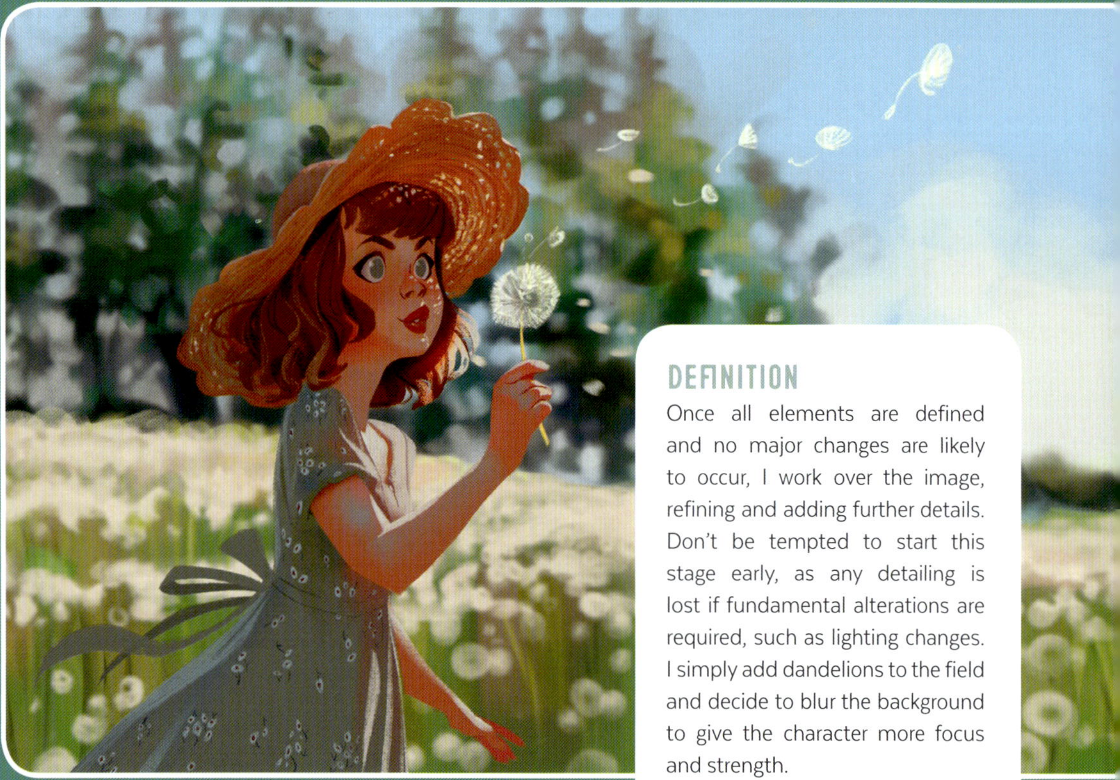

DEFINITION

Once all elements are defined and no major changes are likely to occur, I work over the image, refining and adding further details. Don't be tempted to start this stage early, as any detailing is lost if fundamental alterations are required, such as lighting changes. I simply add dandelions to the field and decide to blur the background to give the character more focus and strength.

FINAL TOUCHES

To finalize the design, I darken the character slightly and add finishing details to the background and dress of the character.

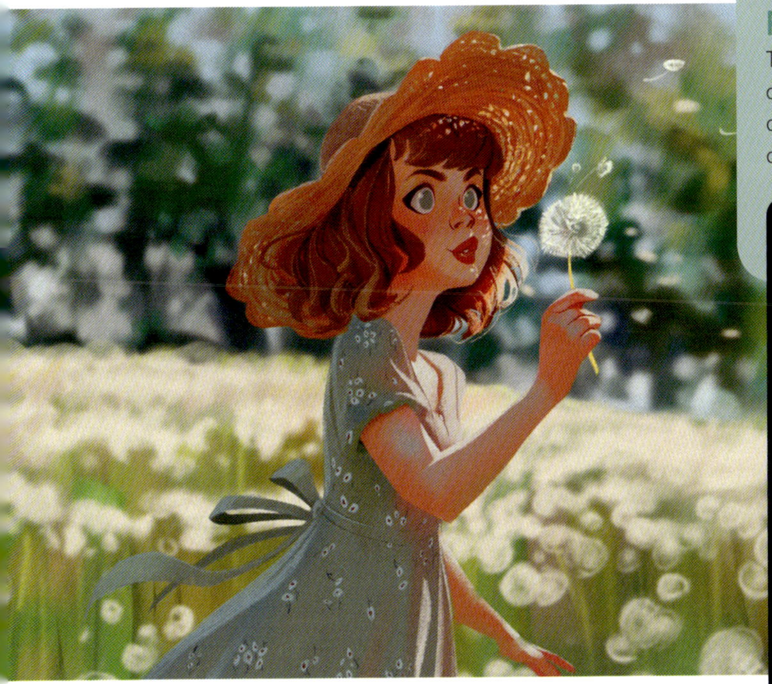

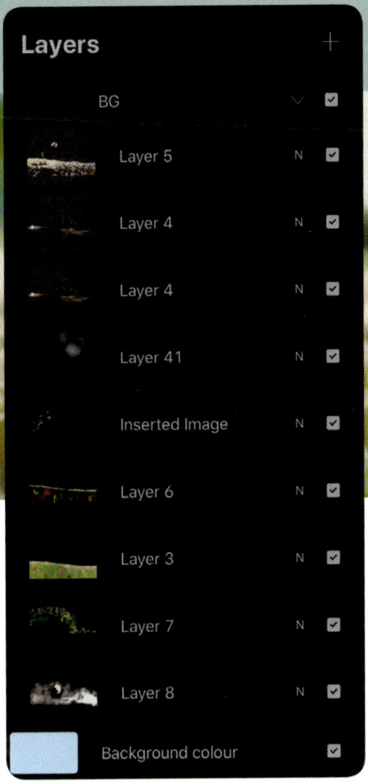

These are the layers I used for the character

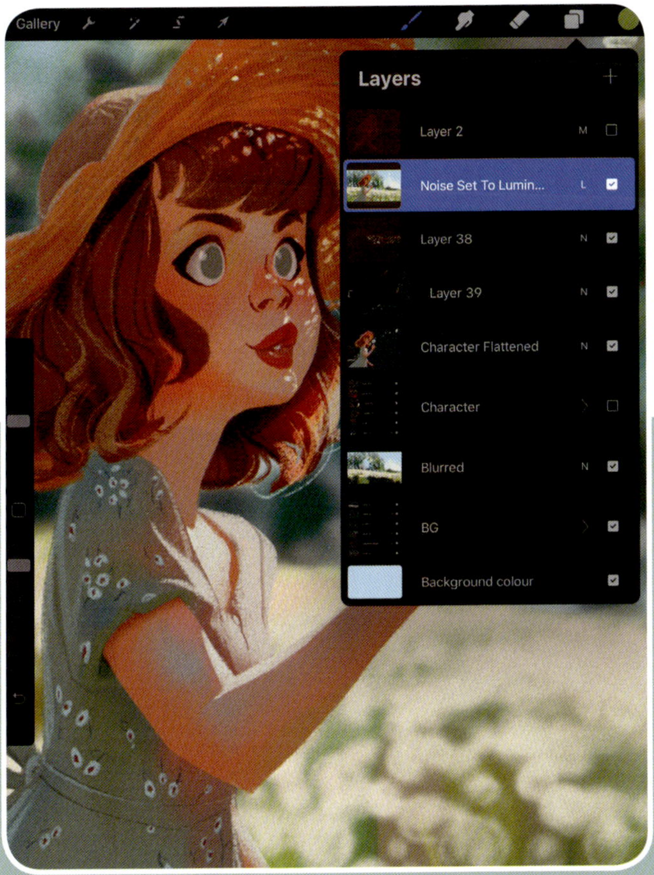

ADDING A LITTLE NOISE

This menu will appear when swiping down with three fingers in Procreate. You can then choose to "Copy All." In Photoshop this can be done with a shortcut: for PC, use Shift+Alt+Ctrl+E and for MAC, use Shift+Option+Cmd+E. By copying and pasting all into a new layer, final effects can be added with ease. To this piece, I add some noise and set the layer to "Luminance," and with this final detail the design is complete.

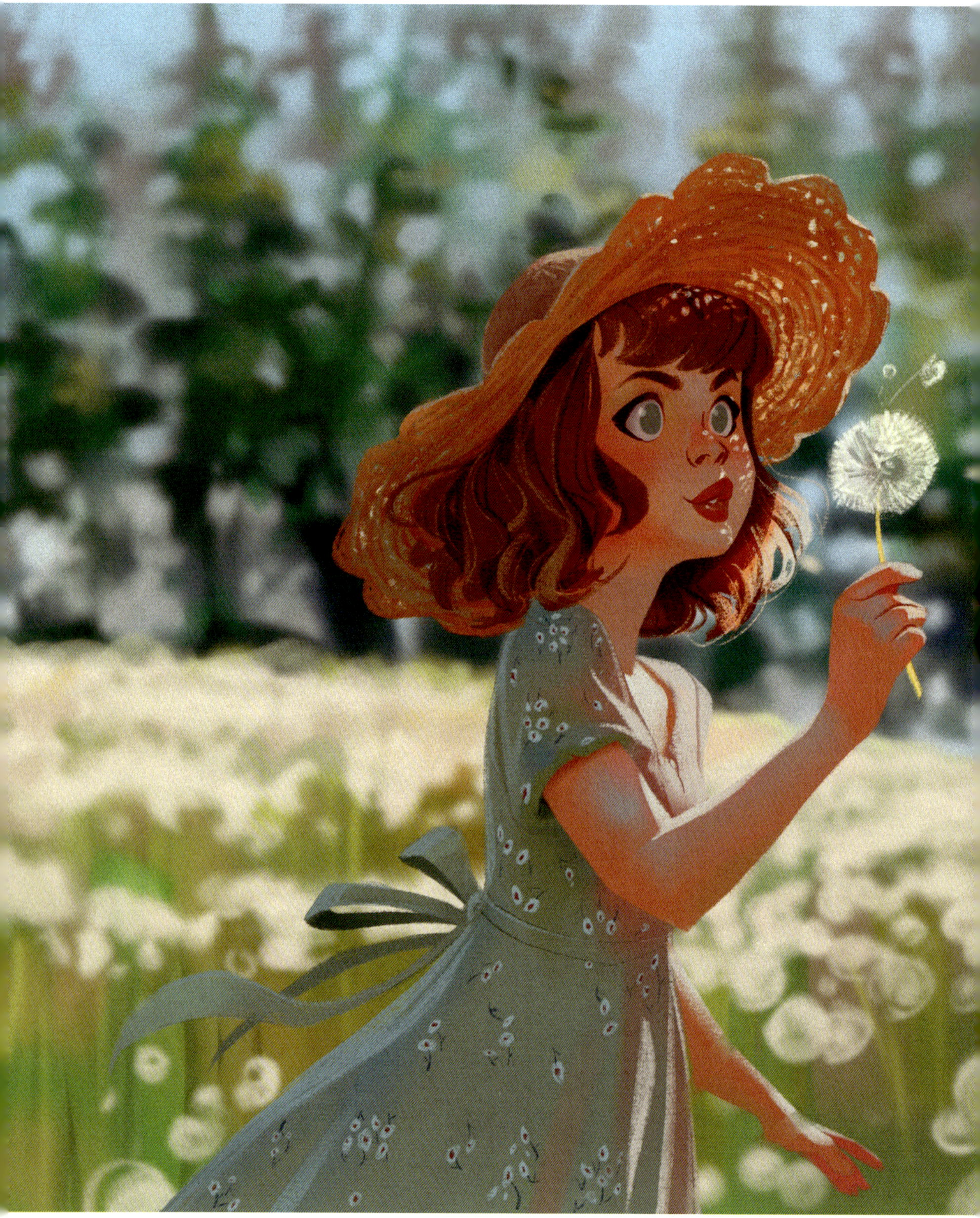

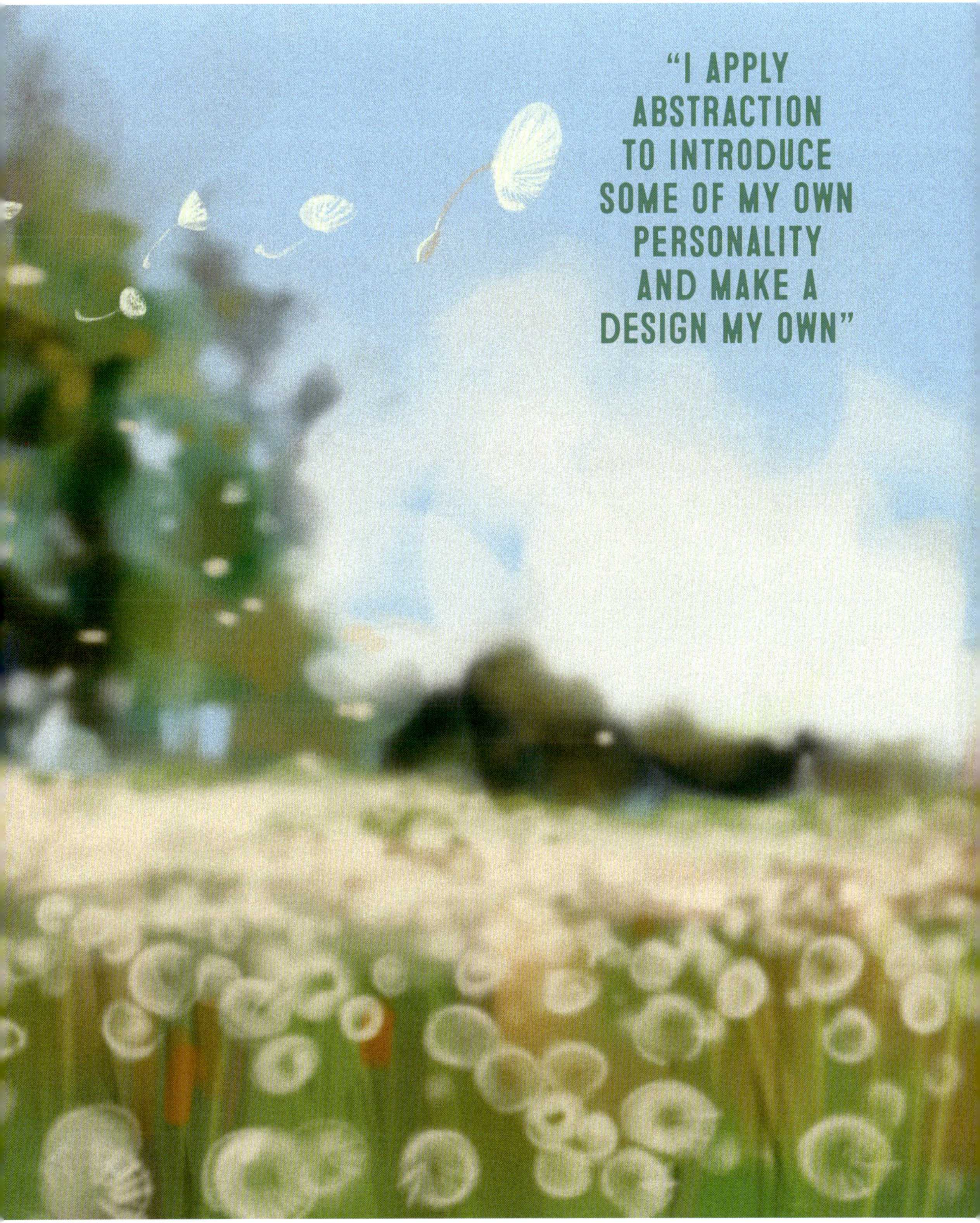

"I APPLY ABSTRACTION TO INTRODUCE SOME OF MY OWN PERSONALITY AND MAKE A DESIGN MY OWN"

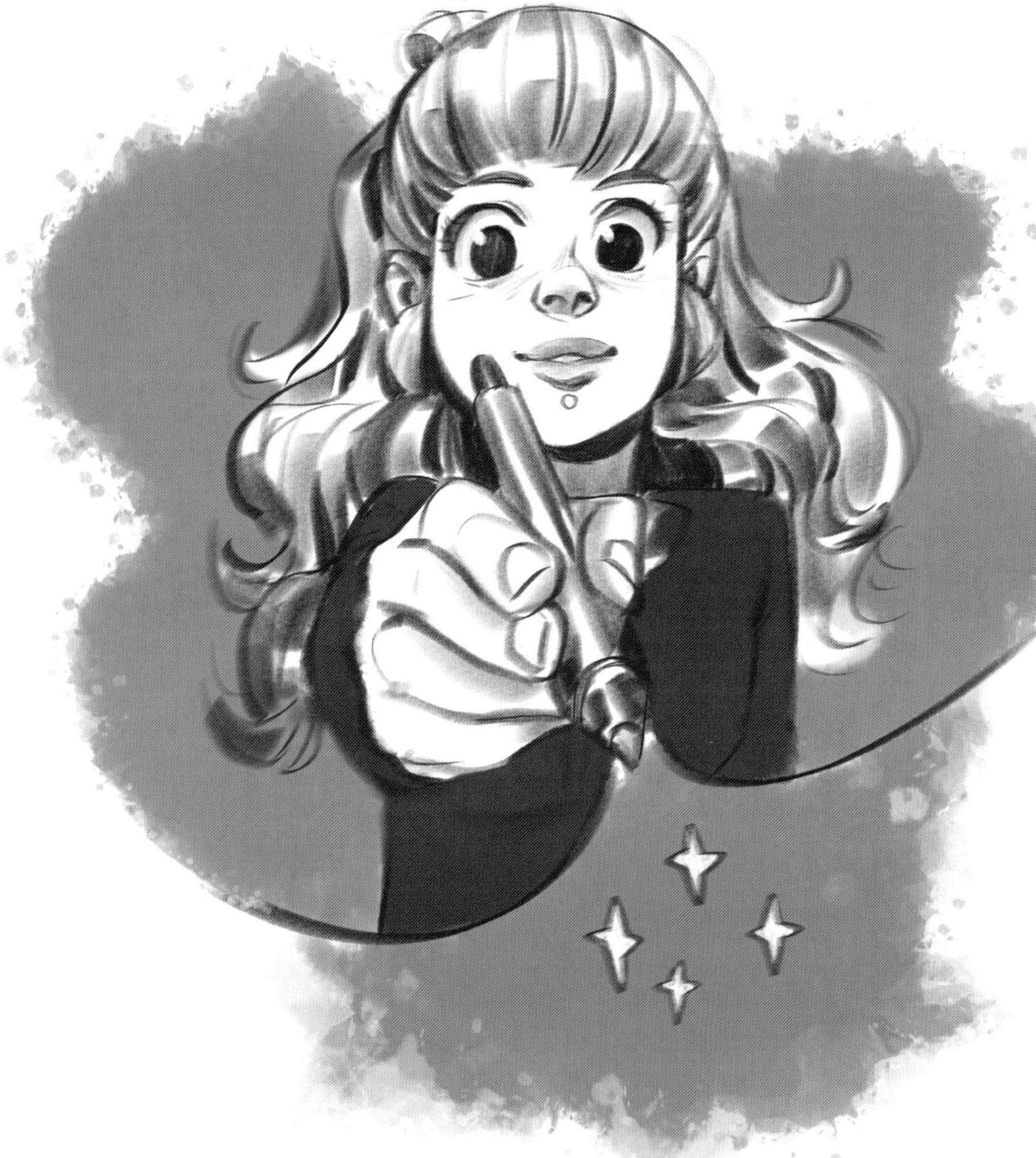

DIGITAL TECHNIQUES & INSIGHTS

In this chapter, I share in detail how I work digitally, discussing some of the most important techniques and tools needed to understand and unlock the possibilities that working digitally offers.

MASKS

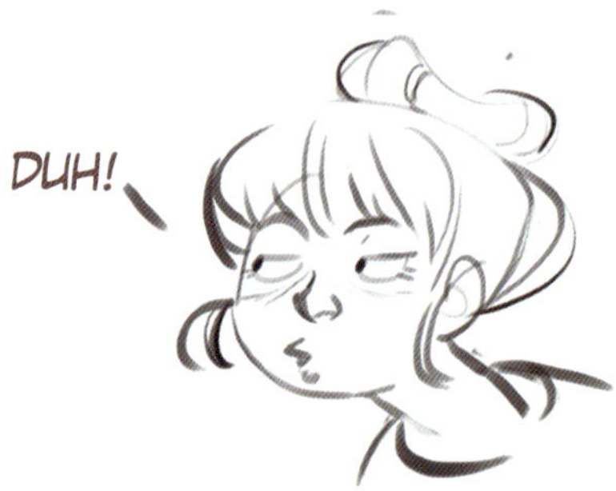

Masking tools in Photoshop make it possible to "mask" and hide part of your image, to allow for more flexibility when working digitally. They can be used in many different projects to create effects and finishes.

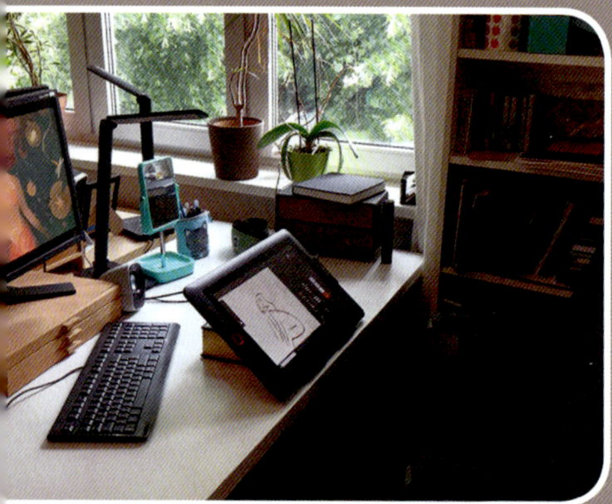

Start with a flat background – it could be painted or perhaps even a photo, as I have used here.

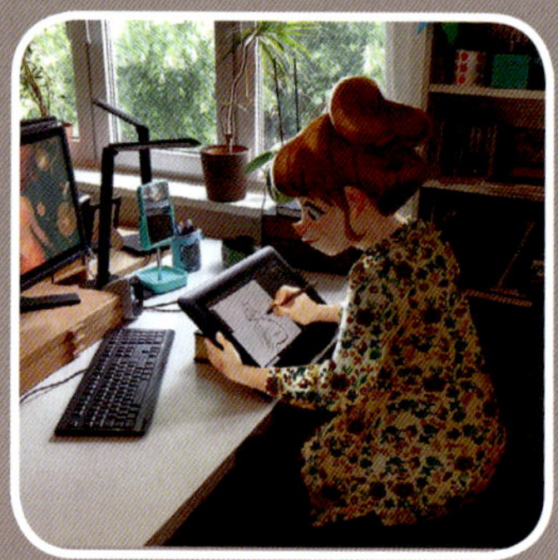

Next, add a character. To make the character fit the scene, parts of the character or scene may need to be adapted or erased.

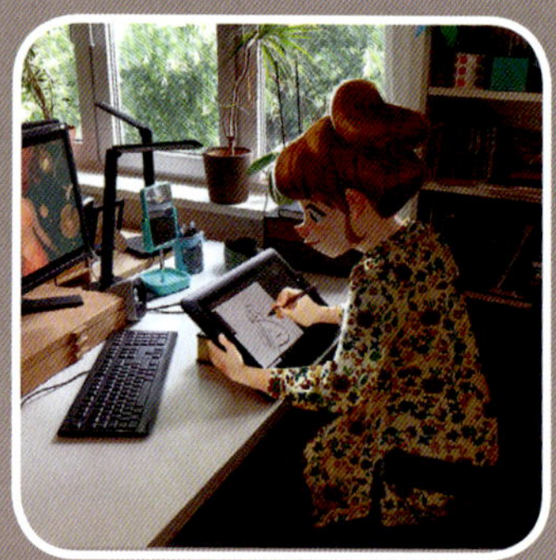

This can, however, be a very tedious process, and it doesn't leave much room for mistakes – once pixels have been deleted, they're permanently gone!

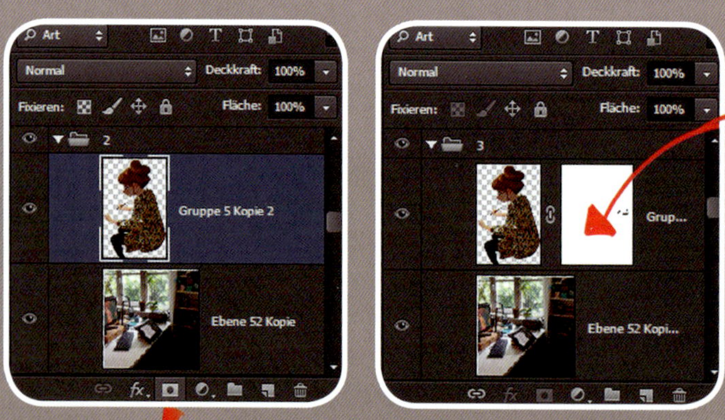

Alternatively, create a mask and paint in grayscale by clicking on it (color changes automatically to grayscale). Painting in black hides the drawing underneath, while white reveals it! Painting softly in gray creates translucent areas, which can also have many uses.

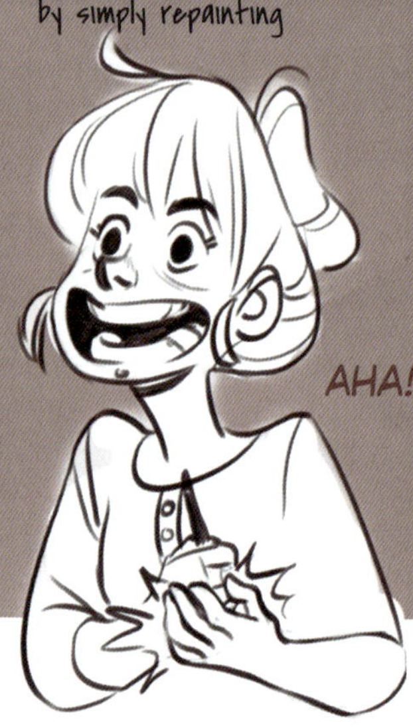

Here's another example of how I like to use masks:

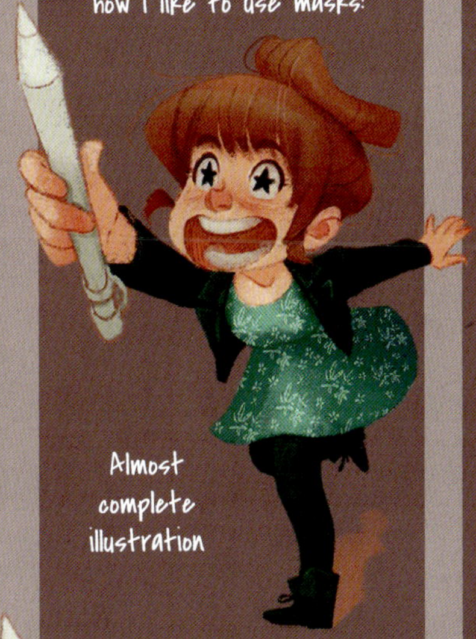

Almost complete illustration

Finished with masks! Volume is added with shadow and light, and subtle saturation completes the piece

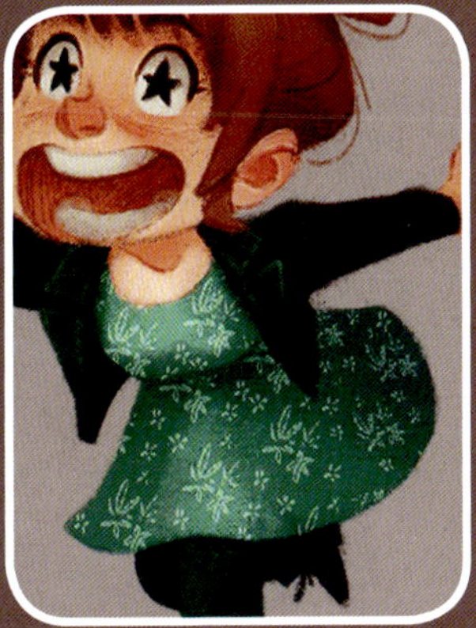

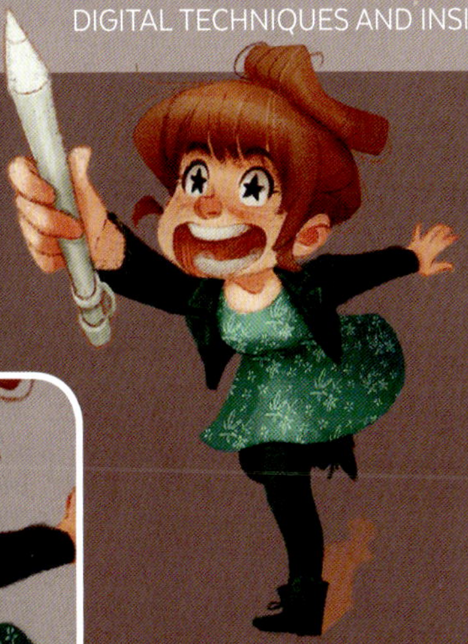

Painting with masks offers a quick and easy way to add depth and pop to a final image. Make sure to play around a bit!

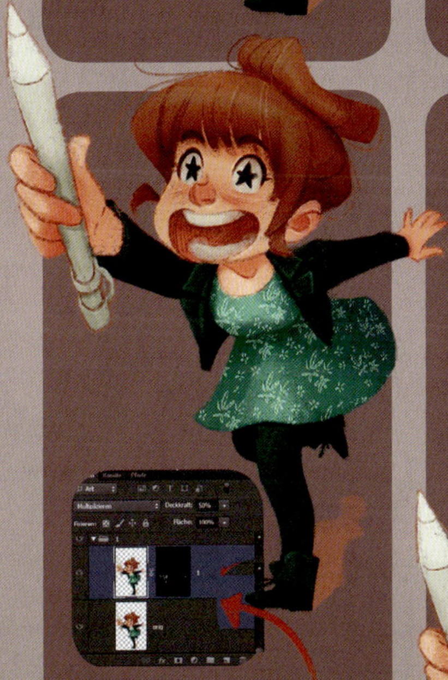

STEP 1

I duplicate the original layer and set it to Multiply. I then add a layer mask that I fill black, causing the duplicated darker image to disappear. Next, with the layer mask selected, I paint with white and darken some areas to add volume.

STEP 2

I again duplicate the original layer and set it to Soft Light blending mode, which makes the colors a bit more saturated. As I don't want all colors to be saturated, I use the same procedure and only add the brighter colors where I want them by painting on the layer mask.

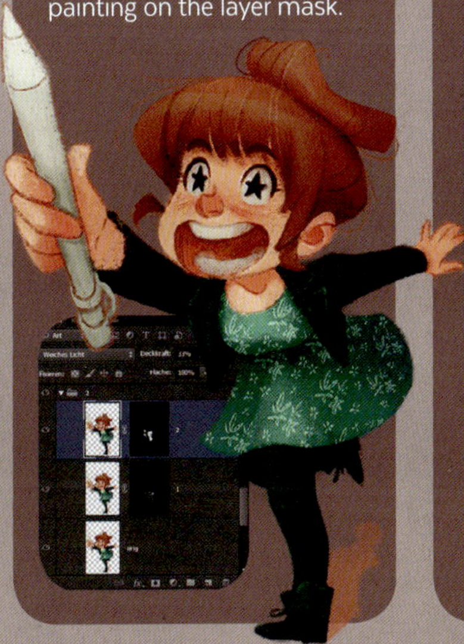

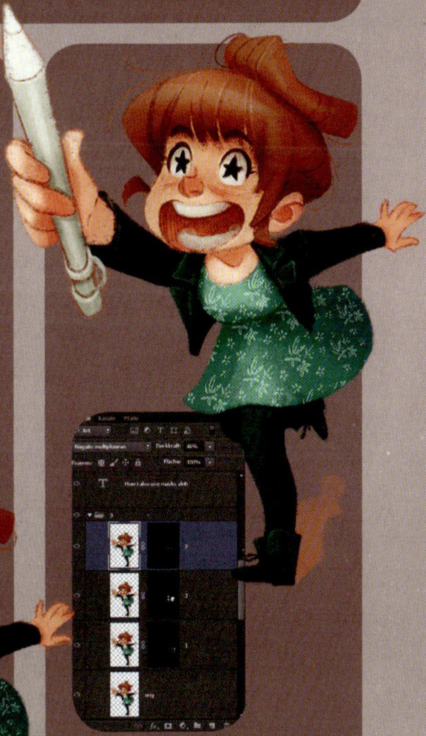

STEP 3

Using the same method, I lighten some areas, with the layer set to blending mode Screen.

CLIPPING MASKS

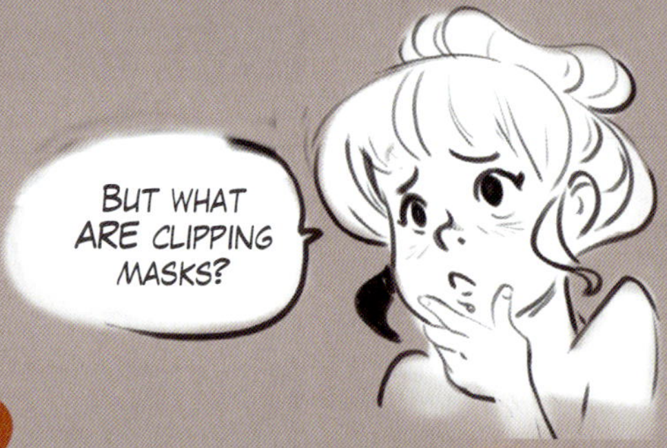

When using clipping masks, it is best to start with all the elements on separate layers. The original sketch can be turned off after creating all the individual shapes and lines. When attempting to use this technique for the first time, I suggest creating a simple design, such as a portrait, as multiple layers can become very confusing.

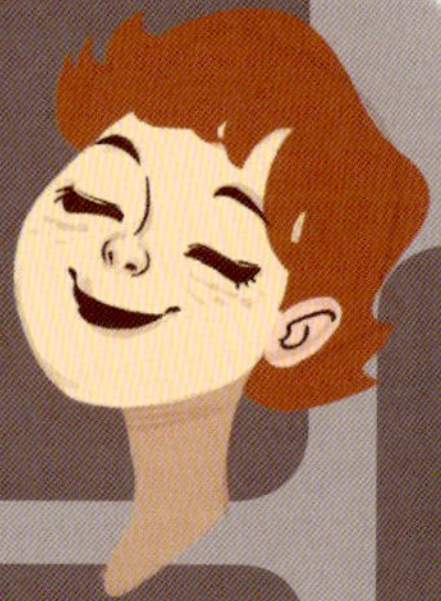

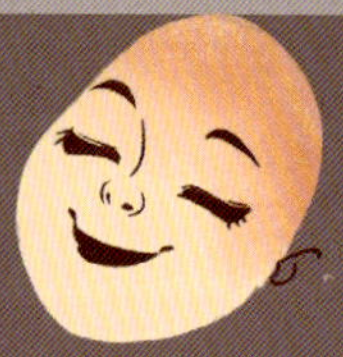

CLIPPED

Clipping masks are normal layers "clipped" on to a layer below.

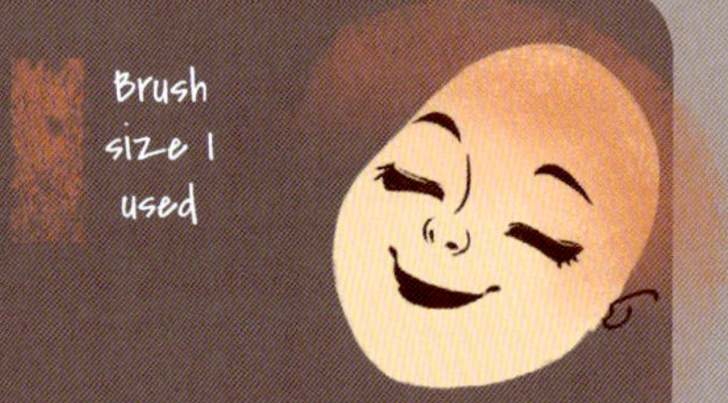

The unclipped layers would look like the image seen here. A clipping mask uses the shape underneath to cut away the excess shading. This is useful to achieve smooth shading with a subtle texture, as this is best created with a big brush.

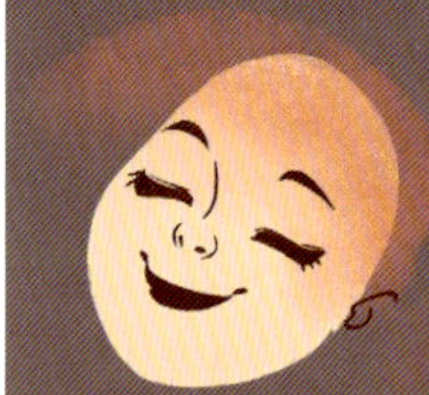

UNCLIPPED

To make a clipping mask, select the layer on top of the layer it should clip to and press Ctrl+Alt+G (it can be unclipped with the same shortcut.) Alternatively, right-click the chosen layer and select "Create clipping mask" in the options.

It is possible to create multiple clipping masks on top of one layer

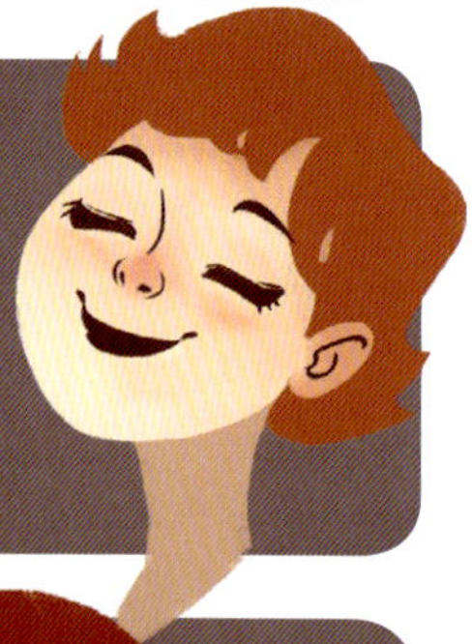

Clipping masks make it easy to paint without destroying the existing painted areas – simply layer on top of the layers until satisfied and edit them by gently erasing any mistakes. Once complete, flatten all clipping mask layers by selecting the bottom layer and pressing Ctrl+E.

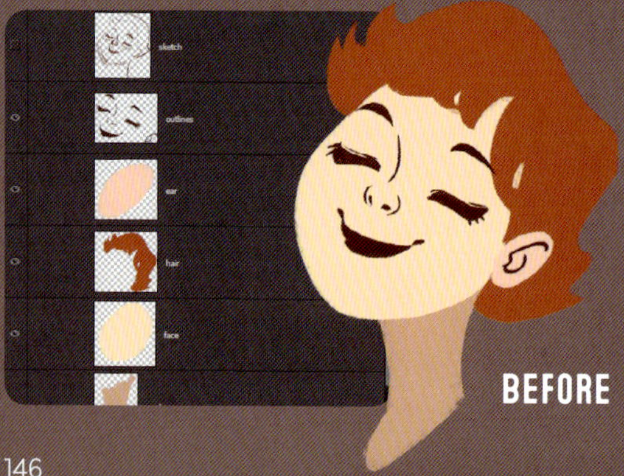

BEFORE

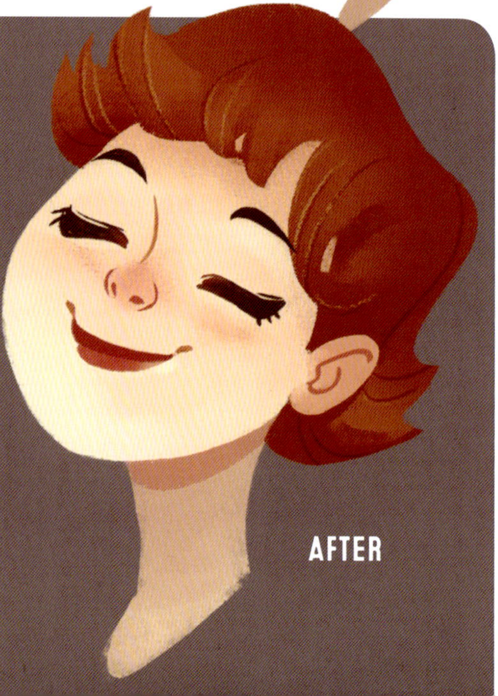

AFTER

ALPHA LOCK

Alpha Lock can be used in a similar way to clipping masks. However, the big advantage of using Alpha Lock rather than clipping masks is that there isn't the same potential for complicated layer chaos. Applying Alpha Lock on a layer "locks" the pixels on the layer, allowing only those on the layer to be painted. While using Alpha Lock is far tidier than clipping masks, clipping masks are more versatile.

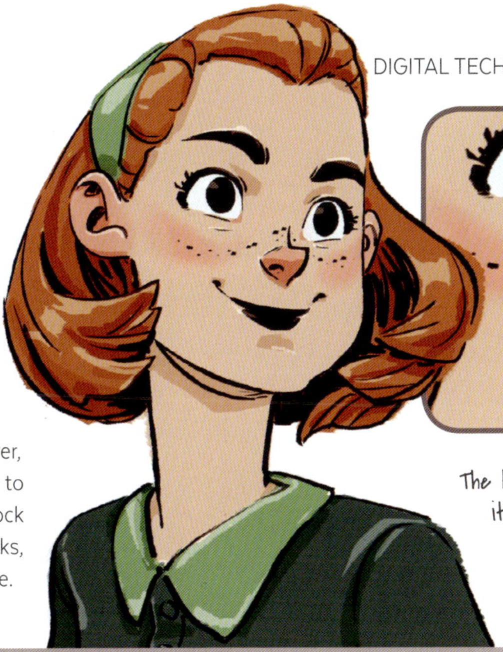

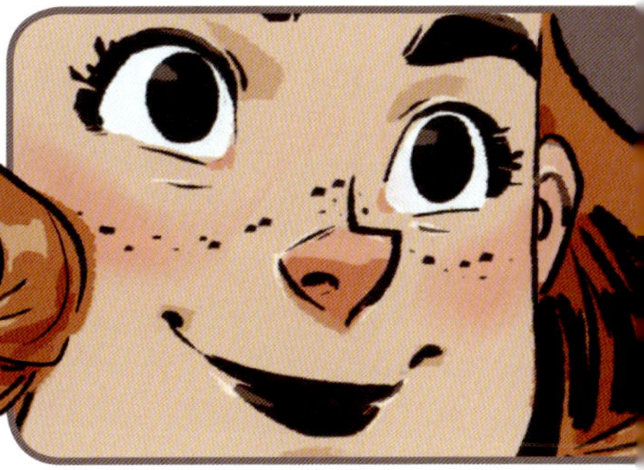

The base painting, with its layers locked

I paint linework with a soft brush in different colors and add slight gradients. The brush is set to Multiply and the opacity is reduced to allow the colors underneath to shine through

I add gradients to the locked shadow layer by painting onto it with a soft brush

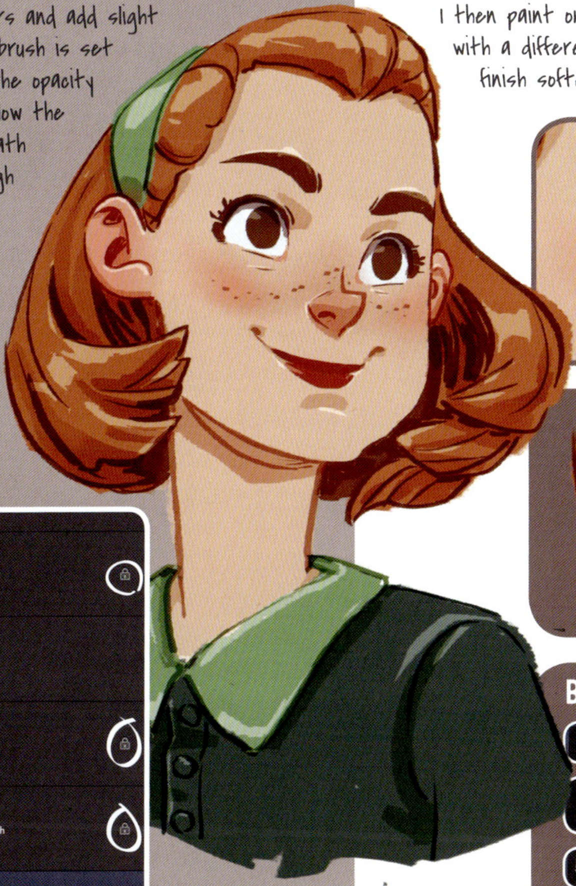

I then paint on the locked blush layer with a different color to make the finish softer and more subtle

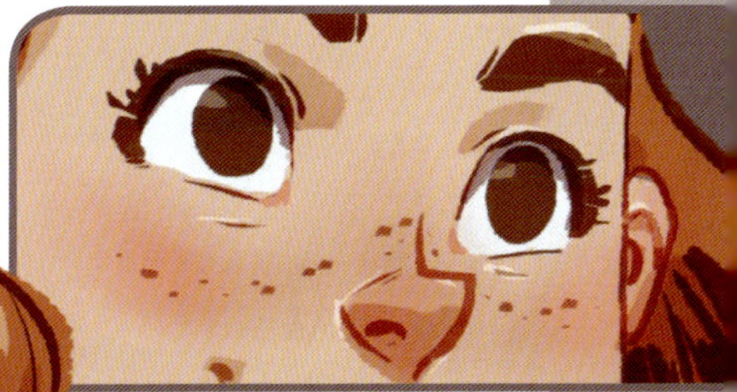

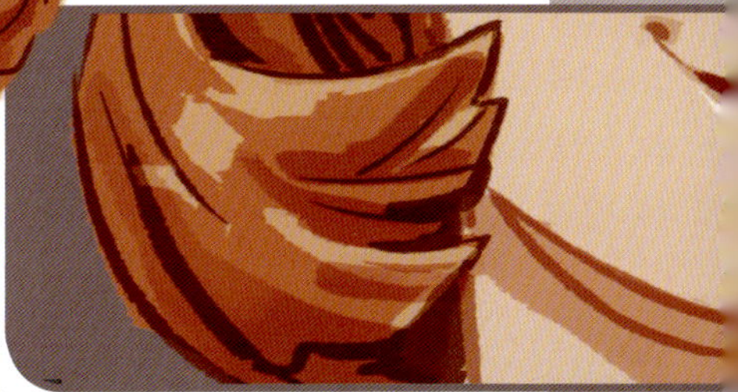

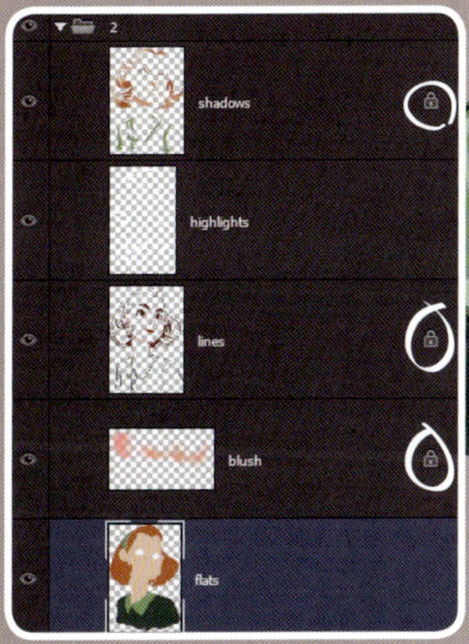

BRUSHES USED:

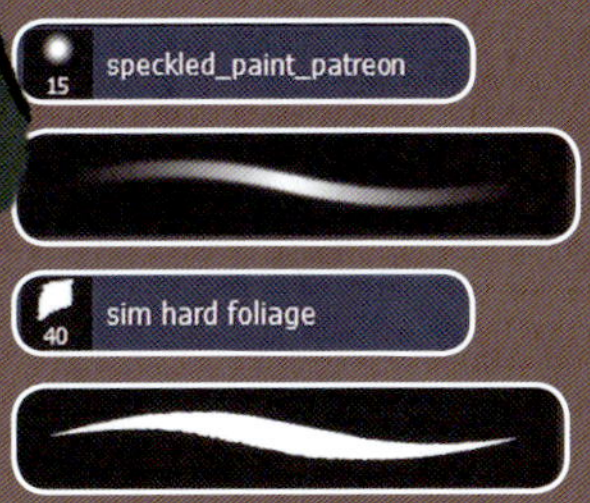

CREATING LINELESS CHARACTERS

I use the following Photoshop workflow to create clean color-blocked characters with no outlines.

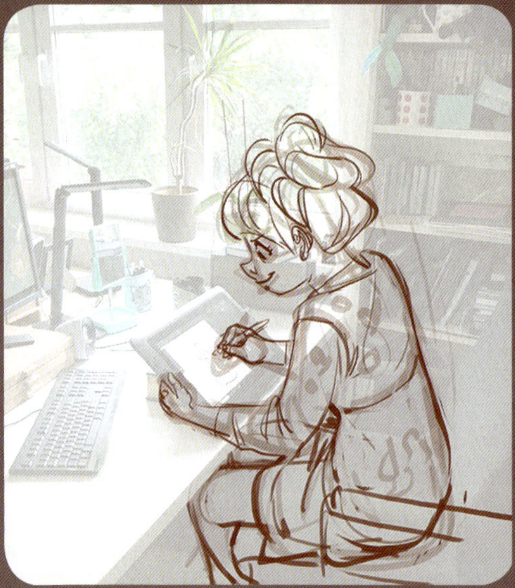

Refine the initial sketch, so that all necessary elements are accurately defined.

This is a layer heavy approach! Most elements have their own layer for better editing. It is important to keep a logical order – the ear on top and the hand holding the pen at the bottom. Think of it as if you are assembling the character from pieces of cardboard.

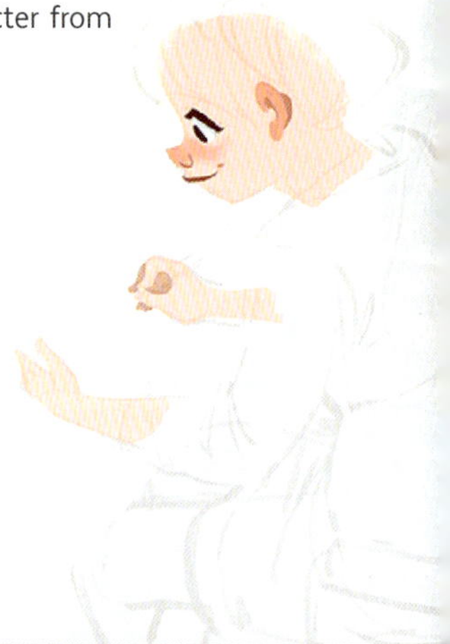

I like to add facial details at an early stage because it keeps me motivated! To create a rosy nose and cheeks, I apply red and then erase gently with a low opacity on the eraser.

When blocking in colors, I consider the lighting and think of the foreground and character as light, the middle ground as medium, and the background as dark. These slight lighting variations avoid the design appearing flat. To add further depth, I use a large brush with a lowered opacity; alternatively an air brush is also a valid option.

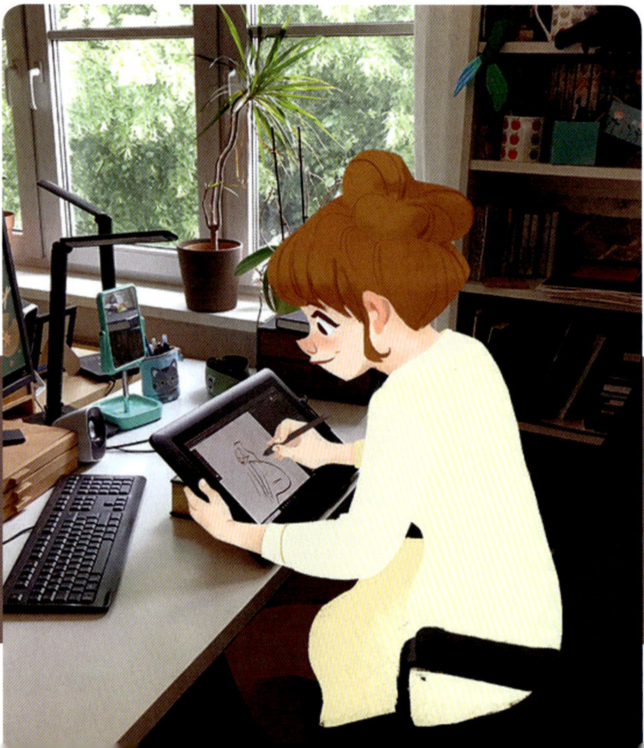

Next, I unify the elements with gradients and introduce gentle shading. Shading is easiest to undertake with clipping masks because it can be counter-erased and it is easier to edit the bottom shape if that remains a flat color.

When drawing folds, I select the base clothing color and set it to Multiply

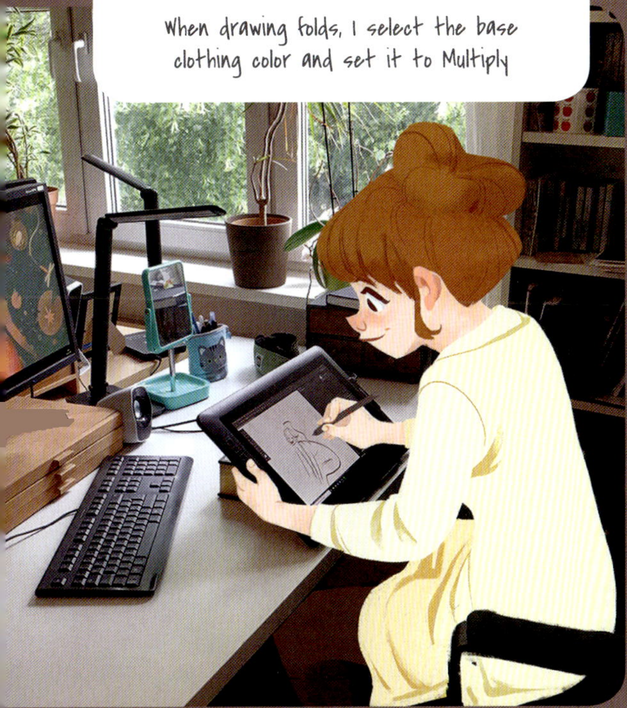

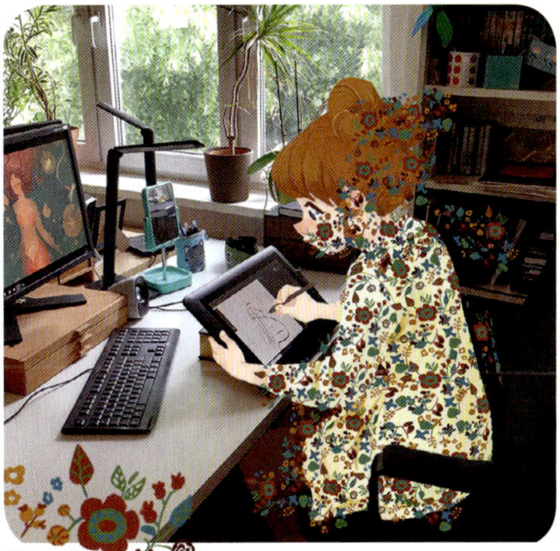

For the pattern on the dress, I draw a small section of the design and then duplicate and transform it multiple times and apply with clipping masks

To finish, I play with layer effects. I duplicate the character's grouped layers, flatten and then set to different blending modes, and erase parts to shade and darken or lighten parts in a gentle way.

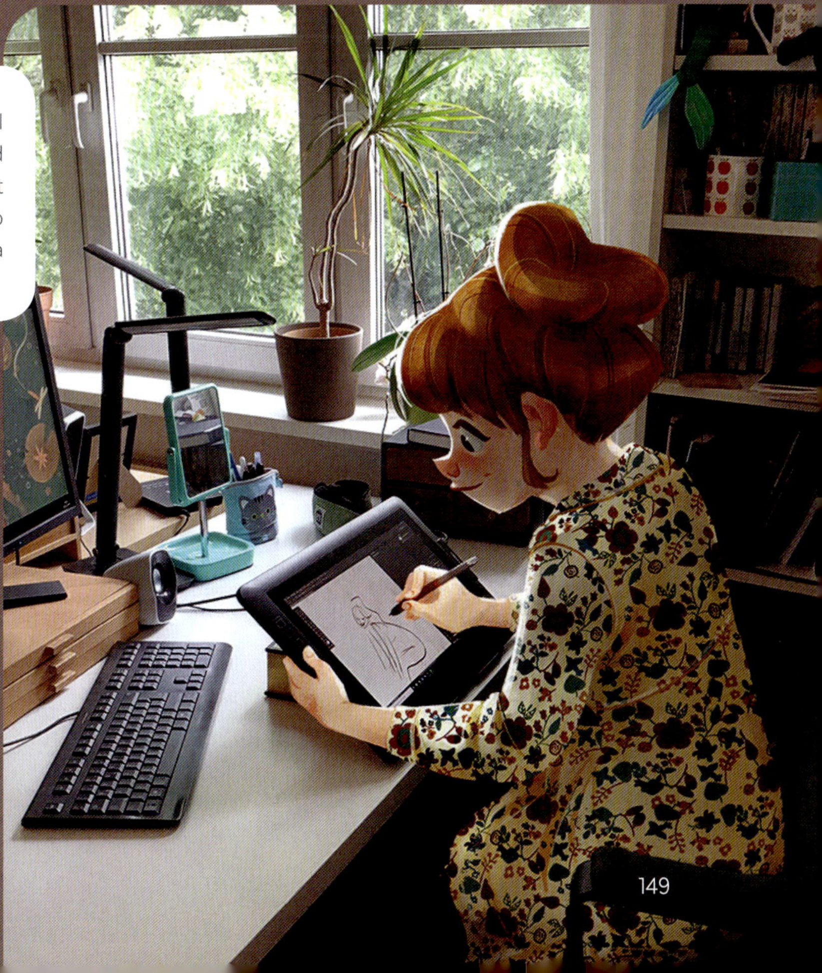

"I LIKE TO ADD FACIAL DETAILS AT AN EARLY STAGE BECAUSE IT KEEPS ME MOTIVATED!"

DIGITALLY CORRECTING WATERCOLOR PAINTINGS

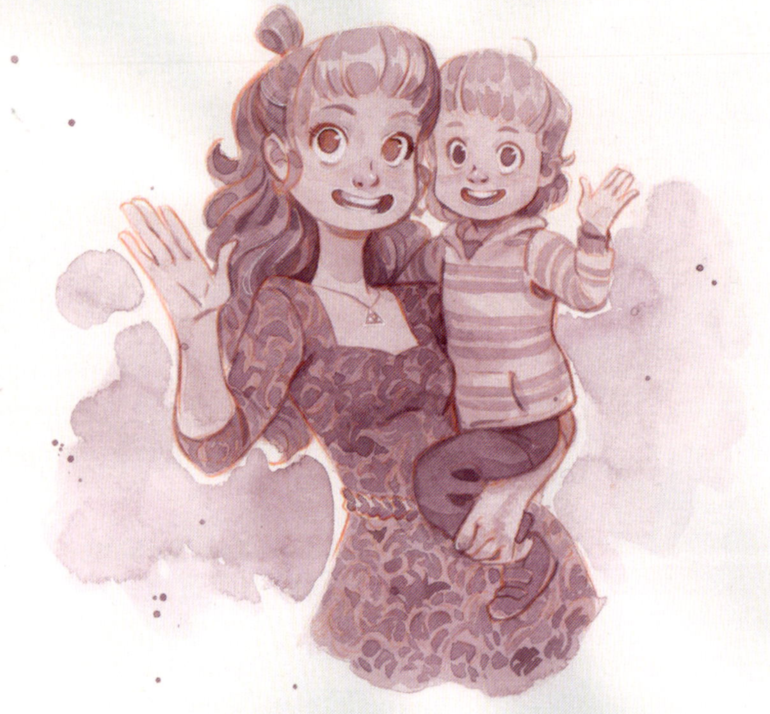

When scanning watercolor paintings, the image on screen often requires a few corrections to make it look as brilliant as the original. For example, the colors often look dull and shadows can be seen from the ripples in the paper caused by the watercolor paints.

I use a Canon CanoScan LiDE 100 flatbed scanner and it serves me well, so I highly recommend it. However, some corrections are always required. I use the following method to adjust my scans in Photoshop.

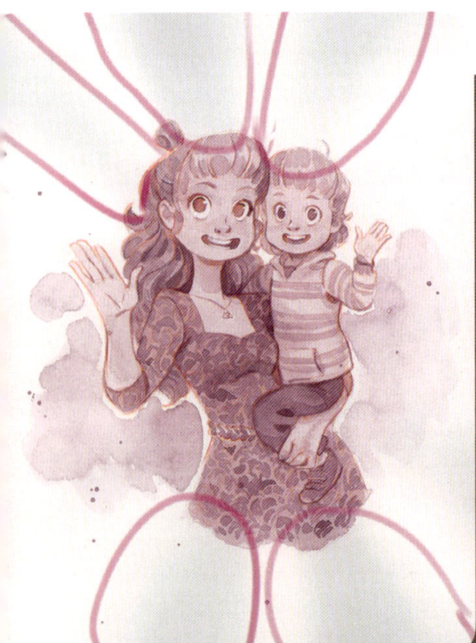

To remove the shadows and help the whole design to pop a little more, I start by selecting the adjustment layer, Levels.

After selecting Levels, a small window will appear, where the Eyedropper tool can be selected. Using the Eyedropper tool, click on the background area of the image and it will lighten the whole image so that the clicked-on area will turn white.

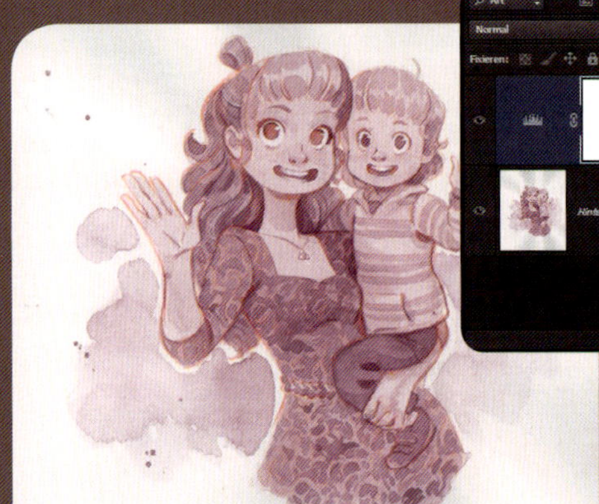

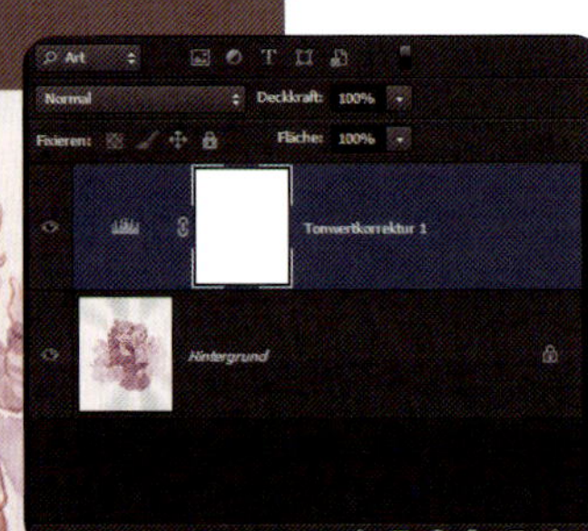

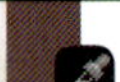

There are three different Eyedroppers. This is the correct icon to select

This process is called white balancing – try clicking on different points on the image to see the different results. I click on the darkest of shadows I want to whiten.

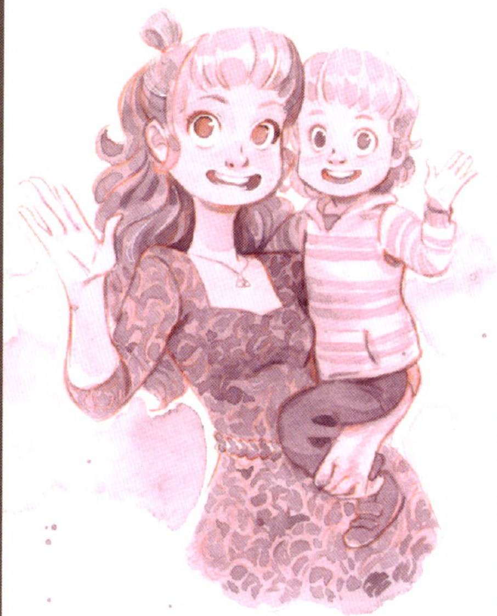

After the white-balancing process, the whole image is lightened and the shadows are gone. This change is only visible with the adjustment layer visible. The original drawing hasn't been changed.

Take a "picture" of what is visible by selecting everything, then copying and pasting it onto a new layer.

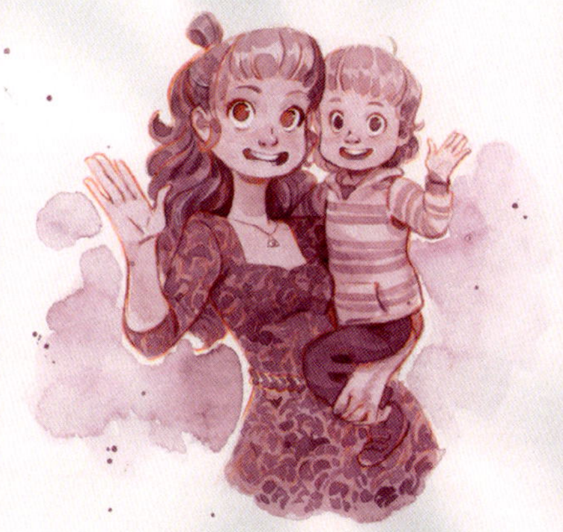

Set the new copied image layer to Multiply to help the image pop and darken it without also darkening the unwanted shadows. I turn the lightened adjustments level layer off because I decide it makes the image a bit too white.

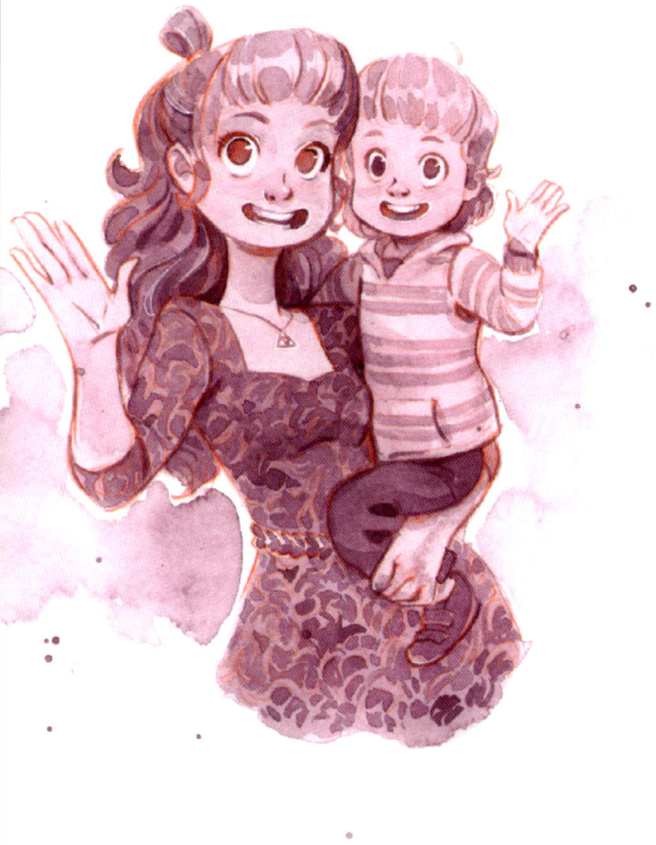

Next, I once again balance white levels with a new adjustment layer, but this time I just whiten the paper slightly so that the image looks bright and clean, except for traces of shadows.

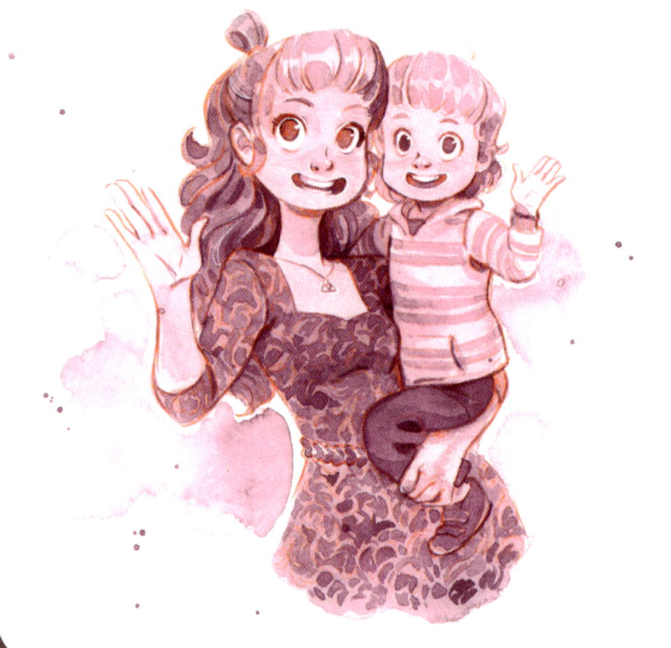

I click on the darkest part of the shadow to balance white levels a little more. Again, the image looks too light and details have been lost, but I have some tricks to get them back!

Create a layer mask, covering the art. By clicking on the layer mask, you can then paint away the desaturated too-bright effect on the art. The beautiful details of the watercolors are retained and just the desaturated effect of the white balancing is removed.

This method can be used for pencil drawings too — it's the easiest way to get rid of dirt and touch up the drawing at the same time!

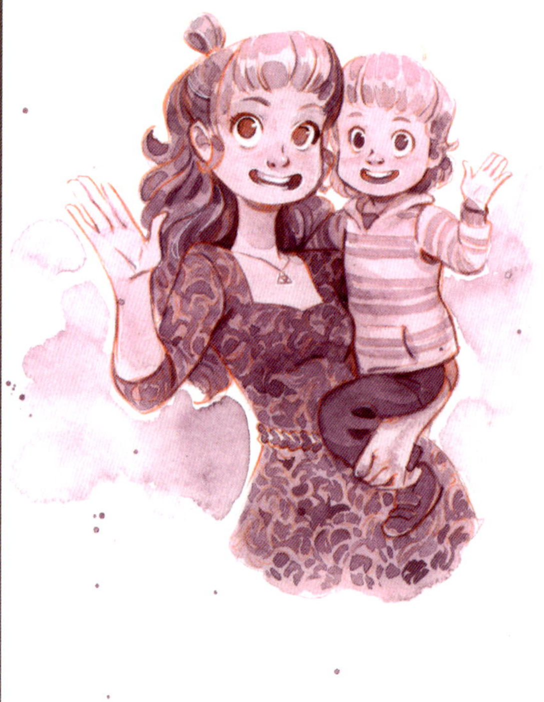

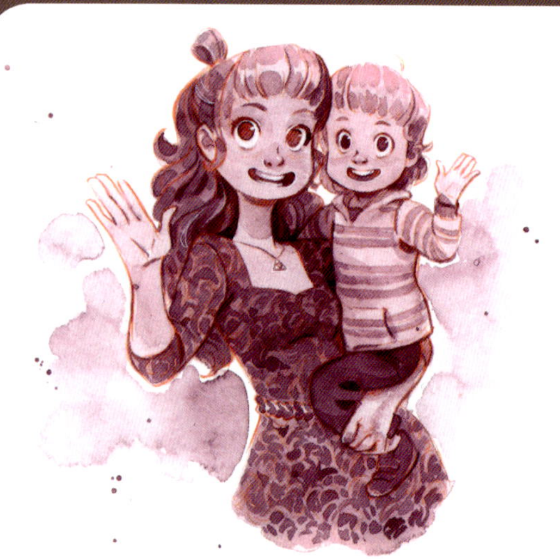

Lastly, I add more contrast by copying the image and setting it to Multiply. All these steps cause the image to become quite saturated, so I reduce the saturation on a final adjustment layer.

This whole process takes me about five minutes, and each step cleans up the image and intensifies the painting.

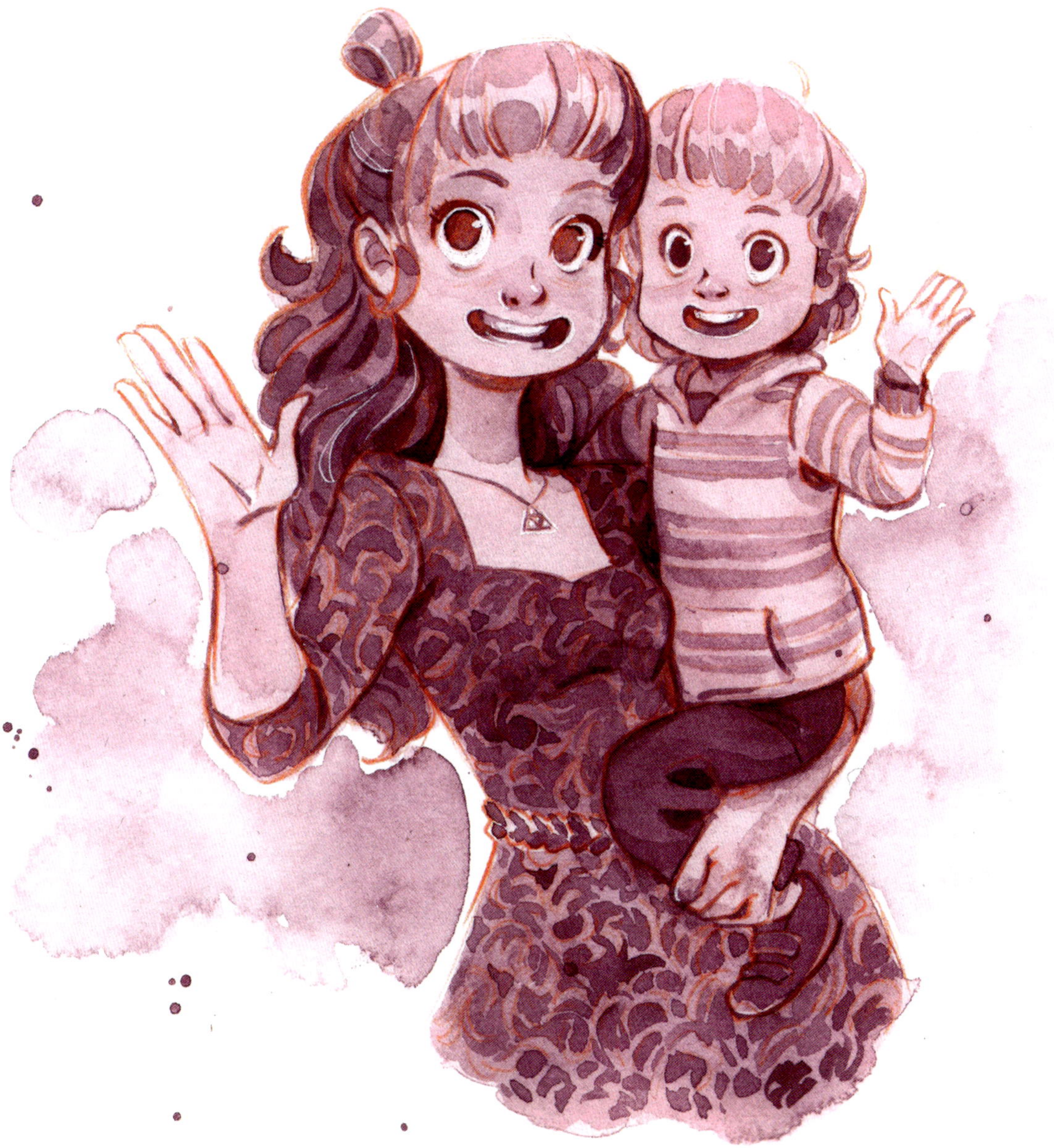

PROCREATE TIPS AND TRICKS

As well as Adobe Photoshop, I use Procreate software in my digital workflow. There's always lots to learn when using new software, so here are a few tips and tricks to get you started!

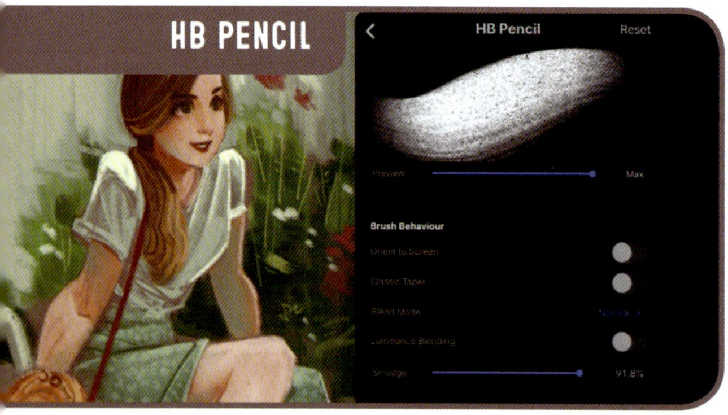

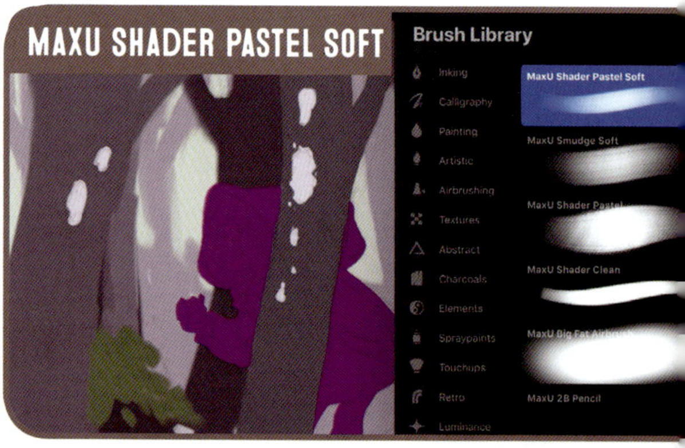

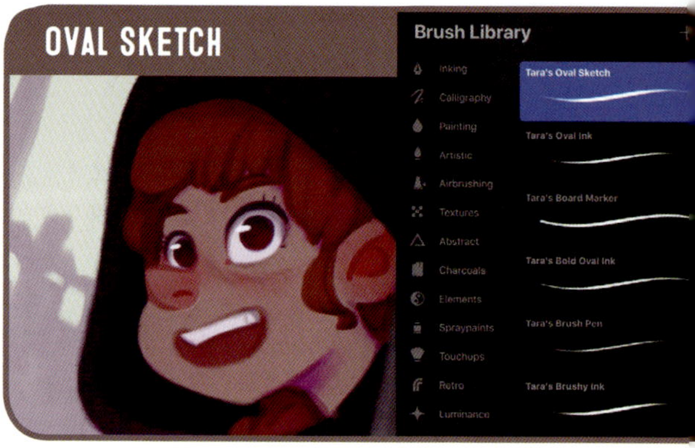

BRUSHES

In Procreate there are three brushes I use a lot:

MAXU SHADER PASTEL SOFT
FROM MAX ULICHNEY'S ESSENTIAL MAXPACK BRUSH SET

I love its soft shading and I also use it to block in shapes.

OVAL SKETCH
FROM THE DIZZYTARA'S SKETCH & INK PROCREATE BRUSHES SET

I like using this brush for detailing and outlining.

HB PENCIL
FROM PROCREATE'S ORIGINAL COLLECTION

I tweak the size of the brush to 140% to create a chalky pencil effect. To alter the size, simply go to "Brush Presets".

QUICK MENU

It is very useful, especially while sketching, to be able to flip the canvas, as flipping the canvas can help to highlight fundamental design mistakes that may have been missed. Fortunately, the canvas can be flipped easily with the use of a useful quick menu that offers immediate access to a selection of tools and options, including adding a new layer or clearing a layer.

The quick menu can be found here:
Actions > Preferences > Gesture Controls

I have set my quick menu to appear on a four-finger tap but it can be set to whatever command is preferred. It's also possible to customize lots of other shortcuts to improve workflow; for example, I changed my Eyedropper tool to a touch command.

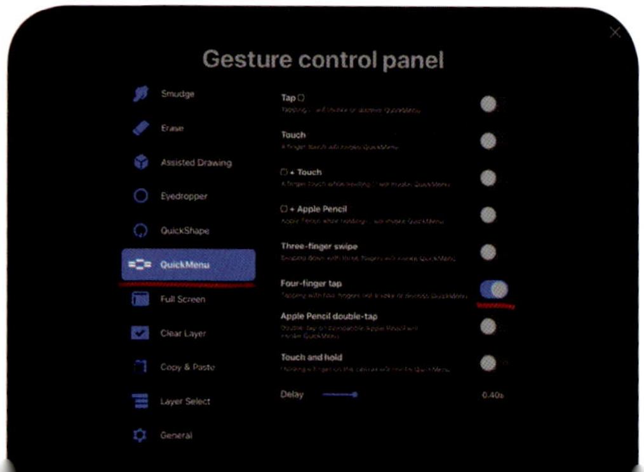

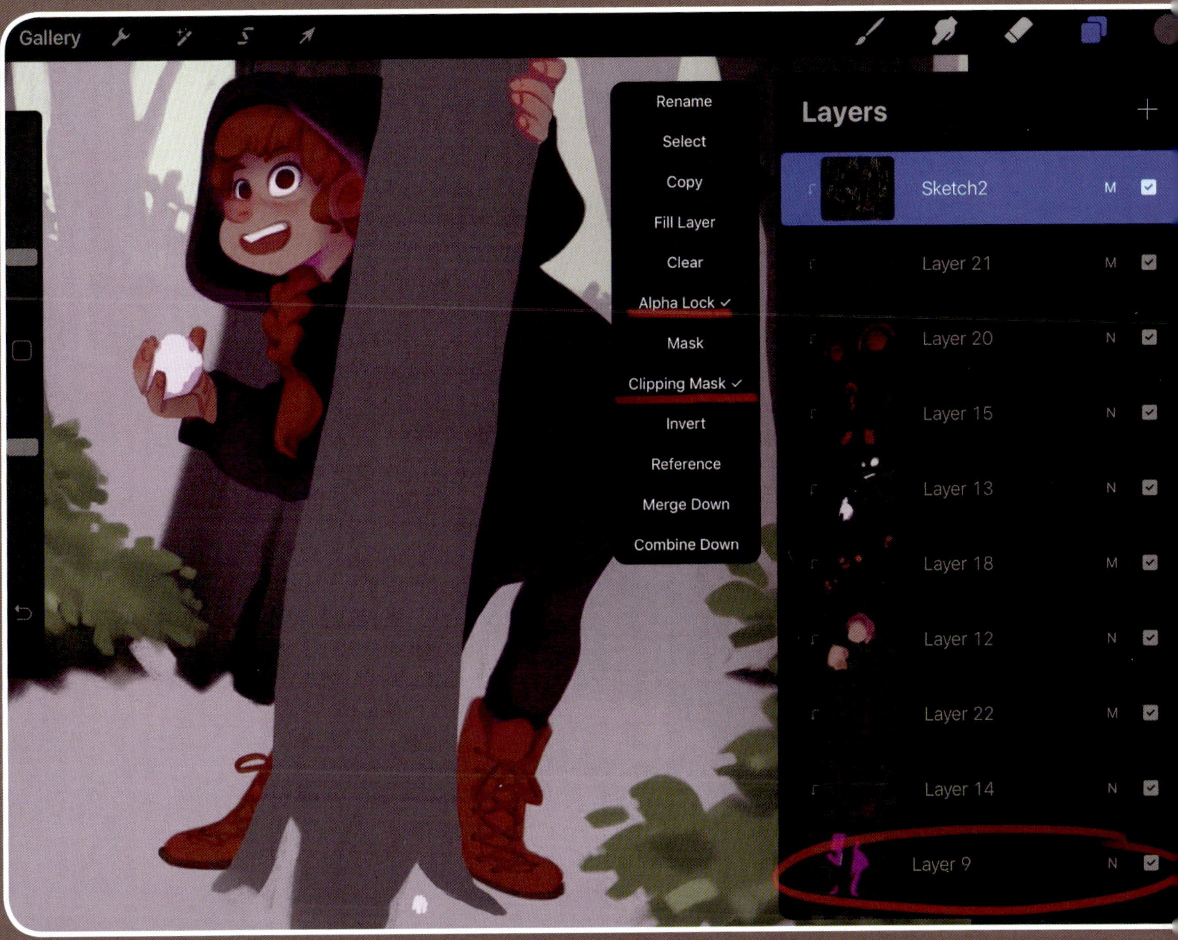

CLIPPING MASKS AND ALPHA LOCK

I have always loved working with clipping masks and Alpha Lock in Photoshop, so I was thrilled when they were added to Procreate!

I use layers set to clipping masks on top of my main shape, shown in the image above as Layer 9. This way, I don't need to worry about painting over the edges of the main shape on all the layers set to clipping masks on top of it. Within these layers I use Alpha Lock (again to avoid painting over the borders of a shape) but this only applies to layers with the checkered background. I define the layer's shape, then set it to Alpha Lock, and paint is only applied within the borders.

Selections can be useful too, but they slow my workflow, so I rarely use them.

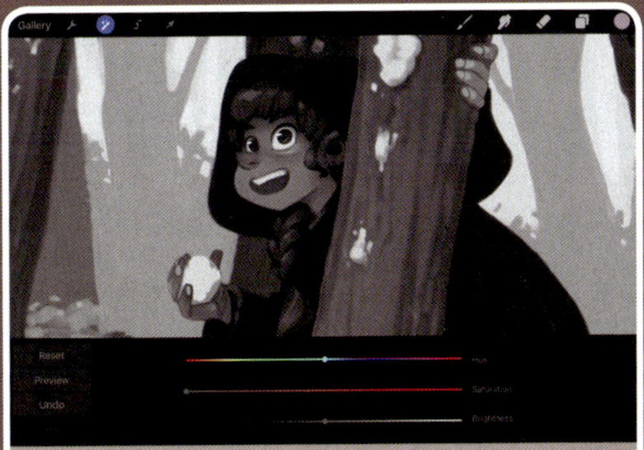

NOISE

Adding a little noise is something I like to do at the end of finalizing a painting. The noise effect is simply a colored grain effect, that, when applied, gives the whole piece an organic and slightly blurred finish. Three-finger tap the menu, and copy and paste all visible layers onto a new layer, then add "Noise."

DIGITAL MEETS TRADITIONAL

Here I demonstrate how I digitally paint a traditionally drawn sketch. Combining both media improves my workflow, as I can take my favorite aspects of both and achieve the outcome that works best for me and my style.

BACKGROUND DESIGN INSPIRED BY A PHOTOGRAPH BY @ SASHA_AND_ESCHER

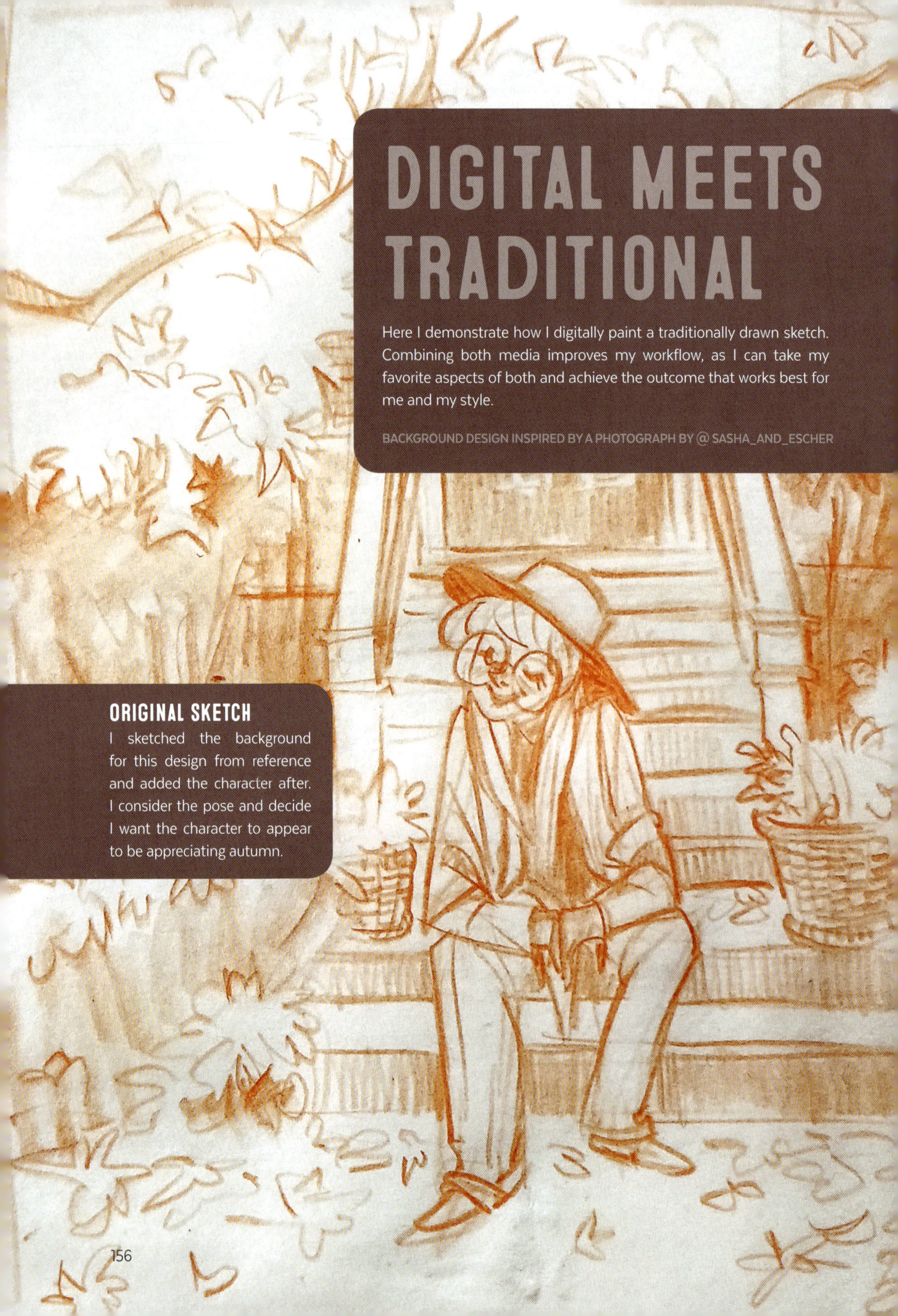

ORIGINAL SKETCH

I sketched the background for this design from reference and added the character after. I consider the pose and decide I want the character to appear to be appreciating autumn.

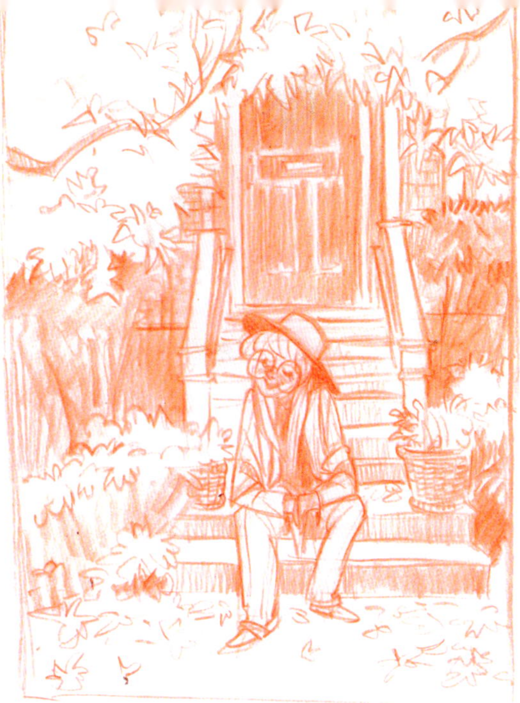

SCAN

To start the process, I scan the original sketch at 600 dpi.

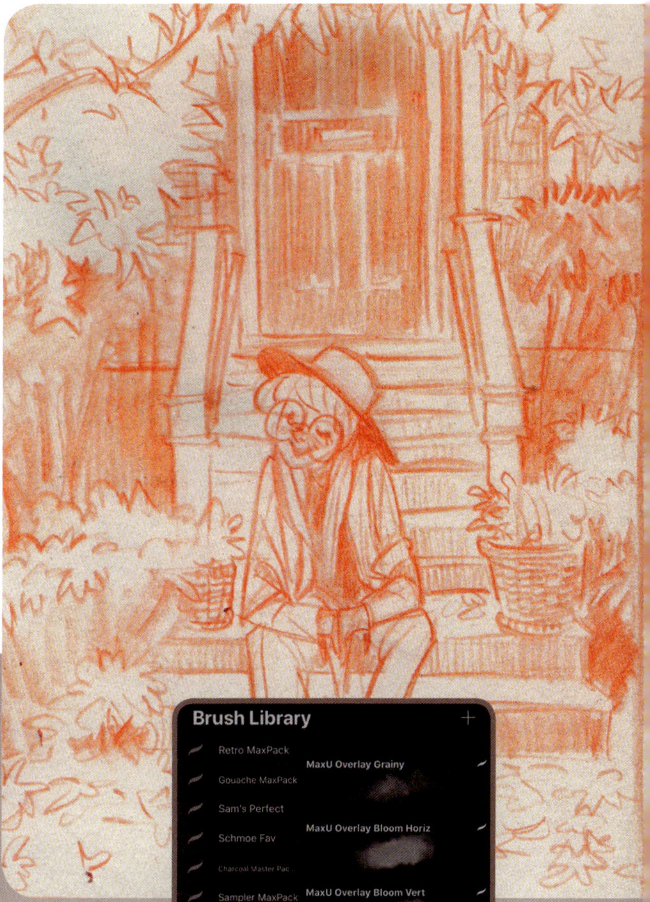

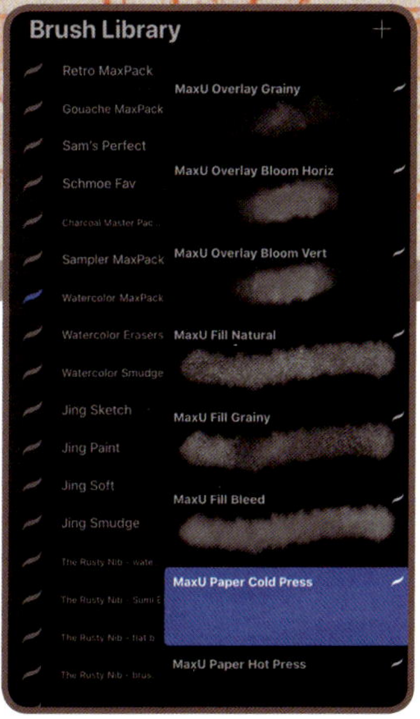

WARM BASE

With the image open in Procreate, I add a subtle paper texture background to give the design a warm tint. I use the MaxU Paper Cold Press brush, shown here on the right.

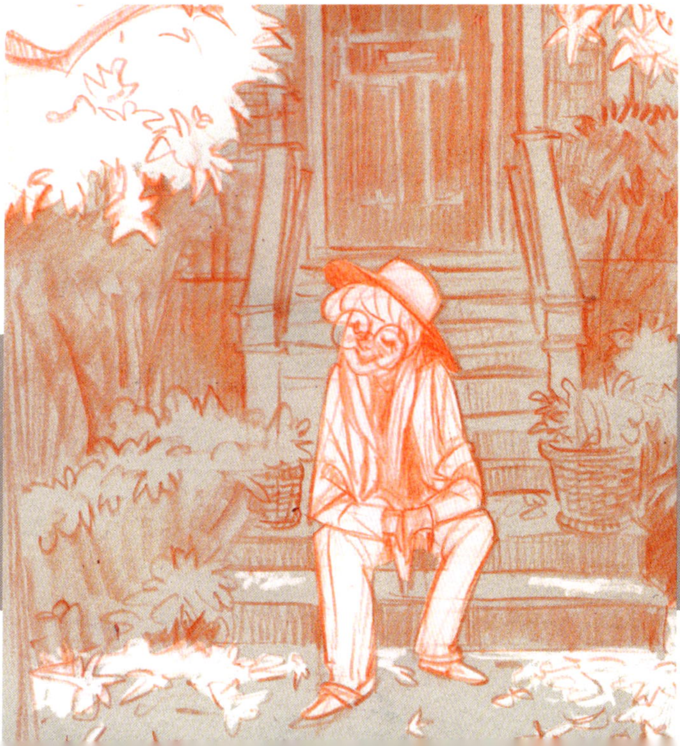

DEFINING GROUNDS

Next, I paint the foreground elements white to separate the background and foreground.

BUILDING BACKGROUND

Under the solid white foreground, using watercolor brushes shown below, I layer earthy base colors to build the background scene.

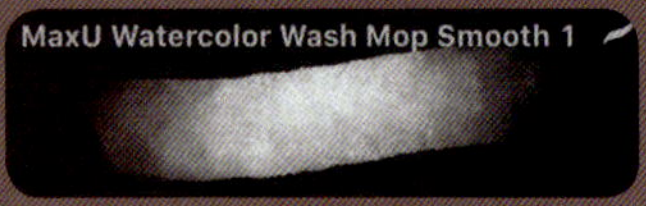

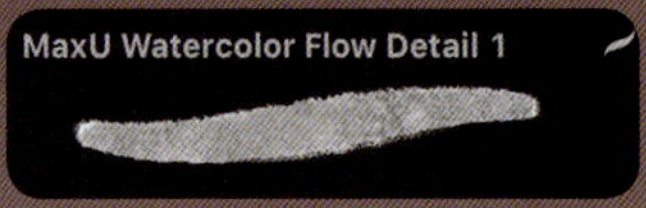

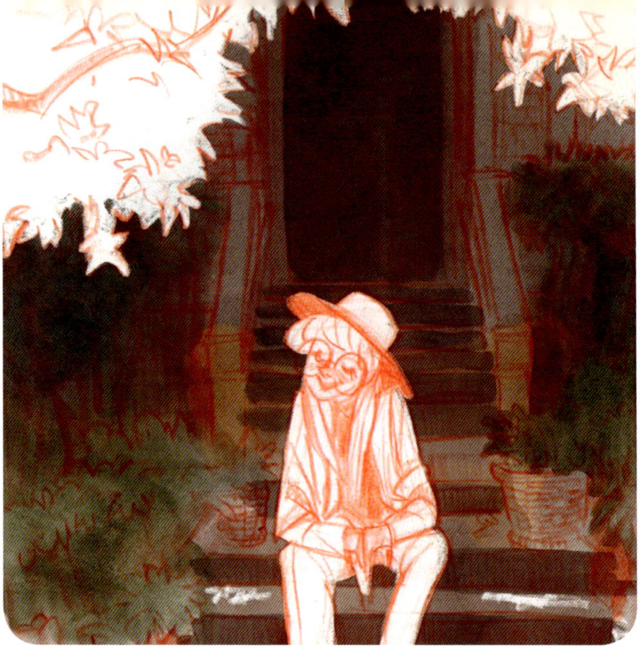

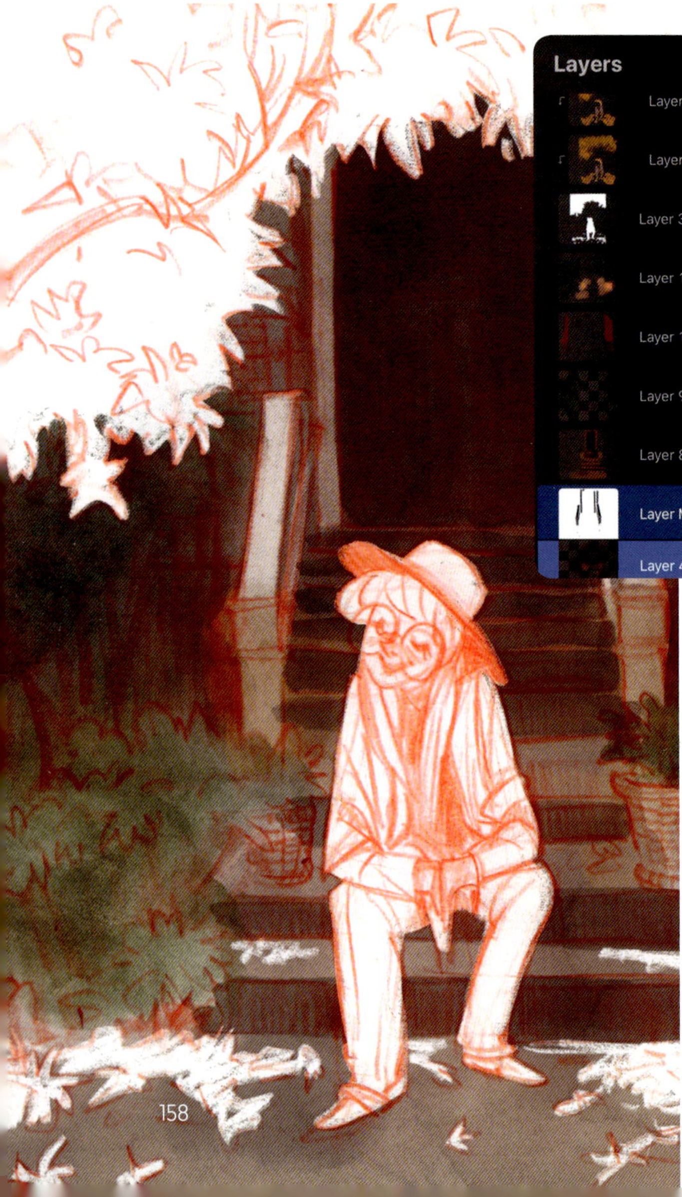

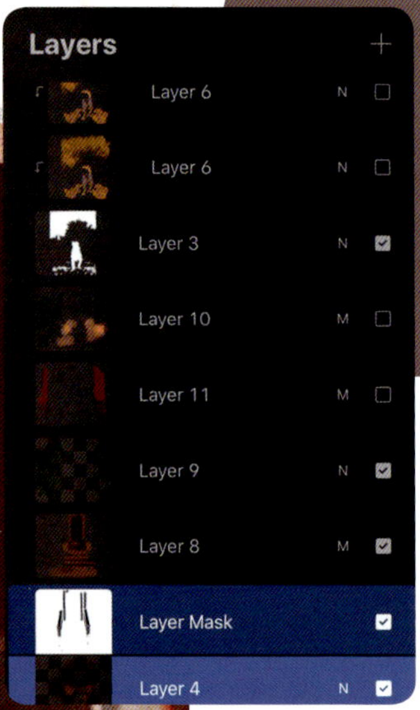

LIGHTENING

With a layer mask, I remove some of the color from parts of the handrails and door frame to lighten them and frame the character a little.

FOREGROUND COLOR

I then start adding warm seasonal color to the foreground foliage. The linework is on a separate layer on top of all layers and set to Multiply.

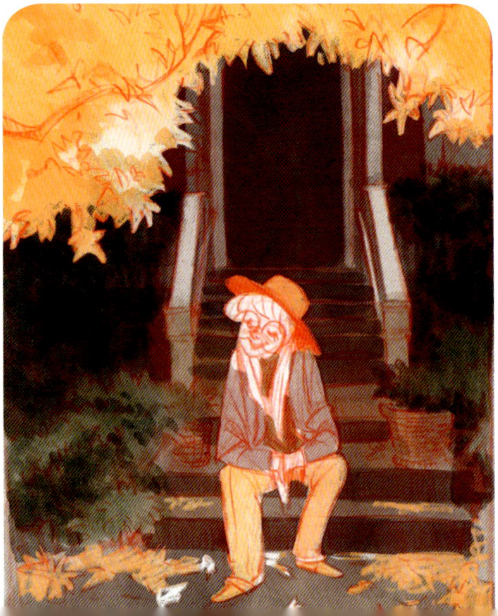

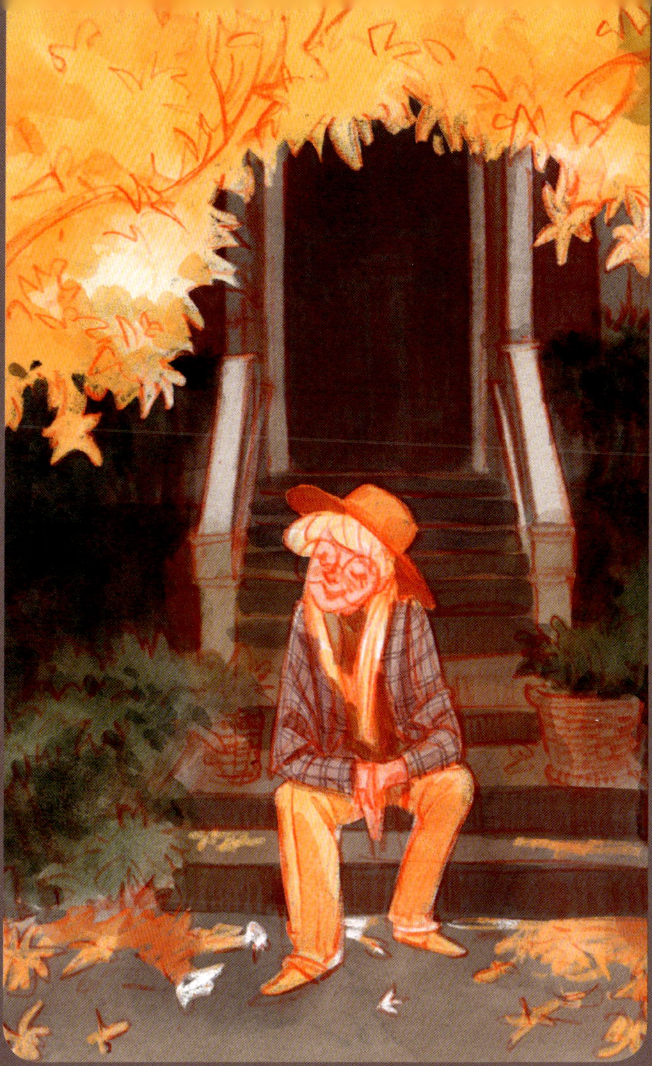

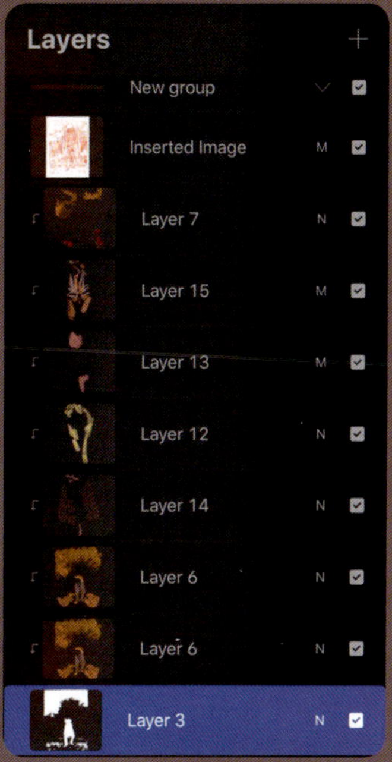

LAYERING COLOR

I continue to add color by layering up the layers on top of each other. All new layers are clipped onto the white layer, with the background layers sitting underneath.

SHADING

I add shadow to the colors in the background by painting on a layer set to Multiply. I then add further shading to the rest of the foliage in the middle ground and begin to add details.

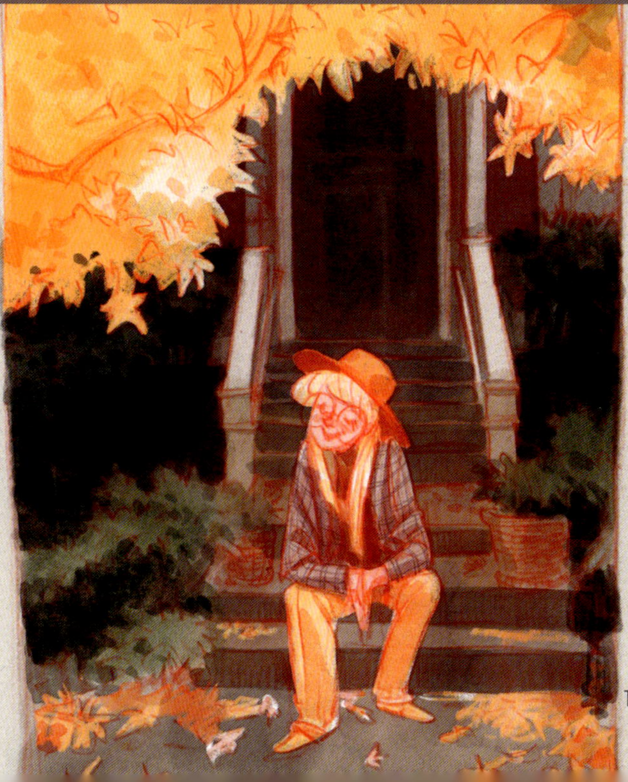

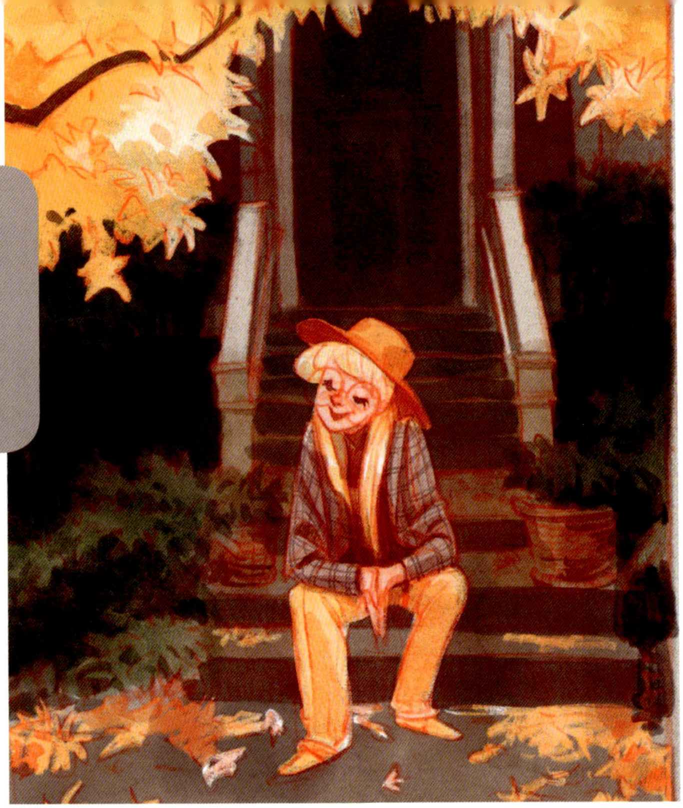

DETAILING

I apply further details all over the piece using the chalk brush below.

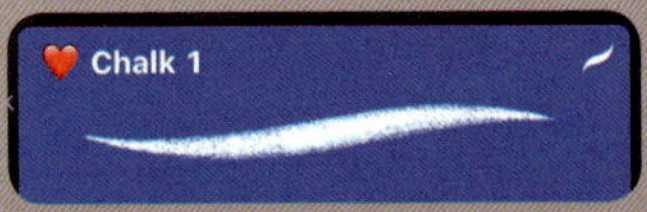

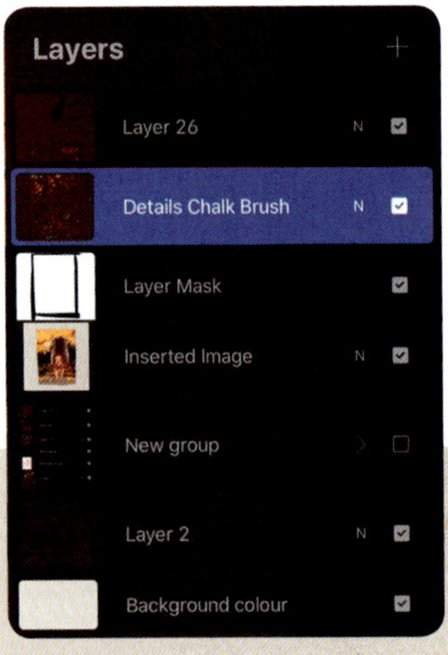

All layers in this group are turned off (except the texture layer at the bottom)

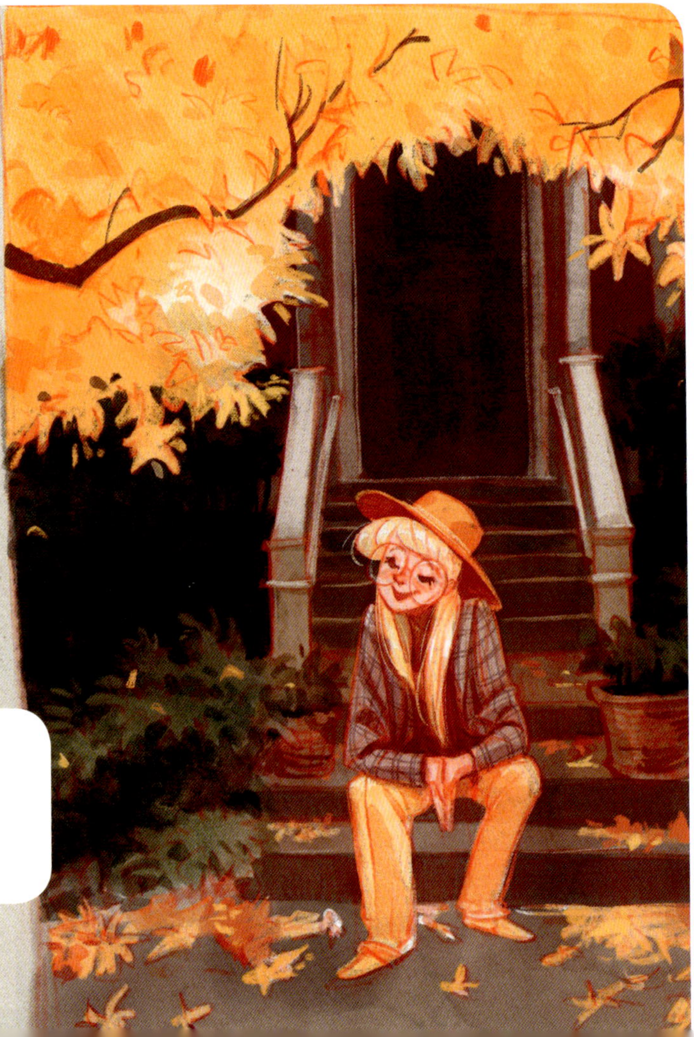

FINALIZING

Finally, I add the last details and clean-up with a layer mask on a flat image of all the layers.

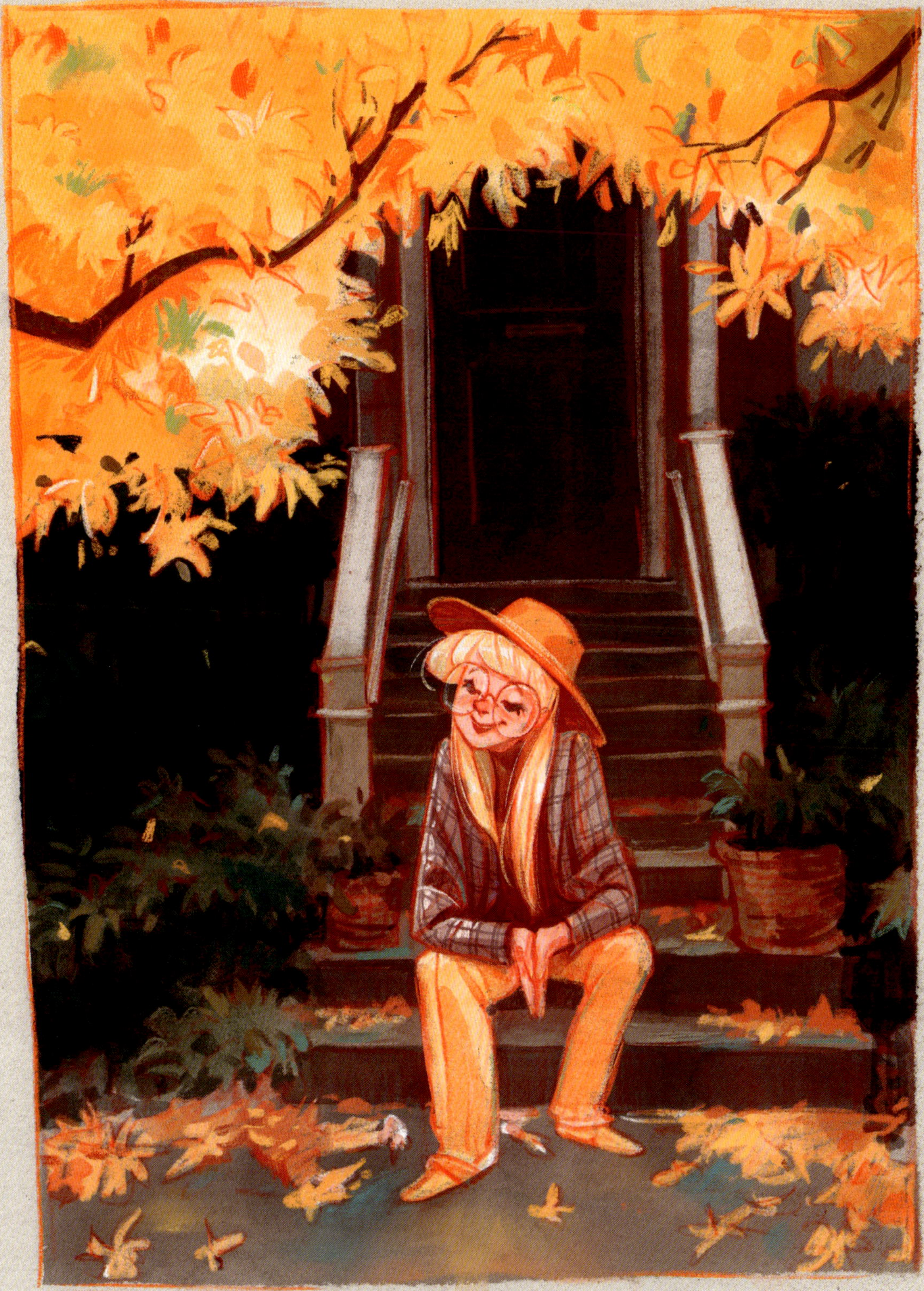

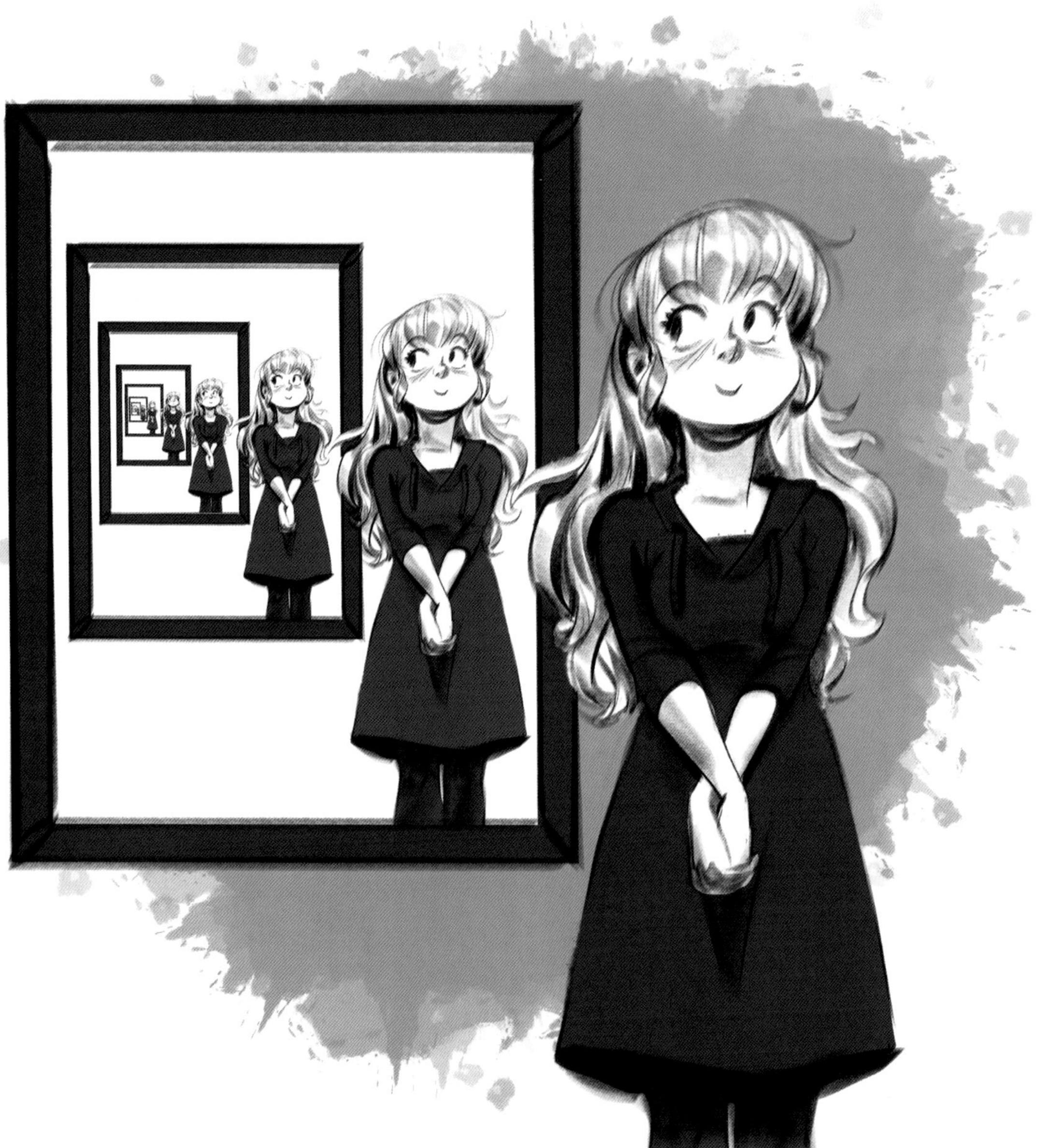

GALLERY

Walk with me through a collection of my recent art. I'm very proud and happy with the following pieces. Each one has taught me something new and provided a stepping stone toward my unique style, which I feel I am coming closer to. In recent times, I have found workflows that suit me well, and make me want to create even more. I love how I can create art while learning so much along the way!

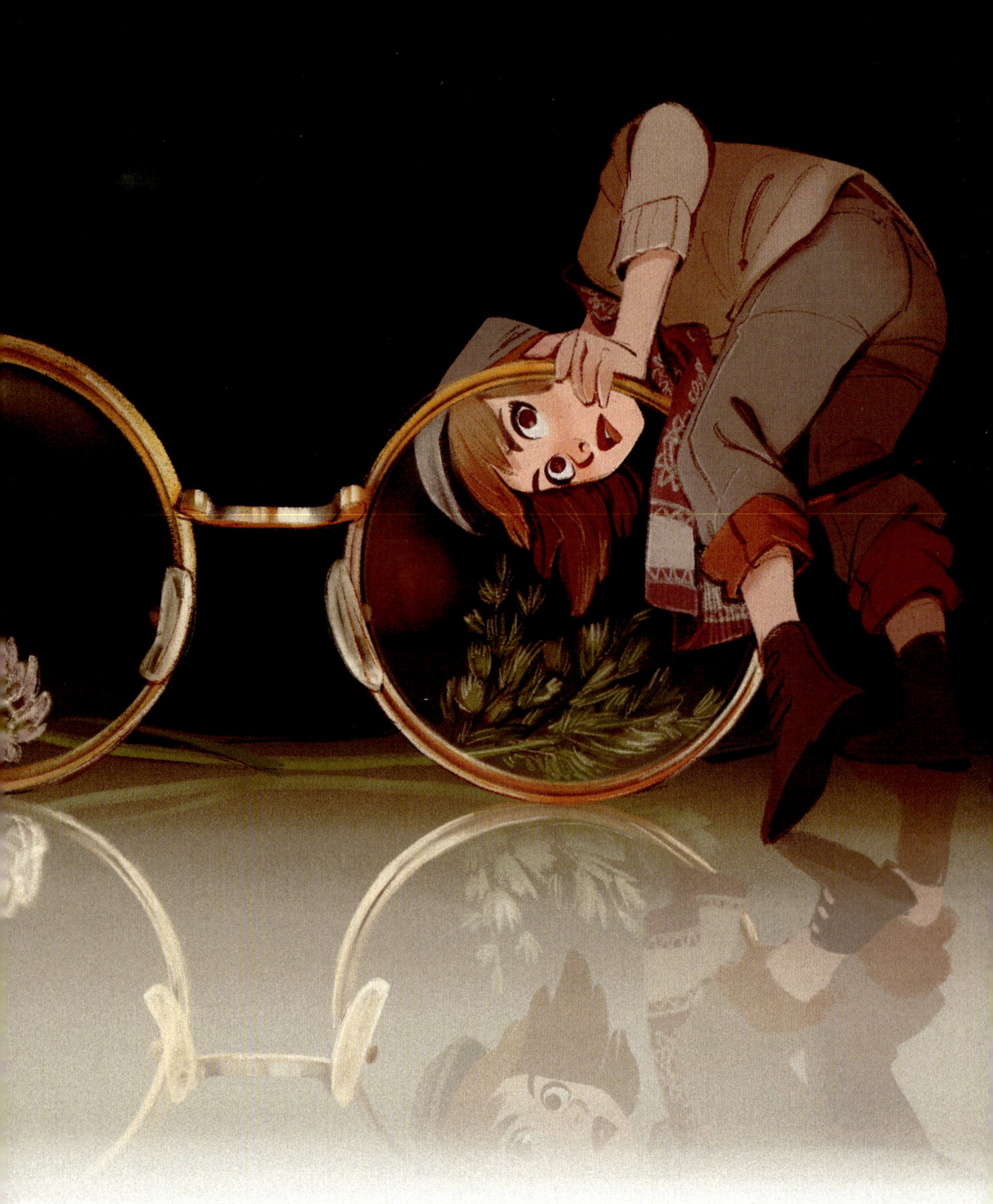

TAKE A LOOK

Sometimes an idea just jumps out at you when you see an interesting photo. Inspired by a photograph by @mydreammountainhouse

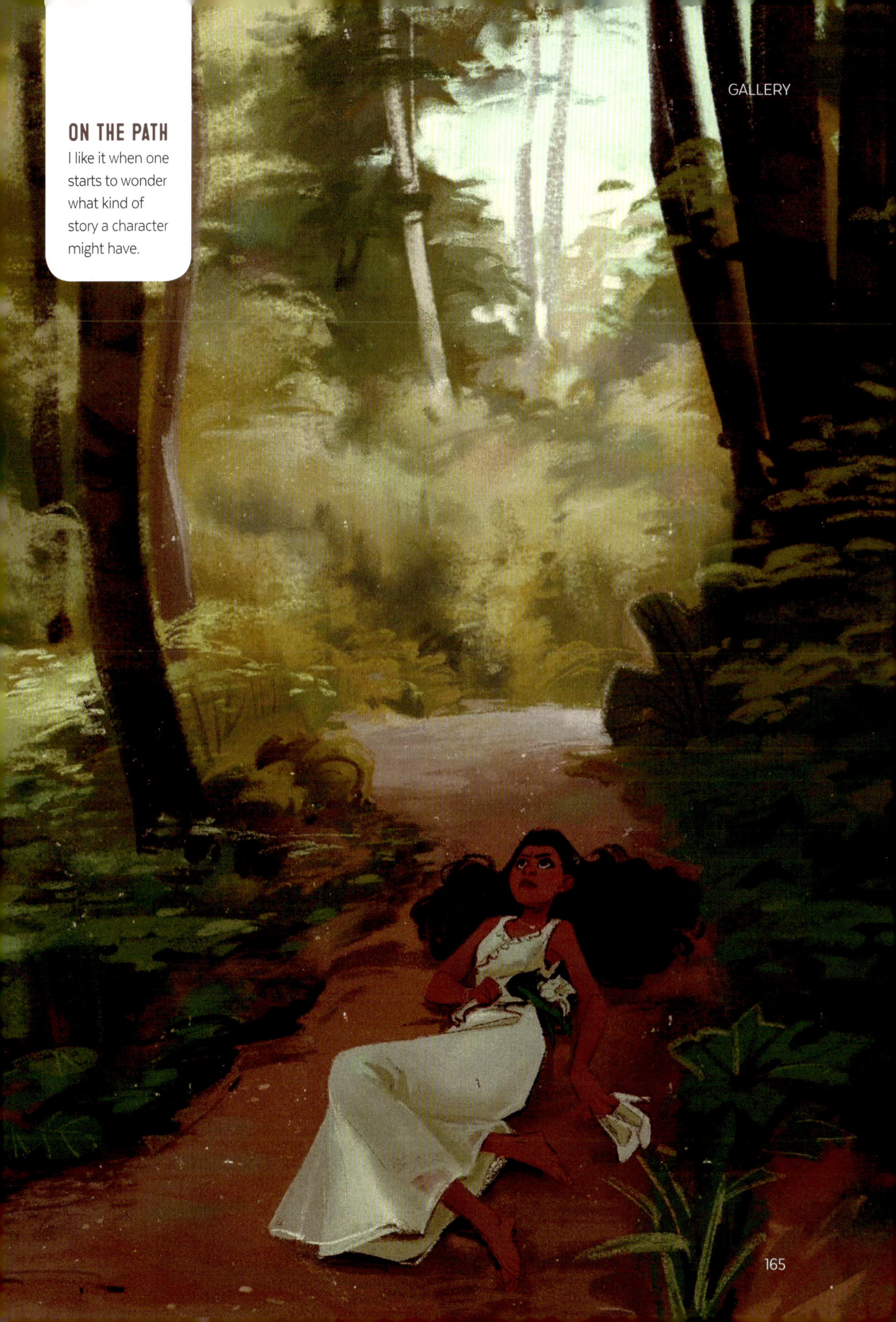

ON THE PATH

I like it when one starts to wonder what kind of story a character might have.

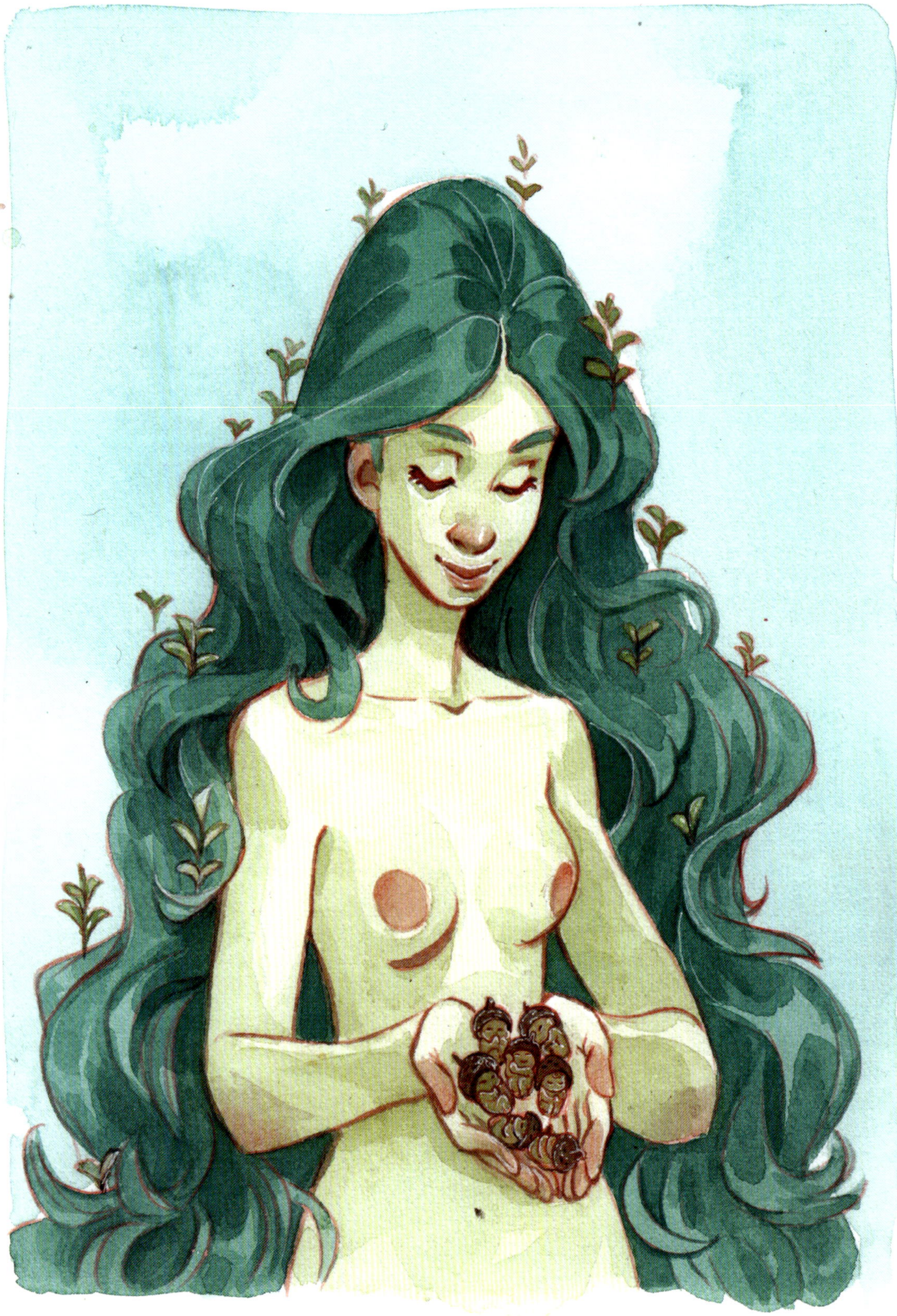

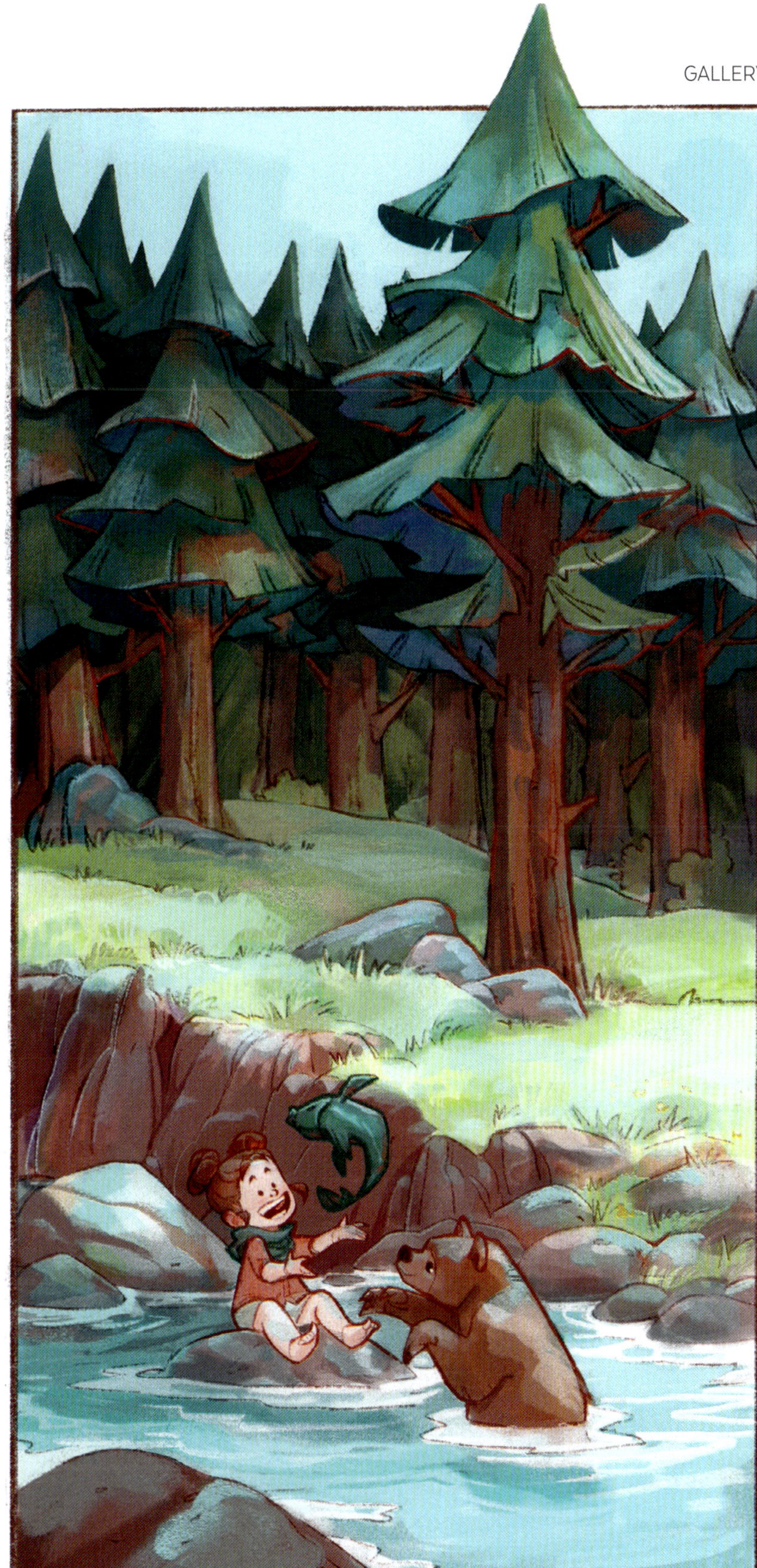

MOTHER
I love the idea of acorns being little babies.

AT THE RIVER
Drawing animals and kids as friends is always a treat!

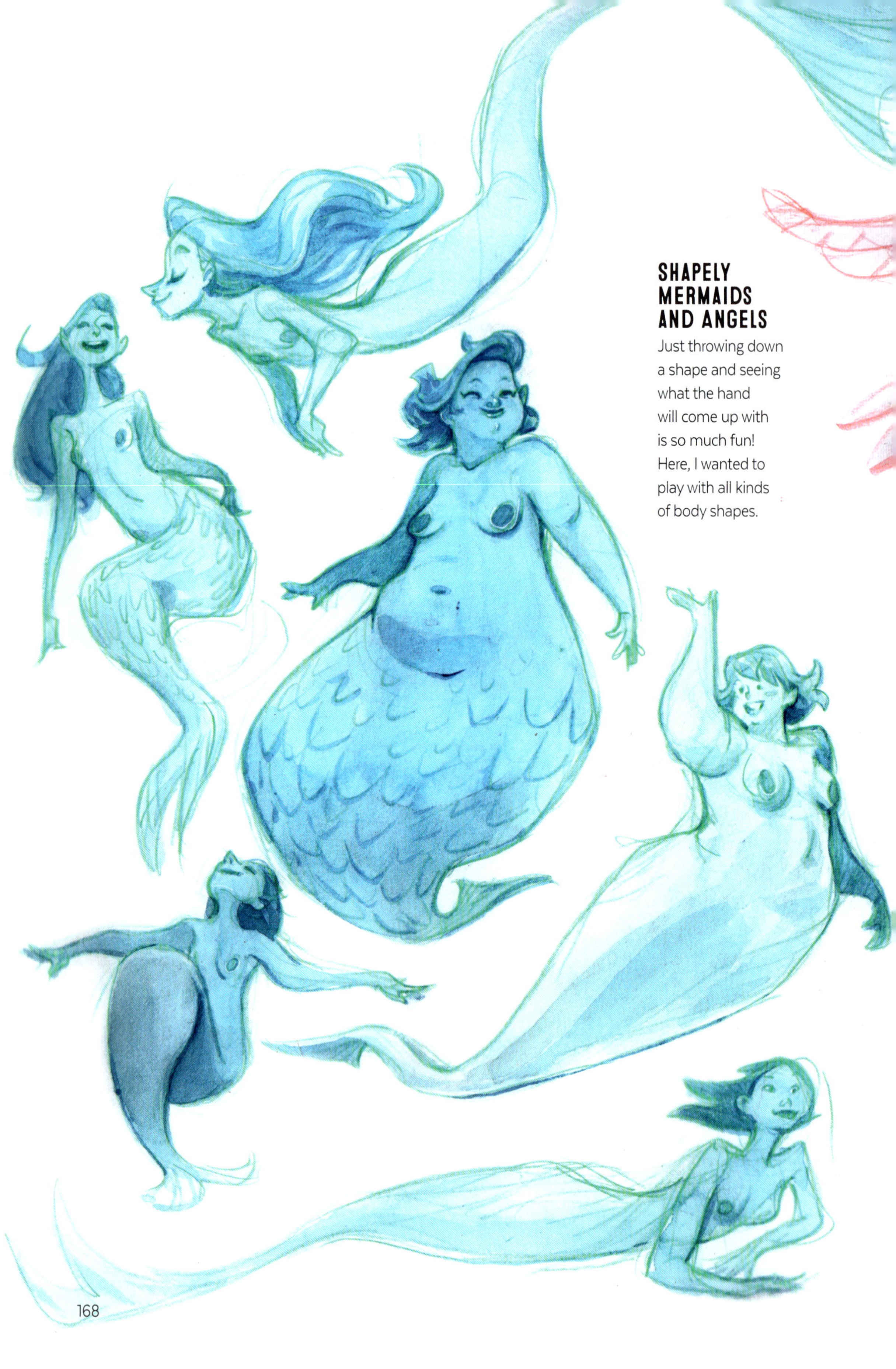

SHAPELY MERMAIDS AND ANGELS

Just throwing down a shape and seeing what the hand will come up with is so much fun! Here, I wanted to play with all kinds of body shapes.

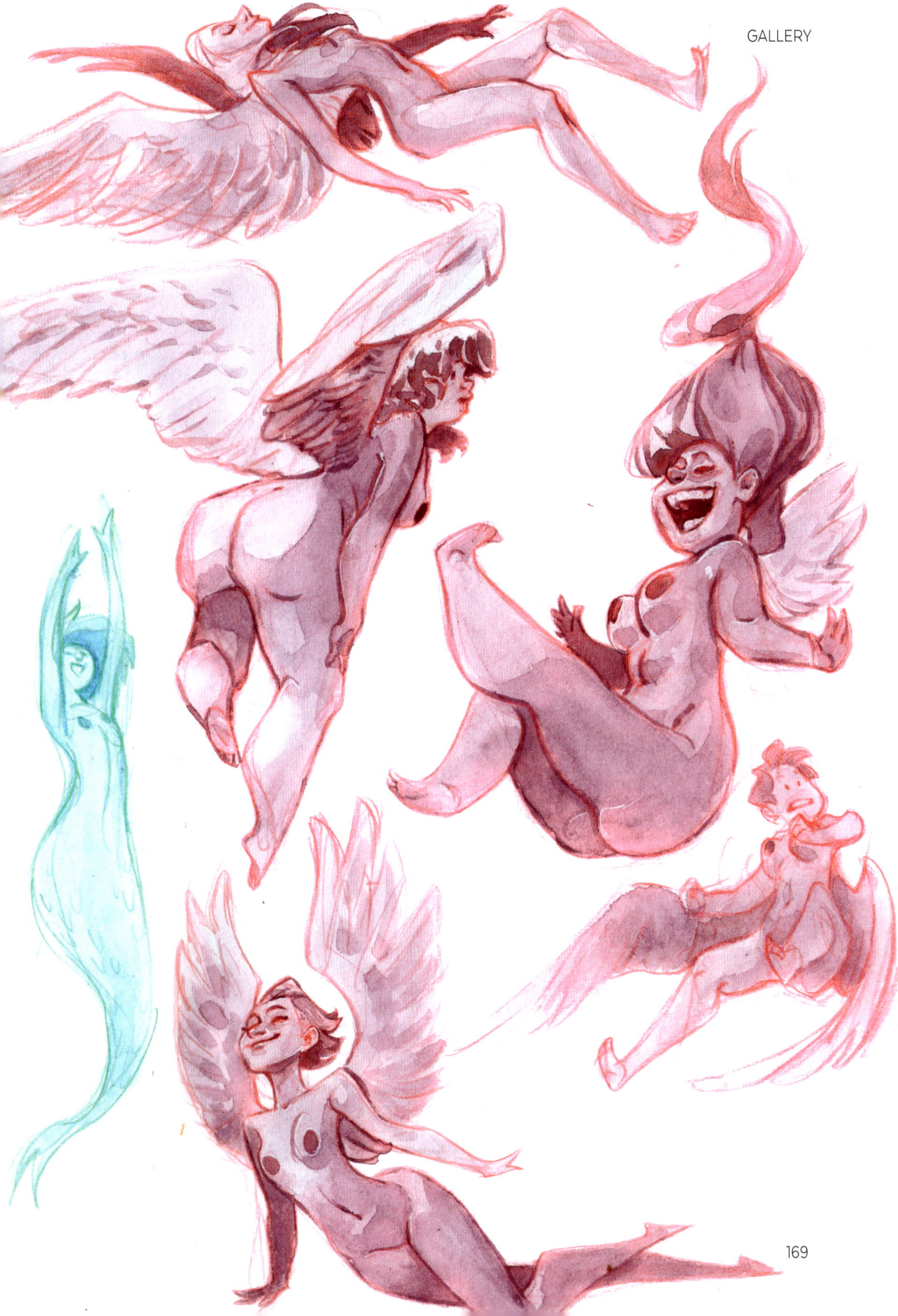

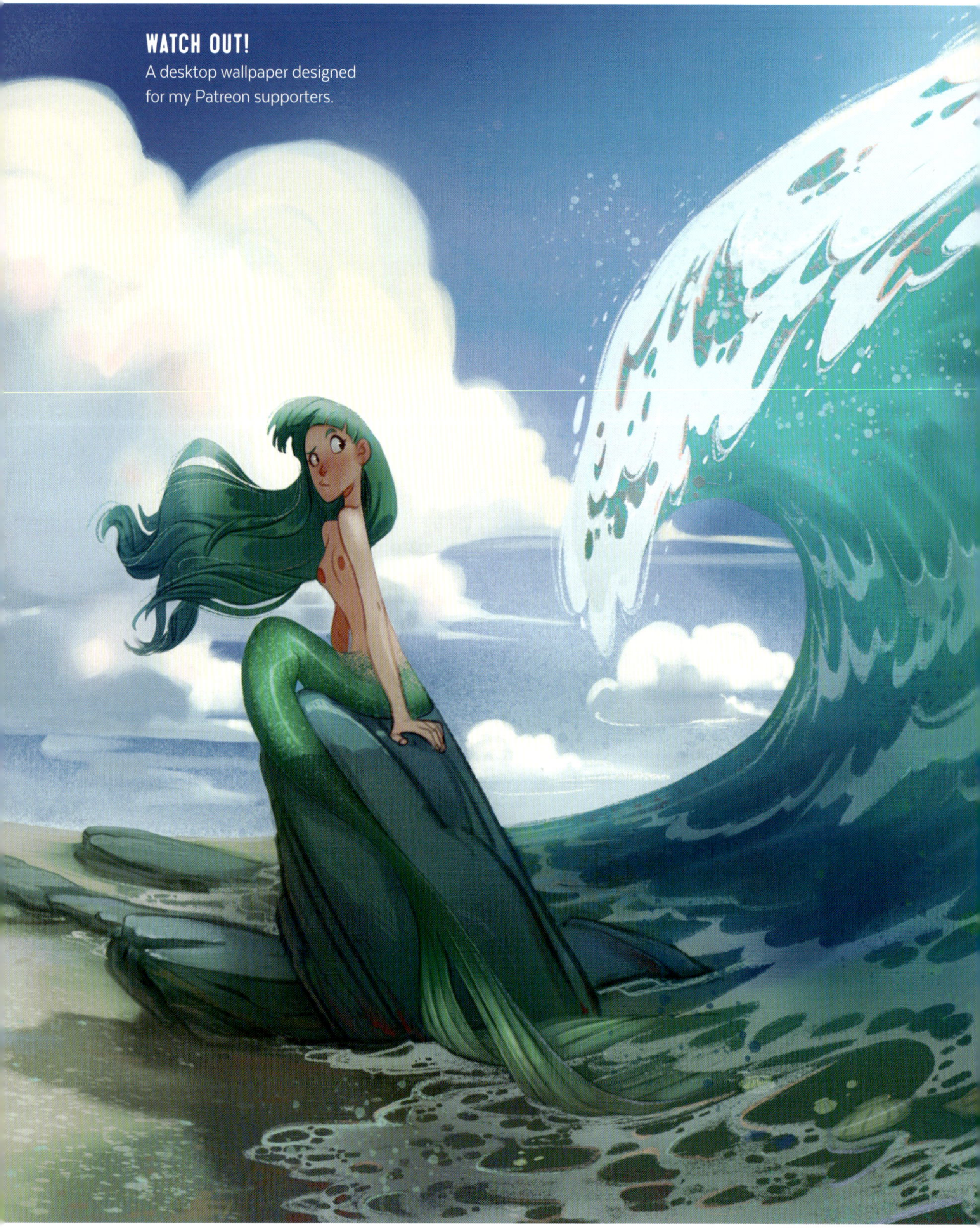

WATCH OUT!

A desktop wallpaper designed for my Patreon supporters.

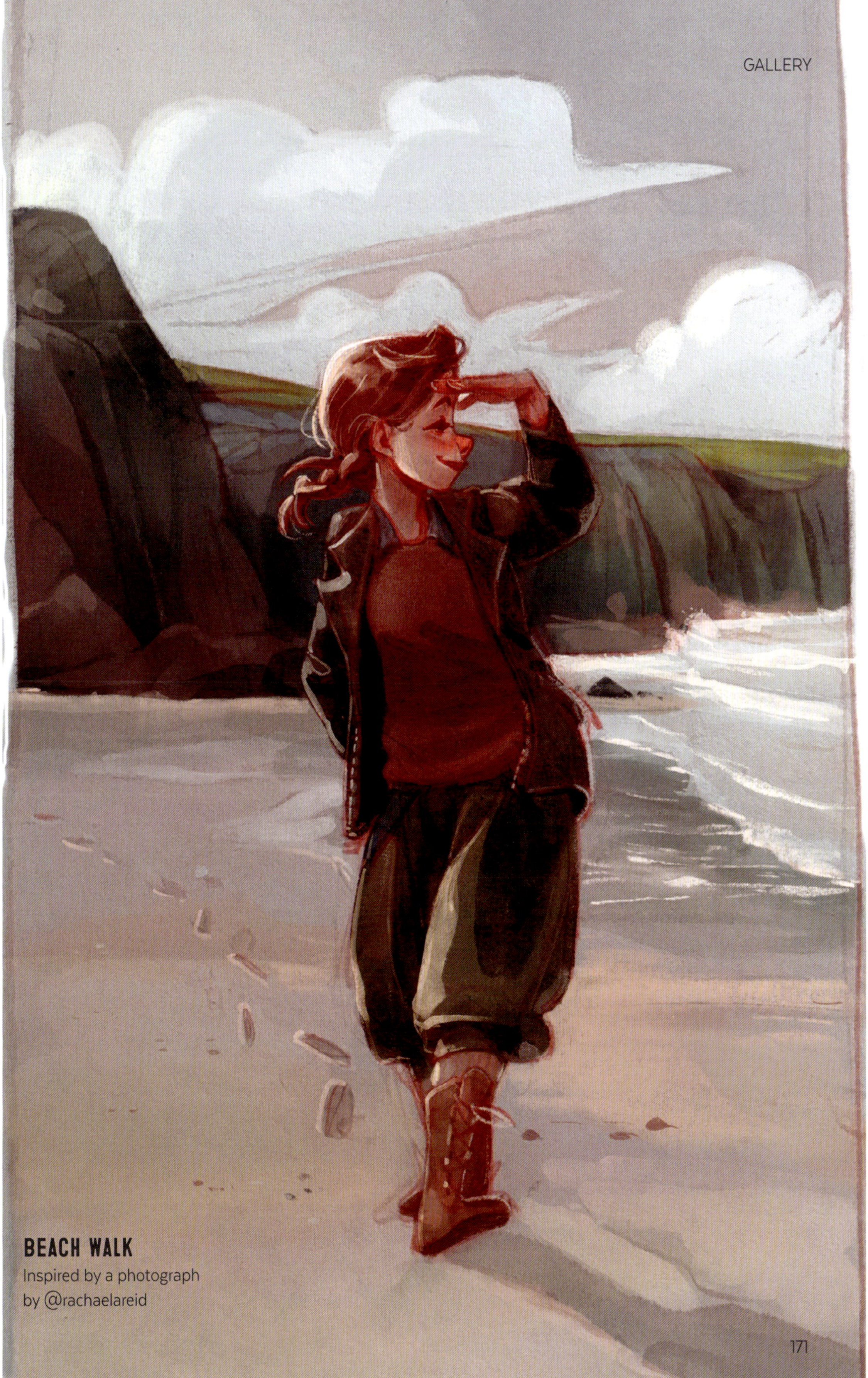

BEACH WALK
Inspired by a photograph
by @rachaelareid

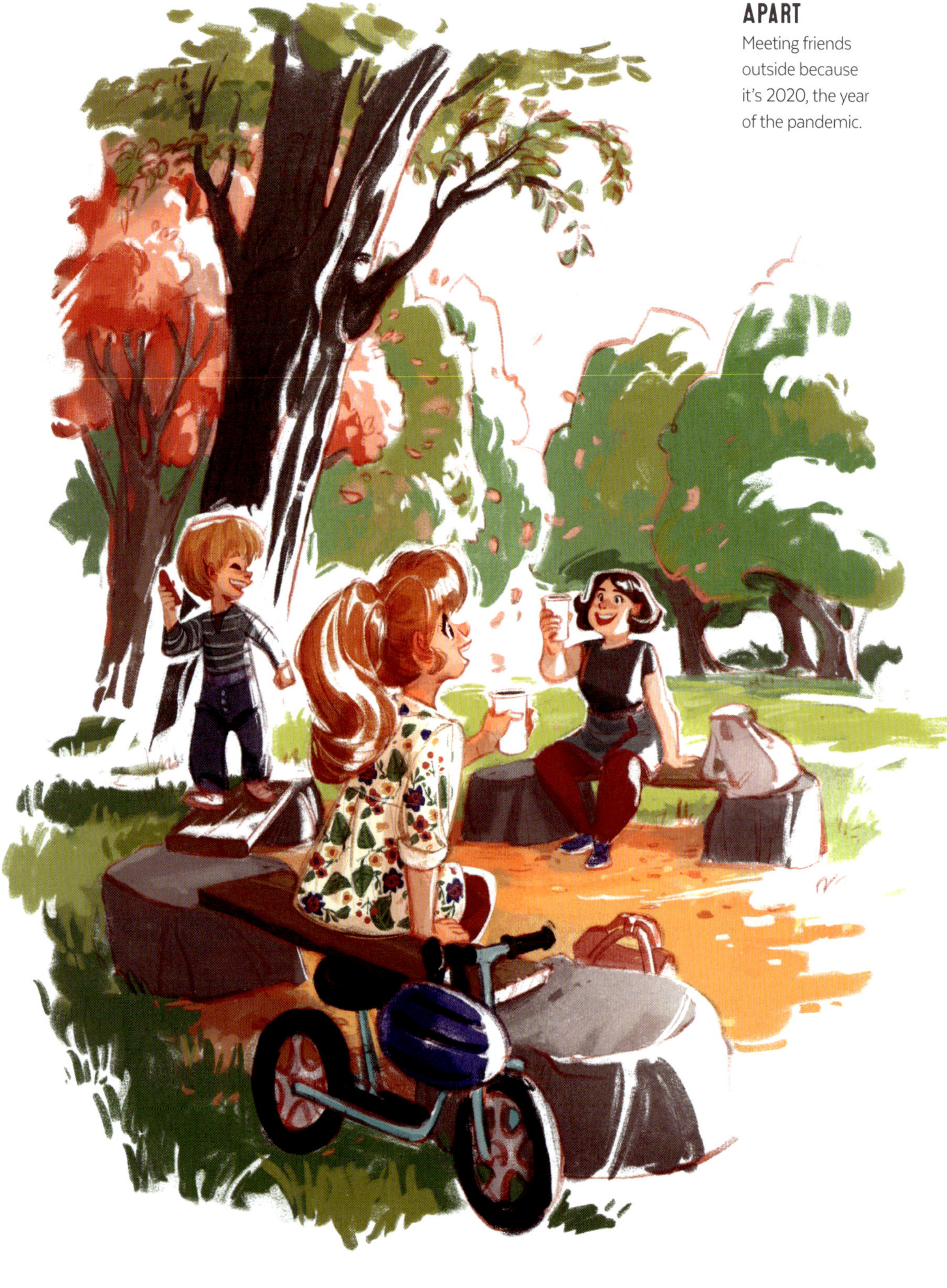

TWO METERS APART

Meeting friends outside because it's 2020, the year of the pandemic.

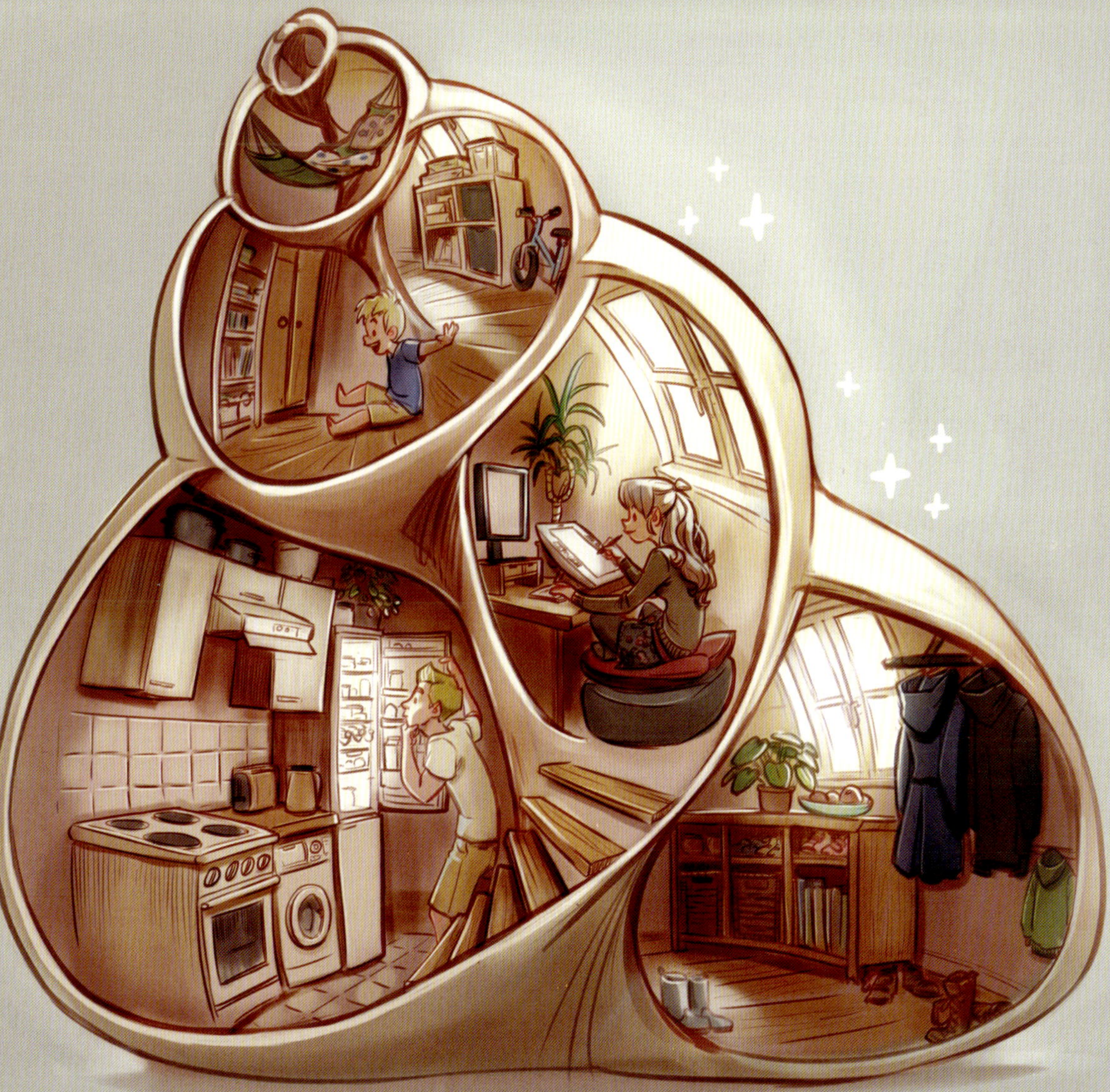

OUR SHELL

I wanted to capture the feeling of pulling back from the world in 2020. And, to me, hiding like a little snail didn't feel too bad.

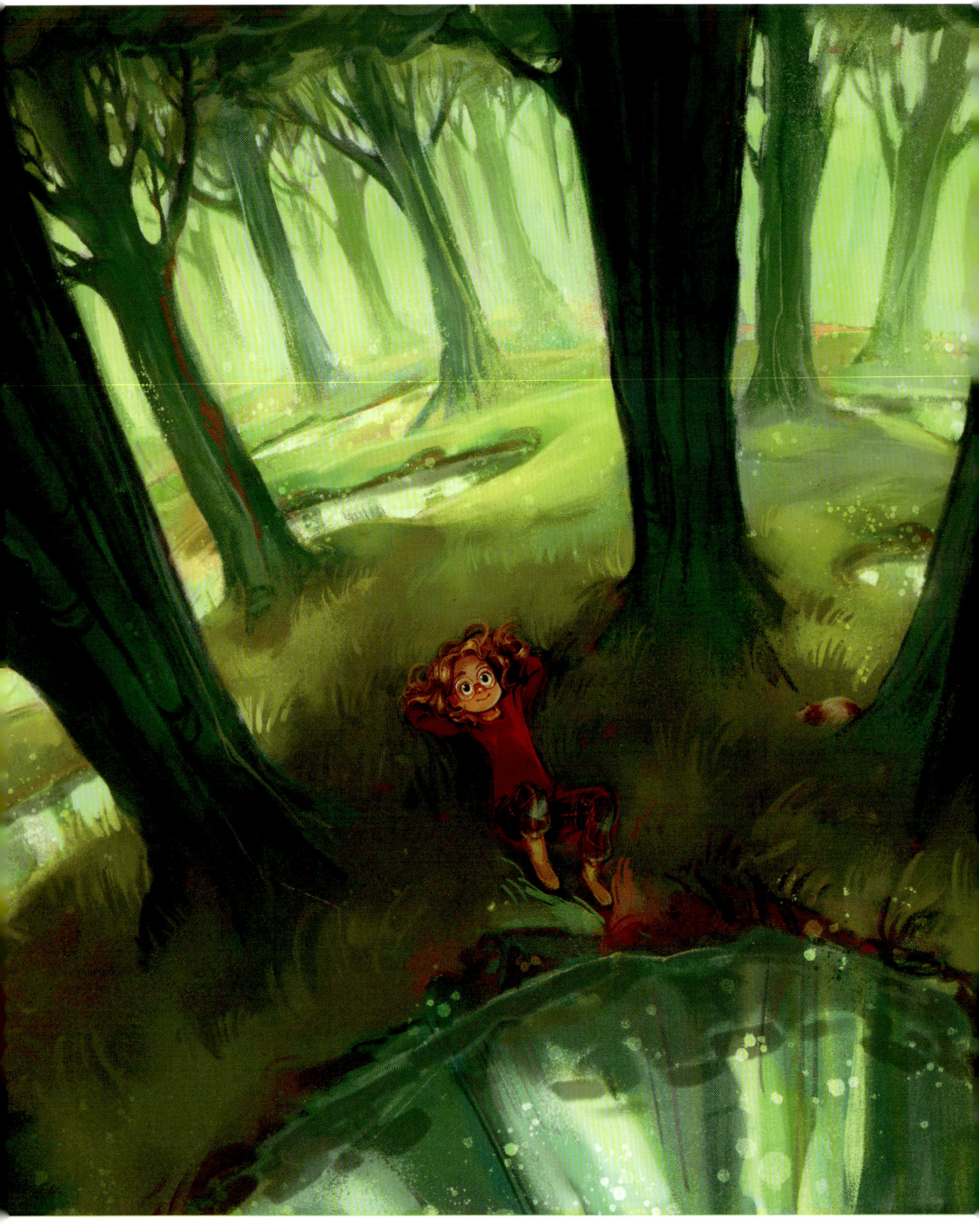

THE WOODS BETWEEN WORLDS

This piece is inspired by a place from *The Magician's Nephew* by C.S. Lewis that I always wanted to visit. Each pool leads to another world!

SHAPELY CERVITAURS

Sometimes, I love to just work intuitively and go with the flow!

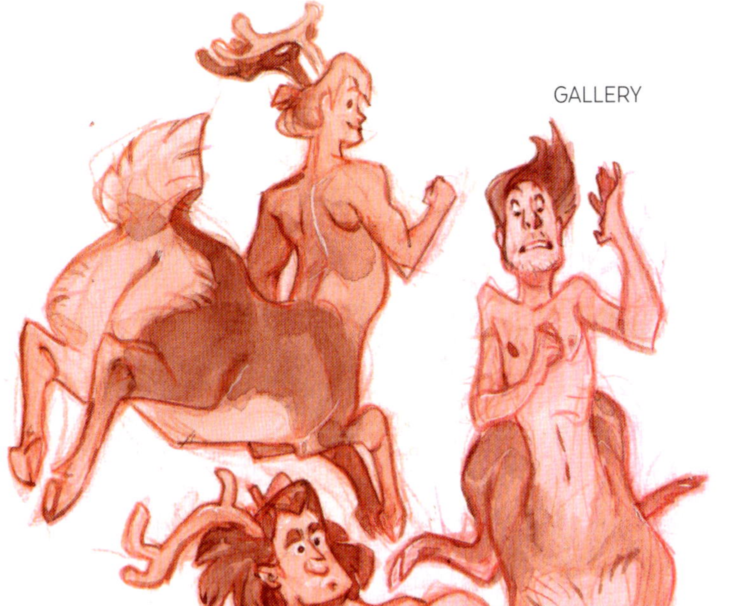

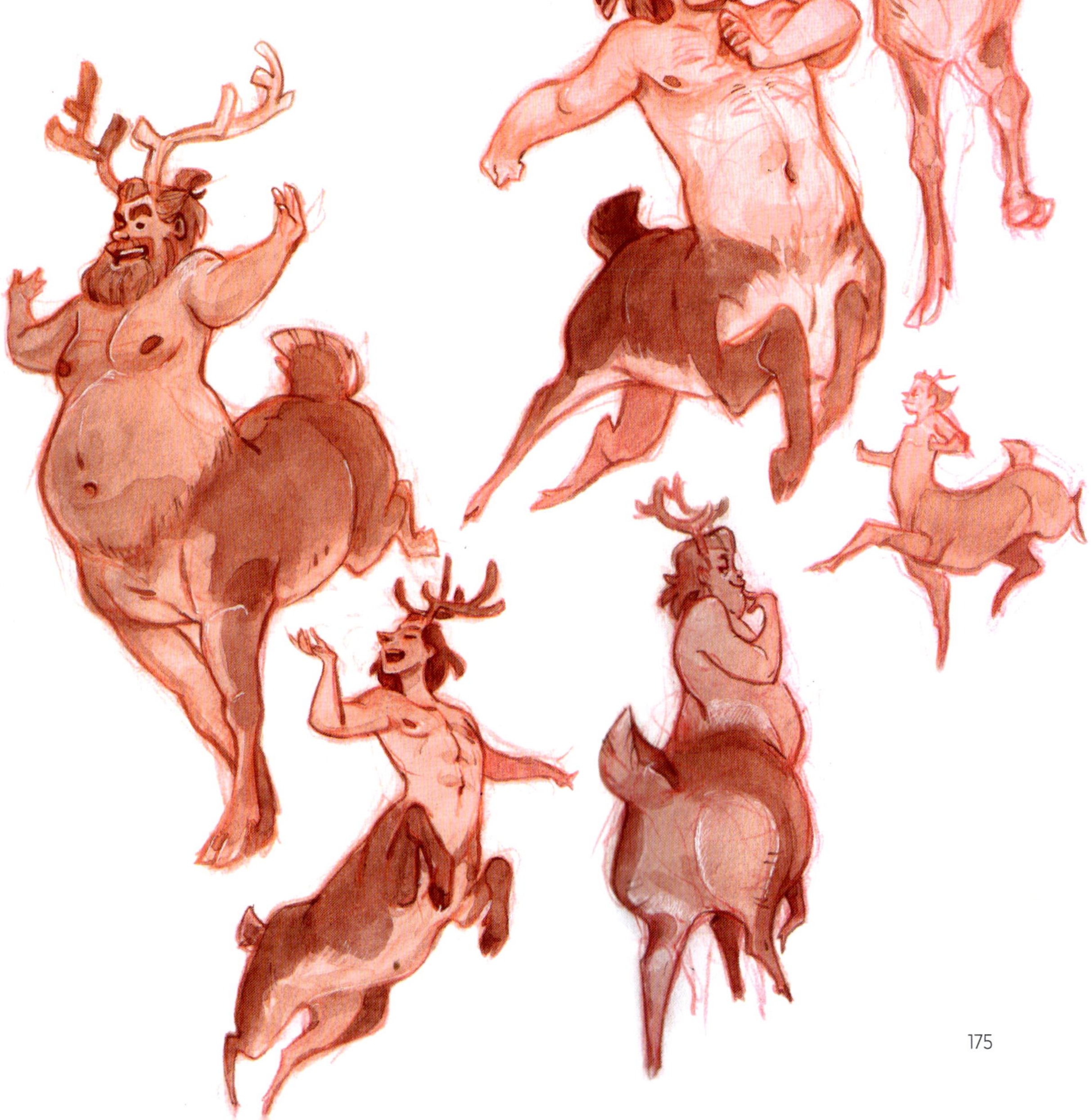

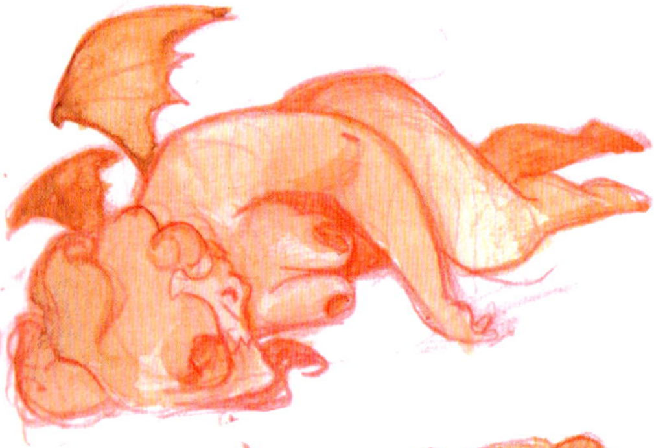

JERIANIE'S WOODS

I follow photographer and illustrator, Jerianie, on Instagram and I am always inspired by her beautiful photos of woods – I would love to go there!

SHAPELY DEVILS

My favorite design of the group is the devil sitting down.

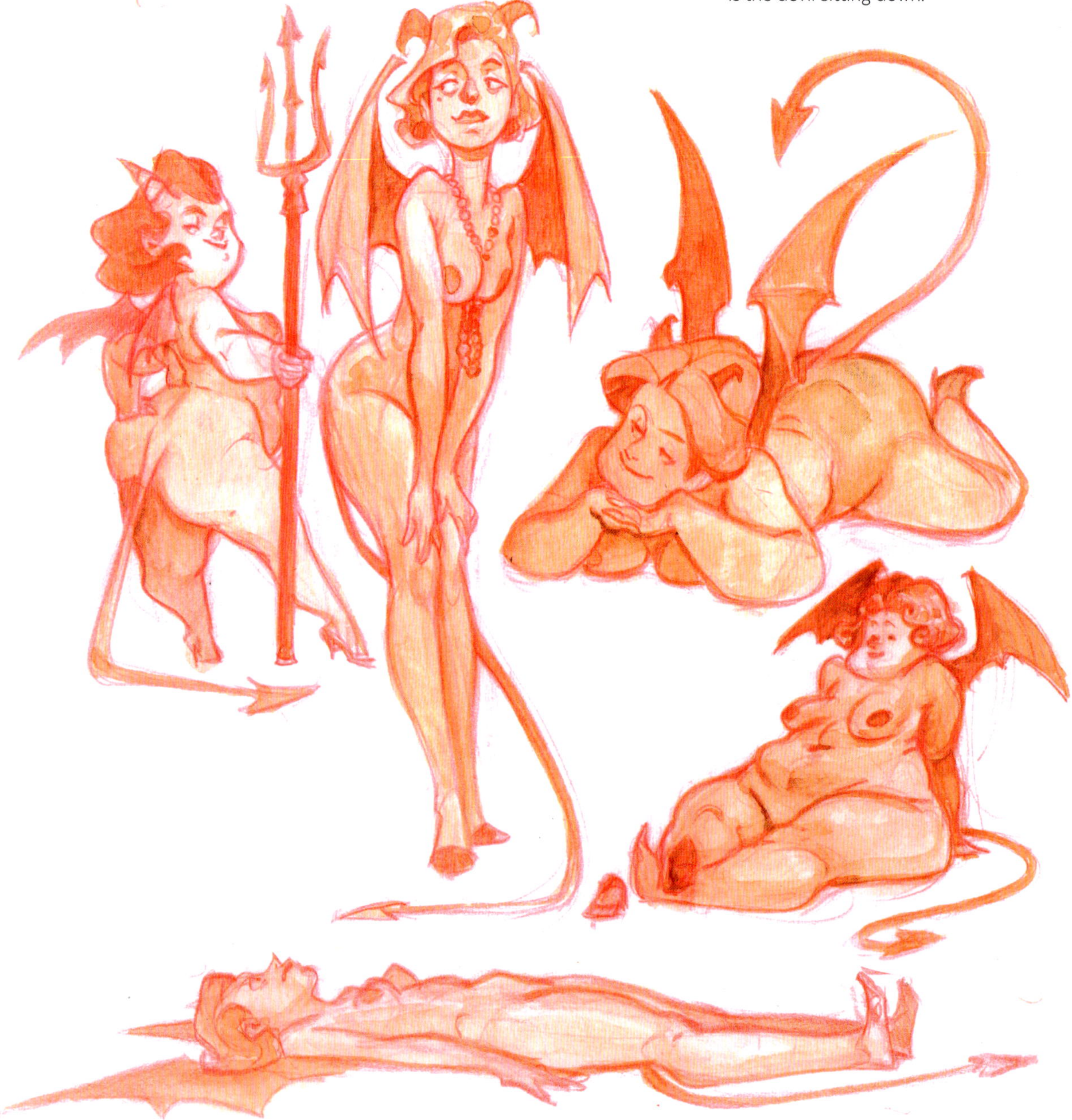

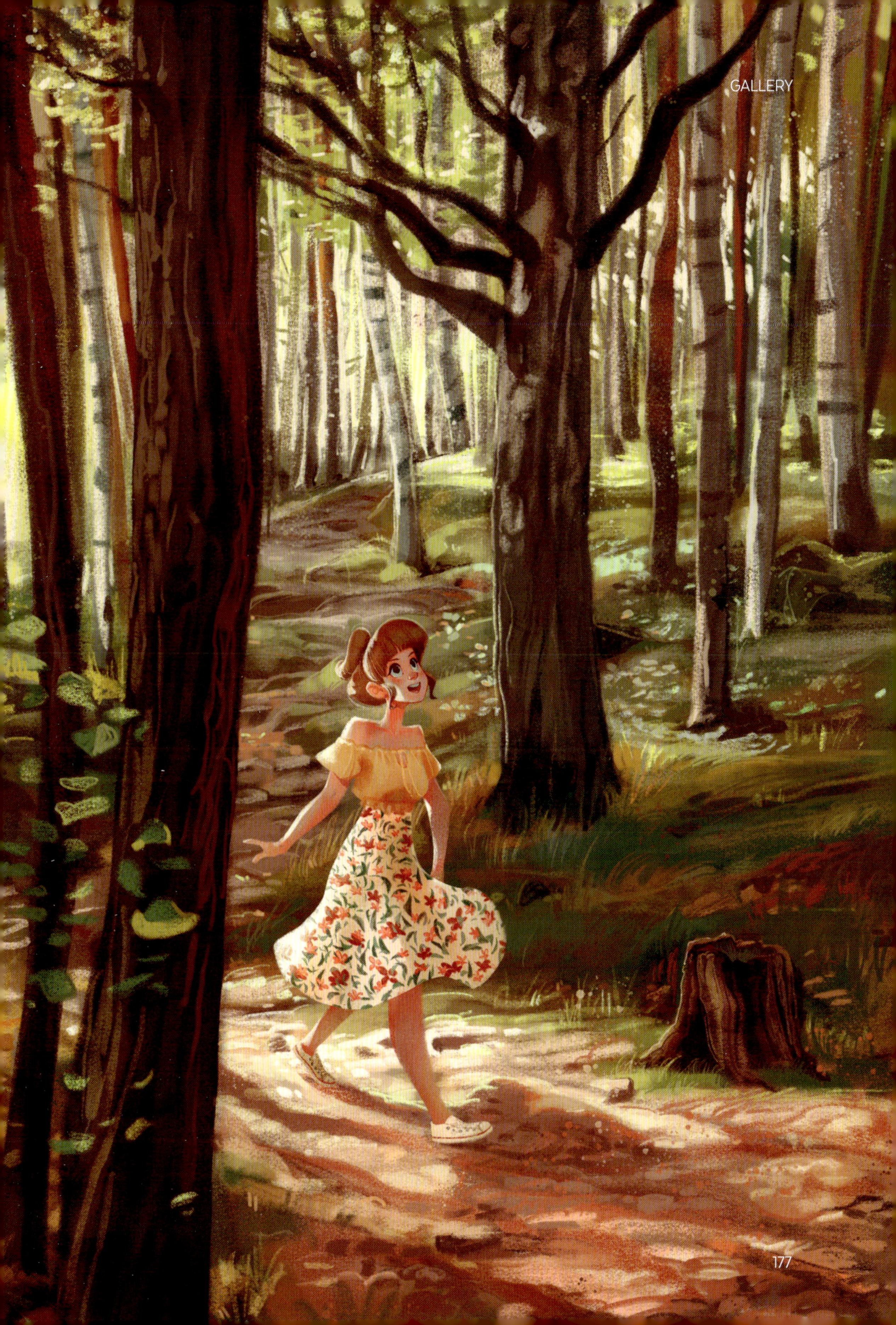

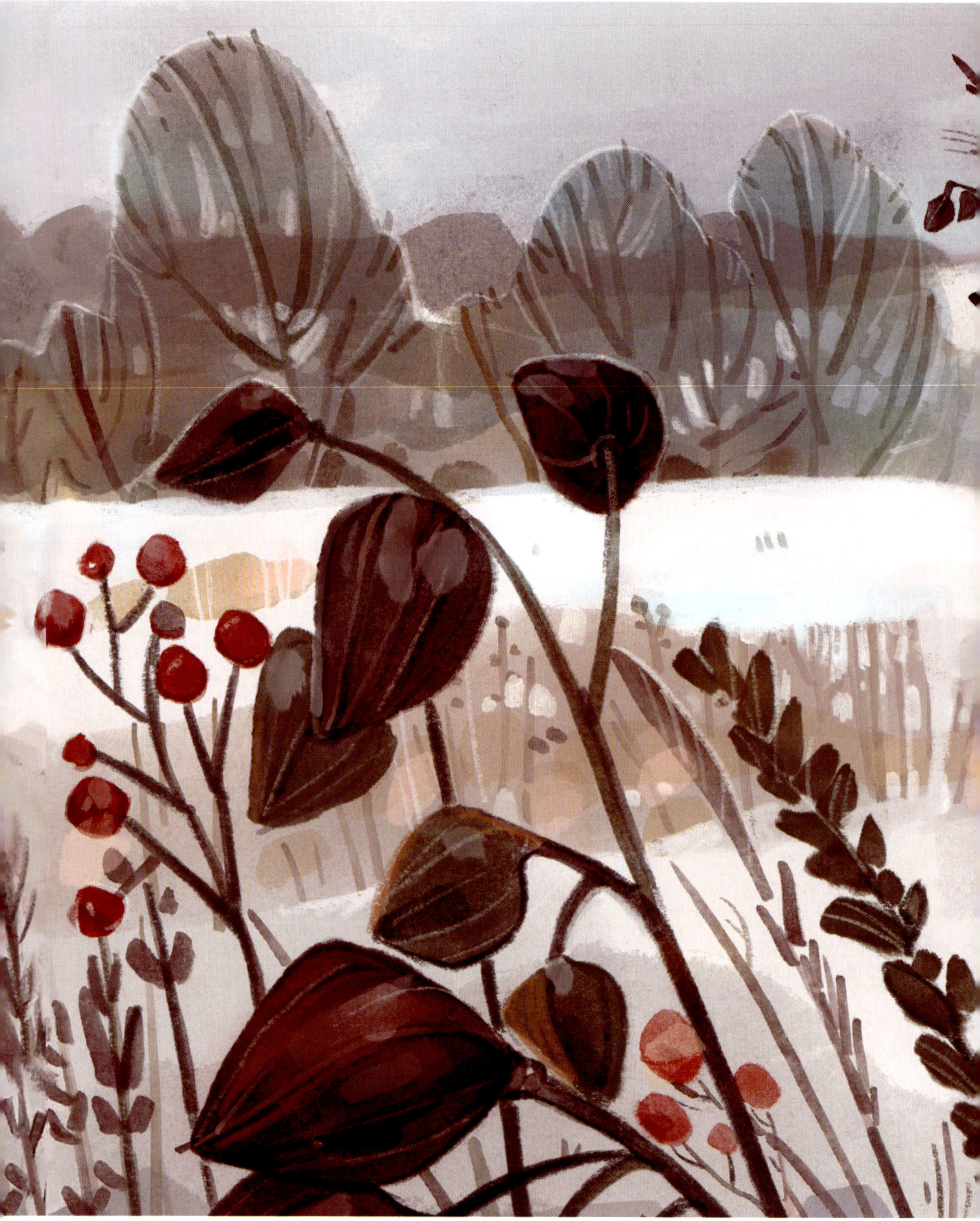

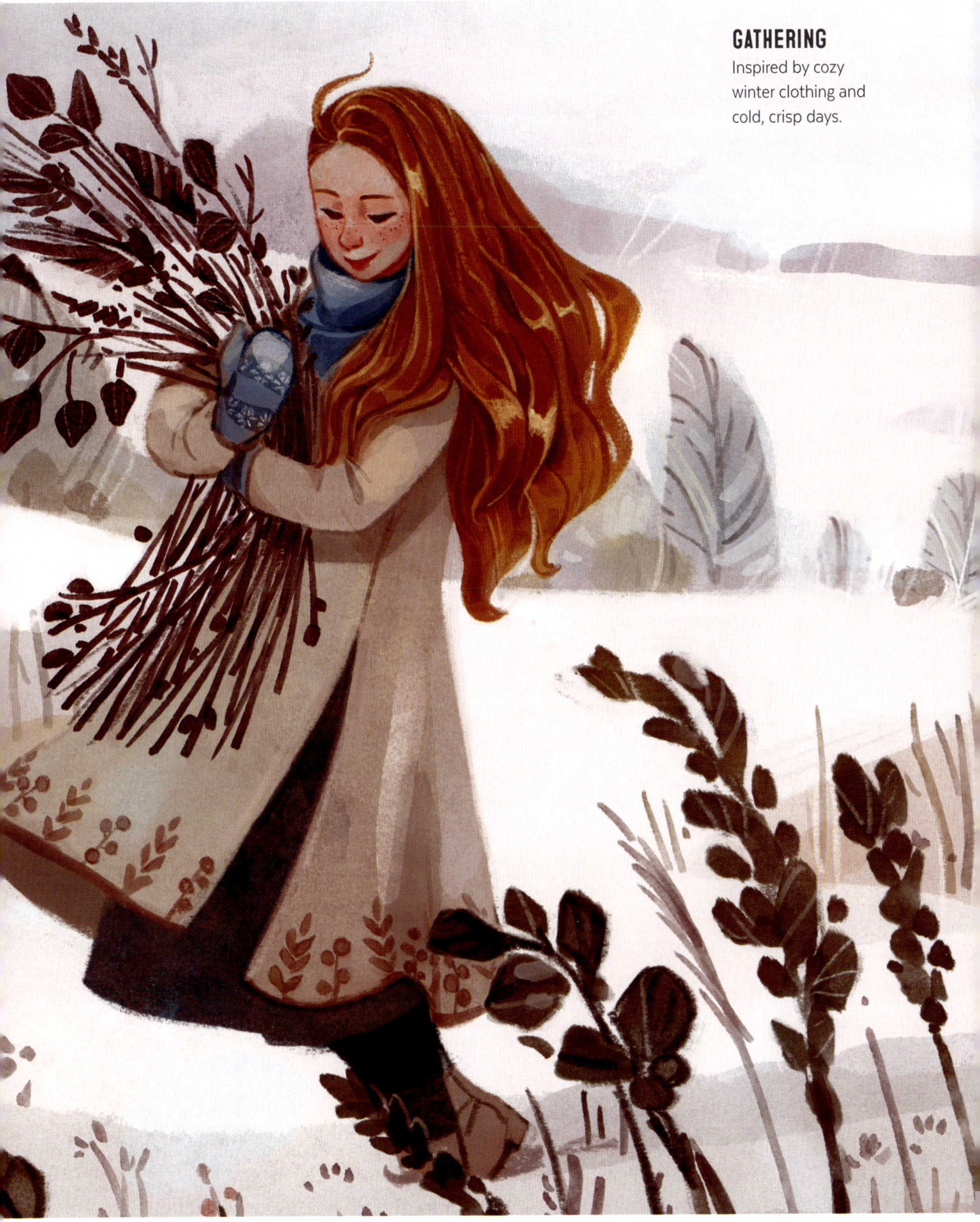

GATHERING
Inspired by cozy winter clothing and cold, crisp days.

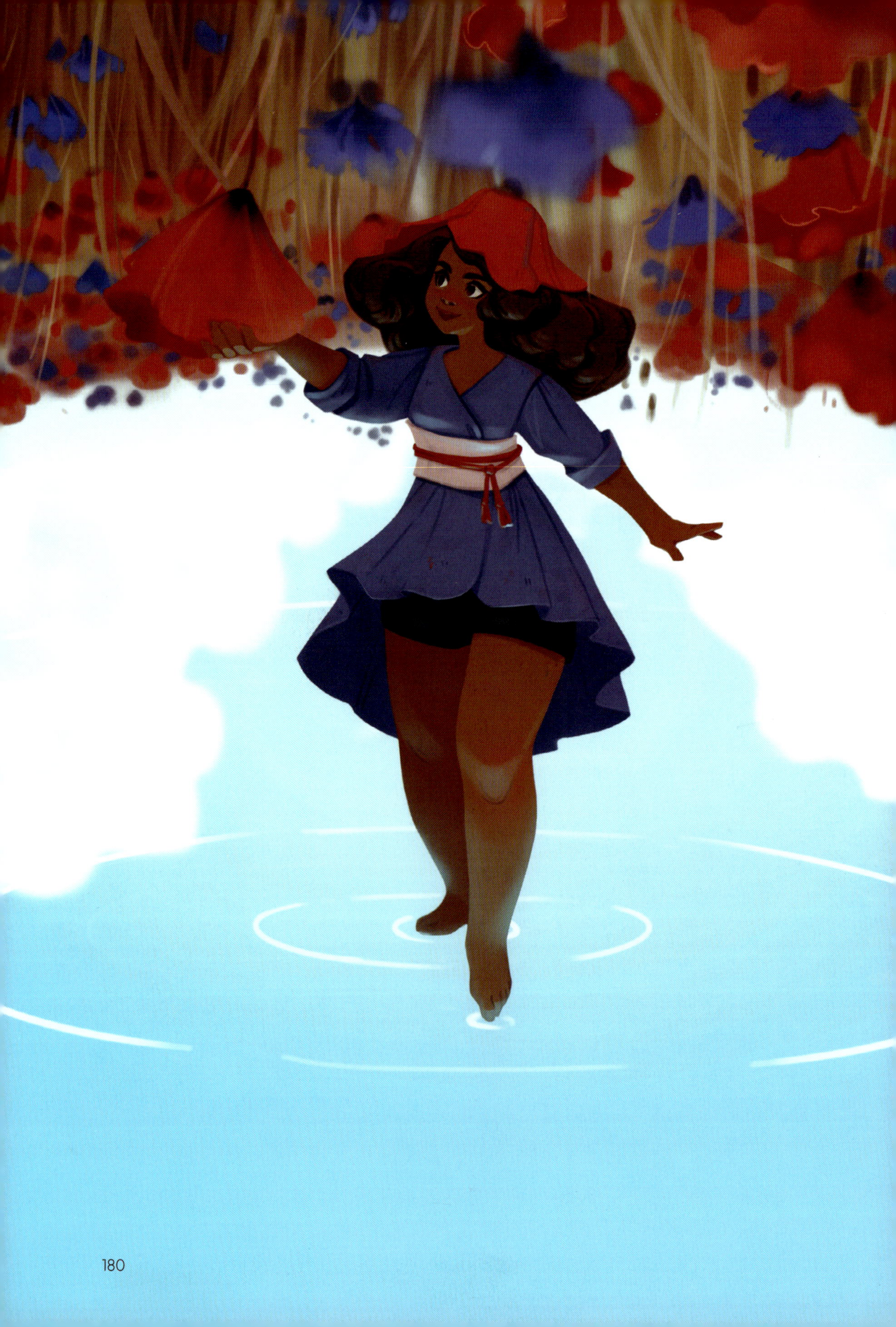

POPPY HAT
Wearing a field of flowers in a dream. Inspired by a photograph by @augenbl.icke

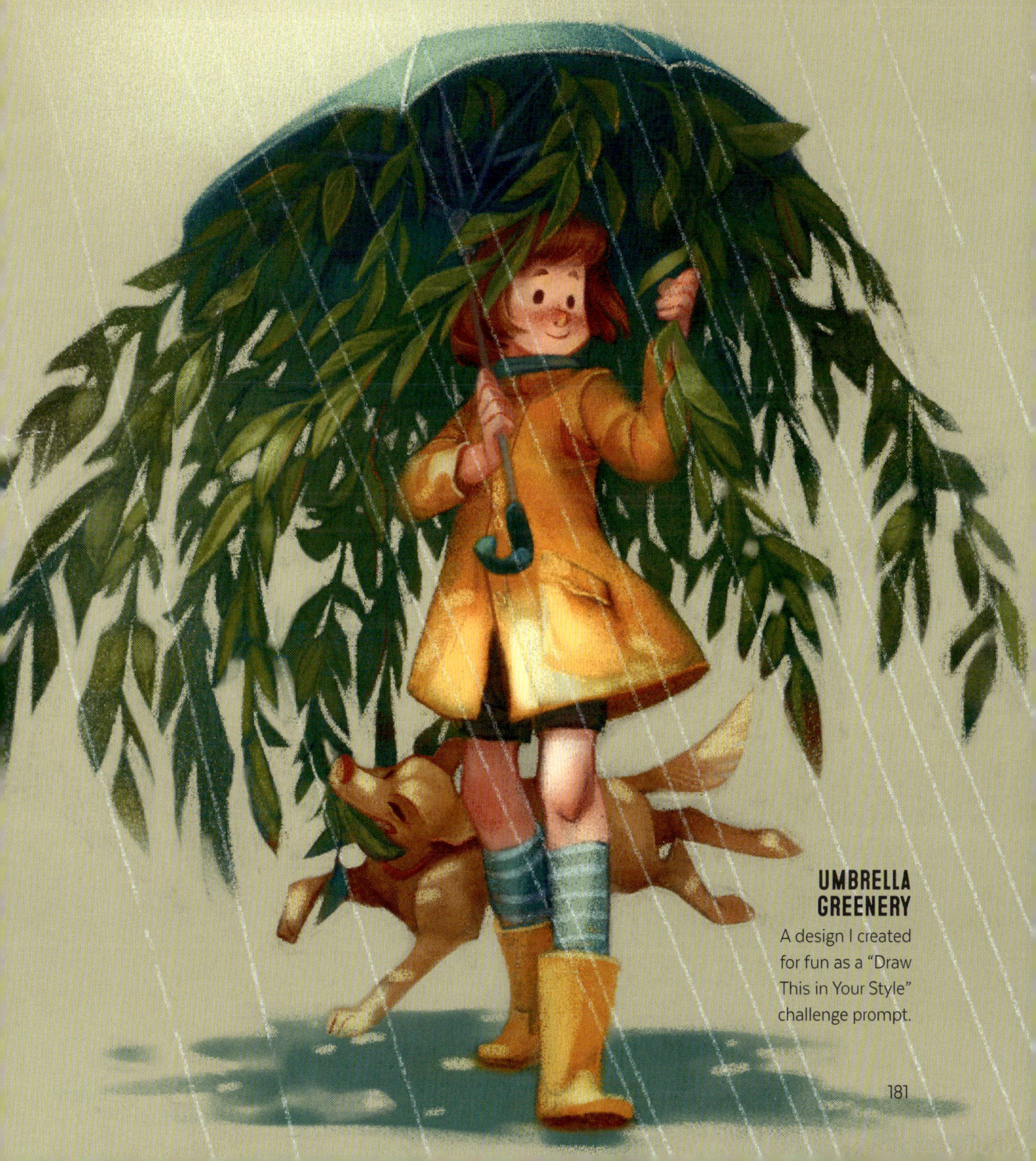

UMBRELLA GREENERY
A design I created for fun as a "Draw This in Your Style" challenge prompt.

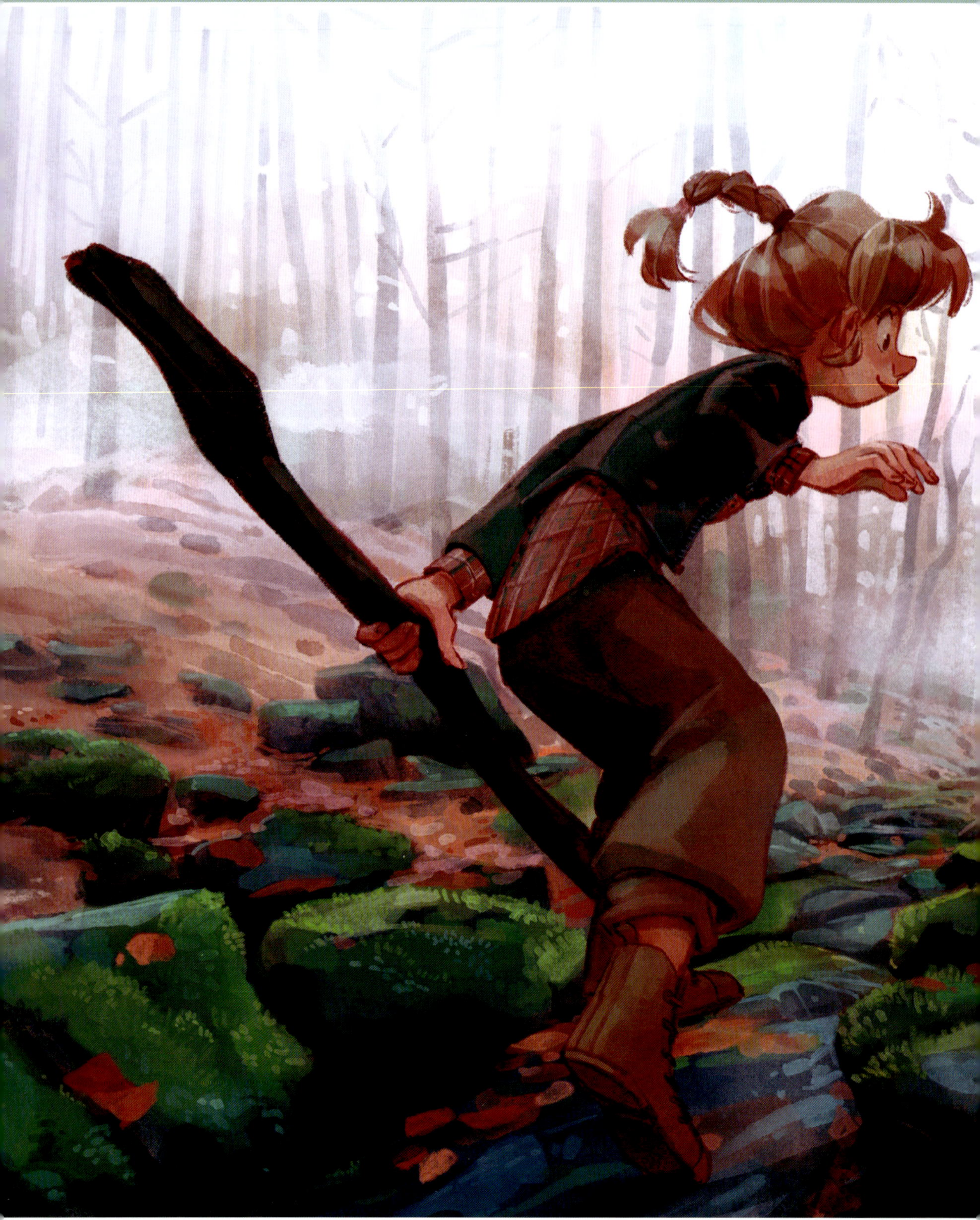

THANK YOU

Firstly, I must thank the most important people in my life: my family. My husband, for giving me the room to create and for being there to bounce ideas off. It was because of him that I considered crowdfunding, such as Patreon and Kickstarter, as a possibility for my own professional growth. My son Remus, for always inspiring me and bringing meaning and joy (and chaos) to my life.

Thank you to my lovely art friends – I love our community and the support we give each other. With special thanks to Olga, Rino, and Irina for helping with the freelance section of the book. I would also like to thank all of the artists who take beautiful photos that inspire me and spark fresh ideas.

And, of course, last but certainly not least, thank you to my followers and Patreons for helping to make this second book possible! I appreciate your continued support and questions, which help me to continue to become a better artist.

Thank you!
Simone

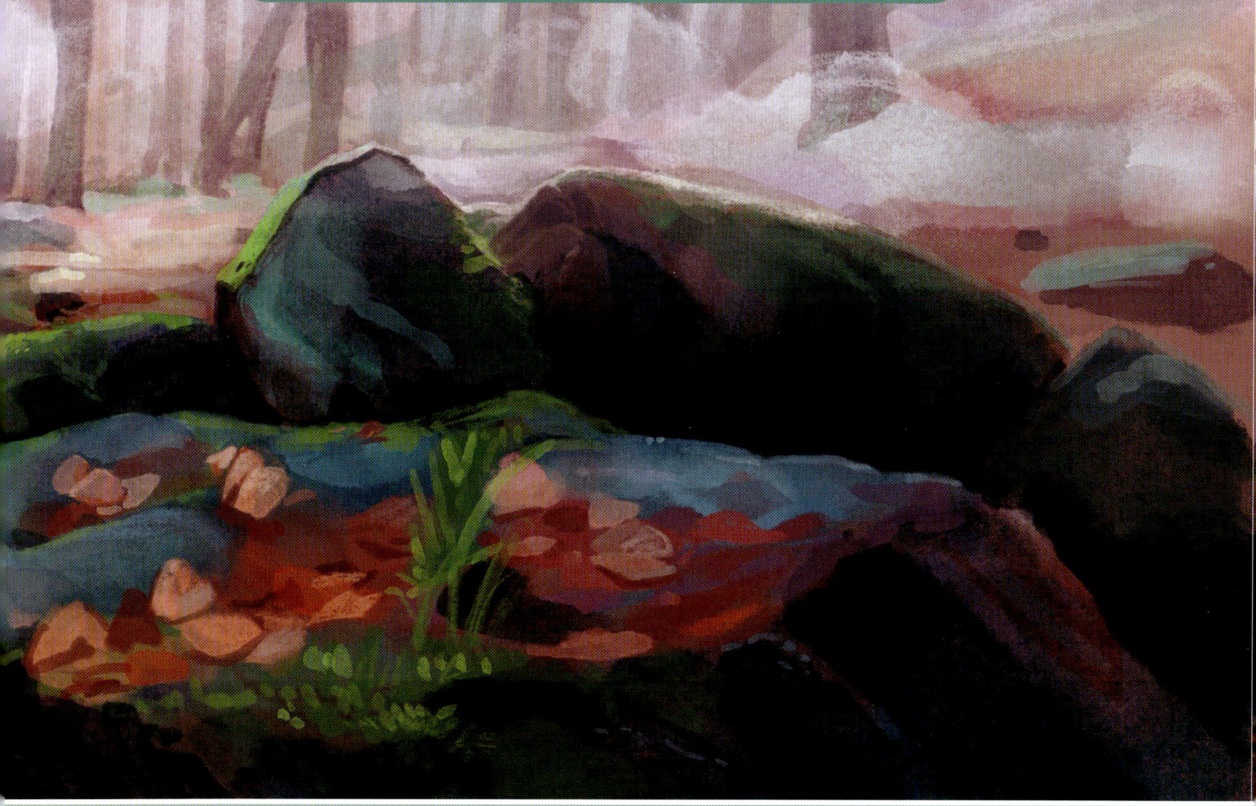

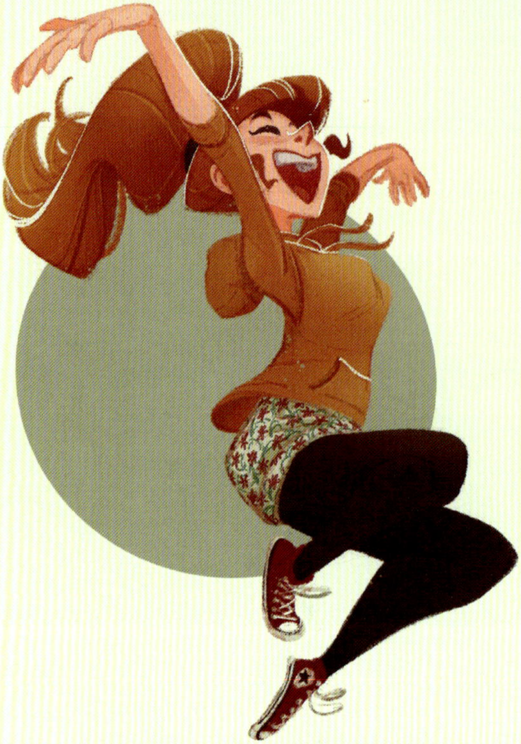

ABOUT 3DTOTAL PUBLISHING

3dtotal Publishing is a trailblazing, creative publisher specializing in inspirational and educational resources for artists. Our titles feature top industry professionals from around the globe who share their experience in skillfully written step-by-step tutorials and fascinating, detailed guides. Illustrated throughout with stunning artwork, these best-selling publications offer creative insight, expert advice, and essential motivation. Fans of digital art will enjoy our comprehensive volumes covering Adobe Photoshop, Procreate, and Blender, as well as our superb titles based around character design, including Fundamentals of Character Design and Creating Characters for the Entertainment Industry. The dedicated, high-quality blend of instruction and inspiration also extends to traditional art. Titles covering a range of techniques, genres, and abilities allow your creativity to flourish while building essential skills.

Well-established within the industry, we now offer over 100 titles and counting, many of which have been translated into multiple languages around the world. With something for every artist, we are proud to say that our books offer the 3dtotal package:

LEARN | CREATE | SHARE

Visit us at 3dtotalpublishing.com

3dtotal Publishing is part of 3dtotal.com, a leading website for CG artists founded by Tom Greenway in 1999.